CRITICAL TERMS FOR MEDIA STUDIES

Edited by W.J.T. MITCHELL
and MARK B.N. HANSEN

THE UNIVERSITY OF CHICAGO PRESS   Chicago and London

The University of Chicago Press, Chicago 60637
The University of Chicago Press, Ltd., London
© 2010 by The University of Chicago
All rights reserved. Published 2010
Printed in the United States of America

18 17 16 15 14 13 12 11 10   1 2 3 4 5

ISBN-13: 978-0-226-53254-7 (cloth)
ISBN-10: 0-226-53254-2 (cloth)
ISBN-13: 978-0-226-53255-4 (paper)
ISBN-10: 0-226-53255-0 (paper)

Library of Congress Cataloging-in-Publication Data

Critical terms for media studies / edited by W. J. T. Mitchell and Mark
Hansen.
    p.   cm.
    Includes index.
    ISBN-13: 978-0-226-53254-7 (cloth : alk. paper)
    ISBN-10: 0-226-53254-2 (cloth : alk. paper)
    ISBN-13: 978-0-226-53255-4 (pbk. : alk. paper)
    ISBN-10: 0-226-53255-0 (pbk. : alk. paper)
    1. Literature and technology. 2. Art and technology. 3. Technology—
Philosophy. 4. Digital media. 5. Mass media. 6. Image (Philosophy).
I. Mitchell, W. J. T. (William John   Thomas), 1942– II. Hansen,
Mark B. N. (Mark Boris Nicola), 1965–
PN56.T37C75 2010
302.23—dc22

                                        2009030841

Contents

Introduction

W. J. T. MITCHELL AND MARK B. N. HANSEN

"Media determine our situation." With these lines, German media scientist Friedrich Kittler begins his influential historical theorization of media, *Gramophone, Film, Typewriter*. Packed into Kittler's statement is a crucial claim: that media form the infrastructural basis, the quasi-transcendental condition, for experience and understanding. Like the strata of the seeable and sayable that, in French philosopher Michel Foucault's archaeology of knowledge, make knowledge possible in a given historical moment, media broker the giving of space and time within which concrete experience becomes possible.

This broad claim forms the motivating insight behind this volume of essays devoted to "critical terms" for the study of media. In today's intellectual climate, it would be no exaggeration to cite media as a central topic of research in the humanities and the humanistic social sciences, and for precisely the reason indicated by Kittler. Media can no longer be dismissed as neutral or transparent, subordinate or merely supplemental to the information they convey. Rather, an explosion of work by a diverse group of scholars representing a host of fields, disciplines, and interdisciplines has attested to their social and cultural agency. Not surprisingly, in the wake of this work, "media studies" has emerged as a viable research area, under rubrics like Comparative Media Studies (at MIT) and Literature, Communication, and Culture (at Georgia Tech), and as the focus of an ever-expanding range of research initiatives across the globe.

Despite this process of institutional consolidation, however, media studies remains an amorphous enterprise, more of a loosely associated set of approaches than a unified field. One can find practitioners who apply statistical methods to analyze audience response to media content and others who focus on the political impact of media consolidation and deregulation. "Media studies" embraces researchers who study virtual reality environments, hypertext fiction, materialist anthropology and culture, the history of information theory, precinematic devices, the institution of print, and word frequency in Greek literature. Indeed, the circle could be expanded to embrace any practice involving material artifacts, which is to say, the vast majority of practices in the humanities and humanistic social sciences. We are, it seems, all practitioners of media studies, whether we recognize it or not.

The question, then, becomes how we delimit media studies and, perhaps more profoundly, what is to be gained by such delimitation. Turning to Wikipedia (why not, given the key role played by new computational technologies in making the inescapability of media, well, inescapable), we find one strategy for dealing with the amorphous state of media studies: minimal definition. "Media Studies," the entry begins, "is the study of the constitution, history, and effects of media." It goes on to divide media studies (usefully, to be sure) into two traditions: on the one hand, "the tradition of empirical sciences like communication studies, sociology and economics," which "generally focus on Mass Media, their political, social, economic and cultural role and impact in creating and distributing content to media audiences"; on the other hand, "the tradition of humanities like literary theory, film/video studies, cultural studies and philosophy," which "focus on the constitution of media and question . . . [how] they shape what is regarded as knowledge and as communicable." Media studies thus comprises any study of media, within any discipline or interdiscipline, and may be subdivided according to the conventions governing research in those fields. These conventions group into two categories—the empirical and the interpretive—which, though far from homogeneous, designate two broad methodological approaches to media as the content of research.

We do not discount the value of such taxonomies. But we and the authors represented in this volume take a somewhat different tack. Rather than focusing on media as the *content* of this or that research program, we foreground a range of broader theoretical questions: What is a medium? How does the concept of medium relate to the media? What role does mediation play in the operation of a medium, or of media more generally? How are media distributed across the nexus of technology, aesthetics, and society, and can they serve as points of convergence that facilitate communication among these domains? Expressed schematically, our approach calls on us to exploit the ambiguity of the concept of media—the slippage from plural to singular, from differentiated forms to overarching technical platforms and theoretical vantage points—as a third term capable of bridging, or "mediating," the binaries (empirical versus interpretive, form versus content, etc.) that have structured media studies until now. In a minimal sense, what the emergence of the collective singular *media* betokens is the operation of a deep, technoanthropological universal that has structured the history of humanity from its very origin (the tool-using and inventing primate). In addition to naming individual mediums at concrete points within that history, "media," in our view, also names a technical form or formal technics, indeed a general mediality that is constitutive of the human as a "biotechnical" form of life. Media, then, functions as a critical concept in something like the way that the Freudian unconscious, Marxian modes of production, and Derrida's concept of writing have done in their respective domains. Though a distinct innovation, this general concept of mediality that we are proposing reveals thinkers from Aristotle to Walter Benjamin to have been media theorists all along. Sophocles had no concept of the Oedipus complex, but after Freud it becomes difficult to think about Greek tragedy without reference to psychoanalytic categories. Shakespeare had no concept of media, but his plays may be profitably studied as specific syntheses of varied technical, architectural, and literary practices. The very concept of media is thus both a new invention and a tool for excavating the deepest archaeological layers of human forms of life. It is our collective attentiveness to this deep, technoanthropological universal sense of media that allows us to range across divides (characteristically triangulated) that are normally left unbroached in media studies: society-technology-aesthetics, empirical-formal-constitutive, social-historical-experiential.

As an illustration of the approach to media we are proposing, consider the case of Arnold Schwarzenegger's election in 2003 to the governorship of California. Schwarzenegger's victory has often been attributed to his status as a Hollywood star, as if that somehow guaranteed success. But this explanation, in our view, falls far short. If it were adequate, we would have to explain the fact that the vast majority of governors and other political officeholders in this country are not actors or other media celebrities, but practitioners of that arcane and tedious profession known as the law (see Peter Goodrich's essay on this topic below). If Hollywood stardom were a sufficient condition to attain political office, Congress would be populated by Susan Sarandons and Sylvester Stallones, not Michele Bachmanns and Ed Markeys. Something other than media stardom was clearly required. And that something was the nature of the legal and political systems that give California such a volatile and populist political culture, namely the rules that allow for popular referendums and, more specifically, make it relatively easy to recall an unpopular governor. California has, in other words, a distinctive set of political mediations in place that promote *immediacy* in the form of direct democracy and rapid interventions by the electorate. It is difficult to imagine the Schwarzenegger episode occurring in any other state.

But there is more to this particular media event. Schwarzenegger was not just any Hollywood star but an internationally known "action hero." He had attained iconic status first as a prize-winning bodybuilder whose sculpted physique reminds us that one of the earliest media of human expression is the malleable physical body itself. Schwarzenegger's standing as an icon of power and action gave him a decisive advantage over an incumbent who was widely perceived as weak and passive in the face of the various crises California was facing. This perception was reinforced—"re-mediated," as it were—by the mass media themselves. In one notable layout in the *New York Times*, just weeks before the recall vote, Schwarzenegger was shown above the fold surrounded by adoring fans, while Gray Davis appeared in a smaller photo below the fold playing bingo with a senior citizen. If ever a photo layout telegraphed (and arguably helped to produce) the ultimate result of an election this was it. One wonders if a similar layout in the January 28, 2008, *Times*, which juxtaposed Barack Obama, engulfed in an adoring crowd, with Hillary Clinton, alone on a stage, addressing a distant audience, had a similar predictive and productive effect.

The California recall election illustrates the need for a multidimensional, "triangulated" approach to media events and phenomena. This one involved a "perfect storm" of political, technical, and aesthetic forms of mediation: the international circulation of cultural icons converged with the aesthetics of masculine body images at a specific historical moment in a regional political culture with particular electoral conventions. A simple appeal to Schwarzenegger's celebrity status will not do.

+   +   +

"The treatment of *media* as a singular noun . . . is spreading into the upper cultural strata," Kingsley Amis observed in 1966. And at or around that moment, when it becomes possible to speak of media in the singular—as something other and indeed more than a simple accumulation of individual mediums—media studies emerges as a quasi-autonomous enterprise. The passage from content to medium, from a plurality of divergent contents to the collective singular, lies at the heart of what is arguably the first and still most influential effort to articulate a comprehensive theory of media. In *Understanding Media* (1964), Marshall McLuhan famously identified the medium and the message, or rather, he defined the message as the medium itself. From McLuhan's standpoint, a medium impacts human experience and society not primarily through the content that it mediates but through its formal, technical properties as a medium. The example he proffers in a central section of *Understanding Media* is the lightbulb, which, despite having no content of its own, profoundly impacts social life, literally illuminating the darkness and thereby extending the time of human social interaction. "Understanding media," then, does not mean just (or primarily) understanding individual mediums—electricity, the automobile, the typewriter, clothing—but rather something like understanding *from the perspective of media*. Media, become singular, forms an abstraction that denotes an attentiveness to the agency of the medium in the analysis of social change.

McLuhan urges us to focus on media independent of its ties with content, and in the process redefines media itself as content, not just a vehicle or channel. Though some, perhaps many, practitioners of media studies find this deeply problematic, McLuhan's redirection is foundational for "media studies" in the sense in which we employ it here. For precisely this reason, his approach has a capaciousness that can encompass the multiple and historically disjunctive origins of the term *media* as well as related terms like *medium* and *mediation*. Etymologically, our term *media* is not just the plural of *medium*. According to its first entry in the *Oxford English Dictionary*, it derives from the postclassical Latin *media*, which, centuries before its modern singular use, denoted the voiced stops *b*, *g*, and *d* in Latin and Greek grammar. In this first entry, *media* carries several definitions: in addition to "a voiced stop in ancient Greek," or more generally "a (voiced) unaspirated stop," it refers to "the middle layer of the wall of a blood vessel or lymphatic vessel" and "a principal vein . . . in the basic pattern of insect wing venation." It is only in the etymology of a second entry that *media* as the plural of *medium* is mentioned. Definitions of the modern *medium*, derived from the Latin for "middle, centre, midst, intermediate course, intermediary," are broken into two categories: (1) "something that is intermediate between two degrees, amounts, qualities, or classes," and (2) "a person or thing which acts as an intermediary," whether a token of exchange, a material used in artistic expression, a "channel of mass communication," the "physical material . . . used for recording or reproducing data, images, or sound," a "substance through which a force acts on objects at a distance or through which impressions are conveyed to the senses" (including "the substance in which an organism lives"), or a spiritualist who communicates with the dead. From the sense involving mass communication, the dictionary notes, "a new singular has arisen."

It seems clear that *media* as a collective singular noun is somehow tied to the emergence of the mass media—from the eighteenth century's investment in paper as the medium of circulation and sociality, to the nineteenth century's invention of electricity as the medium of phenomenality, to the newspapers of the later nineteenth century and the television of the twentieth, forms through which information itself is mediated. In all of these cases, what is at stake is something more than the form of a specific content, and thus something that exceeds the pluralization of the term *medium*. Something that opens onto the notion of a form of life, of a general environment for living—for thinking, perceiving, sensing, feeling—as such. With this, the early modern meaning of medium as intervening substance seems not only to make a disguised reappearance but to do so in a manner—which is to say, with a generality—capable of sustaining the integrity of the term *media* across its various disjunctions and periodic reinventions. As a term denoting the "pervading or enveloping substance" in which human organisms live, *medium* designates a minimal relationality, a minimal openness to alterity, a minimal environmental coupling (in the terminology of contemporary ethological cognitive science), that appears somehow central to our understanding of ourselves as "essentially" prosthetic beings. Following the morphing of *medium* into the collective singular *media*, this minimal relationality comes into focus for itself: thus media studies can and should designate the study of our fundamental relationality, of the irreducible role of mediation in the history of human being.

Indeed, this generalized sense of media is at the heart of McLuhan's conceptualization of media as "extensions of man." By linking media—and the operation of mediation as such—to the historically changing sensory and perceptual "ratios" of human experience, McLuhan underscores the fundamental correlation of the human and the technical. Though never an explicit theme, this correlation animates his conception of media as a prosthesis of human agency, and it implicates the logic of human embodiment in media history in a way that makes common cause with some important contemporary media theorists and philosophers of technics. It anticipates, for example, the work of cultural critic N. Katherine Hayles, for whom disembodiment is an ideology that facilitates all-too-easy circulations of information without regard to cultural and material realities. In Hayles's view, information always operates in conjunction with bodies, whether these be computational embeddings or phenomenological embodiments, and careful study of the imbrications of bodies and machines serves to underscore our fundamentally prosthetic mode of being.

In a slightly different register, McLuhan is the recognized source for Friedrich Kittler's media science, which as Kittler suggests, can be understood as a working out of the impossibility of understanding media, where media forms the infrastructural condition of possibility for understanding itself. Indeed, we propose that McLuhan cuts a path between these two positions: for him, in contrast to both Hayles and Kittler, it is the coupling of the human and the technological that holds primacy;

while imbricated in myriad, complex ways, human enaction and technological materiality remain two distinct forms of informatic embodiment, two distinct processes of materialization that, no matter how much they may converge, retain their respective autonomy. For McLuhan, the human body can neither be understood as a first or primary medium, as some posthumanist critics propose, nor relegated to the status of merely optional receiver of technically mediated information, as Kittler proposes. Rather, the body for McLuhan comprises the non–self-sufficient "ground" for all acts of mediation, including those (the vast majority of mediations) that expand its agency beyond the "skin." The body, in sum, is a capacity for relationality that literally requires mediation and that, in a sense, cannot be conceptualized without it.

In this respect, McLuhan's work converges with the position of another important media critic, French philosopher Bernard Stiegler. Following the work of his compatriot, paleontologist André Leroi-Gourhan, Stiegler advances a complex argument for the "co-originarity" of technics and the human; the break that gave rise to the human as a distinct species, that is, was the invention of technics (or the technics of invention)—the use of objects not simply as tools but as tools to make other tools. The contemporaneity in the fossil record of protohuman remains and primitive flint tools supports Stiegler's theorization of the human as, from the start, a prosthetic being. Human beings, he claims, evolve by passing on their knowledge through culture. Technics, then, is of the essence, the medium for human life. The human and the technical coevolve, and media, in both its singular form, as a quasi-autonomous giving of the sensible, and its plural form, as a constantly evolving set of concrete exteriorizations of the human, designates something of their relation. And it does so in two distinct yet tightly correlated registers: as an always concrete articulation of the conjunction of human sensory and perceptual ratios with the technical processes that broker or mediate the givenness of space and time for human experience, and as a general condition for human life at any moment of its evolution.

It is important that we stress just how much this conceptualization of media as an environment for the living differs from conceptions of the medium/media as a narrowly technical entity or system.[1] Before it becomes available to designate any technically specific form of mediation, linked to a concrete medium, *media* names an ontological condition of humanization—the constitutive operation of exteriorization and invention. The multitude of contemporary media critics who focus on the medium—and media in the plural—without regard to this ontological dimension run the risk of positivizing the medium and thus trivializing the operation of mediation. Whether this leads toward an antihumanist technological determinism (Kittler) or the unending media-semiosis of Jay Bolter and Richard Grusin's "remediation" (itself, fundamentally, a remediation of McLuhan), what is lost in the process is a broader sense of the existential stakes, of how these operations of mediation tie in with the form of life that is the human.

We should also emphasize that our invocation of "the human" is not an attempt to resuscitate some ahistorical human essence, much less a traditional humanism. One of the key implications of thinking of media (tools, artifacts, codes, etc.) rather than language as constitutive of human life is that the assumption that the human is metaphysically distinct from other forms of life is called into question. Birds, bees, and beavers produce a kind of natural architecture; animals communicate with one another and with us. A more exact sense of what we mean by "the human" would emphasize the sense in which humanity is a work in progress, a radically historical form of life distinguished not simply by "media" but by cycles of media innovation, invention, and obsolescence. For in media, to paraphrase the Bible only slightly, we live and move and have our being. And they do not remain static, but constitute a dynamic, historically evolving environment or ecosystem that may or may not sustain a recognizable form of human life indefinitely. The most obvious medium in which the human species dwells is the earth's atmosphere, and that, we know, is undergoing drastic, man-made modifications. Human beings now have a greater impact on the environment than rain. It would not be too far-fetched to think, then, of the present project as emulating meteorology's study of dynamic interactive weather patterns, as an effort toward a "mediarology" that would track the pressure systems and storm fronts that crisscross the man-made world of symbols we have created.

+ + +

Though written by authors with differing commitments to "media," not to mention highly diverse scholarly investments, the essays in this volume all share some minimal commitment to the broader context of the operation of media and mediation. Each evaluates the role played by media and its cognates within certain conceptual frameworks and lineages, again of markedly diverse scale, that have been and remain central to research in the humanities and humanistic social sciences. The authors represented here take seriously the "middleness" evinced by the term *media* and seek to position media studies as an intermediary or mediator not simply within extant disciplinary formations but across and between disciplines. Without necessarily mandating a concrete shift in emphasis from media as artifactuality to media as process of mediation, these essays exemplify that work of mediation.

We have divided the essays into clusters, premised on three general approaches to media: in the first part of the book, the authors come at the question of media by way of *aesthetics*, which concerns the realm of the senses, the body, and the arts, and places individual human experience at the center; in the final part, with reference to *society*, emphasizing the place of media in making communication and collective relationships possible; and in the middle section, via *technology*, with a focus on the mechanical aspects of media and the way that innovations and inventions transform the condition of both individual and social experience. These categories are to some extent arbitrary, and many of the terms that appear under one rubric could easily be transferred to another. Our point is not that these approaches are sealed off from one another but just the reverse. We want to foster an integrated approach that overcomes the balkanization of the field of media studies, which makes it difficult for scholars interested in, say, politics and mass media to find common ground with the aesthetes who are concerned with the place of affect and perception.

We also want to overcome the notion that any one of these rubrics provides the "determining instance" that governs the other two. This is especially important with regard to technology, which is so often placed in the role of cause, with the other domains cast as effects. When Kittler writes, "Media determine our situation," we know that he means media technology: computers, typewriters, fiber-optic cables, phonographs, printing presses, and so on. We instead start from the premise that media are themselves mediated—constituted, that is, by a three-way set of exchanges among the dimensions of individual subjectivity, collective activity, and technical capability. This premise allows us to resist the seductive fallacy of technical determinism, which has haunted media studies from the outset. "The French Revolution," declared William Hazlitt, "might be described as a remote but inevitable result of the art of printing."[2] Our aim is to slow down the drawing of conclusions from a dazzling observation of this sort. Why, we would ask, is this "result" *both* "inevitable" and "remote"? If the printing press leads inescapably to revolution, why did it do so only in France, when the "art of printing" was also highly developed in the Netherlands and England? What sort of causal chain has been compressed into the word "result"? Is the printing press a necessary or sufficient condition for modern revolutions? Probably the former, certainly not the latter. Other conditions must be in place: an educated, literate public capable of consuming the products of the art of printing, as well as a taste for the pleasures of reading. Political and institutional arrangements—the licensing of print shops, regulation of the press, constraints on the ownership of printing houses—can vary considerably across political and cultural traditions. One might even reverse Hazlitt's formula, noting that "the repression of press freedom in the 1790s was a transatlantic development in the aftermath of the French Revolution."[3] Similarly, the utopian speculations about cybercommunities during the rise of the Internet in the 1990s have since been moderated considerably by recognition that cyberspace, like any other media landscape, does not simply dictate the nature of individual experiences or social relationships but is itself subject to legal and political manipulation, economic exploitation, and individual variability of usage.

At the same time, though, we want to acknowledge that technology and science are prime movers in the history of media innovation, even when they encounter resistance from individuals and social formations. New ways of communicating, of fabricating forms and images, and of expressing ideas are largely driven, or made possible, by new gadgets and gizmos. Insofar as media studies is a historical discipline, it is driven by an obsession with invention and innovation: How did the invention of metal casting transform Roman sculpture and Chinese bell temples? How did the invention of mechanically imprinted coins affect ancient economies? How did the movement from stone inscriptions to papyrus, or from pictographic to alphabetic writing, change the conditions of communication across large distances and the administration of colonial regimes? What difference has the invention of television made to the American judicial system and the venerable theatrical traditions of the courtroom?

These questions suggest some of the complexity of thinking across the fields of media studies, regarded here as encompassing the domains of human perception, social, political, and economic arrangements, and technoscientific inventions. Rather than impose a language of cause and effect, we propose a language of necessary (but not sufficient) conditions, a vocabulary of catalytic effects and conflicted situations rather than determining forces. This seems appropriate, if only because one of the most conspicuous features of media studies, considered as a singular field, has been its failure to communicate across the borders that divide the technophiles, the aesthetes, and the sociopolitical theorists. Paul Starr's magisterial history of the mass media in nineteenth-century America betrays nothing but disdain for the "culture industry" models of the Frankfurt school, and it contains not a single reference to the work of Noam Chomsky, Marshall McLuhan, or Robert McChesney. Rosalind Krauss's work on the "post-medium condition" of recent artistic practices has little to say about the transformed state of communicative technologies in the period in question. And Chomsky's "propaganda thesis," which takes American mass media as the hegemonic instruments of corporate capitalist elites, shows little interest in the aesthetic and symbolic features of these media, reducing them to machines for "manufacturing consent."

We cannot promise that we have overcome, in this volume, all of these failures to communicate, but we have tried to assemble an array of topics and scholarly interventions that make these failures more visible and perhaps set the stage for further discussion. In this sense, we hope that these essays remain faithful to the thought of some of the founders of media studies, especially Marshall McLuhan (explicitly) and Walter Benjamin (implicitly). For McLuhan, the concept of media embraced the totality of technical, social, and aesthetic reality. Because he portrayed the media as technical devices that interacted with the human sensorium, the physical world, and the sphere of social life, he has often been accused of being a "technical determinist," but in truth his more common strategy was to examine the complex dialectics of technical inventions. McLuhan's famous thesis about media as "extensions" of the senses is coupled with a recognition that they are simultaneously "amputations" of the organs they extend. Writing (as Plato first noted) must be understood both as an "aid to memory" and as a tool that may cause oral memory to atrophy. Similarly, the computer (as Bernard Stiegler argues in chapter 5) is the most powerful exteriorization of memory technology in the history of media, but it may be transforming the nature of "natural" human memory in far-reaching ways.

This is one reason that we take *memory* to be a keyword in media studies. It is one of those terms that reveal vividly the need for a theory of media as a collective singularity, a convergence of psychological, social, and technical domains. Memory, which is usually understood as an interiorized and innate psychological faculty, has, from the standpoint of media studies, been understood as a crossroads of aesthetics, technology, and society since ancient times. Mnemosyne was, for the Greeks, the muse of all the temporal arts—poetry, music, and history—and of the human power that assured the remembrance of famous men and magnificent deeds. Mnemotechnics, the training of memory as a psychological faculty, is also a technology of the eloquent speaking body in performance, hence the medium for producing cultural continuities, tradition, myth, and collective identity. Interior memory technologies, then, were understood as constellations of external media: words and images, tastes and sounds, cabinets and retrieval systems, marks on objects and bodies, buildings and statues, computers and clocks, coins and credit lines. All were vehicles for memory, and all move (or remain in place) in radically uneven, unpredictable ways depending on the situations into which they are inserted and the exteriorizations that enable their functioning. Media studies, therefore, is as concerned with subjective, mental life as it is with machines, codes, and communities. It deals not only with extensions of the human sensorium, but with their introjections into the structures of feeling and forms of life that constitute human subjectivity and collectivity.

Within this volume, each essay addresses a "critical term." These, as previously noted, we have grouped under the rubrics of aesthetics, technology, and society, as shown in the table below.

AESTHETICS	TECHNOLOGY	SOCIETY
Art	Biomedia	Exchange
Body	Communication	Language
Image	Cybernetics	Law
Materiality	Information	Mass Media
Memory	New Media	Networks
Senses	Hardware/Software/Wetware	Systems
Time and Space	Technology	Writing

The alert reader will object that many terms are missing from this list: structure, sign, spectacle, surveillance, screen, site, surface, style, simulation—just to take the S's. Our aim, however, was not to construct an exhaustive glossary, but to commission in-depth essays on a limited set of terms that seem crucial to the current state of discussion in media studies.[4] The authors were urged to reflect on the historical trajectory of the terms while at the same time engaging with their contemporary inflections. Some of the terms (Law, Communication, the Body) have ancient pedigrees. Others (Mass Media, Cybernetics, Biomedia) are relatively young. And one (New Media) explicitly emphasizes contemporary innovation, while acknowledging that (from a technical standpoint) media have always been entangled in cycles of innovation and obsolescence, innovation and renovation—from the invention of writing, printing, and artificial perspective to the invention of photography, television, and the Internet.

It bears repeating that most of these terms could have been placed under more than one heading. Writing, for instance, could be moved from Society to Technology with little trouble, while Communication could be switched from Technology to Society. Other terms seem obviously to fit one category. Art, for instance, might resist a transfer from Aesthetics to Technology. Nonetheless, artists have, since time immemorial, used, abused, and manipulated technology, though that contact has often been seen as lowering of the status of both art and artist. The terms gathered under Aesthetics, in fact, seem particularly conservative and tied to abiding traditions, while those under Technology involve concepts that seem relatively new (including, with perhaps astonishing redundancy, the term Technology itself). Again, our goal is not to produce a fixed framework for thinking about media, but to erect a house of cards that can be (and is always necessarily being) reshuffled into an indefinite number of combinations. The point is really to suggest three entryways into the labyrinth of media, with the understanding that each will sooner or later lead to the other two.

This raises an even more basic question about our approach to media and media studies. Why "triangulate" at all? And is this particular triangulation—Society, Technology, Aesthetics—the only conceivable way of organizing a set of articles on basic concepts in the field? Part of the answer is that we want to avoid the seductions of binarism, the prevalent rhetorical fallback in polemical and preanalytical discourse: past and present, new and old, art and technology, society and the individual, subject and object, space and time, nature and culture, ancient and modern. We especially want to avoid the presentism that plagues so much of "new media" studies today. Our aim is to take the field back beyond the "digital revolution" of the last twenty years to its deeper origins in antiquity and early modernity, and to think of media history as highly differentiated both spatially and temporally. Thus, Alex Galloway's article on Networks begins, not with the Internet, but with the net that Clytemnestra throws over Agamemnon.

A more elusive reason for triangulating the topic of media has been our intuitive sense that media themselves are always and everywhere understood by way of tripartite models. Consider, to list just the obvious examples: sender-channel-receiver (in communication theory), symbol-index-icon (in semiotics), image-music-text (in Roland Barthes's aesthetics), opsis-melos-lexis (in Aristotle's analysis of mimesis), and symbolic-imaginary-real (in Lacan's analysis of psychic "registers"). Think also of the structure of a syllogism, where the "middle term" is called the medium.

But beyond these abstractions, our search for what Roland Barthes termed the "third meaning" is driven by the practical reality of media events, operations, and environments. The triangulation of our topic, then, is a way of emphasizing the "middleness" of media studies, its role as a go-between, a mediator, in relation to the numerous other disciplines where it has had an impact, from ancient mosaics to digital images, from the code of human law to the code of life itself. Among these triangulations is, of course, the idea of media and the medium itself. Are "the media" one thing or many? Singular or plural? What are the relations between the singular, specific "medium" and the constellation of things known as "the media"? To grasp the horns of this dilemma, we broach the venerable concept of "mediation" as such, with its pedigree in Hegelian philosophy, dialectics, and critical theory. If, to this point, we have focused on the opening out of *media* (as the plural of *medium*) through the historical and semantic operation of its singularization, we must now devote ourselves to exploring how the third term, *mediation*, itself mediates—and multiplies levels of mediation between—the separate processes designated by media in the singular and media as a plurality of mediums.

+   +   +

Though it stretches back to ancient times, where it denoted a means of dispute resolution in matters of commerce, mediation acquires the value on which we are here drawing with the development of German Idealism (Hegel) and dialectical materialism (Marx and Engels). For Hegel, mediation was the abstract operation through which the dialectic pursued its forward march. Proceeding through the sublation (*Aufhebung*) of individual contradictions (pairings of thesis and antithesis), the dialectic of reason or spirit (to cite *The Phenomenology of Mind*) itself comprises the ongoing and processural operation of mediation necessary for Absolute Knowledge to emerge triumphant as the culminating product both of philosophical logic and world history. If Marx and Engels do not actually turn this operation on its head, they do correlate it with actual reality in a manner unimaginable for Hegel: in their work, mediation designates the primary form of relation and reconciliation between contradictory forces in a society, between the material domain and culture, base and superstructure. This analysis, found in the mature work of Marx and Engels, emerges from Marx's early understanding of mediation as labor, where labor mediates between a worker's body and nature and, more generally, between the human realm and natural world. Following the expropriation and reification of labor power, it is capital itself which becomes the agent of mediation: the capitalist determines the exchange value of labor, thus transforming labor power into a commodity.

Much of the attention devoted to Marxist theory after Marx and Engels has focused on the mediation between base and superstructure and the degree of agency available to social actors within monopoly capitalism. One lineage, running more or less directly from the later Marx through Lukács to Althusser, emphasizes the role ideology plays in the operation and consolidation of capital. On this account, there is little possibility for agency since consciousness itself is "the imaginary rela-

tionship to a lived reality"; if consciousness is perforce "false consciousness," the logic of this position runs, there simply is no possibility for
the social actor to gain an understanding of her own repression. In media studies, this lineage finds an instantiation in the Frankfurt school's
conceptualization of the culture industry, which through an account of
the one-dimensional ideological function of the mass media likewise di-
minishes the possibility for social agency.

Another lineage, originating with Antonio Gramsci's innovative conceptualization of hegemony (as an alternative, more flexible account of
state power) and branching off in various directions—including the Birmingham school of cultural studies (Raymond Williams and Stuart Hall),
the work of Ernesto Laclau and Chantal Mouffe, the work of the Italian
school (from Lazzarato to Hardt and Negri), and recent efforts to unite
Marxism and media studies—retains a stronger emphasis on mediation,
and thus a more robust conceptualization of social agency. For these diverse theorists, mediation names the highly dynamic process through
which individual and collective social actors engage with the forces of
capital as lived reality; according to these thinkers, the hold of capital
cannot be absolute, or (following Althusser) absolutely antihumanist,
for the precise reason that it can be maintained (that is, continuously
rearticulated) only through its impact on social actors.

To illustrate the value of this dynamic sense of mediation for articulating the range of what media studies is and can be today, let us return to Kittler's proposal that "media determine our situation." Bearing in mind our exploration of the paradoxical double case of media, we
can now approach this claim more concretely. By "media," Kittler clearly
means a plurality of mediums, an empirical accumulation of things, and
by "determine" (*bestimmen*), he seems to mean something more akin to
the late Marx's account of determination (the operation of the base on
the superstructure, or the infrastructure of capital on the consciousness
of the social actor) than to the more dynamic Gramscian conception. For
Kittler, that is, media seem to determine our situation (the possibilities
for action within a certain technico-historical infrastructure) in a manner not altogether different (notwithstanding a fundamental reversal of
values) from the Frankfurt school's account of the culture industry: human experience and agency is, at best, the positive effect of a media system but more likely "mere eyewash," the "optional output" he envisions
in his introduction to *Gramophone, Film, Typewriter*.

The essays in this volume engage Kittler's proposal. But when we
posit as the inaugural proposition for our media studies that media determines our situation, the shift from media as an empirical collection
of artifacts and technologies to media as a perspective for understanding

allows us to reassert the crucial and highly dynamic role of mediation—social, aesthetic, technical, and (not least) critical—that appears to be suspended by Kittler. Without jettisoning the crucial finding of Kittler's work (and of much of the archaeological work in contemporary media studies)—that media do have agency and do necessarily constrain experience—we seek to reintegrate the empirico-transcendental agency of media into the larger social domain, the domain of mediation, within which culture and life actually happen. In concert with contemporary Marxist theorists of media like Matthew Fuller, we propose that media studies names something other than an activity performed on a certain kind of object or content. As a mode of understanding, a perspective from which to engage our world, media studies rehabilitates understanding from Kittler's antihermeneutical critique (a critique shared by others, e.g., Gumbrecht) precisely by resituating it. What is to be understood is not media in the plural, but media in the singular; and it is by understanding media in the singular—which is to say, by reconceptualizing understanding from the perspective of media—that we will discover ways to characterize the impact of media in the plural. Whether they can be considered to be modes of understanding in themselves, such characterizations will involve much more than a unidimensional account of the technics of a given medium; indeed, by pursuing a generalization of technics along the lines suggested by Stiegler (as the correlate of human life), such characterizations necessarily involve mediations among the domains we have quite artificially dissociated here: society, aesthetics, technology. That these mediations themselves require yet another kind of mediation—critical mediation—is, in the end, the very burden of this volume and its neo-McLuhanesque injunction to understand from the perspective of media. Rather than *determining* our situation, we might better say that media *are* our situation.

Notes

1. Mention should be made here of the concept of "media ecology," pioneered by Neil Postman, who followed McLuhan in thinking of media not merely as means of communication (through which messages are transmitted), but also as environments (within which forms of life are developed).

2. William Hazlitt, *The Life of Napoleon*, 6 vols. (Boston: Napoleon Society, 1895), 1:56.

3. Paul Starr, *The Creation of the Media: Political Origins of Modern Communications* (New York: Basic Books, 2004), 79.

4. For a more extensive list of keywords in media studies, see the short articles by University of Chicago students collected at http://csmt.uchicago.edu/glossary2004/navigation.htm.

AESTHETICS

+ + + + + + + + + + + + + + +

1 :: ART

Art is the exploitation of the medium.
OGDEN, RICHARDS, AND WOOD, *The Foundations of Aesthetics*

Art is a notoriously difficult concept to define. The unruly condition of contemporary artistic activity challenges many received notions about *art* as a class of objects or set of practices. Fine artists no longer confine themselves to the use of traditional media and materials, so the identity of fine art can no longer be assured simply by an account of its making. Icons, themes, and technologies of mass media show up with increasing frequency in fine art imagery, so no clear divide between popular media and those of fine art can be established on thematic grounds either. At the same time, ideas of what an artist is or what the role of fine art might be are constantly changing. Classical notions of beauty, harmony, and proportion have largely vanished, along with displays of formal skill; or, at the very least, they are no longer required to make an artwork. Equally absent are expressions of tender feelings, religious and spiritual themes, and such once-familiar genres as portraiture, landscape, and still life. In short, the characteristics that long distinguished fine art from ordinary objects or mass media—the use of special materials, particular kinds of imagery, and aspirations toward higher values—are no longer definitive.

The foundational moment for modern art comes with the Industrial Revolution. But in Western culture, notions of art have a longer history, and a brief overview provides some insight into the dual legacy that seems to have confounded the idea of "art" in our time. Traditional production in the decorative arts has been involved in a sustained—if sometimes fractious—exchange with mass media and the fine arts. In this history, *media* means two things: the materials of production and the broader context of media culture.

In the modern to contemporary period, the prevailing belief is that the distinctive identity of art derives from the unique ability of individual artists to give formal expression to imaginative thought. This tenet seems unlikely to disappear, though it has been modified considerably; art is now as often constituted as a practice or activity as it is by the production of rarified objects. In tracing the concept of art as a viable category, several threads need to be followed: attitudes toward the media of production and imagery, the role and function of art, and the concept of the artist.

In traditional cultures, the techniques and activities of fine art are not distinguished from other kinds of form-giving. Pottery, clothing, and religious and ceremonial objects are often carefully made and elaborately decorated but without being separated from their function within secular or sacred cultural activities. Individuals with artistic talent were certainly appreciated in the ancient world—by classical times, sculptors and painters gained fame and reputation through their works—but art was a concept associated with *techne*, or applied skill. Individual talent was not linked to the expression of personal experience or feeling. The modes and motifs of classical aesthetics followed dictates of form. A few individual artists are known through historical accounts and associations (e.g., Praxiteles, a sculptor who worked in the fourth century BCE), but the moden idea of originality is of more recent origin.

In medieval monasteries and workshops, art was still not distinguished from the application of skills to specialized tasks. Illumination, calligraphy, elements of painting, drawing, and bookbinding, as well as stained-glass work, stone carving, and other applied arts contributed to church decoration of a high artistic order. Yet imagination was a concept outside the realm of such activity. Practical manuals stressed technical perfection, offering recipes for inks and paints or models to be copied. Finely made textiles, furnishings, and decorative objects served wealthy and powerful patrons, but not until towns and cities sprang up within expanded economies and emerging political and social systems was there a developed market for works that were not commissioned or controlled. The notion of art offered for sale as an autonomous commodity was almost unknown, even if artistic skills were prized and works commissioned from talented craftsmen.

The idea of the artist as a gifted individual gained prominence in Renaissance culture, as a symbol and symptom of humanistic thought. Leon Battista Alberti's brief treatise *On Painting* (1436) stressed training in perspective, anatomy, and geometry, along with the art of composition. His sources were the ancients, with Aristotle's poetics and classical rhetoric in literary texts presented as the wellspring from which painters who practiced the "highest art" should draw their inspiration. Media in the literal sense were relegated to craft production even as the notion of invention, with its emphasis on originality, began to ascend. A century later, in the high Renaissance, Giorgio Vasari's *Lives of the Artists* (1550) consolidated a paradigm of the artist as genius and original thinker. With Leonardo da Vinci and Michelangelo Buonarroti as examples, this ideal took hold in a way that has never lost its grip on the Western imagination. Art as the expression of individual genius affirms the very concept of originality and virtuoso capability. A direct line connects the Renaissance figure of the artist as a personality ruled by the planet Saturn, and thus tinged with madness or melancholy, with the later Romantic artist at odds with culture and society. Even in the present day, an aura of alienation is considered characteristic of artistic temperament.

The invention of the printing press in the fifteenth century challenged the identity of works of art as unique, individually crafted objects. Woodblock printing, though not capable of anything like the volume of production that would come with industrialization three centuries later, was quickly put into the service of every conceivable kind of expression, from scandal sheets and news broadsides to scientific texts dependent on visual illustrations as a primary mode of knowledge production. The role of the artist continued to be blurred with that of the engraver or other tradesman skilled in printing or graphic arts, and, in an era where distinctions between popular and fine arts served little purpose, the identity of art was expanded.

Printing remained a slow and laborious process throughout the sixteenth, seventeenth, and eighteenth centuries. Several hands were involved—an artist's original drawing was usually engraved (and thus interpreted) by one skilled artisan and printed by another. Prints made by indifferent, anonymous craftspersons were produced through the same media as those of renowned artists such as Pieter Breughel, Rembrandt van Rijn, and William Hogarth. Each of these artists made his reputation through prints distributed within a widespread commercial market. These once-popular mass-media images now are considered fine art, raising questions about the changes in status brought by historical perspective; later generations may discern sufficient artistry in various commercially driven productions of our times to overturn the categorical distinctions that now prevail. The distinction between fine art and popular graphics sometimes depends on whether a work was initiated by an artist or brought to market through the agency of a commercial publishing partner. But such differences are not necessarily perceptible in either the imagery or object.

Our contemporary concept of fine art is closely bound to nineteenth-century ideas, particularly Romanticism, with its emphasis on artistic imagination and emotion. Images of nature, nightmares, and other excesses prevailed in this period as signs of cataclysmic power, beyond the rule of rational thought. The visionary artist William Blake championed the ability of art to open the doors of perception. Art became an instrument through which to refute the claims of Enlightenment thought and its emphasis on rationality. The Romantic artist often took the stance of being at odds with mainstream culture and its conventions. The image of the artist driven by feelings, often working in isolation, scorned or misunderstood, found ample support in the works and deeds of Eugene Delacroix and Lord Byron, exemplary among others, who seemed to embody the wildest dream of artistic life. Imagination became the catchword of the era, and Percy Bysshe Shelley's essay "Defence of Poetry" (1822) made a passionate argument for the essential contribution of poetic imagination to the generation of new knowledge and creative production. Edgar Allan Poe, by contrast, exposed the myth of this cliché in his own essay on the deliberate craft of literary labor, "The Philosophy of Composition" (1846).

Aesthetics, as an area of philosophical inquiry, focused on questions of taste and value in the late eighteenth century, though the specific properties of individual media remained largely a concern of artists. Gotthold Lessing's influential essay *Laocoön: An Essay on the Limits of Painting and Poetry* (1766) reflects the sensibility of the writer-playwright as much as a philosophical disposition. Immanuel Kant's formulation of autonomy (as distinct from moral obligation or selfish desire), though adopted by later philosophers and social critics as a way to describe art practice as a discrete domain of cultural activity, was concerned with media mainly as an abstraction. When G. W. F. Hegel formulated his aesthetics with a hierarchy of progress toward a spiritual condition, media were linked to material but without the engagement with specificity inherent in Lessing's earlier tract. The posthumous publication of Hegel's *Philosophy of Fine Art*, in 1835, had little traction on the critical investment in media and materiality central to modernism's formal bent. Central tenets of German Idealism (e.g., beauty as equivalent to truth) persist. But attention to specific properties of media find a materialist expression among the writings and works of late Romantics (Pre-Raphaelites), Symbolists, and early Futurists in ways that were not explicit in an Idealist philosophical formulation.

Romanticism comes into being as the Industrial Revolution is transforming European culture in radical ways, automating labor and production on an unprecedented scale. Thus the distinction between rational thought and imaginative expression aligned with a contrast between mechanistic labor and artistic innovation—and with a contrast between mass-reproduced works and unique, hand-executed originals. The less obvious problem of the role of art in an era of administered culture (where applied logic and bureaucracy were perceived as oppressive) would come to the fore only later, though signs of this struggle are ubiquitous in early Romantic expression. Art takes on the force of a secular religion, auratic and charged with a salvific mission in the face of the perilous condition into which humankind is being led by the coming of machines and the end of traditional forms of labor and life.

The historical dialogue of art media and mass production reached a crucial point in the early nineteenth century. Industrialization exponentially extended the capabilities of mechanical print production, and these transformations were accompanied by changes in the concept of art. Visual culture was changing radically and rapidly. A mediated world of high-volume, mass-produced print artifacts sprang into being. An unprecedented number of social transactions became linked to printed objects, as train tickets, theater posters, menus, bills, trade cards, and other graphic ephemera began to be part of people's daily routines. Mass-circulation printed matter—newspapers, journals, cheaply made books, and novels—created new social spheres and communities of readers. By the 1830s the "penny press" was reproducing engravings of fine works of art from antiquity, motivated in part by a belief in the moral benefit of exposure to classical masterpieces. But if an engraving of a statue like the classical *Laocoön* could be had for a penny, then how was the value of a work of art to be established? Enormous pressure arose to define art as something other—not mass-produced or commercial but finer in form, rarer in production values, and particular in its uses of media. In dallying with media other than those abrogated to art for its specialized use, the argument went, art risked being overwhelmed, sold out, or lost in the rising tide of visual noise that clamored for attention in the streets, on the kiosks, and in the shopwindows of stationers, booksellers, and framers.

One celebrated case exposed the way crucial questions regarding the definition of art were posed by uses of the new media of reproduction and publicity. When the renowned British painter John Everett Millais, a member of the Royal Academy, allowed his painting *Bubbles* to be used to advertise Pear's soap, an enormous debate ensued. The image of a velvet-suited boy with angelic features enraptured with floating soap bubbles, painted in 1886, became the basis of the first advertising campaign to enlist a work of established fine art. Some artists and critics accused Millais of abasing the sanctity of art and sullying his own reputation in allowing his painting to be linked with commerce. Once used as a soap advertisement, *Bubbles* was no longer a work of art, purists declared. Others saw the popularization of images of fine art as a social benefit. Late-nineteenth-century British and American culture was permeated with the ideals expressed in the works of Matthew Arnold, who considered fine art to be the best expression of the highest values of civilization. Exposure to works of poetry, music, art and architecture were believed to be ennobling and uplifting, and the mass reproduction of Millais's image brought it before a wide public. In any event, works of art could not be separated from systems of distribution, consumption, and use, and the relations of art and commerce, inextricably linked to media and reproduction, continued to engender debates.

The early-nineteenth-century belief in art as a means of liberation had grown jaded by midcentury. A radical social vision of reform—and faith in the power of art as an instrument of cultural change—gave a realist painter like Gustave Courbet a very different conviction about the role of his work. In a spirit shared by the great novelists of the period— Honoré de Balzac, George Eliot, and Emile Zola—practitioners of realism believed in the social efficacy of artistic work. Social reform of child labor, living conditions among the urban poor, and other injustices became the impetus for works of art that took advantage of the power of print and imagery to expose cultural ills. Though works of art had been pressed into the cause of moral reform for centuries, the idea of art as a force for social transformation, not just spiritual improvement, was an idea that gained unprecedented momentum as the cultural effects of industrialization prompted utopian socialist movements.

The links between art and utopian idealism took many forms. The Arts and Crafts movement in Britain, largely inspired by William Morris, launched a nostalgic return to guild production methods of the preindustrial era. Art in this context was to be reintegrated with craft traditions in which individual expression was second to trade skills. But in an era still charged with romantic ideas about individual talent and the rarified character of artworks in relation to industrial products, the Arts and Crafts agenda was filled with contradictions. Though Arts and Crafts workshops rarely sustained themselves economically for more than a few decades, the ideas about art as a holistic, integrated, alternative to the alienated condition of work in industrial circumstances took hold of popular imagination. But by the century's end, even the initiators of the Art and Crafts movement had become reconciled with a role for art in industry, rather than as an alternative to it. The notion of the designer or industrial artist with a commercial and professional identity came into being by the 1890s and early 1900s. Fine art, however, retained its rarified status, even as the terms on which that identity was maintained were constantly questioned by critics and by changing practices. If anything, the growth of new professional identities in design, architecture, and graphic art reinforced the distinction of applied and fine art.

At the end of the nineteenth century a new surge of support for art as a democratic medium accompanied the vogue for chromolithographic posters. Theirs was an art for the people, claimed the producers of the larger-than-life dancers at the Folies Bergère drawn by Jules Cheret and Henri de Toulouse-Lautrec. Advertisements for oatmeal, cigarettes, beer, and bicycles appeared in public spaces, pasted up by bill-stickers competing for space in the crowded urban landscape. The champions of such public art met with cold welcome from citizens inclined toward decorum, many of whom felt that vivid commercial advertising cheapened public space. Battles over control of bill-posting also involved governments intent on controlling the politically inflammatory effects of poster art and reformist groups worried about the corrupting influences of dance hall programs and other images of entertainment. The artistic value of such posters was determined by aesthetic criteria, but more conservative judges felt that any commercial association negated a work's artistic status.

In the 1890s an art-for-art's-sake sensibility dominated the circles and salons from which sprang publications and images that characterized the fin de siècle across Europe and England. While applied arts and new professions in design for industry flourished, the rhetoric of fine art shifted to a self-justification on the basis of aesthetics. Art was to have no purpose but itself, serve no masters but beauty and imagination, and be in the service of individual expression or taste. Though only pale echoes of the decadent sensibility found their way across the Atlantic, a form of bohemianism flourished in American capitals as well as those of Russia, Scandinavia, and Eastern Europe. The flamboyantly witty Oscar Wilde proclaimed, "All art is quite useless," a statement that clearly demarcated aesthetic activity from that of industrial labor or production.

At the same time (and not surprisingly, given the formalism implicit in a focus on aesthetic properties), the idea that artworks were composed primarily of their media and materials came increasingly to the fore. The work of Impressionist artists focused attention on the literal surface of the canvas as early as the 1860s, when Eduoard Manet eschewed the conceits of illusion associated with academic technique. By the 1870s, when Claude Monet's *Impression, Sunrise*, lent its title to the new movement, the group's painters were being accused of exhibiting their dirty paint rags and palettes. But for calling attention to paint and pigment, rather than placing it wholly at the service of an image, they elicited critical support as well as attacks. A theoretical foundation for modern art as medium-based came into focus. In 1890 the French painter Maurice

Denis made a comment that resonated for decades: "Remember that a picture, before being a battle horse, a nude, an anecdote or what not, is essentially a flat surface covered with colors assembled in a certain order." Abstract formalism and attention to materiality became *the* basis of critical approaches to fine art in the Postimpressionist work of Georges Seurat and the Symbolist Gustave Moreau. The influence of mass-media techniques in poster design, combined with the fashion for Japanese prints, likewise called attention to the graphic organization of surface elements in visual work of the final decades of the nineteenth century. And Roger Fry and Clive Bell, early-twentieth-century British writers on aesthetics, made attention to the formal properties of art production paramount. In *Art* (1914), Bell stressed that the one shared characteristic of all fine art was what he termed "significant form"—the capacity to carry meaning through well-composed, skillful expression. This text was written in support of the work of Paul Cezanne, among others, but was attempting to make universal claims for modern work and media.

Bell and Fry were not alone in proclaiming the importance of materiality. In two landmark essays from 1913, "The Word as Such" and "The Letter as Such," Russian Futurist artists Velimir Khlebnikov and Aleksei Kruchenyk stressed the material foundations of art, emphasizing facture, or making, as the primary means through which artistic value (form and meaning) was produced. Russian theorists struggled to define the particular properties that made literature "literary"—and by extension, made art a category apart. Viktor Shklovsky coined the phrase "making strange" to describe the effect of art on the habits of thought that pervaded modern life and consciousness. This may be seen as a version of Blake's earlier "opening of the doors of perception," but defamiliarization, in this case, relied on shock effects rather than the romantic visionary imagination. Nonetheless, the twentieth-century avant-garde extends the romantic sensibility. Avant-garde artists were commited to creating works that flew in the face of convention and tradition. An equally strong impulse toward universal abstraction and an art of ideas also found justification by asserting the autonomy of media. Visual artists as distinct as the Russian Suprematist Kasimir Malevich and the Dutch artist Piet Mondrian pushed formal innovation to new limits in their hard-edged geometric approach. While Malevich aimed to destroy illusion, Mondrian sought the delicate harmonies and balances of a supremely distilled formal rhythm. For both, flat properties of the canvas and the literal surface of the painting were primary factors. For modern art, media were no longer serving as a vehicle or instrument of communication or representation of meaning, but as the very *site* of meaning and experience.

The idea that art might be defined by formal distinctions between traditional studio practice and mass media began to erode with the invention of collage practices. Pablo Picasso's 1913 *Still Life with Chair Caning* contains actual rope, thus challenging distinctions between presentation and representation. Other works he produced in the 1910s included torn newspaper, wallpaper, and other mass-produced printed materials. Not only were mass media and entertainments now subjects for fine art, but mass-media artifacts were materially incorporated into artworks. At the same time, principles of composition, harmony, proportion, and beauty were attacked or eroded. While Picasso's careful arrangements respected traditions of composition, German and Swiss Dada artists soon began making random collages using chance operations. Elements were drawn from a hat, thrown to the floor, or allowed to drift onto a canvas from a great height. With this shift, any possibility of using significant form as a criteria for defining art fell away.

Theoretical recognition of the growing power of visual culture seriously altered critical conceptions of fine art. In the 1930s critical theorist Walter Benjamin composed an essay titled "The Work of Art in the Age of Its Technical Reproducibility," in which he celebrated the arrival of mass media as an antidote to the "aura" that had surrounded original works of art. The essay aligned mass production with an idea of the democratic multiple, which he contrasted with the legacy of religious and sacred art. Benjamin, along with a number of other important members of an intellectual circle referred to as the Frankfurt school, were concerned with the ideological values or belief systems that created myths on which culture operated. While Benjamin celebrated the democratic implications of films and other mass-produced works' being made available to a broader audience, others, notably Theodor Adorno and Max Horkheimer, decried the mind-numbing effects of what they called "the culture industries" of Hollywood, Broadway, and Madison Avenue. Yet these critics all maintained some faith in the ability of art to preserve values that were otherwise lost in the broader culture. An earlier Romantic era had embraced imagination and emotion, but these authors stressed the importance of resistance and defamiliarization, concepts inherited from the avant-garde.

Much twentieth-century art seems to play a game of eluding and outstripping definitions supplied by critics and theorists. Artists cannot resist challenging the premises of such definitions. The artist most responsible for pioneering these radical gestures of conceptual gamesmanship was Marcel Duchamp, who famously submitted an upturned porcelain urinal for inclusion in a 1917 art exhibition. He signed the work with a pseudonym, "R. Mutt," and forever changed the way art was defined.

By choosing, titling, and signing a mass-produced object, Duchamp was suggesting that the identity of art is based on cultural frameworks— that is, that the foundation of art consists in a set of conventions and ideas, not in formal properties or principles of composition or media. This was a radical departure from previously held ideas.

In the mid-twentieth century, the work of critic Clement Greenberg became practically synonymous with modern art, especially in the United States. His essays on abstract art, particularly the work of the group known as Abstract Expressionists, made materials and media central to the definition of what constitutes painting or sculpture. With a rigor that took earlier twentieth-century formalism to its limit, Greenberg wrote in 1940 in the *Partisan Review*, "The arts, then, have been hunted back to their mediums and there they have been isolated, concentrated and defined. It is by virtue of its medium that each art is unique and strictly itself." Flatness, Greenberg determined, was the essential characteristic of painting, and any canvas that betrayed the least hint of spatial illusion was violating that basic premise. In an earlier essay, "Avant Garde and Kitsch," Greenberg had revealed the influence of other critical theorists by arguing passionately for the importance of fine art as a way to resist mass culture. Art, it seemed, had the task of preserving whatever was left of civilization, a charge that was resonant and potent in the face of the rise of fascism in Europe and various forms of totalitarianism elsewhere. A generation of artists took Greenberg's tenets as prescriptive; Morris Louis's poured veils of paint on raw canvas (*Alpha Pi*, 1960), for instance, directly fulfilled the call for work that was entirely about the medium of paint. Greenberg's purity was later perceived as exclusionary and repressive, premised on an ideal of autonomy, or the separateness of art from ideology, that could not be sustained. But he had in fact championed experimental fine art for its combination of aesthetic and cultural values. Greenberg's insistence on visuality extended the earlier modern prohibition against literary references and narrative qualities as much as it expressed hostility to representation or illusion.

The European artists who, in the aftermath of World War II, created the group CoBrA (for Copenhagen, Brussels, Amsterdam) sought to create art that would build world community by drawing on universal principles. One central figure, Asger Jorn, drew on his training as an anthropologist to incorporate the study of signs and archetypal figures as primal elements of visual media. Though these interests seem far from the realms of mass media, a number of these artists became part of the influential Situationist International movement, participating in its investigations of simulation and illusion in contemporary culture. Driven as much by political impulses as aesthetic interests, SI combined serious

Marxist criticism with strategies for transforming cultural life. These included a practice called *détournement*, an early form of what is now called "culture jamming," that consisted of transforming the meaning of mass-produced images and objects through direct intervention in the images or forms of the works. Among its precedents were Dada collage and photomontage and Duchamp's use of mass-produced reproductions. Distinctions between "high" and "low" art—the former aligned with elite taste, the latter with popular audiences—were challenged by the use of old master reproductions or thrift-store paintings, all treated with irreverence in creating works of critical commentary. Fluxus, a more loosely affiliated international network of artists that became established in the early 1960s, became interested in the aesthetics of everyday life. Art became increasingly a matter of participatory performances and ephemeral activities. Fluxus artists honked automobile horns and turned their windshield wipers on and off, rubbed soap suds on cars and themselves, poured streams of water from a great height, and so on. Art, it seemed could get along very well without the production of objects.

The emphasis on ideas rather than forms created a distinction between media culture and fine art in which art took the conceptual high ground. Some Conceptual artists flirted with eliminating visual work altogether. In 1958 Yves Klein, a metaphysically oriented and deeply spiritual artist, made an exhibition titled "Void," comprising an empty gallery. In a 1967 essay, "Paragraphs on Conceptual Art," Sol LeWitt stated that "an idea is a machine that makes art." Conceptual art invoked the idea of "dematerialization," as expressed in the writings of critic Lucy Lippard. Media that would have been unheard of in studio work a century earlier were used to push artistic boundaries. In the early 1960s conceptual artist Piero Manzoni made a limited edition of cans of his own excrement, neatly labeled and signed. Book artist Dieter Rot made pages of cheese and bodily fluids sealed into plastic packaging. Blood, semen, human hair, and other detritus found their place in sculptural installations and visual works throughout the 1960s and 1970s, as barriers to incorporating any and all materials and media into the realm of art fell away completely. Art freed from media constraints assured its identity through other means. Duchamp's basic inventory of defining gestures—the cultural conventions of authorship, institutional sites, or games of value predicated on contracts and beliefs—seemed to work very well to ensure the continuity of art as a specialized realm of production even as the objects or events produced outstripped conventional categories.

Conceptual art and Pop art came to prominence in the same decades. Andy Warhol, a major figure in Pop art, had been trained in commercial art and advertising. He began by making hand-painted images of mass-produced objects but in 1962 took a step that broke down another set of boundaries that had distinguished types of production. Using photographic silk screens of the kind used to make industrial billboards and signs, he created works of fine art in a studio called the Factory. Airbrushes and halftone screens soon made their appearance in studios as well as workshops, and this new intertwining of mass-media culture and fine art threw critics into confusion. Copied from the workings of an emerging celebrity culture, the image of the Pop artist has reinforced a model for dramatic actors and actresses, authors and artists, film stars and rock musicians to the current day. When Warhol, who had become a media figure as well as skillful manipulator of media images, predicted that in the future every person would have their fifteen minutes of fame, he may or may not have foreseen the extent to which that fame would be based on the bold outlines of the artist as a distinctive personality silhouetted against the masses. Art, it seemed, was a celebrity accessory, a high-end fashion statement, a commodity among commodities, to be fetishized along with the artist-personality that produced it.

In an extreme contrast, at least formally, a third major strain of artistic practice emerged in the 1960s that also had implications for the definition of art and for the range of media and materials used in its practice. Minimalism pushed the boundaries of art toward another limit. Minimalist artists made use of mass-produced chunks of steel, glass, felt, or other materials altered only enough to have them register as art. Donald Judd's starkly stated principles of minimalist work, "Specific Objects" (1963), declared all conventions of composition, hierarchy, figure-ground relations, proportions, and surface detail irrelevant to the more significant problems of artistic identity. Robert Morris's cut and draped pieces of felt or Barry Le Va's floor pieces of scattered, broken glass exemplified the movement's reductive aesthetic. The distinction between works of art and those of mass culture depended on removing the industrial materials from use. Austere, difficult, and elegant, Minimalism emphasized properties of art that were inherent in materials and media, but dependent on a conceptual framework. Minimalist art reduced forms to material, banishing expression and emotion, compositional techniques, and any trace of representation or reference.

All three major mid-twentieth-century movements—Pop, Conceptualism, and Minimalism—contributed to the range of possibilities on which contemporary artists draw. Our ideas of the ways "art" distinguishes itself from mass culture are in part dependent on critical positions forged in the debates generated by these movements. In the 1970s identity politics from feminist communities and traditionally marginalized groups brought representational imagery back into the mainstream.

A new, eclectic internationalism was supported by biennials and art fairs, and in a cycle of boom and bust economies, fine art became an investment as well as a status symbol.

In the 1980s postmodern artists engaged in acts of appropriation. They posed strong arguments with the myth of originality that had fueled artistic practice since the dawn of the industrial era. Postmodern critics asserted that all art used images and ideas that had "always already" existed. So appropriating preexisting works from any and all sources—commercial, industrial, historical, or artistic—was the only way to create new works. Richard Prince made prints of the Marlboro man from cigarette advertisements and Sherri Levine rephotographed works by canonical photographers like Edward Weston. They exhibited these as their own works, eschewing the concept of authorship and originality. High postmodernism quickly exhausted its conceits and devices for art making, but in its wake, the rule-bound and highly codified terms of formalism were banished, along with any trace of autonomy as a viable critical concept. In their place came theories of allegory, hybridity, and pastiche that granted wide permission for the most eclectic practices. Contingency, or the situatedness of work within cultural and historical frames, displaced lingering traces of formalist autonomy. Performance art, installation work, new media, photography, projection, ephemeral activist work that left little or no remnant, and works that consisted largely of actions or transactions took their place among the traditions of painting, sculpting, printmaking, and other studio-based art, all of which experienced a late-twentieth-century revival.

Ultimately, however, works of art have to be distinguished from the products of other culture industries that permeate daily life. Often this is as much a matter of framing, site, and presentation as of material, media, or imagery. The spectacularly kitschy sculptures made by Jeff Koons in the 1980s and the elaborately staged performance sculptures of Vanessa Beecroft, using fashion models posed nude, register as art in part through context. Works of art are certainly valued above and beyond the costs of labor or materials used in their production, though *In the Name of God*, a diamond-studded platinum skull made by British artist Damien Hirst (and the most expensive piece of sculpture by a living artist), played with the capacity of fine art to command capital as part of its production. In a striking countermove, Pierre Huyghe and Philippe Parreno acquired and liberated a Japanese anime figure—returning a mass-media brand to a free condition outside of ownership or markets. Clearly these artists understand the mediated condition of their own practices as part of the production of objects and events. Thus the intrinsic value of the media involved shrinks by contrast to the works' value as rarified expressions of human thought, skill, or emotion. The question of which media are specific or proper to the production of art has been answered differently in successive generations. In traditional practice, materials such as fresco, oil paint, watercolor, marble, and bronze were the media through which works of fine art are produced, but in the modern and postmodern periods, media have become the subject and substance of works of art, not merely the means of production.

In the era of digital and electronic arts, new challenges to the boundaries and definitions of art are posed by changes in contexts and circumstances of production and reception. The basic characteristics of digital work are that it is programmable, iterative (open to being issued in new and changing versions), generative (giving rise to new expressions), and frequently networked. While earlier networks of social and economic exchange were intrinsic to the value of works of fine art, the networked condition of digital media allows for works of virtual art that have little or no existence outside of electronic environments. The production of artworks for sale and consumption in the online world Second Life, exemplified by the artists' books editioned within its realms by Richard Minsky, show the critical and economic viability of aesthetic projects conceived entirely within the domain of virtual space. While the existence of these productions first and foremost as files of digital code foregrounds their simulacral, or immaterial, aspect, the elaborate technological infrastructure that supports these activities makes clear the highly material nature of electronic media.

In a work that calls attention to the circuit of human involvement essential to the operation of aesthetic effects, Janet Zweig created a piece titled *The Medium* (2002) for the lobby of the School of Journalism and Mass Communication at the University of Minnesota. It consists of a cozy alcove, scaled for conversation but with a large video screen separating any two individuals who take their places in it. The occupants can speak to each other but only through a camera feed, in which their images are modified by a program that shifts the colors and tones in real time. The result is a hypnotically beautiful series of images, with visual qualities that seem psychedelic, solarized, or impressionistic by turns. The myth of face-to-face communication as unmediated is exposed, as the process emphasizes the subjective quality of perception in any and all circumstances. Our experiences are mediated through the perceptual apparatus, as well as the cultural conditions of our individual subjectivity. Zweig's piece makes a clear case for the emphasis on media as an aesthetic device and art as a specialized form of experience within the larger realms of mediated perception. It thus exemplifies the dictum of the renowned media theorist Marshall McLuhan that the "medium is a *mas-*

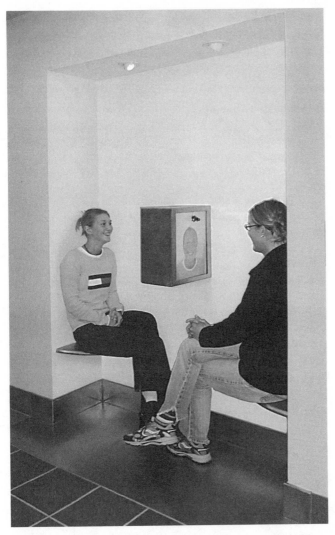

Janet Zweig, *The Medium*, 2002. University of Minnesota School of Journalism and Mass Communication, commissioned by the Art on Campus Program. Photo courtesy of the artist.

sage." But it is the art coefficient that provokes wonder and seduces us into consideration of the way it inflects and shapes meaning.

Works of art can no longer be identified by their media, and the image of the artist has become a founding myth of celebrity and commodity culture. The definition of art in an era of mass media depends on our ability to distinguish works of art from other objects or images in the spheres of media and mass visual production. Art serves no single purpose, cannot be circumscribed by agendas or beliefs. But it provides a continuing space for renewing human imagination and giving expression, in any form, ephemeral or material, to that imaginative capability. Finally, the practice of art becomes independent of objects or things, even of ideas or practices. Art becomes a way of paying attention.

References and Suggested Readings

Beardsley, Monroe. 1966. *Aesthetics from Classical Greece to the Present*. New York: Macmillan.

Berger, John. 1972. *Ways of Seeing*. London: British Broadcasting Corporation; Harmondsworth: Penguin.

Bloch, Ernst, et al. 1977. *Aesthetics and Politics*. London: New Left Books.

Drucker, Johanna. 2005. *Sweet Dreams: Contemporary Art and Complicity*. Chicago: University of Chicago Press.

Drucker, Johanna, and Emily McVarish. 2009. *Graphic Design History: A Critical Guide*. Upper Saddle River, NJ: Pearson Prentice Hall.

Elkins, James. 1999. *The Domain of Images*. Ithaca: Cornell University Press.

Frascina, Francis. 1985. *Pollock and After: The Critical Debate*. New York: Harper and Row.

McLuhan, Marshall. 1964. *Understanding Media: The Extensions of Man*. New York: McGraw Hill.

Mitchell, W. J. T. 1994. *Picture Theory*. Chicago: University of Chicago Press.

Ogden, C. K., I. A. Richards, and J. E. H. Wood. 1974. *The Foundations of Aesthetics*. New York: Haskell House.

Wallis, Brian, ed. 1984. *Art after Modernism: Rethinking Representation*. New York: New Museum; Boston: David Godine.

2 :: BODY   BERNADETTE WEGENSTEIN

No thought, cultural production, or human activity can take place without the body as its source. Yet, while human bodies have been implicated in cultural production since the dawn of the historical record, the body itself has often been treated as a given in critical explorations more focused on concrete artifacts. The reason for this neglect is perhaps obvious. Whereas cultural production varies across time and place, the human body is, or would seem to be, one of the few constants defining human being. When attempting to theorize the body historically, the critic thus faces a burden that does not attend the case of artifacts—the burden of negotiating between the body's organic invariance and its historical specificity.

Even so, the body has been the focus of a minor tradition in historical analysis and is a central topic in much recent thought. It is insufficient, if not downright wrong, some theorists have argued, to view the body as a passive but necessary basis for human activity. As a corrective to that view, they have sought to position the body as the indispensable *medium* of experience, which is to say, as a constituting basis for all experience, including that of its own thematization. To appreciate its centrality within current theoretical discussions in media studies, the body must accordingly be situated within the context of a larger and perhaps more fundamental set of philosophical questions, including whether and to what extent the body is a medium and what the stakes are in considering it as such.

These questions are crucial to the humanistic and historical disciplines that ask what the body means in a culture, how the body produces culture, and to what extent culture produces a certain body. For behind all of these approaches to the body's cultural significance lies the issue of the body's constituting power: from where does the body acquire its capacity to shape and produce culture? The body's role as medium is likewise a fundamental concern for the sciences as they individually and collectively explore the meaning of the body; these same questions come to the fore in medicine, when it asks how to interpret the sick body's symptoms, and in the cognitive and engineering sciences, which explore the body's functionalities and the possibilities of replacing them with artificial devices. In each of these cases, the body is approached not as a static object, an inviolable "natural" entity, but as a dynamic process.

From prehistory onwards, the human body has been invested as an object of aesthetic interest. Throughout the history of the West, parts and attributes of the body have been accentuated by rituals of modification such as tattooing, piercing, masking, and the use of cosmetics and jewelry. While many of these practices, at least in their more outlandish versions, are popularly associated with ethnically marginalized people, they are all features of modern industrialized cultures. And while they serve varied purposes—from initiation to exclusion—they collectively delineate several ways in which the body can be seen as a medium. Thus, in addition to embellishing the body's appearance and allure, the wearing of jewelry and cosmetics evinces its function as a support, like the canvas underlying a painting; tattooing and piercing present the body as a site of inscription; and the masking of the face, together with the practice of cosmetic surgery, which it anticipates, show it as a material to be shaped or carved. A similar differentiation appears in critical practices that aim to expose the tyranny of our cultural drive to perceive the body as beautiful. Body art performances question our societal exclusion of the sick body, the handicapped body, the "other" body; extreme practices of self-mutilation, scarification, or voluntary amputation deploy the body as site of critical inscription; and the anorexic female body, to the extent that it is made to communicate female body image disorder, brings a critical purchase to the body as sculpted material.

In order to differentiate between the body as a static concept—a biological given—and the body as the basis of concrete and historically situated experience, cultural theorists have introduced a distinction between the body and *embodiment*. In *How We Became Posthuman* (1999), N. Katherine Hayles writes, "In contrast to the body, embodiment is contextual, enmeshed within the specifics of place, time, physiology, and culture, which together compose enactment." Embodiment thus refers to how particular subjects live and experience being a body dynamically, in specific, concrete ways. If human bodies are in some cases factual objects to be discovered and analyzed, they are at the same time the very medium through which such knowledge is attained. As an object of analysis, that is, the body is unique in that it is always also the means for analysis. Philosopher Hans Jonas (1982) has perfectly captured this dual status of the body in his claim that only living human bodies can inquire after their own living. The specificity of human embodiment can thus be expressed via the phenomenological differentiation between "being a body" and "having a body": the former, insofar as it designates the process of living the body, the first-person perspective, coincides with dynamic embodiment; the latter, referencing the body from an external, third-person perspective, can be aligned with the static body. Humans, Jonas argues, are unique in that they can experience both modes of embodiment simultaneously. (We shall return to the terrain of phenomenology below, but it is worth noting here how deeply the desire to overcome the separation between these two modes marks the development of phenomenology in the twentieth century, and how critical this accomplishment of phenomenology is to our own contemporary insight into the body's function as medium: the body can serve as medium in the divergent modes remarked above precisely because it is a medium in a deeper, phenomenological sense, which is to say, the medium for experience itself.)

Contemporary technoscience is in a unique position to exploit this phenomenological convergence of first- and third-person perspectives. Indeed, as I shall show below through analysis of examples from contemporary media art, the experience of embodiment today can be altered and enhanced through robotic devices, implants, prostheses, and a variety of other technical exteriorizations of the body. In what amounts to an empirical confirmation of Marshall McLuhan's prophetic insight into the dual function of media—at once extension of the body and amputation—these technical exteriorizations undermine the very distinction between inside and outside, and thus complicate immeasurably the separation of first- and third-person perspectives on bodily experience. While these developments instance what is perhaps most interesting about the body's role as medium, it is important that we not treat them as the cause for this role, and indeed, that we trace the body as medium back through history. Such a historical reconstruction will lay bare the differentiated yet cumulative coevolution of the body and embodiment that informs the phenomenological becoming-medium of the body.

The tension between the body as object and as agent of experience, a tension inherent to human life itself, shapes the history of the body from the very start, and impacts how different cultures at different times have framed the experience of embodiment in highly divergent ways. The irreducible fact of a culturally specific history of embodiment (or, indeed, of multiple such histories) underscores the body's function as medium: the body as medium is the source from which different cultural styles of embodiment emerge. At the same time, this fact of cultural specificity goes a long way toward explaining the process of naturalization that makes one's own embodiment seem "natural" and the style of embodiment characteristic of different historical periods comparatively alien.

To take one historical example, scholars have argued that the perception of and through the body during the European Middle Ages was markedly different from our own. One such interpretation claims that spectacles in the Middle Ages affected audiences in more physical ways than they do in the modernized West, where the *performative* value of a representation—that is, how a representation may affect or produce what it apparently only describes—tends to be replaced by the ultimate meaning or message it is intended to convey. This effect on the body of medieval performances has been called *presence* by William Egginton, and has its prototypical example in the Catholic doctrine of the Real Presence. According to this doctrine, the bread presented at the celebration of the mass becomes, in fact, the body of Christ and not merely a representation of that body—the thing itself and not merely a medium for that thing. Masses of people were said to have rushed into churches during the fourteenth century just to be present at this moment of transubstantiation, a phenomenon that underscores one particular mode in which the body functions as medium, namely, the mediation that operates in the identification of representation and presence. The bodies of the faithful are, in other words, the medium in which representations become material and are experienced, not merely as hidden meanings or messages, but as presences that impact the bodies of believers in concrete, physical ways. While the doctrine of the Real Presence and transubstantiation remains a core element of contemporary Catholicism, it is perhaps still worthwhile to underscore the singularity of the medieval sensibility, a sensibility captured in the frenzy of the masses' embodied experiences and the violence of the imaginary that surrounded the practice of the liturgy. No one has more forcefully underscored the singularity of this sensibility than historian Caroline Walker Bynum, who, after reflecting on the curiously bloody nature of some medieval revelation narratives, concludes that "there is something profoundly alien to modern sensibilities about the role of the body in medieval piety."

Another example of the tension between the body as object and as agent involves the art of healing across cultures. While it may be the case that all cultures use the body as a medium when approaching the problem of healing, the concrete terms of such use point to vastly distinct understandings of embodiment. Western culture since the sixteenth century has developed methods for opening the body and examining it for symptoms of disease or other conditions to be eradicated. In the nineteenth century this enterprise was expanded to include the analysis of microbes. More recently, the ongoing development of medical imaging technologies has improved our access to the body's insides, put the body on display in deeper and ever more inclusive ways, and thus facilitated the exposition of factors contributing to disease. While these and like practices clearly implicate a certain logic of embodiment, their focus on the body as visible object tends to obscure the bodily agency that is at work, for example, in fighting disease. Indeed, for someone accustomed to the practices of Western medicine, with its focus on detecting microbes or producing concrete images of isolated body parts, the very operation of the body as medium might be overlooked.

Medicinal practices in some cultures, by contrast, take other approaches based on fundamentally different assumptions about the nature of the body and its relation to illness. For example, traditional Chinese medicine (TCM), a cluster of millennia-old practices that stem largely from Taoist principles, assumes that the body is an expression of its environment on all scales, from the microscopic to the cosmic. Rather than inspect the individual body piecemeal for specific causes of illness, TCM looks at the balance or harmony within and without the body, and seeks to intervene in order to alter this relation in beneficial ways. Here the tension between body as object and as agent is minimized, if not entirely eradicated.

Yet however much Western practices may obscure embodiment, it remains implicated in ways that cannot simply be eliminated. Indeed, the history of embodiment in the West demonstrates just how central the evaluation of the body and its role as medium have been to philosophy and culture. An especially striking inversion in this cultural and philosophical valuation accompanied the passage from the medieval period to modernity. Scholars from a variety of disciplines have theorized that between the fifteenth and seventeenth centuries European society began developing in ways that stressed modes of embodiment profoundly different from those predominant in the Middle Ages. Medieval historian Georges Duby has argued, for example, that prior to this transition individuals experienced their own bodies as being directly imbued with the meaning of a particular class, group, or religious identification, whereas individuals in the early modern period had already begun to conceive of their bodies as autonomous entities, and of their persons as potentially occupying a variety of positions in society.

This tacit and unthematized experiential shift became codified in philosophical doctrine, specifically in the philosophy of René Descartes, who stipulated the existence of a fundamental divide between body and mind, with the body a passive, inert object inhabited and manipulated by the mind. Although Descartes himself occasionally questioned the categorical nature of this divide (for example, in his writing on the passions), his influence has yielded a deep-seated general tendency in modern Western thought to view the body and its passions as potential obstacles to knowledge. German Idealist Immanuel Kant, for example, used the term *pathological* to indicate those motivations deriving from passion or personal interest that would necessarily distract one from the accomplishment of one's duty, and philosophers ever since have repeated the message in a myriad of forms. This general philosophical picture of the body as passive material that can—indeed, must—be shaped by the morally conscious mind is echoed in cultural and sociological explorations that treat the body as the expression of a social status or particular group. Available as an object for physical and ideological analysis, the body can be deployed to express a person's character and style or to capture her health and well-being.

Modernity inaugurates what Brian Turner has termed a "somatic society," that is, a society that values the body as individual capital. For French philosopher Michel Foucault, the advent of this valuation coincides with a shift from a juridical society to a society of discipline and, more recently, of control. Foucault's distinction concerns the mode in which power is applied to the body. Rather than being punished in public, as it was in the great spectacles of early modernity, the modern body is *self*-disciplined, controlled from within; due to the work of the conscience and the host of disciplines supporting its upsurge, the modern individual finds herself compelled to self-regulate, to submit "voluntarily" to the disciplinary and biopolitical dictates of the state. Thus, for example, modern societies increasingly legislate health in ways that subordinate the individual's bodily well-being to a societal investment in the health of populations.

At the same time, the very modern individuals who may be compelled to conform their practices to the norms of biopower manage to exert a great deal of individual will in the creation of their persons. The modern deployment of the body as expressive medium can thus be seen as closely aligned with questions of individual identity. The medium of the body becomes the subject's own vehicle for communicating gender, age, class, religion, and so on, and is lived as a personal construction and individual property, something to invest in. We can readily point to fitness, healthy nutrition, and the use of enhancement technologies (pharmaceutical or cosmetic) as examples of a modern culture of bodily expression in the spirit of the Foucauldian "care of self."

Notwithstanding the continuity regarding the body as medium (material to be shaped) across the modern period, a shift occurs around the turn of the twentieth century and becomes more pronounced as the century moves forward. Historian Bernard Andrieu attributes this shift, characterized by him as the "epistemological dispersion of the human body," to three correlated developments: the invention of psychoanalysis, the emerging philosophical discipline of phenomenology, and progress within cognitive science. In the wake of these developments, the hitherto disjunct domains of bodily life, the body's "interior" and "exterior," began to signify and to matter in unprecedented ways. For psychoanalysis, the goal was to understand the realm of the unconscious and, specifically, how unconscious experience could produce symptoms in the realm of the body; in short, the body became transformed into a vehicle, indeed a medium, for the mind's hidden desires. With the notion of the unconscious, Freud established the existence of a sphere of interiority and a domain of mental life that simply cannot be detached from the body, in that it expresses bodily urges and is itself expressed in embodied form. Nowhere is the centrality of the body in Freud's vision more apparent than in his conceptualization of the body ego, which is to say, the structure through which the self builds its identity. In *The Ego and the Id*, Freud presents the ego as literally a media artifact, the accomplishment of an act of projection: "The ego is first and foremost a bodily ego; it is not merely a surface entity, but is itself the projection of a surface." The ego, then, is both external and internal—inscribed from the outside (through the expectations of others) and built from expectations and desires arising from inside the subject. In the context of media theory, this duality of the body ego—what we might call its projective basis—is absolutely crucial, for it depicts the body as a mediation, and indeed as a double mediation, insofar as the body mediates its meaning via the gaze of others at the same time as it mediates between the world and the construction of self. For psychoanalysis, in other words, the ego (body ego) *is* (the projection of self as) image and, as such, is particularly responsive to the world of images, which for at least the past century have been created and manipulated by the media. The resulting questions concerning the perception of oneself in the gaze of the other or in the mirror (following French psychoanalyst Jacques Lacan's famous conceptualization of the "mirror-stage") go well beyond the scope of psychoanalysis's understanding of the self. They touch upon fundamental philosophical questions of who the subject is, what her body is, and ultimately, where her body "ends."

The question of autoperception—experiencing the world through one's own skin—is also at the core of phenomenology's concerns. The body becomes a necessary intermediary between the self and the world outside. As French philosopher Henri Bergson formulated it in *Matter and Memory* (1896), the body has the responsibility for organizing relations with the outside through its mediation of images: as a privileged image within a "universe of images," the body selects which images are relevant to it and which to let pass unnoticed. On this account, perception is a subtraction from the totality of images (rather than an addition to it, as it is for an idealist like Kant), and the privileged image that is oneself (i.e., one's embodied place in the universe) is therefore the center of one's being and perception, a literal interface to the world.

In later phenomenological approaches to embodiment, body and world are equally inseparable. Although Martin Heidegger denigrates the body as part of the "inauthentic" everyday subsistence of *Dasein* (the human being considered from an existential perspective), for several other major phenomenologists, from Edmund Husserl to Maurice Merleau-Ponty, the body plays a central role. In *Ideas II*, Husserl speaks of the body as a capacity, an "I can" that is more fundamental than the "I think." Drawing upon and expanding Husserl's analysis, Merleau-Ponty centers his *Phenomenology of Perception* on the motility of the body and reconfigures perception as the accomplishment of an embodied cogito acting in the world. In his final unfinished project, *The Visible and the Invisible*, Merleau-Ponty radicalizes his conception of the body: by jettisoning the subject-object division that persisted in his corporeal transformation of the cogito, he is able to correlate the body and the world through a primordial reciprocity which he calls the "flesh." The famous analysis of the hand touching itself that Merleau-Ponty takes up from Husserl demonstrates the reciprocity of the touching and the touched. The resulting duality of sensation underlies the later division of subject and object and serves to establish the world dependence and nonautonomy of any embodied activity.

Although Husserl had relatively little to say about media, Merleau-Ponty's phenomenology is perfectly suited to conceptualizing the fundamental correlation of human embodiment and media on which several media theorists, from McLuhan to French philosopher Bernard Stiegler, have insisted. Much of Merleau-Ponty's research in *The Phenomenology of Perception* involved phenomena of motor deficiency, and he devoted detailed analyses to instances of prosthetic extension, including driving a car and the famous "blind man's cane." Far from being external artifacts to which we adjust objectively, such prosthetic technologies become integrated into our body image and body schema and seamlessly participate in our motor agency. And while the final Merleau-Ponty had little to say directly about media and the flesh, his ecological or environmental conception of "enworlded" human embodiment has obvious and extremely fruitful implications for media theory (for one development of these implications, see Hansen 2006).

Even as the body's interior sphere became increasingly dependent on the projective and motor exteriorizations explored by psychoanalysis and phenomenology, progress in cognitive science opened significant inroads into the structure and operation of the brain itself. The story of cognitive science in the twentieth century is one of gradual disembodiment. For many proponents of artificial intelligence and artificial life, the human body is no longer the basis for mind, and some scientists even conceive of a future in which the body will be left behind in favor of computational or other machinic embodiment. In her important study *How We Became Posthuman*, cultural theorist N. Katherine Hayles names this tendency to privilege the manipulation of information over specific materiality the "posthuman." Tracing the development of cybernetics from its initial formulation after World War II through its embrace of reflexivity and on into contemporary technoscience, Hayles discerns the ideology underlying this privileging of pattern: bluntly put, disembodiment of information allows for fast and easy translation across divergent systems (see chapter 10, "Cybernetics"). Pushed to the extreme, posthumanism sounds downright frightening, if not starkly antihumanist. In the musings of cognitivists such as Ray Kurzweil and Hans Moravec, the body is simply no longer needed; its "wetware" (flesh and blood) is an obstacle to be overcome through such techniques as cryonics (maintaining the body and life at low temperatures) or computational reembodiment (downloading microthin brain layers onto a hard drive). Viewed in the broader philosophical and cultural context, the term *wetware* can be seen as a rhetorical trick to deemphasize the fundamental imbrication of intelligence and embodiment: by positing body and mind as analogues of computer hardware and software, respectively, the informational approach renders their relation purely functional (see chapter 13, "Hardware/Software/Wetware"). Since the middle of the twentieth century, cybernetic discourses have contributed to this framing of the body/mind problem: the body as material substance is likened to a machine, while its mental capacities are figured as programs. When this position yields cyberfantasies of radical disembodiment and transcendence, as it does in technocultural fads like "extropianism" or cryogenics, the centrality of embodiment reappears with a vengeance. Perhaps more than anywhere else, it is at these moments that we most clearly discern the necessary constraint our embodiment exercises on our deep-seated cultural desires for spiritual transcendence.

A more recent perspective in media theory, oriented against this general tendency, has built on the initiatives of psychoanalysis and phenomenology to criticize and undermine the dualistic assumptions concerning the body and mind in modernity and postmodernity. According to this perspective, the digital revolution at the heart of new media has not eliminated the need to think about embodiment; indeed, the body and questions of embodiment are more relevant than ever today. To understand why this is the case, we must return to the concept of the subject, which has been dominant since early modernity. Specifically, we must ask: What has happened to the subject and her auto-awareness in the digital realm?

It is by now a commonplace that the "logic of the computer" has split the self, leaving in its stead multiple agents or selves capable of interacting with various media at the same time by way of multiwindowed screens. While new media pessimists like Jean Baudrillard and Arthur and Mariluise Kroker, writing in the 1990s, fully expected this logic to lead to cultural schizophrenia and ultimately the loss of the body and our control over it, other scholars have emphasized positive aspects of new media. Psychologist Sherry Turkle, for one, has noted that it provides a virtual space of expression, especially for minorities (women, the handicapped), who are now able to perform or mask cultural and gender difference on the Internet. There is no doubt some truth to both of these views. On the one hand, fragmentation of experience has arguably advanced markedly beyond what Walter Benjamin and his cohort bemoaned, and attention span has likely diminished due to the simultaneous use of different media (as, for example, when a user shuttles between writing and monitoring e-mail in expectation of receiving news from a friend). On the other hand, virtual environments expand our range of possible experience: on sites like ishotmyself.com, for example, one can become a porn star for the day.

Not surprisingly, the virtual realm has also been related to the projective ego and the unconscious. Critics like Allucquére Rosanne Stone argue that virtuality allows us to adopt the role of the "other": when interacting in chat rooms, dating platforms, or massive multiplayer role playing games like World of Warcraft, we can take on personas that differ from our own mundane, embodied selves. This phenomenon has led to concrete cases of Internet addiction, as Turkle's work has shown. On a more abstract level, virtuality reveals that the ego has always been virtual: it is, as psychoanalytic theorist Slavoj Zizek emphasizes, a figure capable of taking on, or projecting itself into, many simultaneous roles. Such innovations in the media-theoretical understanding of human subjectivity resonate with other contemporary theories of the body, for instance, the position in gender theory associated with Judith Butler. In *Gender Trouble* (1990), Butler conceptualizes the gendered body as an instance of mediation: rather than taking the body to be inert matter that underlies and precedes social construction, "gender performativity" entails understanding the body as itself built of reiterated daily performances with which we act out gender roles.

Not surprisingly, this understanding of media as not secondary to some natural body but *constitutive of* bodily experience runs across a host of contemporary disciplines. One powerful tendency in late-twentieth-century thought—a tendency that repurposes Freud's characterization of man as a "prosthetic god"—has been to deconstruct the division between a natural state of human being and its technological, medial usurper (Bernard Stiegler). Indeed, this deconstruction is at the heart of one of Jacques Derrida's most influential early texts, *Of Grammatology* (1967), in which he shows that the "natural" in the work of Jean-Jacques Rousseau is always already inhabited by the need for "cultural" education. Moreover, the thinker understood by many to be the father of modern media theory, Marshall McLuhan, referred to media as "extensions of man," and argued forcefully that they needed to be understood as continuous with the human nervous system. The already-mediated body has entered modern medical practice as well. The emerging practice of neurofeedback has enhanced extant biofeedback strategies with the aid of virtual and digital tools. The practice is intended to help patients deal with certain illnesses and conditions or with chronic pain via their own conscious intervention. In other words, the body and the patient's mediated perception of her body are placed into direct and dynamic interaction for the purpose of effecting change at the somatic level.

The incursion of media into the physical milieu of the body has no more striking example than the explosion of cosmetic surgery in recent decades. Whether in private or for the mass audiences of reality TV, people are undergoing surgical intervention in record numbers in the hopes of altering their bodies to fit standards propagated by the mass media, or to match their "inner body" expectations to the exterior body images circulated by the media. This cultural obsession with bodily perfection now transcends the actual procedures of surgical modification, shaping a "cosmetic gaze" (Wegenstein 2006) through which we look at our own and other's bodies with an awareness of how they could be changed.

At the same time, the media have developed in correlation with the needs of the human subject: as Mark Hansen puts it, they have become "corporealized." The subject's auto-awareness of interacting on more than one level of representation has been pushed to its extreme in the unified platforms of the entertainment industry's theme parks, for example, where film, video game, and comic book franchises are marketed to consumers in fully combined forms, as shown by Angela Ndalianis.

This awareness extends too to the realm of advertising and fashion, as, for instance, in watchmechange.com, a Web site launched in 2007 by the Gap clothing chain. Its header reads, "Make your Body. Make your Face. Get dressed." Visitors to the site are invited to explore the possibilities for reshaping body image, with changes to external elements, like clothing—part of the body's "phenotype," so to speak—addressed in the same way that modifications of genotype are addressed in genetic engineering. We first choose a female or male body type (specifying weight, chest size, skin tone, jaw width, nose type, the distance between one's eyes, and so on) and then the kind of clothes we would like to see ourselves in. At this point, the site instructs us to "get ready to shake it off and try it on," and our alter ego starts a virtual strip performance, dancing and "shaking it off" in the changing room. "Change. It feels good," the site declares. "Change your shirt. Change your pants. Change your look. Change your mind. Change one thing. It could change everything."

This melding of subject and media was also the driving theme of a campaign by the design collaborative KnoWear entitled "The Façade of the Synthetic" (2004). In a series of digital billboards, the group manipulated fashion logos, such as those of Chanel or Nike, so that they appeared to be implanted in the skin of their models, emphasizing the extent to which global brands have "gotten under the skin" of the consumer. More even than the Gap ad, which solicits viewer interaction, this campaign foregrounds the fundamental passivity of our embodiment of media images, and thereby effectively erases the distance between unadorned body and product.

The corporealization of new media technology is evident in other realms as well. An example of "media architecture" is the Blur building (2002), a pavilion on lake Neuchâtel in Switzerland, designed by Diller + Scofidio. Hovering mysteriously over the lake, Blur is a dynamic structure that consists, like the human body, almost entirely of water. More specifically, Blur is a "smart weather" device, using 12,500 spray nozzles covering its infrastructure to produce a cloud of mist that changes its appearance depending on the (unpredictable) weather of the day. But it is also, as Hansen points out, "space that has been made wearable": the very configuration of the building owes much, at any point in time, to the movements and interactions of its inhabitants, and the predominate aesthetic of blur has the effect of making space "cling to" the motile body.

Weather, Diller + Scofidio note, exemplifies, perhaps better than any other phenomenon, our contemporary obsession with control and the anxiety that results from our incapacity to manage our environment. Considered in this context, Blur presents weather not as a solely natural process but as a cultural phenomenon; as the architects themselves put it: "At stake is how we interact with each other through weather, not only as a shared obsession but also as a process of global communication." This example perfectly captures just how profoundly the logic of new media has infiltrated our contemporary conceptualization of the body; but it also pinpoints how thinking about the body has, in turn, opened new elements—indeed a renewed concept—of mediation itself. Architecture, traditionally conceived of as the craft of building dwellings for the body, now reflects a sensitivity to dynamic embodiment. In the wake of new media, architecture need no longer narrowly concern itself solely with erecting separate, exterior structures to house bodies but can position itself as an exteriorization of embodiment, which is to say, as a design practice fundamentally continuous with the body's own status as medium.

The phenomenological conceptualization of embodiment at issue here resonates with McLuhan's analysis of clothing in *Understanding Media*. For McLuhan, clothes must be understood as extensions of the skin, which means that, in addition to changing the appearance of the body, they impact its agency in the external world. Perhaps no media artist has explored this dual capacity more deeply than Italian artist Alba d'Urbano. During the 1990s, d'Urbano experimented with images of her own skin, which she digitized, processed, reshaped, and cut into the pattern of a "skin-suit." In her 1995 project *Hautnah* (German for "close as skin," or idiomatically, "immediate," "very close"), the artist "took off her own skin" in order to offer others the possibility of walking through the world it conceals. One profound effect of this work is to refocus attention on the skin itself as "clothing," that is to say, as medium or exteriorization of the body. In a literal sense, d'Urbano makes clothing from her own skin, exposing the body's nakedness but in a form that can be worn by others as an extension of their skin. As a site of convergence between inner consciousness and outer reality, the skin literally fuses "nature" and "culture," and the genius of *Hautnah* is to reveal how this fusion can be grasped only through mediation—through the imaginary activity of abandoning one's own skin or putting on somebody else's.

Crucial to the critical impact of d'Urbano's exploration of the skin as surface, as the fusion of inside and outside, is her decision to exhibit her "skin-suit" on a coat hanger. This decision reenacts the logic of objectification that has placed women in the role of object to be viewed and that enacts the artist's expropriation of her own skin. In this regard, it is significant that the skin-suit—made of material printed with images of the naked skin of the artist's body—has neither hands, feet, nor face; these interactive body parts have simply been cut off. Is d'Urbano trying

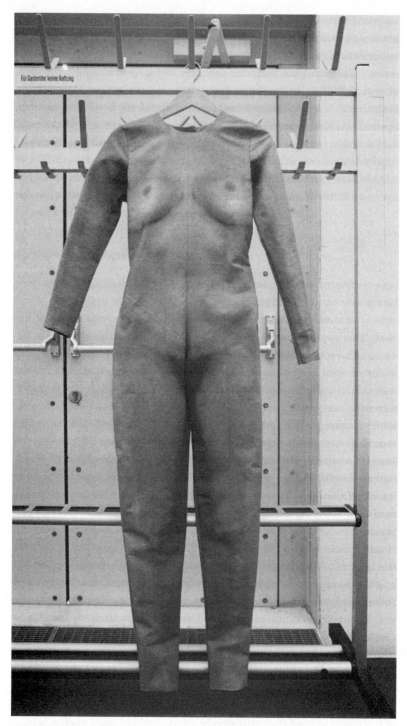

Alba d'Urbano, *Hautnah*, 1995. Installation photo courtesy of the artist.

to tell us that the mediated body no longer needs the parts that render it a motile whole? Can we read the absence of interactivity, represented here by negation, as more than simply a familiar feminist critique of a male-dominated gaze that has torn the female body from its (natural) environment? Can we read it, that is, as an exemplification of the technological possibilities for dissociation and exteriorization—in this case, *of the skin from the body*—that promise to reconfigure our understanding of how the body is always "essentially" mediated?

These examples from new media art and architecture engage in a topology of embodiment that questions the stable distinction between inside and outside. The operative figure for this topology is the Möbius strip, a paradoxical surface constructed by connecting the ends of a planar figure after one of those ends has been given a half twist. The result, while appearing to have two sides, in fact has only one continuous side. If one travels long enough along the surface, one finds one has ended up on the other "side," without ever having crossed over. The Möbius strip has been a standard metaphor for theorists from Jacques Lacan to Elizabeth Grosz, who have used it to conceptualize the body and subjectivity as an indivisible complex, in which the outside flows to the inside without any apparent break. The skin, as a result, is rethought as porous and fluid, the site of encounter and exposure between body and media rather than a site of exclusion and closure. This has been particularly fruitful for feminist thought, in that it has allowed the body to be reconceptualized as a site of cultural inscription without thereby losing its status as a materially substantial entity. A body with such fluid borders—borders that allow a womb to be extended to a test tube, for example—opens the door to a potentially endless series of practices, from reproductive to self-enhancing, all of which open for women a much larger platform of gender identification than has previously been available. Furthermore, and perhaps more profoundly, what these examples signal is how current critical artistic expression has taken embodiment as a vital subject of engagement. While these developments certainly do not serve to establish that the digital age has discovered the body as medium, what they do suggest is that current trends in thinking and engaging technically and artistically with the body aim to redress the predilection toward disembodiment in modern culture.

Let us conclude, then, by returning to our opening questions: Should the body be considered a medium and, if so, what is at stake? What I have tried to show in this brief overview is that the body has always been a medium, and indeed, that it is the most primordial medium, the basis for all subsequent forms of mediation. Different times and different cultures deploy the mediality of the body in radically different ways, and the fundamental contribution of understanding the body as medium is to reveal the extent to which the resulting body practices are rooted in culture. This same cultural rootedness pertains to practices that are ostensibly most "objective," for example, practices that analyze the body as an object of science. While it is perhaps easy for the scientist to forget the cultural specificity of her approach to the body, this specificity remains central to our proper understanding of the body's mediation of life. As I have suggested, this reality takes center stage in more recent conceptualizations of the body in theoretical work and in media art and architecture where the overriding task has been to redress a previous tendency to overlook embodiment when looking at the body—to overlook, in other words, how the body is always our most fundamental medium of knowledge and experience.

References and Suggested Readings

Bergson, Henri. 1990. *Matter and Memory*. Trans. N. M. Paul and W. S. Palmer. New York: Zone Books.

Hansen, Mark. 2004. *New Philosophy for New Media*. Cambridge, MA: MIT Press.

———. 2006. *Bodies in Code: Interfaces with Digital Media*. New York: Routledge.

Hayles, N. Katherine. 1999. *How We Became Posthuman*. Chicago: University of Chicago Press.

Jonas, Hans. 1982. *The Phenomenon of Life: Toward a Philosophical Biology*. Chicago: University of Chicago Press.

Merleau-Ponty, Maurice. 1969. *The Visible and the Invisible*. Trans. Alphonso Lingis. Evanston, IL: Northwestern University Press.

Ndalianis, Angela. 2005. *Neo-Baroque Aesthetics and Contemporary Entertainment*. Cambridge, MA: MIT Press.

Stiegler, Bernard. 1998. *Technics and Time 1*. Trans. Richard Beardsworth and George Collins. Stanford, CA: Stanford University Press.

———. 2009. *Technics and Time 2*. Trans. Steven Barker. Stanford, CA: Stanford University Press.

Wegenstein, Bernadette. 2006. *Getting under the Skin: Body and Media Theory*. Cambridge, MA: MIT Press.

Zizek, Slavoj. 1992. *Looking Awry*. Cambridge, MA: MIT Press.

3 :: IMAGE

W.J.T. MITCHELL

What is the relation of images and media? It is commonplace to remark (usually with alarm) on the overwhelming number of images that bombard people who live in modern media cultures, which in an age of global media means almost all cultures. When a globally significant event occurs (war, natural disaster), a "storm of images" sweeps across the planet (to echo a *New York Times*' account of the media coverage of Hurricane Katrina in September 2005). New technologies such as the Internet and global television, coupled with the digitization of images, seem to accelerate these storms, heating up the mediasphere and flooding television watchers with "gross and violent stimulants" in the form of images.

The remainder of mass-media culture is devoted to the production of the imagistic equivalent of junk food: instant celebrities, pop stars, sports heroes, politicians, and pundits, whose "images" are carefully cultivated by publicists and whose misfortunes and personal failings provide the centerpiece for entertaining scandals when the supply of violence, catastrophe, and other serious news runs low. As Marshall McLuhan noted, the news is always bad, dominated by images of destruction, sorrow, and grief: "if it bleeds, it leads." But that is merely the sour or salty form of junk food, balancing the sweetness of commercials, which bring "good news"—promises of pain relief, beauty, health, and sexual prowess (punctuated by ominous warnings about side effects).

When it comes to mass media, then, one seems compelled to agree with the Canon camera commercial in which tennis star Andre Agassi asserted that "image is everything." Or with the contrary message, from a later Coca-Cola campaign: that "image is nothing." Or, perhaps, with the deeper truth revealed in an advertisement for Sprite: that "thirst is everything." Whatever the truth of images in media might be, then, we will have to reckon with their radically contradictory reputation as "everything" and "nothing," the most valuable and powerful elements of the messages transmitted by media, or the most trivial, degraded, and worthless. To understand their paradoxical status, we will have to take a longer view of images in media, asking what they are and why it is that, since time immemorial, they have been both adored and reviled, worshipped and banned, created with exquisite artistry and destroyed with boundless ferocity.

Images did not have to wait for the arrival of modern mass media to acquire this all-or-nothing status. The three great religions of the book, Judaism, Christianity, and Islam, agree on two things: that human beings are created "in the image" of God, and that human beings should not make images, because human-made images are vain, illusory things. One should not take the Lord's *name* in vain, but his *image* is inherently contaminated by vanity and hollowness. The second commandment is absolutely clear on this matter:

> Thou shalt not make unto thee any graven image, or any likeness of any thing that is in heaven above, or that is in the earth beneath, or that is in the water under the earth. Thou shalt not bow down thyself to them, nor serve them. (Exodus 20:4–5, King James Version)

Ingenious commentators through the ages have tried to read this as a ban only on the idolatrous worship of images, not on the production of images more generally. But the language of the commandment is clear. It rules out the creation of images of any sort, for any reason. Perhaps there is a "slippery slope" principle underlying this zero-tolerance policy, a conviction that, sooner or later, images will turn into idols if we allow them to be created in the first place.

Clearly the prohibition on graven images has not worked very well. There may be some aniconic cultures that have succeeded in keeping some kinds of images out of sight (the Taliban are an interesting case), but most cultures, even officially iconoclastic ones such as Judaism and Islam, tolerate innumerable exceptions to the ban (think of the gigantic portraits of Islamic saints and heroes, from the Ayatollah Khomeini to Osama bin Laden).[1] And Christianity, with its spectacular rituals and televangelism, not to mention its encyclopedic repertoire of iconic figures—saints, angels, devils—and the central tableau of the Passion of Christ, himself the incarnate "image of God," has long since given up any real interest in the second commandment. Roman Catholic Christianity perfected the art of mass distribution of holy images as early as the Middle Ages, creating those forerunners of mass-media spectacle known as cathedrals. Cathedrals were sometimes erected, moreover, on the ruins of Greek and Roman temples which had been dedicated to the worship of pagan idols. Modern, secular, "enlightened" cultures have been no better when it comes to erection of cult images and sacred icons: The atheists of the French Revolution erected a statue to the Goddess of Reason; godless Communism produced its own pantheon of heroic idols, from Marx to Lenin to Stalin to Mao; fascism's führer cult borrowed from the iconography of paganism and Norse mythology, transforming German burghers into Wagnerian gods and goddesses; and in the United States, the American flag is routinely treated to rituals of political sanctification. All American politicians must drape themselves in the flag or include it in their photo opportunities, while enormous amounts of overheated rhetoric are expended to head off the (extremely rare) practices of flag desecration.

There are important differences between the role of images in modern mass media and more traditional ways of circulating images to large bodies of people. The invention of photography, cinema, television, and the Internet has brought about a degree of image saturation in global culture that was unimaginable in earlier times. This has led a number of scholars to postulate a "pictorial turn" in modern culture, a qualitative shift in the importance of images driven by their quantitative proliferation.[2] First came the mechanical reproduction of images, exemplified, as Walter Benjamin argued, by the recording technologies of photography and cinema; then electronic communication (Marshall McLuhan's central focus) via "real-time" broadcast and communication media such as radio, television, and the Internet; and most recently biocybernetic reproduction. Biocybernetics, the newest technology of image-production in the sphere of what has come to be called "biomedia" (see chapter 8), is exemplified by the production of those "living images" we call clones. Cloning has reawakened all the ancient phobias and taboos regarding the creation of images because it seems quite literally to introduce the prospect of "playing god" by taking over the role of making creatures.

The relation of images to media, then, is a highly sensitive barometer of the history of technology, perhaps because the repertoire of image types (faces, figures, objects, landscapes, abstract forms) has remained relatively stable even as the technical means of reproducing and circulating them has been altered radically. The invention of new means of image production and reproduction, from the stamping of coins to the printing press to lithography, photography, film, video, and digital imaging, is often accompanied by a widespread perception that a "pictorial turn" is taking place, often with the prediction of disastrous consequences for culture. A history of the relation of images and media, then, clearly has to be wary of binary narratives that postulate a single decisive transition from "traditional" or "ancient" media to "modern" or "postmodern" forms. The history of media technology suggests that it has been subject to important innovations from the very beginning, since at least the invention of writing. The invention of metal casting was a decisive innovation in ancient Rome and China. The invention of oil painting in Renaissance Europe created a revolution in the circulation of images, freeing them from their muralistic attachment to architecture and transforming them into movable property, commodities to be exchanged and sold and copied in the new industry of reproductive engraving. The invention of artificial perspective produced a new relationship between image making and empirical sciences such as geometry and surveying.

While technical innovation is a crucial element of media history and its relation to images, however, it is not the only factor. Political, economic, and cultural influences also play a role. Media are not just materials or technologies but social institutions like guilds, trades, professions, and corporations. The history of mass media in the United States is very different from that of Europe, despite the fact that both sides of the Atlantic are using much the same technologies—movable type, offset printing, electronic tubes, and fiber-optic cables.

What does seem to remain constant across the cycles of media innovation and obsolescence is the problem of the image. The deeply ambivalent relationship between human beings and the images they create seems to flare up into crisis at moments of technical innovation, when a new medium makes possible new kinds of images, often more lifelike and persuasive than ever before, and seemingly more volatile and virulent, as if images were dangerous microbes that could infect the minds of their consumers. This may be why the default position of image theorists and media analysts is that of the idol-smashing prophet warning against Philistines—the exemplary ancient idolaters, since reincarnated in modern kitsch and mass culture. The same critic will, however, typically be engaged in elevating certain kinds of images in selected types of media to the status of art. Aesthetic status is often credited with a redeeming effect on the degraded currency of images, as if the image had somehow been purified of commercial or ideological contamination by its remediation within certain approved media frameworks (typically, art galleries, museums, and prestigious collections). Even a nakedly commercial image from mass culture can be redeemed in this way, as the silk screens of Andy Warhol demonstrate.

As a critical term in the study of media, however, *image* has to be subjected to a more dispassionate analysis, one that brackets the question of value at least provisionally. For the remainder of this essay, therefore, I will concentrate on defining the image and its relation to media in a way that will help us to understand why images have the power to elicit such passion.

First, a definition: An image is a sign or symbol of something by virtue of its sensuous resemblance to what it represents. An image or "icon," as the philosopher C. S. Peirce defined it, cannot merely signify or represent something; it must also possess what he called "firstnesses"—inherent qualities such as color, texture, or shape that are the first things to strike our senses—(what Erwin Panofsky called the "pre-iconographic" qualities of an image, the things we perceive before we are even concerned about what the image represents).[3] These qualities must elicit a perception of resemblance to something else, so that the object produces a double take: it is what it is (say, a piece of painted canvas), and it is like another thing (a view of an English landscape). Where this likeness or resemblance is to be found, and what exactly it consists in, is often a matter of dispute. Some locate it in specific properties of the object, others in the mind of the beholder, while others look for a compromise. Some philosophers have debunked the entire notion of resemblance as too vague to be the foundation of any referential or significant relationship, since *everything* can be said to resemble everything else in some respect or other.[4] The perception of resemblance may turn out to be a *result* of image making rather than a foundation for it; Picasso famously told a critic who complained that his portrait of Gertrude Stein did not look like her, "Don't worry. It will."

We experience the image as a double moment of appearing and recognition, the simultaneous noticing of a material object and an apparition, a form or a deformation. An image is always both there and not there, appearing *in* or *on* or *as* a material object yet also ghostly, spectral, and evanescent. Although images are almost automatically associated with the representation of objects in space, it is important to recognize that some form of temporality is built in to our encounter with any image: phenomenologists note what we might call the "onset" of an image, the event of its recognition, and the "second look" or double take that Wittgenstein called "the dawning of an aspect."[5] An image may also bear other signs of temporality—a date of origin or production (central to the ontology of photographs), a historical style, a depicted narrative (as in history painting), or a labyrinthine interiority that leads the beholder on a pursuit of its depths, as when we observe a drawing coming into the world, drawing out of invisibility the trace of something that is coming into view. Images often appear in series, as in the Stations of the Cross, which narrate the story of the Passion of Christ and call the spectator to enact a ritual performance. And we must not forget that the image has always been, even before the invention of cinema, an object that is potentially, virtually, or actually in *motion*. The real-time images of a camera obscura move if the objects in them move, and their stillness (like that of webcam or surveillance photos) is nevertheless suffused with time (which, in the contemporary examples may be documented, to the millisecond, in an accompanying time stamp). The silhouettes projected on the walls of Plato's cave are cast by a moving *procession* of sculpted images. The entire history of dramatic performance is bound up with what Aristotle called *opsis* (spectacle), *lexis* (words), and *melos* (music). Actors on stage do not represent themselves; they imitate—that is, produce *images* of—characters and actions through costume and gesture in a setting that is also a scenographic image, because of either the set designer's artistry or the imaginative activity of the spectator (as in Shakespeare's famous call, from the pit of the Globe Theater, to "imagine yourself in the fields of France").[6] The very first image, in biblical tradition, is a sculpted object made of clay that does not remain inert but has life and motion breathed into it by its creator.

So the image is the uncanny content of a medium, the shape or form it assumes, the thing that makes its appearance in a medium while making the medium itself appear as a medium. It remains in memory as a place or face encountered, a landscape or a body, a ground or a figure, a repeatable gesture or "movement image." This is why an image can appear in a narrative or poem as well as in a painting, and be recognizable as "the same" (or at least a similar) image. A Golden Calf, for instance, can be "remediated," appearing in a text, a painting, and (in its proper appearance) in a statue.[7] Images (in contrast to "cultural icons") are not that special or unusual. They are everywhere, a kind of background noise to everyday life. They can rise out of accidental perceptions as well intentional acts, so that we see a face in the clouds, or (as Leonardo da Vinci recommended) look for landscapes and battle scenes in the splashes of mud thrown against a wall by passing carts.

Everything about the relation of images and media, then, seems to expose contradictory tendencies. They can be representational and referential, or "abstract" (a purely geometric circle becomes, with a single well-placed mark, a face with a smiling mouth). Their range of formal possibilities extends from the strictly defined shape to the chaotic jumble, from a geometrically precise design to a Minimalist scatter piece. They can appear as formal, deformed, or *informel*, a readily standardized stereotype or a hideously deformed caricature, a ghostly illusion for the superstitious or a testable scientific model for the skeptical observer. They can be found in architecture as well as in pictures. They can provide maps of empirical reality, or of Neverlands and utopias. They can be achingly beautiful, ugly, monstrous, wondrous, cute, ridiculous, enigmatic, transparent, or sublime. They can be, in short, anything that human imagination, perception, and sensory experience is capable of fashioning for itself as an object of contemplation or distraction.

And this is one of the most puzzling things about the concept of the image. Although we generally think of images first as material pictures or objects in the world, tangible things that can be created and destroyed, we also routinely speak of them as *mental* things—memories, fantasies, dreams, hypnagogic reveries, hallucinations, and other psychological phenomena that can be accessed only indirectly, through verbal descriptions or graphic depictions. What is the status of the "mental image" from the standpoint of media studies? Certainly if *memory* is regarded as a medium, then images will be an important element of the content of memory, along with narratives, lyrics, words, and phrases. Whenever we try to give an account of mental images, we seem compelled to resort to some external, material apparatus as the model for the mind—a theater or cinema, a *musée imaginaire*, a camera obscura, a computer, a camera. We find it difficult to talk about the mind without comparing it to a medium of some sort, often a medium that entails the internal display, projection, or storage and retrieval of images. It is as if, alongside the images *in* media, we have images *of* media that we internalize as subjective pictures of our own mental processes—the mind as photographic apparatus or blank slate, as Freud's "mystic writing tablet," set to receive impressions. In this sense, all images, no matter how public and concrete their staging, are mental things, in the sense that they depend upon creatures with minds to perceive them. (Some images, decoys, for instance, reach below the threshold of human consciousness to attract the attention of animals.)

Of course, in bringing up the mind as a medium for the storage and retrieval of images, one is immediately confronted with the fact that all the minds we know about are housed in *bodies*. To speak of mental images is automatically to be led into the problem of embodiment, and the material world of sensuous experience, whether it is the generalized "human body" of phenomenology or the historically marked and disciplined body of race, gender, sexual orientation, disability, and biomedical technology (see chapter 2, "Body"). Our pursuit of the image across media seems endless and perhaps circular, beginning in the real world with concrete pictures and representational objects in all manner of media, moving rapidly into the mental lives of the producers and consumers of these media, then returning to their physical existence in concrete circumstances. From the standpoint of media theory, then, it is perhaps inevitable that images become the central element of media functions, the thing that both circulates through all conceivable varieties of media as an appearance or communicated content, and emerges from this flux in the moment of secondary reflection to provide models for the entire process. The image, in other words, is both at the center and the circumference of the problem of media: images always appear *in* some medium or other, and we cannot understand media without constructing images *of* them.

Senses and Signs

The default meaning of image is "visual image," though that very phrase suggests that images can be apprehended by, and addressed to, other, nonvisual senses. Acoustic, tactile, gustatory, and even olfactory images are unavoidable notions, and they satisfy the same basic definition of imagery: they are signs or symbols by way of sensuous resemblance, bundles of analog information carried by different sensory vehicles, received by distinct perceptual channels. A sugar substitute doesn't merely "signify" sweetness but awakens the sensation we associate with sugar. When Nutrasweet learns to simulate the granular, crystalline appearance of sugar as well as its taste on the tongue, it will be a more perfect icon. Algebraic notations such as "equals," "is congruent with," and "is similar to" are, as Peirce noted, icons in the sense that they make a highly abstract relation of resemblance or equivalence immediately visible. When the channels or senses are crossed or confused, we speak of "synesthetic" images, colors heard as sounds or vice versa. The ordinary vocabulary of music invokes visual and graphic analogies such as color, line, and gesture, and verbal "echoes," assonance, alliteration, and rhythmic figures and rhymes are fundamental to the way that aural images arise in the sound of words.

Returning to the default, it is a commonplace in media studies to use phrases like "visual media" or "visual art" to mean roughly the same thing: forms such as painting, photography, sculpture, cinema, and television that are treated as fundamentally addressed to the eye. These are commonly distinguished from "verbal media"—literature, books, newspapers (the "print" media)—the distinction almost invariably accompanied by ritual lamentation over the decline of literacy and the displacement of reading by spectatorship. But a moment's reflection suggests that the situation is not quite so simple. First, all the examples of "visual media," and especially the mass media, turn out to be *mixed* media that combine visual and acoustic images, sights and sounds, pictures and words. Second, the so-called print media have, from their beginnings, included printed *pictures* and other graphic images. Moreover, print itself, as a material medium, is taken in by the eyes. The choice of typeface or font is itself a choice about the "look" of a text. Marshall McLuhan famously argued that the Gutenberg revolution was the transformation of a previously oral culture into a visual culture. The linear process of reading, he suggested, was closely aligned with the development of the linear, geometrically defined space of artificial perspective.

When we talk about "verbal" and "visual" media, then, we are confusing two quite different distinctions, one involving semiotics (the classification of signs) and the other involving the senses. On the terrain of signs, the difference between the verbal and visual is the difference between what Peirce would call a symbol, an arbitrary and conventional sign, and an iconic sign, which signifies by virtue of its sensuous resemblance to what it stands for. Most examples of print media (say, newspapers and magazines) deploy both words—verbal signs that are to be read as arbitrary symbols—and visual images, iconic signs that are scanned for their resemblance to things in the world.

On the terrain of the senses, by contrast, the verbal/visual distinction is that between hearing and seeing, speaking and showing, oral and visual communication. The distinction between signs and codes fades into the background; icons and symbols can appear on *either* side of the divide. Conventional, arbitrary symbols can be addressed to the eye or to the ear, as can iconic signs. Media based in "visual images" comprise the full range of print culture, and media based in "acoustic images" cross the boundaries of speech and music. The figure below will clarify the intersection of the double distinction between signs and senses that underlies the often confusing categories of verbal and visual media.[8]

The Digital Image

No account of the image in media studies would be complete without some discussion of the "digital image." Some scholars have argued that the arrival of computer-processed images has produced a radical transformation in the ontology of the image, altering its fundamental essence as an object of human experience. One line of thinking holds that digital images (in contrast to traditional, chemical-based photographs) have lost their causal, indexical linkage to "the real," becoming untethered ap-

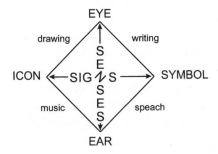

pearances subject to willful manipulation. This was, of course, always a possibility with hand-made images, which often represented things that no one had ever seen. (The emphasis on *manipulation,* a term that carries within it the image of the human hand, is interesting in relation to the fingers figured in *digital*.) If we confine the question to the history of photography, it seems clear that both the profilmic event and the dark-room process have always been manipulable, if not with the ease and rapidity provided by programs such as Photoshop. Nonetheless, digital images, like the photographs of torture at Abu Ghraib prison, seem to retain their credibility. In general, we might say that claims about a photograph's connection to "the real" are heavily dependent upon what precisely counts as the relevant notion of the real, and upon attendant circumstances, such as who took the picture when. Photographs are not taken "on faith" in a courtroom: their veracity must be vouched for by secondary testimony and human witnesses. The aura of self-evidence that hovers about images in any medium, their sensuous presence or "firstness" (to recall Peirce's terminology), can lend them an easy credibility that may be the occasion for a sense of their faithfulness to the real, or (for the very same reason) can make them objects of suspicion. If digitization has produced a change in the ontology of images, it might, then, be more plausibly sought in the changed conditions of their "being in the world"—the changed conditions of their production and circulation, the exponential increase in the number of images, and the rapidity of their transmission, especially via the Internet.

Another, even more radical claim for the novelty of the digital is that it has rendered the image "in its traditional sense" obsolete. The image, recoded as pure numerical information, is, in principle, quite independent of the human body and its senses. The sensuous "firstness" of the image and its reliance on the analog code of infinitely differentiated impressions and similitudes is replaced by a language that is read (and written) by machines. The old regime of sensuous images is reduced to mere surface appearance or "eyewash," to use Friedrich Kittler's term; what is important and real are the ones and zeros of the binary code. Unsurprisingly, this argument is often accompanied by a dark, dystopian vision of a "posthuman" order. If man was created in God's image and God was remade in man's, with the onset of secular humanism, it makes a kind of sense that the invention of artificial intelligence and "thinking machines" would mark the end of the human and the image altogether. The posthuman imaginary postulates robots and cyborgs—biomechanical hybrids—as the emergent life-forms of our time. "Man" and "woman" have become obsolete categories—stereotyped image classes—to be replaced, one hopes, by actually existing men and women.

The postulation of the digital image as a radical break with the past has not gone unchallenged. The liveliest images of the posthuman digital age continue to be located in the future, in science fiction films and novels (both traditional genres).[9] The numerical or "digital infrastructure" beneath the "eyewash" of analog experience remains the province of technicians, not ordinary users, who treat digital images in much the same way as analog images (except easier to copy and distribute). It is sometimes claimed that digitization introduces a component of interactivity between the beholder and the image that was unavailable to traditional images: one can "click" on a hot spot in a digital image and go to another one, or change the look of the image, or open up a textual gloss, or even (in Lev Manovich's concept of the "image-interface" and the "image-instrument") treat the image as a control panel for the manipulation of information. Yet interactivity and immersion have been features of image culture at least since Plato's cave or the invention of carnival. As for the obsolescence of the analog image, one cannot help but notice that, at the precise moment when a stream of alphanumeric ciphers is unveiled as the deep truth of the digital "matrix" in the film by that title, the digits align themselves into the analog human shapes of the "agents" of the Matrix. All the counting and calculation and computation that underlies the digital image comes home to roost, finally, in what Brian Massumi has called "the superiority of the analog." If the ones and zeros did not add up to an image that massages the familiar and traditional habits of the human sensorium, it is unlikely that the digital revolution would have gained any traction at all.

This is not to argue that, when it comes to images, there is nothing new under the sun. But whatever this newness is, it will not likely be well described by a binary history that separates the digital image from all that proceeded it. For one thing, the very idea of the digital is ambiguous. Nelson Goodman argued that what makes a code digital is not numbers or counting but the use of a finite number of characters or elements, differentiated without ambiguity from one another. The alphabet, under this definition, is digital. Mosaic tile would count as a digital medium, as would the benday dots of newspaper images. But if digitization is confined to systems using numbers, and specifically to the binary system that underlies computer processes, then something of the specificity of contemporary digital imaging may be discerned. Mark Hansen argues, contra Manovich, that

> it is not simply that the image provides a tool for the user to control the "infoscape" of contemporary material culture . . . but rather that the "image" has itself become a process and, as such, has become irreduc-

ibly bound up with the activity of the body. Specifically, we must accept that the image, rather than finding instantiation in a privileged technical form (including the computer interface), now demarcates the very process through which the body, in conjunction with the various apparatuses for rendering information perceptible, gives form to or *in-forms* information. In sum, the image can no longer be restricted to the level of surface appearance, but must be extended to encompass the entire process by which information is made perceivable through embodied experience. This is what I propose to call the *digital image*. (Hansen 2004, 10)

I would agree with everything in this passage except for the tense of the predicates; the image, I would suggest, *has always been* bound up with the body, but that interconnection is now made evident by the onset of digital imaging, in the sense of binary computation. Just as photography revealed unseen and overlooked visual realities, an "optical unconscious" in Walter Benjamin's phrase, and just as cinema produced both a new analysis and a historical transformation of human visual experience, digital imaging may be uncovering yet another layer of the perceptible cognitive world that we will recognize as having always been there. We know that the most archaic images have always involved "a process . . . bound up with the activity of the body," that they have always given form to information. But now we are in a position, thanks to the invention of digital imaging, to know it in a new way. Our situation may be very like that of Alberti, who understood that artists had already known how to represent depth, foreshortening, and other practical equivalents of perspective, but whose treatise, *Della Pittura*, made these practices accessible in a new way to systematic, mathematical analysis and unforeseen extrapolations.

New technical media certainly do make for new possibilities in the production, distribution, and consumption of images, not to mention their qualitative appearance. Artists, as Marshall McLuhan observed, are often at the forefront of experimentation with the potential of new media, and earlier media innovations such as photography and cinema, which were widely regarded as inherently hostile to artistic expression, are now firmly canonized as artistic media of the first importance. But media innovation is driven by other factors as well: by technoscientific research, by the profit motive, and by emergency situations such as war. If researchers like Paul Virilio and Friedrich Kittler are correct, one cannot understand stereophonic sound without considering the guidance apparatus developed to allow bomber pilots to fly "blind" in a fog, the movie camera without considering its evolution from the machine gun, or the Internet without considering it origins in military communication. One must recognize, however, the conservative trajectory of these inventions, their tendency to return to the "firstnesses" of sensuous, analog experience. The bomber pilot's stereo headphones find their cultural vocation as a means to mediate the image of realistic acoustical space, the sound of an orchestra in a concert hall. The staccato shots of the machine gun become the photographic shots that together form a "movement-image" of the human body in action (or a "time-image" of a body doing nothing at all, as with the still images that convey the story in Chris Marker's classic film *La Jetée*). The Internet becomes a metamedium that incorporates the postal system, television, computer programming, the telephone, newspapers, magazines, bulletin boards, advertising, banking, and gossip. Images continue to arise and circulate in these new media, metastasizing and evolving so rapidly that no conceivable archive could ever contain them all.

It seems unlikely, then, that any new technology is going to render images, or sensuous firstnesses, resemblances, or analog codes, obsolete. The persistence of these qualities is what ensures that, no matter how calculable or measurable images become, they will maintain the uncanny, ambiguous character that has from the first made them objects of fascination and anxiety. We will never be done with asking what images mean, what effects they have on us, and what they want from us.

Notes

1. See Bland (2000) on the role of images in Jewish culture.

2. See Boehm and Mitchell (2009), Mirzoeff (2000).

3. Peirce's icon should not be confused with what we have been calling "cultural icons," which are images that have a special importance (religious icons, idols, patriotic symbols). The icon in Peirce's sense is merely a sign by resemblance.

4. See Nelson Goodman, *The Languages of Art*, for the most sustained critique of the notion of resemblance as a basis for representation.

5. Wittgenstein, *Philosophical Investigations*.

6. *Henry IV, Part I*, Prologue.

7. See Jay David Boulter and Richard Grusin, *Remediation: Understanding New Media* (Cambridge, MA: MIT Press, 2000).

8. I have confined this discussion of sensory modalities to the eye and ear, what Hegel called "the theoretic senses." A fuller analysis would suggest that the proper categories are not *eye* and *ear* but the *scopic* and *vocative* drives, which combine eye/hand and ear/mouth. It would also note that vision itself is constituted as the coordination of optical and tactile sensations. We could not see anything if our sensory-motor system had not learned to navigate the world by moving through and touching it. See my article "There Are No Visual Media," in *Media Art Histories*, ed. Oliver Grau (Cambridge, MA: MIT Press, 2007), 395–406.

9. Similarly, the hyperbolic rhetoric surrounding the invention of new, immersive 3-D im-

ages, billed as "virtual realilty," seems to have subsided or become a staple of cinematic remediation in various forms of special effects.

References and Suggested Readings

Benjamin, Walter. 2002. "The Work of Art in the Age of Its Technical Reproducibility." In *Walter Benjamin: Selected Writings*, vol. 3, *1935–1938*, ed. Howard Eiland and Michael W. Jennings, 101–33. Cambridge, MA: Harvard University Press.

Berkeley, George. 1709. *An Essay towards a New Theory of Vision*. London.

Bland, Kalman. 2000. *The Artless Jew: Medieval and Modern Affirmations and Denials of the Visual*. Princeton, NJ: Princeton University Press.

Boehm, Gottfried, and W. J. T. Mitchell. 2009. "Pictorial versus Iconic Turn: Two Letters." In *The Pictorial Turn*, ed. Neal Curtis. London: Routledge.

Goodman, Nelson. 1976. *Languages of Art*. Indianapolis: Hackett.

Hansen, Mark. 2004. *New Philosophy for New Media*. Cambridge, MA: MIT Press.

Kittler, Friedrich. 1999. *Gramophone, Film, Typewriter*. Stanford, CA: Stanford University Press.

McLuhan, Marshall. 1964. *Understanding Media*. New York: McGraw-Hill.

Manovich, Lev. 2002. *The Language of New Media*. Cambridge, MA: MIT Press.

Mirzoeff, Nicholas. 2000. *An Introduction to Visual Culture*. London: Routledge.

Mitchell, W. J. T. 1994. *Picture Theory*. Chicago: University of Chicago Press.

Mitchell, William J. 1992. *The Reconfigured Eye*. Cambridge, MA: MIT Press.

Peirce, C. S. 1931–58. "The Icon, Index, and Symbol." In *Collected Works*, vol. 2, ed. Charles Hartshorne and Paul Weiss. Cambridge, MA: Harvard University Press.

Wittgenstein, Ludwig. 1953. *Philosophical Investigations*. New York: Macmillan.

4 :: MATERIALITY BILL BROWN

The thorn lodged in your swollen thumb is matter; the thought lodged in your mind is not. Yet that discrepancy can be troubled by any admission that thoughts are the outcome of, say, electrochemical impulses, or even (to borrow a medium-inspired trope) the effect of synapses within a neural network. No matter how immaterial you understand your thoughts to be, you can't help but grant that they have some neurophysiological ground. Which is simply to say that the process of thinking has a materiality of its own.

This hardly means that you should abandon the original distinction (phenomenological or epistemological or ontological) between thoughts and thorns. Rather, it's a way to begin recognizing how, both in ordinary language and more specialized language, *materiality* can refer to different dimensions of experience, or dimensions beyond (or below) what we generally consider experience to be. Like many concepts, *materiality* may seem to make the most sense when it is opposed to another term: the material serves as a commonsensical antithesis to, for instance, the spiritual, the abstract, the phenomenal, the virtual, and the formal, not to mention the immaterial. And yet *materiality* has a specificity that differentiates it from its superficial cognates, such as physicality, reality, or concreteness. When you admire the materiality of a sweater, you're acknowledging something about its look and feel, not simply its existence as a physical object. When you complain of another sweater that it lacks this materiality, you're not asserting its immateriality. And if, after machine-washing the first sweater, you allow that you have witlessly destroyed its materiality, you mean that you've altered some of its physical qualities, not that you have eradicated the object tout court. Nonetheless, the obfuscation of an object can be the requisite result of gaining greater access to its material components—dramatizing its materiality, let us say—especially when that access has been technologically mediated. Magnetic resonance imaging (MRI) can show us the material within objects—the brain tissue within the skull and thus, perhaps, the material source of some pathological condition—but it does so at the expense of skin and bone. You might say, then, that this visualizing medium at once materializes and dematerializes the human body.

Such permutations should be kept in mind when considering any declaration about the dematerialization, via digital encoding, of the material world. Nonetheless, insofar as such declarations register genuine change—change in what we experience and how we do so—they merit attention, not least because they inhabit a tradition (extending from Karl Marx and Max Weber to Guy Debord and Jean Baudrillard) within which the process of modernization or of postmodernization has been understood as one of abstraction. It could well be argued, moreover, that the digital's apparent threat to materiality helped provoke a new materialist turn that began to thrive in the 1990s within a variety of disciplines: anthropology, art history, history, cinema studies, the history of science, and literary and cultural studies. Within media history, media theory, and cybercultural studies, this provocation has focused attention on the materiality of the medium, of information, and of communication, inspiring research on a wide range of topics, from the material substratum of media to the human body's interaction with technology to the socioeconomic systems which support that interaction (see, e.g., Gumbrecht and Pfeiffer 1994; Lenoir 1998; Mitchell and Thurtle 2004).

Materiality thus glimmers as a new rapier, cutting two ways. On the one hand: Doesn't the medium (be it telegraphy or photography or television or digital video) elide the materiality of the object (or the violence, or the degradation) it represents? On the other: Aren't you ignoring the materiality of the medium itself, the material support, the medium's embeddedness within particular material circumstances, its material ramifications? No matter how variously the term may be deployed, *materiality* has come to matter with new urgency.

Whatever the urgency, when we think about media and materiality it may be difficult not to begin by wrestling with some very basic questions: What do scholars mean when they assert that one medium or another has a dematerializing effect? What do scholars do when they attend to "the materiality of communication"? What might scholars accomplish through a materialist analysis of media? And a corollary bonus question: What sort of materialism would help us assess the materialites of dematerializing media? What critical act is comparable to that casual yet cataclysmic moment in a movie theater when you happen to glance backward and see . . . a funnel of light that streams from the projector?

The Dematerialization Hypothesis

Describing the "dematerialization of material culture," the archaeologist Colin Renfrew laments the current separation "between communication and substance," the image having become increasingly "electronic and thus no longer tangible." Because "the electronic impulse is replacing whatever remained of the material element in the images to which we became accustomed," the "engagement with the material world where the material object was the repository of meaning is being threatened." All told, "physical, palpable material reality is disappearing, leaving nothing but the smile on the face of the Cheshire Cat" (Renfrew 2003, 185–86). This is a dystopian wonderland where we're left with only traces of a physical world, a world somehow vaporized by electronic media. In Baudrillard's more familiar version of the tale (inseparable from the tale of postmodernity), the image has come to have "no relation to any reality whatsoever; it is its own pure simulacrum"; within the era of the hyperreal, then, "materiality" makes sense only insofar as it marks some bygone era.[1]

Yet this melodrama of besieged materiality hardly requires a postmodern setting. Indeed, according to the philosopher Ernst Cassirer (writing in the 1940s):

> Physical reality seems to recede in proportion as man's symbolic activity advances. Instead of dealing with the things themselves man is, in a sense, constantly conversing with himself. He has so enveloped himself in linguistic forms, in artistic images, in mythical symbols or religious rites, that he cannot see or know anything except by the interposition of this artificial medium.[2]

"Medium," in this argument, names that which prevents some more *immediate* access to "things themselves"; thus media by definition have a dematerializing effect. And yet, of course, Kant argued that "dealing with the things themselves" is an impossibility within human experience because things themselves (things in themselves) remain elusive; we know the world only as it is mediated by perceptual categories (time, space, cause and effect, and so on). We know the world, moreover, only as it is mediated by the senses, one of which—touch—seems to provide some privileged access to the physical; indeed, the immaterial/material distinction often asserts itself (as in Renfrew) as the difference between the visible and the tangible. It might finally prove useful to avoid the discrepancy between the phenomenal and the material—to describe instead the phenomenon of materiality, or the *materiality-effect*, the end result of the process whereby you're convinced of the materiality of something (be it the stone on which you stubbed your toe or the handle you're about to grab within an immersive VR system). But the discrepancy must remain operative for any basic discussion of the materiality that lies beyond or beneath the experiential, be it the swirling components of the atoms of your desk chair or the silicon chips within your computer or the approaching storm that's visible on radar but not yet out the window.

When critics view media as a threat to materiality, they generally mean that our human experience of materiality has been compromised, and they thus extend paradigmatic claims about modernity, which tend to retroproject some prelapsarian intimacy with the real. Of course, the development and transformation of media are constitutive of modernity variously understood: as the experience of industrialization and urbanization, or of rationalization and bureaucratization, or of technologization and massification (the emergence of mass culture).[3] The grand sociological accounts of modernity—by Émile Durkheim, Max Weber, and Georg Simmel—all consider the increase in abstraction to be a chief characteristic of the modernizing world.[4] Simmel took the medium of money to be the master trope for, and a dominant force of, the increasing abstraction and rationalization of social and psychological life, not just because (as Marx would have it) the particularities of any object or action disappear within the regime of value (all qualities being translated into quantities), but also because money facilitates the preponderance of calculation. (The electronic transfer of money, from Simmel's point of view, would simply be another chapter in the history of its dematerialization.)[5] Among those who heard Simmel lecture (including Cassirer, Walter Benjamin, and Sigfried Kracauer), Georg Lukács both absorbed the claim and embedded it within the Marxist paradigm that Simmel himself eschewed. Describing the effects of the commodity form once it saturates society, he concludes that the inevitable "rational objectification conceals above all the immediate—qualitative and material—character of things as things."[6]

Even such a hasty genealogy suggests why, when it comes to assessing the abstracting force of media, both money and the commodity form are frequently invoked. (For the intellectual legacies informing the utopian claims for digital technologies, see Coyne 2001.) In his influential article "The Traffic in Photographs," the photographer and critic Allan Sekula argued for the close correspondence of the effects of photography and of commodification. "Just as use value is eclipsed by exchange value," he wrote, "so the photographic sign comes to eclipse its referent."[7] The argument develops from a fascinating essay, "The Stereograph and the

Stereoscope," in which Oliver Wendell Holmes Sr. (the American physician and essayist who also invented the hand-held stereoscope) claims that, with the advent of photography, *Form is henceforth divorced from matter. In fact, matter as a visible object is of no great use any longer.* Sekula analogizes Holmes's assertion to Marx's claims about the mediatory power of the money form to transpose a heterogeneous world into a world of equivalences: "Just as money is the universal gauge of exchange value, uniting all the world['s] goods in a single system of transactions, so photographs are imagined to reduce all sights to relations of formal equivalence" (23). Very much in step with Sekula, Jonathan Crary charted the new "autonomy and abstraction of vision" that accompanies the shift from geometrical to physiological optics, and the development of photography, which reshapes "an entire territory on which signs and images, each effectively severed from a referent, circulate and proliferate." Both money and photography are "magical forms that establish a new set of abstract relations between individuals and things." The new visual experiences of the nineteenth century are "bound up" in "theories of vision that effectively annihilate a real world."[8]

New media always seem to provoke this old melodrama. One of the ironies of the digital regime (in the visual register) has been the extent to which photography and film are now reputed to have had intimate contact with the material world: at least photography has an indexical relation to its subject; at least analogical media don't translate the world into numbers and quality into quantity. As Lisa Gitelman has argued, any "putative dematerialization . . . can only be experienced in relation to a preexisting sense of matter and materialization." Thus (in the auditory register) "what often seems so startling about digitization and distributed networks is their supposed power to *de*materialize and differently commodify information" in contrast to "the once startling power to capture, to materialize and differently commodify sound" (Gitelman 2006, 86). And digital media lay claim to overcoming material decline: analog recording (on, say, magnetic tape) may more precisely inscribe and reenact the original vibrations, but digital recordings don't suffer the same physical deterioration. Analog artifacts (films, videos, photographs, recordings, books) have been converted into digital form not just to provide more extensive access but also to preserve them. Yet digital media are themselves subject to deterioration—just think of the bum DVD you received from Netflix—because they still require physical support.

Of course, one effect of this now-rampant conversion is the dematerialization of the original medium itself; all media may eventually be homogenized within the hegemony of the digital. At the outset of *Gram-*

ophone, Film, Typewriter, in his much quoted overture on optical fiber networks, Friedrich Kittler asserts that

> the general digitization of channels and information erases the differences among individual media. Sound and image, voice and text are reduced to surface effects, known to consumers as interface. . . . Inside the computers themselves everything becomes a number: quantity without image, sound or voice. And once optical fiber networks turn formerly distinct data flows into a standardized series of digitized numbers, any medium can be translated into any other. With numbers, everything goes.[9]

Kittler's assertion itself reanimates the logic with which the effects of other media have been described, in particular their effects on art. In André Malraux's imaginary museum, a collection of photographic reproductions dissolves the material specificity of the artistic medium—the fresco, the enamel miniature, the woodcut. Before Malraux, Benjamin had argued that art's technological reproducibility, while emancipating the experience of art from material and social constraints, had extinguished the "aura" of the artwork—its uniqueness, its historical specificity, and its spatial relation to the spectator, both its cultural and its material embededness.[10]

But with regard to both photography and film, Benjamin also believed that these new technologies had the capacity to enrich the perceptual field, disclosing "physiognomic aspects" of the material world—"hidden details in familiar objects," "new structures of matter"—that lay beyond quotidian consciousness.[11] And Kracauer (1997) championed film's ability to effect a redemptive reification, to register a material world that lies beneath other representations or interpretations of it. Indeed, Andreas Gursky's large-format photographs confront you with aspects of built space that no walking tour of Paris or Hong Kong could. And the digital enlargement of a Whitman manuscript gives you access to physical details that, with the page in your hand, would remain imperceptible. Like the microscope and the telescope, which, on Simmel's argument, enable us to overcome distances only while making us aware of the extent of those distances, media in general have a history of exposing the limits of our accustomed access to the world we inhabit—the limits of the material everyday. The "most remote," suggested Simmel, "comes closer at the price of increasing the distance to what was originally nearer" (Simmel 1978, 475–76).

When it comes to these dialectics of nearness and distance, of materialization and rematerialization, you could do worse than say of media what Simmel said about art, that it "changes the field of vision," bringing us "closer to reality" even as it distances us "from the immediacy of things," allowing "the concreteness of stimuli to recede." He made his claim without ignoring Kant's point, insisting that no realism (artistic or scientific)

> can dispense with an *a priori*, with a form that—springing from the needs of our nature—provides a robe or a metamorphosis for the world of our senses. This transformation that reality suffers on its way to our consciousness is certainly a barrier between us and its immediate existence, but is at the same time the precondition for our perception and representation of it. (473)

Of course, any new medium can radically alter our recognition and representation of such barriers.

The Materiality of Communication

You can concur with Mark Poster that "the material infrastructure of the sign"—both the relation between signifier and signified and the relation between sign and referent—has been "drastically reconfigured" by new media without bemoaning or celebrating the loss of some aboriginal materiality.[12] Indeed, no matter how many digital images you take of the thorn in your thumb, it remains there, and should you print those images, the medium turns out to have amplified (not annihilated) "palpable material reality."

But the dematerialization hypothesis persists—at times a nightmare, at times the "human dream of transcending materiality" or "the final scientific-technological realization of the Gnostic dream of the Self getting rid of the decay and inertia of material reality."[13] The hypothesis persists not least because of the historical development of the cybernetic paradigm itself, the way that early research in cybernetics conceptualized information as disembedded and disembodied. In her archaeological story of how information lost its body, Katherine Hayles shows how the Cartesian mind/body distinction reappeared as the distinction between materiality and information, between informational pattern and material instantiation, to the point where embodiment seemed to be beside the point.[14] (See chapter 10, "Cybernetics.") Information, delaminated from any specific material substrate, could circulate—could dematerialize and rematerialize—unchanged. The very definition of information, she argues, has enabled people to consider it "as a kind of immaterial fluid that circulates effortlessly around the globe while sill retaining the solidity of a reified concept."[15]

And yet information (and our access to it) relies on the physical support of communication technologies: integrated circuits depend on a silicon substrate; different optical fibers have different properties and serve different functions; any wireless communication depends on truckloads of wire. But when scholars address the materiality of media, they focus on more than physical infrastructure; they're tracking what Hayles calls the "materialities of embodiment" in several different registers, working, you might say, to rematerialize media by exhibiting the physical interaction that occurs between humans and technology and disclosing the multilayered histories that lie within any technology of communication. As the recently founded Research Centre for Material Digital Culture (University of Sussex) suggests, not only individual scholars but also institutions have assumed different versions of Hayles's archaeological task, asking "what material properties, what symbolic properties, what affective or sense perceptive regimes and what political economies" inform new media. Such work registers an impulse within the broader field of media studies (work on early cinema or on the history of the book, for instance) and within the field of science studies (a materialist epistemology that grants a consitutitive role, in the production of scientific theory and scientific fact, to the layout of laboratories and the character of instruments).[16]

One approach to rematerializing is to ask about the constituent mediations that instantiate any image, sound, or text. Matt Kirschenbaum, in an online exchange, argues that

> a bibliographical/textual approach calls upon us to emphasize precisely those aspects of electronic textuality that have thus far been neglected in the critical writing about the medium: platform, interface, data standards, file formats, operating systems, versions and distributions of code, patches, ports, and so forth. *For that's the stuff electronic texts are made of.*[17]

Some sense of such stuff (the mediating structures of digital communication) becomes recognizable in Mark Napier's interactive Shredder 1.0, which is at once simple and startling: when you enter a URL, Shredder retrieves the specified Web page but with its HTML code altered, its graphics and text radically distorted.[18] The work extends art's attention to its own media (as in *Tristram Shandy*), but the act of defamiliarization remains independent of any specific content; the artwork's only message is the mediations of the medium. It may be the case that "new media are doing exactly what their predecessors have done: presenting themselves as refashioned and improved versions of other media."[19] But Napier means to disrupt the ease with which older media have become analogues for new media:

Why Shred the Web?

The web is not a publication. Web sites are not paper. Yet the current thinking of web design is that of the magazine, newspaper, book, or catalog. Visually, aesthetically, legally, the web is treated as a physical page upon which text and images are written.

Web pages are temporary graphic images created when browsing software interprets HTML instructions. As long as all browsers agree (at least somewhat) on the conventions of HTML there is the illusion of solidity or permanence in the web. But behind the graphical illusion is a vast body of text files—containing HTML code—that fills hard drives on computers at locations all over the world. Collectively these instructions make up what we call "the web." But what if these instructions are interpreted differently than intended? Perhaps radically differently?

Run through this disorganizing process, the Web site of the Chicago School of Media Theory (http://csmt.uchicago.edu/home.htm) produces congested graphics, words, and code, unintelligible, oscillating between the distorted and the serene, the semantic and the merely graphic:

```
ng>02.02.20
04</strong></span><br />
The
```

Although this refunctioning (which changes with every reentry of the URL) can yield impressive visual results, this is Net art that most consistently foregrounds the layers of mediation through which words and images become, as many critics would say, "embodied" on the computer screen.

This rhetoric of embodiment has been essential in efforts to describe media's materiality. And the human body itself (in its Cartesian distinction and beyond that distinction) has repeatedly served as the ground for assessing the materiality of media, both new and old (see chapter 2, "Body"). The telegraph, for instance, was understood to make "communication independent of embodied messengers," to separate thought from the body, and thus to jeopardize, among other things, "racial barriers defined in terms of bodily difference."[20] But new media would seem to grant the embodied "recipient" of information a newly active role—indeed the role of the medium (let us say) that must "produce" the analogue of the "physical page upon which text and images are written." Grounding his argument in both phenomenology and neurobiology, Mark Hansen provides a sustained account of how "*the framing function* of the human body" forges an image out of information that would otherwise remain "formless." He thus grants one version of the dematerialization hypothesis—the homogenizing, dematerializing effects of digitization, a process that dislodges any image from its traditional spatial coordinates, a process that remains mere process until the "affective body" makes sense of the flow it has arrested and stabilized. The human body thus becomes the source for "giv[ing] body to digital data."[21] All told, then, new media differently dramatize the phenomenological process by which the human subject makes sense of the environment. More recently Hansen (in line with the very late work of Merleau-Ponty) has argued that new media foreground not just the "correlation of embodiment and technicity" but also the technicity of bodily and psychic life, indeed what he terms the "essential technicity of being."[22]

Such technicity has been dramatized very differently by "biomedia," a term Eugene Thacker deploys to caption the work being done in bioinformatics, nanomedicine, and biocomputing, where boundaries between the biological and the technological have dissolved (see chapter 8, "Biomedia"). The "dry lab" and the "wet lab" mirror one another, and computational biology finds its specular completion in biological computing: the use of DNA molecules, because of their combinatory potency, to solve computational problems.[23] Biocomputation may be in its early stages, but it is widely and popularly recognized as the next computational wave. Reporting on research being done in 2002 at the Weizmann Institute of Science, *National Geographic* observed that "scientists have devised a computer that can perform 330 trillion operations per second, more than 100,000 times the speed of the fastest PC. The secret: It runs on DNA."[24] The field of genetics has shown that biological life depends on the storage and processing of "information" to the point where it now makes sense to wonder whether the body is best understood as a network (Thacker 2004, 31). It is as though information has found a body, and that body turns out to be *yours*. In this post-Cartesian universe, arguments that insist on the embedded and embodied character *of* information give way to experiments exhibiting the body *as* information.

Materialism

As should be clear at a glance, this recent work, which conceptually rematerializes media squares unevenly with the materialist tradition. In his most basic materialist conception of history, Marx asserts that "the mode of production of material life conditions the general process of social, political and intellectual life," which is to say, economic structures are the foundation of cultural formation and transformation. But the "changing materialist content of materialism," as Raymond Williams has phrased it, gives rise to a widespread conviction that even as economic relations determine social and cultural forms, so too do these forms determine those relations.[25] The economy shapes our contemporary media landscape, but that economy itself has taken shape—assumed its global spatiality and instantaneity—as a result of new media. Indeed, the psychological, social, and political effects of technological communication have been so profound (and so profoundly internalized by human consciousness) that they often remain imperceptible.[26] Still, as Williams argues in his attack on Marshall McLuhan, technological determinism readily becomes a formalism that isolates technology from the socioeconomic history of its production, discounting the way that inventions depend on human decisions (and thus on social and economic motivations).[27] Kittler may be right to insist that "media determine our situation," but every medium itself emerges from a determinate situation, one formed by technological, ideological, physical, economic, legal, political, and other determinants.

Attention to materiality within media studies shares the objectives of a "new materialism" that has distinguished itself from historical materialism, structuralism, and semiology by reengaging phenomenology (the embodied phenomenology of, say, Henri Bergson, as well as the materialist phenomenology of Benjamin), by focusing on material culture, and by drawing attention to a materiality of the signifier, now understood as the signifying effects of matter itself. Thus Timothy Lenoir argues that "attention to the materiality of inscriptions themselves will demonstrate the extent to which inscription devices actually constitute the signifying scene in technoscience" (1998, 12). Within the field of anthropology, competing symbolic and materialist approaches once reduced "objects to being either economic and utilitarian goods or semiotic vehicles," eliding the materiality of those objects and thus failing to recognize materiality itself as a signifying component.[28] For literary and cultural studies, objects could come into view only by moderating the focus on the subject: the editors of *Subject and Object in Renaissance Culture*, for instance, were abashed at how assiduously their field had elided objects and the material world in the service of representing the early modern era as the period of "the rise of subjectivity, the complexity of subjectivity, the instability of subjectivity."[29]

The critical focus on materiality has often had to resist the explanatory power of forms, structures, and systems in much the same way that materiality often makes sense as a mark and measure of resistance (as that which resists). But one can imagine some ideal materialism that displays the multiple orders of materiality—or the order of materialities—between a phenomenological account of the interface between user and technology, an archaeological account of the physical infrastructure of the medium, and a sociological account of the cultural and economic forces that continue to shape both the technology itself and our interactions with it. Because we live in world that is less than ideal (a world that is, in a word, material), such a display seems unrealizable, and also, of course, less than ideal. For all its attention to materiality, the ambition would inevitably suffer from the fact that, as Cornelius Castoriadis has argued, individuals apprehend materiality through a specific "socialization of the psyche," a "corporeal imagination" shaped by history and culture.[30] Within a culture where form and matter (like mind and body) have been differentiated so powerfully, often it is only some breakdown in your habitual interactions with the world that makes its materialities (and yours) suddenly meaningful. In the effort to apprehend the materiality of media, then, you could do worse than to tap the space bar with your sore thumb.

Notes

1. Jean Baudrillard, *Simulacrum and Simulation*, trans. Sheila Faria Glaser (Ann Arbor: University of Michigan Press, 1994), 6.

2. Ernst Cassirer, *An Essay on Man* (New Haven: Yale University Press, 1944), 26. For a more popular account of dematerialization, see, for instance, John Balderston's 1927 stage version of *Dracula* (New York: Liveright, 1960), where Van Helsing explains that "science can now transmute the electron, the basis of all matter, into energy, and what is that but the dematerialization of matter? Yet dematerialization has been known and practiced in India for centuries. In Java I myself have seen things" (25–26).

3. I am eschewing any definition of media within this essay, but here I want to register the fact that Kittler, among others, has defined the city itself as a medium. See Friedrich A. Kittler, "The City Is a Medium," trans. Mathew Griffin, *New Literary History* 27, no. 4 (1996): 717–29.

4. These accounts of abstraction can be descriptive without being evaluative. Even critics of modernity cannot denigrate abstraction tout court. Democracy, for instance, depends on individuation without individualization: your class, gender, and ethnicity disappear as you become homogenized into a simple abstract citizen.

5. Graeber argues that tokens of exchange were virtual *before* they were considered material. See chapter 15 in this volume.

6. Georg Lukács, *History and Class Consciousness: Studies in Marxist Dialectics*, trans. Rodney Livingstone (Cambridge, MA: MIT Press, 1971), 92. Just as one can understand Martin Heidegger's *Being and Time* as an extended response to Lukács, both posing and answering the question of what unreified being might be, so too one can understand his lecture on "The Thing" as an effort to pose and answer the question of what the "thingness of things" could possibly mean. For Heidegger, though, the point of departure is not the commodity form but the technology (radio, film, television) that has eradicated distance (both nearness and remoteness).

7. Allan Sekula, "The Traffic in Photographs," *Art Journal* 41, no. 1 (Spring 1981): 22.

8. Jonathan Crary, *Techniques of the Observer: On Vision and Modernity in the Nineteenth Century* (Cambridge, MA: MIT Press, 1990), 13–14.

9. Friedrich A. Kittler, *Gramophone, Film, Typewriter*, trans. Geoffrey Winthrop-Young and Michael Wutz (Stanford, CA: Stanford University Press, 1999), 1–2.

10. Walter Benjamin, "The Work of Art in the Age of Its Technological Reproducibility" (third version), trans. Harry Zohn and Edmund Jephcott, in *Walter Benjamin: Selected Writings*, vol. 4, *1938–1940*, ed. Howard Eiland and Michael W. Jennings (Cambridge, MA: Harvard University Press, 2003), 253–57. On "aura," see Miriam Bratu Hansen, "Benjamin's Aura," *Critical Inquiry* 34, no. 2 (January 2008): 336–75.

11. Walter Benjamin, "Little History of Photography" trans. Edmund Jephcott and Kingsley Shorter, in *Walter Benjamin: Selected Writings*, vol. 2, *1927–1934*, ed. Micahel W. Jennings, Howard Eiland, and Gary Smith (Cambridge, MA: Harvard University Press, 1999), 512; Benjamin, "Work of Art," 266.

12. Mark Poster, *What's the Matter with the Internet?* (Minneapolis: University of Minnesota Press, 2002), 132.

13. Dan Thu Nguyen and Jon Alexander, "The Coming of Cyberspacetime and the End of Polity," in *Cultures of the Internet: Virtual Spaces, Real Histories, Living Bodies*, ed. Rob Shields (London: Sage, 1996), 99; Slavoj Zizek, *On Belief* (New York: Verso, 2001), 33. All but needless to add, the apparent realization of this dream has had considerable impact on the conceptualization of gender, ethnicity, and sexuality.

14. Of course Aristotle located the substantial (that is, the essential) in form, not in matter.

15. N. Katherine Hayles, *How We Became Posthuman: Virtual Bodies in Cybernetics, Literature, and Informatics* (Chicago: University of Chicago Press, 1999), 246. Mark Hansen has shown how contemporary theory effectively vaporizes the material otherness of technology by transposing it into textuality. See *Embodying Technesis: Technology Beyond Wrting* (Ann Arbor: University of Michigan Press, 2000).

16. See, for instance, the "Material Texts" book series from the University of Pennsylvania Press, which draws attention to the history of the book understood as the history of writing, printing, and reprinting; titles include Fernando Bouza's *Communication, Knowledge, and Memory in Early Modern Spain* (trans. Sonia López and Michael Agnew; Philadelphia: University of Pennsylvania Press, 2004), Juliet Fleming's *Graffiti and the Writing Arts of Early Modern England* (Philadelphia: University of Pennsylvania Press, 2001), Meredith McGill's *American Literature and the Culture of Reprinting, 1834–1853* (Philadelphia: University of Pennsylvania Press, 2002). For a crucial overview of early print culture, see Adrian Johns, *The Nature of the Book: Print and Knowledge in the Making* (Chicago: University of Chicago Press, 1998). For an important emphasis on practice, see Bradin Cormack and Carla Mazzio, *Book Use/ Book Theory* (Chicago: University of Chicago Press, 2005). In the case of science studies see, for instance, Bruno Latour and Steve Woolgar, *Laboratory Life: The Construction of Scientific Fact* (1979; Princeton: Princeton University Press, 1986); Bruno Latour, *Science in Action: How to Follow Scientists and Engineers through Society* (Cambridge, MA: Harvard University Press, 1988); Peter Gallison, *How Experiments End* (Chicago: Univesity of Chicago Press, 1987) and *Image and Logic: A Material Culture of Microphysics* (Chicago: University of Chicago Press,1997); and David Baird, *Thing Knowledge: A Philosophy of Scientific Instruments* (Berkeley: University of California Press, 2004).

17. Matt Kirschenbaum, "Materiality and Matter and Stuff: What Electronic Texts Are Made Of," www.electronicbookreview.com/thread/electropoetics/sited (accessed July 26, 2005).

18. Shredder 1.0, see http://www.potatoland.org/shredder/shredder.html. For a discussion of the piece, see Mark Tribe and Reena Jana, *New Media Art* (Köln: Taschen, 2007), 70–71. In her own effort to bring the materiality of media into view, Katherine Hayles has published a book, *Writing Machines* (Cambridge, MA: MIT Press, 2002), whose ridged cover and oscillating typography and layout are reminders of how physical form alters information.

19. J. David Bolter and Richard A. Grusin, *Remediation: Understanding New Media* (Cambridge, MA: MIT Press, 1999), 14–15.

20. Paul Gilmore, "The Telegraph in Black and White," *ELH* 69, no. 3 (2002): 806.

21. Mark B. N. Hansen, *New Philosophy for New Media* (Cambridge, MA: MIT Press, 2004), pp. 11, 13. The body, in Hansen's argument, is fully sensuous and affective, irreducible to the merely ocular. See, esp., pp. 197–232.

22. Mark B. N. Hansen, *Bodies in Code: Interfaces with Digital Media* (New York: Routledge, 2006), 79.

23. Eugene Thacker, *Biomedia* (Minneapolis: University of Minnesota Press, 2004). Molecular computing was first described in L. M. Adleman, "Molecular Computation of Solutions to Combinatorial Problems," *Science* 266, no. 5187 (November 11, 1994): 1021–24. On the analysis of networks "in nature," see T. S. Gardner, D. di Bernardo, D. Lorenz, and J. J. Collins, "Inferring Genetic Networks and Identifying Compound Mode of Action via Expression Profiling," *Science* 301, no. 5629 (July 4, 2003): 102–5.

24. Stefan Lovgren, "Computer Made from DNA and Enzymes," http://news.nationalgeographic.com/news/2003/02/0224_030224_DNAcomputer.html (accessed February 25, 2002).

25. Raymond Williams, *Problems in Materialism and Culture* (London: Verso, 1980), 122.

26. A point made very differently in Marshall McLuhan, *Understanding Media: The Extensions of Man* (New York: McGraw Hill, 1964); Friedrich Kittler, *Discourse Networks 1800/1900*, trans. M. Metteer and C. Cullens (Stanford, CA: Stanford University Press, 1992); and Avital Ronnell, *The Telephone Book* (Lincoln: University of Nebraska Press, 1991).

27. Raymond Williams, "The Technology and the Society," in *Television: Technology and Cultural Form* (1974; London: Routledge, 2003).

28. Webb Keane, *Signs of Recognition: Powers and Hazards of Representation in an Indonesian Society* (Berkeley: University of California Press, 1997), 32.

29. Margreta de Grazia, Maureen Quilligan, and Peter Stallybrass, eds., *Subject and Object in Renaissance Culture* (Cambridge: Cambridge University Press, 1996), 5–11. On the place of objects in the Humanities more broadly, see the essays collected in Bill Brown, *Things* (Chicago: University of Chicago Press, 2004); on the place of objects in social theory, see Andreas Reckwitz, "The Status of the 'Material' in Theories of Culture: From 'Social Structure' to 'Artefacts,'" *Journal for the Theory of Social Behavior* 32:2 (2002): 195–217.

30. Cornelius Castoriadis, *The Imaginary Institution of Society*, trans. Kathleen Blamey (Cambridge, MA: MIT Press, 1987), p. 334. Throughout, my use of "embeddedness" has meant to invoke the rhetoric with which the materiality of new media is often discussed. Thus, when the sociologist of the global city, Saskia Sassen, turns her attention to the Internet, emphasizing the materiality of the most apparently dematerialized communication system, she focuses on how the Internet is "embedded" in social practices, institutional environments, and local scenes. "Electronic Markets and Activist Networks: The Weight of Social Logics in Digital Formations," *Digital Formations: IT and New Architectures in the Global Realm*, ed. Robert Latham and Saskia Sassen (Princeton: Princeton University Press, 2005), pp. 54–88.

References and Suggested Readings

Brown, Bill, ed. 2004. *Things*. Chicago: University of Chicago Press.

Castoriadis, Cornelius. 1987. *The Imaginary Institution of Society*. Trans. Kathleen Blamey. Cambridge, MA: MIT Press.

Coyne, Richard. 2001. *Technoromanticism: Digital Narrative, Holism, and the Romance of the Real*. Cambridge, MA: MIT Press.

Gitelman, Lisa. 2006. *Always Already New: Media, History, and the Data of Culture*. Cambridge, MA: MIT Press.

Gumbrecht, Hans Ulrich, and Pfeiffer, K. Ludwig, eds. 1994. *Materialities of Communication*. Trans. William Whobrey. Stanford, CA: Stanford University Press.

Kracauer, Sigfried. 1997. *Theory of Film: The Redemption of Reality*. Princeton, NJ: Princeton University Press.

Lenoir, Timothy, ed. 1998. *Inscribing Science: Scientific Texts and the Materiality of Communication*. Stanford, CA: Stanford University Press.

Mitchell, Robert, and Thurtle, Phillip, eds. 2004. *Data Made Flesh: Embodying Information*. New York: Routledge.

Renfrew, Colin. 2003. *Figuring It Out*. London: Thames and Hudson.

Simmel, Georg. 1978. *The Philosophy of Money*. Trans. Tom Bottomore and David Frisby. London: Routledge.

5 :: MEMORY BERNARD STIEGLER

Introduction by Mark B. N. Hansen

"The Internet age is one of hypomnesis constituting itself as an associated technical milieu." In his wide-ranging history of the concept of memory, Bernard Stiegler aims toward a moment—one that he suggests we are currently living—in which the "industrial model" of memory undergoes fundamental transformation. From Stiegler's vantage point, what is crucial about today's technical memory aids—iPods, smart phones, GPS navigators, and PDAs, not to mention the Internet—is their intimate articulation with anamnesis, a term Stiegler borrows from Plato and uses to designate the embodied act of remembering. Everything hinges on how hypomnesis, the technical exteriorization of memory, articulates with anamnesis, and Stiegler's history of memory can be understood as a history of the changing ecology of these terms. Today's computational technical memory aids—digital *hypomnemata*—differ from the industrial hypomnemata of technical recording (photography, phonography, cinematography) in that they create an "associated hypomnesic milieu" in which "receivers are placed in the position of senders." Rather than dissociating consumption from production, as did broadcast mass media (from phonography to global real-time television), today's microtechnologies and the social networking practices they facilitate connect them: if you can use these technologies to consume, Stiegler suggests, you can also use them to produce.

This is why Stiegler sees digital memory aids as instigators of an "ecology of associated hypomnesic milieus." And it is also why he thinks they have more in common with writing than they do with broadcast media like film and television. Just as the literate citizen learned to read and to write by embodying the practices of literacy through a more or less arduous process of formation, so too the digital citizen acquires facility in networked communication by embodying a procedural logic that views sending and receiving as symmetrical and coimplicated activities. In both cases, the payoff of the process of formation is a capacity to create, to use a standardized technicity for self-expression; this capacity, Stiegler suggests, stands in direct opposition to the mode of passive reception endemic to the broadcast media. The new ecology of associated hypomnesic milieus that Stiegler calls for would accordingly inaugurate a new conjugation of technics and memory that would succeed *mnemotechniques* (the artificial storage of individual memories that characterizes hypomnesis from ideogrammatic writing to the print revolution) and *mnemotechnologies* (the embedding of memories within technological systems that systematically order memories according to their own logics). By renewing the possibility for self-expression, and hence for self-exteriorization, today's digital hypomnemata restore a positive dimension to our coevolution with technics. We might even say that they fuse mnemotechniques and mnemotechnologies, furnishing artificial supports for individual (and collective) memories that exist within and are nourished by a larger mnemotechnological milieu—the system of the Internet.

Stiegler's invocation of contemporary digital hypomnemata comes only at the end of a long interrogation of memory, and its constitutive relation to technics, in Western history. From his first book, *Technics and Time*, vol. 1, *The Fault of Epimetheus* (1994), to his latest work on Foucault's conception of "care" (*Prendre le soin*, vol. 1, 2008), Stiegler has concerned himself with the "essential" correlation of the human and technics. Drawing on the work of French paleontologist André Leroi-Gourhan, Stiegler interprets the coincidence of protohuman fossil remains and primitive flint tools to mean that the human is the species that evolves not simply genetically but extragenetically (or, as he puts it, *epiphylogenetically*, "by means other than life"): the human evolves by exteriorizing itself in tools, artifacts, language, and technical memory banks. Technology on this account is not something external and contingent, but rather an essential—indeed, *the* essential—dimension of the human. As Stiegler explains in his essay, this account of technics provides a necessary counterpart to that of Plato, which, despite its insight into the value of artificial memory (in the *Meno*), ultimately dismisses it as false (in the *Phaedrus*). It is this dismissal, Stiegler argues (following his teacher, Jacques Derrida), that informs the antipathy of Western philosophy to the theme of technics.

With respect to memory, this essential, protohistorical correlation of the human with technics appears in the form of "retentional finitude." It is because our memories are finite that we require artificial memory aids, and the ensuing ecology of "natural" and artificial memory, of anamnesis and hypomnesis, has, since its initial theorization by Plato, characterized the differing function and valuation of memory across our history. If we learn from Plato—or rather, from one side of Plato—that artificial memory is a *pharmakon*, a gift that is also a threat (since dependence on artificial memory makes the training of our own memory less imperative), we learn from Derrida that technical exteriorization or supplementation is an intrinsic, irreducible dimension of the logic and function of memory as such. It is this technical contamination of memory that allows the latter to be historicized, split into distinct epochs of what Stiegler, following Derrida (and the linguist Sylvain Auroux), calls "grammatization": the exteriorization of memory in the form of discrete marks, traces, or *grammé* that forms the hypomnesic milieu for anamnesis. As Stiegler notes, these epochs include those of the stone tool, of ideogrammatic writing, of the alphabet, of analog and digital recording, and now of digitization and the Internet. As different historically specific configurations of anamnesis with technics, these epochs individually and collectively demonstrate that there is no memory that is not hypomnesic. This, again, is why everything hinges on how hypomnesis is articulated with anamnesis.

The dependence of memory on artificial aids makes the question of technology an irreducibly political question. As Stiegler puts it, the hypomnesic milieu can either be "associated" with or "dissociated" from anamnesis (the embodied act of memory). When they are associated with anamnesis, hypomnemata facilitate the deployment of memory in the constitution of meaningful symbolic practices and communal formations; by contrast, when they are dissociated from anamnesis, they advance the interests of the culture industries (Adorno and Horkheimer) and of "control societies" (Deleuze), which work to transform human beings into mere consumers, passive recipients of prepackaged and standardized commodities and media fluxes who have no hope of becoming producers. Put more simply, reliance on artificial memory aids makes us vulnerable to manipulation if the technologies of memory are controlled by industries intent on exploiting our desire for their gain; yet on the other hand (and in accordance with their *pharmacological* logic), these same memory aids hold the promise of expanding our capacity to produce meaning and to form communities open to the future (this is what Stiegler, following the philosopher Gilbert Simondon, means by "transindividuation"). Once again—and this comprises the fundamental message of Stiegler's complex and nuanced history of (technical) memory—everything hinges on how hypomnemata are articulated with anamnesis, and on the political struggles that must and can only be waged through the technologies that at once empower us and threaten our individual and collective agency.

+ + +

The Industrial Exteriorization of Memory

We have all had the experience of misplacing a memory-bearing object— a slip of paper, an annotated book, an agenda, a relic or fetish. We discover then that a part of ourselves, a part of our memory, is outside of us. This material memory, which Hegel named objective, is partial.[1] But it constitutes the most precious part of human memory; in it the totality of the works of spirit (or mind), in all guises and aspects, takes shape. Following Plato—especially the Plato of *Phaedrus*—we call recollection through externalized memory *hypomnesis*.

To write a manuscript is to organize thoughts by externalizing them in the form of traces, that is, symbols whereby thoughts become repeatable, transmissible, *actual* objects of reflection: in short, knowledge. To sculpt, to paint, or to draw is to initiate an encounter with the tangibility of the visible, to see with one's hands while giving-to-be-seen; it is to train the eye of the beholder and, thus, to sculpt, paint, and draw this eye—to *transform* it.

Human memory is originally exteriorized, which means it is technical from the start. It took shape first as a lithic (or stone) tool, two million years ago. A spontaneous memory support, the lithic tool is not, however, made to store memory; not until the late Paleolithic period (before 10,000 BCE) do conscious methods of memory storage, properly called *mnemotechniques*, appear. Ideogrammatic writing, springing up after the Neolithic period, leads to the alphabet—which today still helps the business manager remember a meeting or a relative's birthday. Only now, the personal calendar is an apparatus—the personal digital assistant (PDA). It is no longer simply a method of memory storage, a mnemotechnique, but instead a full-fledged *mnemotechnology*, a technology that systematically orders memories.

Originally objectified and exteriorized, memory constantly expands technically as it extends the knowledge of mankind; its power simultaneously escapes our grasp and surpasses us, calling into question our psychical as well as our social organization. This is particularly apparent in the transition from mnemotechniques to mnemotechnologies—from individual exteriorizations of memory functions to large-scale technological systems or networks that organize memories. Today, memory has become the major element in industrial development; everyday objects increasingly serve as supports of objective memory and, consequently, as forms of knowledge. But the new *technological* forms of knowledge, objectified in equipment and apparatus, conversely engender a loss of knowledge at the very moment one begins speaking of "knowledge societies," "knowledge industries," and what has come to be known as "cognitive" or "cultural" capitalism. To the extent that participation in these new societies, in this new form of capitalism, takes place through machinic interfaces beyond the comprehension of participants, the gain in knowledge is exclusively on the side of producers.

We are in constant relation with mnemotechnological apparatuses of all kinds, from televisions and telephones to computers and GPS navigation systems. These cognitive technologies, to which we consign a greater and greater part of our memory, cause us to lose ever-greater parts of our knowledge. To lose a cell phone is to lose the trace of the telephone numbers of our correspondents and to realize that they are no longer, or perhaps never were, in psychical memory but only in that of the apparatus. Faced with this situation, we must ask if the massive industrial development of mnemotechnologies does not in fact represent a systematic loss of memory, or, more precisely, a displacement of memory: a displacement that renders our memory the *object* of knowledge-control, that positions memory as the mnemotechnological system on which the control societies theorized by Gilles Deleuze operate.[2]

The Question of Hypomnesis

The backdrop of this hypothesis is an ancient concern in philosophy, which, as we have mentioned, was exposed by Plato as *hypomnesis*, and which Michel Foucault (1997) would reactivate as *hypomnémata*.

We exteriorize ever more cognitive functions in contemporary mnemotechnical equipment. And in so doing, we delegate more and more knowledge to apparatuses and to the service industries that network them, control them, formalize them, model them, and perhaps even destroy them. To the extent that they exceed our grasp, the forms of knowledge particular to these technologies lead toward an "obsolescence of the human"; in the face of their hegemony, we find ourselves more and more at a loss and internally empty.[3] Thus, the more the automobile is improved, the less we know how to drive. Eventually, the GPS driving assistant will replace the driver altogether; we will lose control over our own sensory-motor schema as such guidance becomes automatic, a formal element of the navigation system. The more we delegate the small tasks that make up the warp and woof of our lives to the apparatuses and services of modern industry, the more superfluous *we* will become: we will lose not only our know-how but also our knowing-how-to-live-well. The only thing left for us will be the passivity of blind consumption, devoid of knowledge and its rewards. We will become impotent if not obsolete—so long as knowledge is what empowers humanity.

Service economies supported by technologies formalize and manage our hyperindustrial era, which effectively restages what Plato describes as hypomnesis. If what we call industrialization, broadly conceived, is the generalization of a mnemotechnological reproducibility of the motor behavior of producers, *hyperindustrialization* is the generalization of a mnemotechnological reproducibility of the motor behavior *of consumers*. Like the producer—who is rendered a "proletarian" as his gesture is reproduced and his know-how passed into the machine—the consumer is divested of knowing-how-to-live-well and, in the same stroke, de-individualized through hyperindustrialization.[4] The consumer, in short, becomes nothing more than an instance of purchasing power, which is to say of heedless consumerism, and thus an "agent" in the heedless destruction of the world.

In "Plato's Pharmacy," Jacques Derrida (1981) based a major part of his "deconstruction of metaphysics" on his reading of Plato's *Phaedrus*. Derrida showed how this dialogue poses a sophistic *hypomnesis* of writing against a philosophical *anamnesis*—a "recollection" or "reminiscence," which, for Plato, denotes an intelligible, necessary, and true form of knowing. Following his description, in *Of Grammatology*, of the trace as a logic of the supplement, he exposes and undermines Plato's attempt to *oppose* interior memory and its exterior traces: it is impossible, he shows, to oppose living memory to externalized, dead memory (*hypomnematon*) since externalized memory, as a supplement, constitutes living memory as knowable.[5] Consequently, Derrida argues, the static oppositions of Western metaphysics must be replaced by dynamic compositions: one must think in terms, not of hierarchies or totalizing systems, but of processes—in particular, the process Derrida theorizes as *différance*.[6]

For all that, it is clear that the exteriorization of memory, and the resulting loss of memory and knowledge that Socrates describes in the *Phaedrus*, is experienced today in our daily lives, in all the aspects of our existence, and, more and more often, in our feeling of powerlessness, if not impotence. And it is experienced, remarkably, at the exact moment when the extraordinary mnesic power of digital networks makes us all the more attuned to the immensity of human memory, which seems to have become infinitely reactivatible and accessible.[7]

This tension between our desire to resist the privileging of interior memory and the present experience of exteriorization as memory loss renders the question of hypomnesis a political one. What is at stake in hypomnesis is a combat: a combat for a politics of memory and, more precisely, for the constitution of *sustainable hypomnesic milieus*. Once it has reached the hyperindustrial stage, the exteriorization of memory and of knowledge at once furthers their limitless impact and strengthens the forces that can implement their control. Consider the cognitive and cultural industries of control societies that formalize neurochemical activity and the sequences of nucleotides: the inscription of the neurobiological substrates of memory and knowledge in the history of what must be analyzed as a *process of grammatization*—the most recent stage of which is biotechnologies, with nanotechnologies soon to follow—patently raises the question of a biopolitics of memory.

Grammatization as "the History of the Supplement"

By grammatization, I mean the process whereby the currents and continuities shaping our lives become discrete elements. The history of human memory is the history of this process. Writing, as the breaking into discrete elements of the flux of speech (let us invent the word *discretization* for this possibility), is an example of a stage in the process of grammatization (see chapter 21, "Writing").

To rephrase Derrida's analysis of the trace as the logic of the supplement, there is no interiority that precedes exteriorization; rather, the interior as such is distinguished and configured in the very course of what paleontologist André Leroi-Gourhan describes as a process of exteriorization.[8] As Leroi-Gourhan explains, and as Derrida's analysis confirms, this configuring distinction is constantly displacing itself; in so doing, it continually sets up new relations between psychical individuals and collective ones—new processes of the formation of "psychical and social individuation," in the sense Gilbert Simondon (2007) confers to this expression when he stipulates that memory is the "associated milieu" of such individuation.[9]

With the advent of mnemotechnics, the process of exteriorization as technical becoming is concretized in a history of grammatization.[10] The process of grammatization as the *technical history of memory* is the process through which hypomnesic memory repeatedly relaunches the constitution of an anamnesic *tension of memory* exteriorized in the works of the spirit (or mind). In each case, anamnesis is made dependent on a specific regime of hypomnesic memory. In sum, each epoch of psychosocial individuation configures itself by means of its own form of discretization. This process of self-configuration is borne out by the epochs we have already considered: those of the lithic tool, the transition to ideogrammatic writing, the alphabet, and digitization.

With the Industrial Revolution, the process of grammatization suddenly surpassed the sphere of language, of *logos*, and came to invest the sphere of bodies. First of all, the gestures of producers were discretized in view of their automatic reproduction. At the same time, mechanical and apparatus-dependent reproducibilities of the visible and the audible—which so interested Benjamin—made their appearance and ushered in the age of mass media.[11]

This grammatization of gesture, which is the basis of what Marx describes as the process of proletarianization—of the loss of know-how—will continue with electronic and digital apparatuses to a point at which *all* forms of knowledge will be grammatized in the guise of cognitive mnemotechnologies. From linguistic knowledge—technologies and industries of language processing—to knowing-how-to-live or behavior in general, knowledge becomes discreticized through technologies and industries of language processing, user profiling, and the grammatization of affects; what results is the cognitive capitalism of today's hyperindustrial service economies.

Grammatization is the history of the exteriorization of memory in all its forms: nervous and cerebral memory, first linguistic, then auditory and visual; bodily and muscular memory; biogenetic memory. Thus exteriorized, memory becomes the object of sociopolitical and biopolitical channels of control; as a result of economic investments on the part of social organizations, psychical organizations get reconfigured as elements of and by means of mnemotechnical organs, including machine tools and other automata, including household equipment.[12] (Adam Smith analyzed as early as 1776 the effects of the machine on the mind of the worker.[13])

If we were to restage the question posed by the *Phaedrus* in the hyperindustrial epoch of the mnemotechnological object, we would discover that the question of hypomnesis constitutes the preliminary approach to proletarianization, insofar as the proletariat is an economic actor without memory and, so, without knowledge. Having relinquished that knowledge to the gesture-reproducing machine, but without any knowledge of its workings, the proletariat becomes a slave once again.

To examine the question of technical memory today is to again address hypomnesis, as both the question of the proletariat and that of a process of grammatization in which, now, it is the consumer who is deprived of memory and knowledge: it is to study the stage of a generalized proletarianization brought on by the generalization of hypomnesic technologies. The "truth" of Plato's *Phaedrus* would thus be found in Marx, provided two supplementary conclusions be drawn: First, that Marx himself does not identify the hypomnesic nature of technics and human existence, which means that he cannot think of human life as fundamentally exteriorized—as life by means other than life. And second, that Plato's inaugural struggle against sophistics over the question of memory and its technicization is the very heart of that political struggle which, from time immemorial, goes by the name of philosophy. The reevaluation of the scope of hypomnesis in Plato, as well as its deconstruction in Derrida, might then become the basis of a renewed political project of philosophy where the main stakes are in technics.

Human Memory as Epiphylogenesis

If philosophy begins with Plato, it becomes concretized in his battle with the sophists over the question of memory as mnemotechnics (hypomnesis, but also rhetoric and language technologies based on *logographics*). Philosophy's first question is memory, that is, knowledge conceived as anamnesis, and it is the process of grammatization that provokes the question. Grammatization is here constituted negatively, as Plato affirms anamnesis in reaction against the sophistic practice of hypomnesis in writing, which he defines as a technicization of linguistic memory that creates false knowledge (*Gorgias*).[14] Platonic philosophy apprehends technics in general as pseudoknowledge (which knows only contingent, sensible, and accidental becoming) and posits true knowledge as the knowledge of the necessary, that is, of intelligible essences of being qua immutability.

Grammatization is unthinkable in the context of the oppositions conceived by Plato on the basis of the polarization of anamnesis and hypomnesis: being versus becoming, the soul versus the body, intelligible thought in the immortal soul versus the sensible thought of the mortal body (the seat of the passions and the trap of the fall). All of these oppositions come down to the clash between *logos* and *technē*, rational formulae and technical knowledge. To oppose psychical living memory and technical dead memory is to generate this whole inductive series. Conversely, by rethinking memory as a process of grammatization in which living and dead compose without end, we are able to move beyond these oppositions bequeathed by Plato to Western philosophy.

Human archaeology and paleontology offer a way of responding to the Platonic opposition of anamnesis and hypomnesis with a theory of memory that views technicity as constitutive of life as ex-sistence, that is, as desire and as knowledge. On such a view, the process of becoming human can be characterized by the appearance of simultaneously hypomnesic and anamnesic *epiphylogenetic* memory: memory that is at once the product of individual epigenetic experience and the phylogenetic support for the accumulation of knowledge that constitutes the intergenerational cultural phylum.[15]

Let us review how, according to Leroi-Gourhan (1993), this epiphylogenetic memory emerged. *Zinjanthropus boisei*, a protohuman fossil, was first discovered in the Olduvai Gorge of northern Tanzania in 1959; the earliest specimen was found to be 1.75 million years old (later discoveries in the same region push the history of bipedal primates back to at least 3.6 million years ago). The creature would have weighed about thirty kilos and was a true biped, with an occipital hole perpendicular to the top of its cranial box and rear limbs freed for mobility. Its limbs were destined to make tools and to express, that is, to *exteriorize*, and indeed, there is evidence of contemporaneous tool use. Based on these facts, Leroi-Gourhan (1993) argued that what constitutes the humanity of the human—the crucial break in the history of life—is the process of the exteriorization of the living. What had up to then been a crucial element of life, namely activities of predation and defense, passed outside the domain of the living: the struggle for life—or rather for existence—was no longer limited to the basic Darwinian scheme. Unique among the animals, the human alone conducts this struggle with nonbiological organs: the artificial organs of techniques. That is why we can now characterize the human struggle for existence as a spiritual one, a struggle that takes place in a domain other than the living.

Human life is no longer simply biological: it is a technical economy of desire sustained by hypomnesic technical milieus, symbolic milieus in which drives find themselves submitted to a principle of reality that requires the postponement of their satisfaction.[16] As a result of this symbolic mediation, an economy arises through which the energy of the drives is transformed into *libidinal* energy, that is, into desire and sublimation. Technical memory sustains this hallucinatory economy through the epiphylogenetic object, as fetish as well as support of narcissistic reflection.[17] Freud, whose theory of the unconscious is a theory of memory and its censorship, constantly circles around this question without being able to formalize it. Because he ignores the constitutive role of technics, his best efforts lead him into a position of neo-Lamarckism, where memory passes from one generation to another by altogether mysterious means.[18]

We owe to Leroi-Gourhan the thesis that technics is a vector of memory. He showed that a crucial biological differentiation of the cerebral cortex, the opening of the cortical fan, took place in the passage from what he called the Australanthropian to the Neanderthal. He also showed that, from the Neanderthal onward, the cortical system was practically at the end of its evolution: the neural equipment of the Neanderthal is remarkably similar to ours. Nevertheless, from the Neanderthal to us, technics evolves to an extraordinary extent. We may conclude from this that technical evolution no longer depends on biological evolution. Technical differentiation since the Neanderthal has occurred outside and independent of the biological dimension, the "interior milieu" in which, according to Claude Bernard, the constitutive elements of the organism thrive.[19] The process of exteriorization is in this respect the process of the constitution of *a third layer of memory*.

In the wake of the neo-Darwinism arising from molecular biology, and also of the research conducted by Weismann in the late nineteenth century,[20] consensus has been that living sexuated beings are constituted by two memories, that of the species (the genome, which Weismann calls "the germ") and that of the individual—somatic memory, rooted in experience and located in the central nervous system. This latter memory has been observed in organisms as basic as freshwater snails and as proximate to us as the chimpanzee. But humans, and humans alone, have access to a third memory supported and constituted by technics. A piece of flint, for example, takes shape through the organization of inorganic matter: the technician's gesture ingrains an order transmitted via the inorganic, introducing for the first time in the history of life the possibility of transmitting individually acquired knowledge in a nonbiological way. This technical memory is epiphylogenetic; in it, individual epigenetic experience provides phylogenetic support for the intergenerational cultural phylum.

It is because his knowledge is a function of this primordial exteriority of memory that the slave boy Meno in Plato's dialogue of the same name draws the figure of a geometrical object in sand: to think his object, he must exteriorize it by organizing the inorganicity of the sand, which thus becomes the space and the support of the projection of a concept.[21] However mutable it may be, the sand that receives this inscription can conserve the characteristics of the figure more durably than can the mind of the slave boy. Because the boy's mind is essentially fluid, his thoughts are constantly passing away and effacing themselves; in a word, he is retentionally finite. His memory constantly snaps; his attention is drawn toward new ones; and he has a hard time "intentionalizing" the geometrical object—taking it in from the perspective of its organic identity, its necessity, its innermost essence, in sum, its *eidos* or form.

The drawing, as hypomnesic memory, is therefore indispensable to this potential philosopher, the slave boy, and to his passage into action, that is, his anamnesis. It constitutes a crutch for understanding, a space of intuition entirely produced by the gestures of the slave tracing in the sand the figured effects of this reasoning.[22] The sand holds "in view" the results of the slave's intuition and understanding; it thus facilitates the extension and construction of the geometrical proof. But the Platonic opposition between the intelligible and the sensible, between *logos* and *technē*, which became more insistent in the dialogues following the *Meno*, made this technical support literally impossible. As a result, Western metaphysics took shape as the denegation of the originary technicity of memory.

Epiphylogenesis, in becoming the process of grammatization, engenders mnemotechnics which, starting with the Industrial Revolution, produced analog and digital mnemotechnologies; today, these latter are being reconfigured within microtechnologies, biotechnologies, and nanotechnologies.

From Writing to Digitalization

While technics in general constitute for mankind an originary milieu of epiphylogenetic memory, not all technologies are designed to store memory traces. A flint stone is designed to cut meat, to work up matter. It just happens that in addition, and spontaneously, it is also a vector of memory. It is, however, only in the course of the late Paleolithic era that mnemotechnics in the strict sense of the term appear on the epiphylogenetic horizon, in the form of mythograms—supports of ritual narratives—and tattoos on the bodies of sorcerers—the first instruments of calculation. And it is only in the Neolithic era that the conditions proper to grammatization as hypomnesis lead to the evolution of the letter, by way of the transformation of ideographic systems of numbering and the recording of the social memory of the great empires that emerged from agriculture and sedentarity.[23]

Strictly speaking, alphabetization constitutes the Greek city-state; it creates the conditions for communal living as the rules of life are exteriorized and objectified in the form of a written text accessible to all citizens. The political medium takes the form of collective memory, and historical society is born.

The Greek alphabet is a system of diacritical signs—fewer than thirty characters—which can be used by anyone in the role of reader or writer. Its use introduces the possibility of later generations' gaining literal access to what took place in the history of society and in thought. Even today, to read the *Meno* in the Greek of the Platonic era is to be placed in immediate relation with Plato's thought. Literal hypomnesis (the inscription of Plato's text) constitutes the materiality of Plato's thought, and of Western thought more generally: it is the alphabetical organization of access to memory. This is the conclusion reached by Husserl at the end of his life.[24]

The alphabet is the first mnemotechnique that is orthothetic in nature. *Orthotès* means exactitude, and *thesis* means position: alphabetical statements are "ortho-thetical" because they posit in exact spatial form the past time of the speech they record. Alphabetical writing is the *literal synthesis* of linguistic memory; as such, it configures a properly historical temporality.

At the end of the fifteenth century, the printing press, as the first mechanical technique of reproduction, amplified and transformed the effects of this synthesis. The sudden proliferation of books made it necessary for readers to look to new systems for navigating accumulated knowledge. These include library catalogs, indexes, and bibliographies, files made possible by the printed book's foliation, its pagination, its summaries, tables of contents, and glossaries. A process of teleguided reading thus began to take shape, through the implementation of techniques that underlie today's electronic editorial supports and random-access search systems. With the development of contemporary techniques of information processing, a veritable automatic activity of memory will, in the near future, accomplish the exteriorization of the functions of the cerebral cortex and, more globally, of the nervous system.

As Elizabeth Eisenstein has shown, the most important political consequence of the printing press was the Reformation.[25] The printing press made it possible for everyone to have personal access to the Bible translated by Luther into German. Max Weber has shown that the circulation of printed material made possible by the print revolution is also what allows, through the practice of calculation and the circulation of accounting registers, the advent of capitalism.[26]

The nineteenth century saw the development of analogic orthothetical mnemotechniques that enabled the synthesis of visual and aural perception. Like the alphabet, photography and phonography conserve and transmit, exactly, an element of the past—in this case, the light- and sound-wave frequencies produced by an object of perception are recorded via a technological hypommnesic apparatus. Just as I cannot doubt my access to the very thought of Plato when I read the *Phaedo* in the original Greek, when I listen to a recording of the voice of Sarah Bernhardt, my emotion stems from the certitude that I am hearing, not an image of what may have been her voice, but her voice itself. And likewise when I gaze at the face of Baudelaire photographed by Nadar.

These new orthotheses take up the mnesic function which up to then was assigned to sculpture, painting, monumental architecture, and the arts of memory studied by Frances Yates.[27] As a result, they can store and reconstitute more varied and more extensive elements of the past than those stored and reconstituted by the book. These orthotheses developed rapidly in the twentieth century in the form of cinematography, radio broadcasting, and television: this comprises the birth of what Adorno and Horkheimer named the "culture industry."[28] Broadcasted audiovisual temporal objects, which, as they flow by, coincide with the flowing consciousnesses to which they are addressed, form and condition the collective flow of masses of consciousnesses: in this way, they constitute audiences. Controlling the temporal flow of mass consciousness allows the culture industries to control behavior, for instance, to guarantee the consumption of products that the process of permanent innovation (the principle underlying industrial production) constantly releases into the global market.

This power stems from the specificity of analog orthothetic recording, where, in contrast to the literal synthesis of linguistic memory, machines do the coding and decoding. This marks a fundamental shift in the economy linking creator and receiver: in the case of the literal synthesis, one cannot be a reader without being able to write; in the case of analog recording, one can—and typically does—receive audiovisual messages without having the ability to produce them oneself. Thus, industrialization—defined as the separation of producers and consumers—comes into being. Here we have an example that confirms just how fundamentally human memory, which is always both psychical and social, is a technical competency.

Analog orthothetic techniques create the possibility of an industry of audiovisual temporal objects that deploys mass channeling of attention and thereby wields undeniable economic as well as political power—literally a psycho-power. It extends the sway of biopower that Foucault attributed to the disciplinary society and inaugurates a new stage of grammatization—one that, for Adorno and Horkheimer, is tantamount to massive social regression.

In order to amortize the huge productive apparatuses constituted in the development of machinism, industry has since the beginning of the nineteenth century progressively installed a "society of consumption."[29] Such a regime is meant to address the problem posed by permanent innovation: the necessity to absorb new industrial productions for which society is not spontaneously prepared.[30] Industrial society presupposes the permanent modification of the behavior of individuals, who are less and less citizens and more and more consumers; the commodity has become the main operator of the socialization of individuals, and it is in this respect that the media are essential to industrial democracies. Media outlets are vectors conducting society toward the permanent adoption of consumable novelty by means of which capitalism subsists.

Ernest Renan has shown that every society is founded upon the adoption of a fictive past that effaces the differences in the origins of individuals and facilitates the identification of a common future through a politics of memory and forgetfulness.[31] Schooling is the hub of this process, instituting behavioral programs transmitted as knowledge in literal synthesis. For Pierre Nora, who has also studied the politics of education, the process of adoption involves the constitution of places of memory. This is why education has been radically transformed by the psycho-power developed by industrial society through its analog media: by replacing the institutions of programs—grammar schools, high schools, and universities—with the program industries, it effectively creates a new mechanism of adoption.

In the present era, however, this entire apparatus is redeployed to take advantage of the convergence of analog technologies of communication and digital technologies of the information industries. Digital orthothetic synthesis made its appearance during the second half of the twentieth century in the form of information processing; today, at the beginning of the twenty-first century, it takes form in electronic apparatuses of all kinds: video cameras, mobile telephones, and voice recorders that are no longer analog. Digital technologies arose out of information industries that themselves developed through the strategic commodification of information as stability; as that which allows us to orient ourselves in an ever-changing situation, information thus constitutes a new system of cardinality.

Memory and Information

The industrial economy of information becomes a reality starting in the nineteenth century. Charles Louis Havas prefigured the full-scale industrial apparatus for the exploitation of information when, in 1835, he exploited the then new telegraphic network to create the first press agency. To the extent that it is a commodity, information correlates time and value and thereby upsets historical time. As essential elements in the apparatus through which the mercantile production of memory becomes global and quotidian, networks of current events necessarily function at the speed of light. This is because the value of information as commodity drops precipitously with time (in contrast to that of knowledge, which remains constant or increases over time).

The industries of communication achieve ever greater sway by merging with the information industries. Mass broadcasting implies the concentration of the means of production: the cost of a televised image can be amortized only if it is broadcast to millions of spectators. Thus, relatively few images are needed to supply the global network of television stations that produces the raw material of memory by designating information as "eventful." What results from this selection process and near-instantaneous transmission of information is the industrial fabrication of the present: an event becomes an event—it literally takes place—only in being "covered." Industrial time is always at least coproduced by the media. "Coverage"—what is to be covered—is determined by criteria oriented toward producing surplus value. Mass broadcasting is a machine to produce ready-made ideas, "clichés." Information must be "fresh" and this explains why the ideal for all news organs is the elimination of delay in transmission time.[32]

Information is transmitted at the speed of light. Analog and digital orthotheses make this possible, in contrast to the literal orthothesis, which implied a delay, an essential belatedness between what can be called the event (or its seizure) and its reception or reading. It is precisely at the level of the seizure of information and in its processing that the analogically or digitally in-formed event is submitted to the logic of light-time. Access to the networks or vectors of industrial memory requires the existence of entry and exit organs, called interfaces or terminals: the technical advances of photography rapidly lead to belinography,[33] then to cinematography, and finally to the live teletransmission of images, while the pairing of telegraphic and phonographic principles issue into the telephone, and then into live radio broadcasting. Just as the network of light-time does away with the belatedness between the seizure of an event and its reception by infinitesimally reducing the time of its transmission, so too does the analog or digital instrument eliminate all belatedness between the event and its seizure.

With an effect of the real (of presence) resulting from the coincidence of the event and its seizure and with the real-time or "live" transmission resulting from the coincidence of the event seized and its reception, a new experience of time, collective as well as individual, emerges. This new time betokens an exit from the properly historical epoch, insofar as the latter is defined by an essentially deferred time—that is, by a constitutive opposition, posited in principle, between the narrative and that which is narrated. This is why Pierre Nora can claim that the speed of transmission of analog and digital transmissions promotes "the immediate to historical status":

> Landing on the moon was the model of the modern event. Its condition remained live retransmission by Telstar. . . . What is proper to the modern event is that it implies an immediately public scene, always accompanied by the reporter-spectator or the spectator-reporter, who sees the event taking place. This "voyeurism" gives to current events both their specificity with regard to history and their already historical feel as immediately out of the past.[34]

In writing, the very medium of history, an event typically precedes its seizure, and the latter precedes its reception or reading. This configures the present-ation of the past as the retroactivity of an originary default, of a belatedness of the narrative and of the reception of the event with respect to the time of the event, which nevertheless constitutes itself only in this delayed action. The time of relation, of "narrative," is always belated with respect to what is narrated, is always cited in being recited.

The daily and industrial fabrication of time by a press agency is not a mere account of the news: the current events industries are not satisfied with recording what happens, for then everything happening would have to be recorded. Rather, "what happens" happens only in *not* being everything, through its distinction from all the rest. Information has value only as the result of this hierarchization: only that which is "covered" attains the status of event. This is the plight of memory in general (and the theme of "Funes the Memorious" by Jorge Luis Borgès).[35] Memory must be a selection in the present, and its passing, its becoming past, is its diminution. But in the present account, the criteria of selection become industrial—and the selection takes place in real time, not through this work of time that is history, whether as *Historie* (the facticity of "what happened") or *Geschichte* (its meaning).[36]

The conservation of memory, of the memorable that is itself constituted through selection from within the memorizable, is always already its elaboration as well; it is never the mere reporting of what takes place. What takes place only takes place in not quite actually taking place. One memorizes only by forgetting, by effacing, by selecting what deserves to be retained from all that could have been retained; in the same vein, one memorizes only by anticipating, positively or negatively, that which could have happened (which means that retention is always already protention), and this remains the case despite Freud's insistence that such selection is also, at the psychological level, a repression.[37] The question for psychoanalytic theory is how psychological and social memory can be articulated, given that such articulation is the very condition for the constitution of the superego, at least as long as there is one. An essential aspect of the elimination of deferred time, which is to say, of the work of delayed action, is precisely that it sets off a process of desublimation and disindividuation brought on by the loss of knowledge in the era of industrial hypomnesis.

It can be said that the media coproduces that which takes place, here meaning that it produces its effects and so anticipates what will happen. There is nothing intrinsically novel about this situation: it is the very law of memory that it must precede itself. As a result, the past of the present is never situated behind it but has "always already preceded it" (as Heidegger says) without determining it. Nonetheless, something absolutely new happens when the conditions of memorization, that is, the criteria of effacement, selection, forgetting, anticipation, retention-protention—in a word, of temporalization—become concentrated in a technico-industrial machine whose finality is the production of surplus value. In the wake of this development, what hegemonically rules the activity of memory is the imperative to gain time. Just as abstract, capitalizable money is nothing but the credit accorded the future in advance, so too is memory nothing but the future time of the mass audience. Industrial memory retention is ruled by the law of the audience as a source of credit, in all senses of the term. This law irresistibly predetermines the nature of events themselves: social "actors" anticipate the conditions of the recordability of their acts; their actions become a function of the constraints of this industrial surface of time. In this sense, the media is never satisfied with "coproducing" events. ever more often, they produce them through and through: 9/11 was precisely such a production.

There has today occurred a veritable inversion in the relation between life and media: the media now relates life each day with such force that this "relation" seems not only to anticipate but ineluctably to precede, that is, to determine, life itself. In the rivalry among the media, this relation has become drive-oriented—for such is the law of the sensational—and has promoted both the staging of terrorist acts and the ordinary pornography of television. What this means is that the media today destroys the superego as much as it preserves it, which is to say that it destroys the very condition for the transformation of drives into desire, that is, into social energy.

The Ecology of Hypomnesis: The Time of Associated Milieus

Unlike analog and digital orthotheses, literal synthesis presupposes that the receiver of a textual message is literate. The literal reader is herself an apparatus, "equipped" and independently able to access the content of a literal recording. Assuming that she has spent the number of years needed to instrumentalize, automatize, and machinize the functioning of her memory, the literal reader will have transformed herself, by and for herself, into an instrument of reading.

With analog and digital technologies, however, the functions of coding and decoding are delegated to machines. The video recorder "reads" the videotape and the computer "reads" the file. What is important here is not, however, the instrumentalization of memory, which has ample precedent, but the *displacement* of its initial instrumentality. This displacement fundamentally transforms memory, for with analog and digital technologies, sender and receiver no longer coincide with encoder and decoder. This transformation is obviously not without consequences for reading, which is to say for reading as well as writing memory: when collective memory becomes analog or digital, the relations between statements, the sender's and receiver's, are transformed to a considerable extent. These two poles correspond to what is found at the two extremities of a network: on one side, industrial producers; on the other, consumers.

If the continuous flow of information can cultivate an actual consumerism of memory, the reason lies as much in the delegation of reading and writing skills to machines as in the transformation of memory into a commodity; the latter would be impossible without the former. Such is the organization of the loss of knowledge in industrial hypomnesis: it operates by eliminating—or at least by appearing to eliminate—all opportunity for anamnesis. Hypomnesic milieus without anamnesis are dissociated milieus: they are industrially disorganized, desocialized and desymbolized. The exercise of industrial hypomneses imposes the rules and regulations of the industrial division of work on symbolic life as a whole. This industrialization of the symbolic produces a situation in which society is separated into producers and consumers of symbols. The result is the destruction of the symbolic as such.

A symbolic mnesic milieu is in its structure an associated milieu allowing for the constitution and expression of singularities. In interlocution—the very life of language—a receiver (one who listens, hears, and is destined to a language) is a receiver only to the extent that she can also assume the position of sender (that is, speaking what no one else could). In short, you cannot hear a language unless you are able to speak it, and to speak it in an utterly singular fashion. Language is in this respect consubstantially dialogical: speech as symbolic exchange constitutes a circuit wherein those who receive a symbolic address in the form of words render what they have received in the form of other words spoken to other receivers. In speaking they produce a process of individuation and thereby participate in the transformation of language itself.

This process of psychic and collective individuation requires that the linguistic milieu involve permanent interlocution, that is, the participation of everyone in its becoming. The speaker individuates herself—transforms herself and becomes what she is—through her statements, but these statements also contribute to the transformation of the language in which they are pronounced, precisely following the degree of individuation of the speaker. The psychic individuation of the speaker is in the same movement a collective individuation, constituting the shared language of the speakers who constitute themselves in speaking.

The life of language is in interlocution, and it is precisely interlocution that the audiovisual mass media short-circuit and destroy. The social milieus in which psychic existences individuate themselves and the groups through which they exchange and transform themselves exist in general milieus only to the extent that they are participative: the individuation of the milieu takes place through the individuation of those living within it, and vice versa. Generally speaking, the service economy, of which the media are the main sector, deprives the psychical individual of all opportunity of participation in collective individuation. Because it is rooted in the short-circuiting of its users' knowledge by way of industrial hypomneses, the service economy effectively stunts the development of the individual's life milieu.

But at the end of the twentieth century, the Internet has profoundly modified this situation. Now that it has been integrated into a digital environment, audiovisual memory can be produced through participative technologies *that no longer impose the producer/consumer opposition*. That is why the Internet age is an age of hypomnesis constituting itself as an *associated* technical milieu. It marks the end of the era of dissociated milieus—the escape from milieus that separate the functions of producers and consumers, deprive both of their knowledge, and consequently strip their capacity to participate in the socialization of the world through its transformation.

Gilbert Simondon (1989) speaks of associated technical milieus in his analysis of the tide-propelled electrical power plant: the power plant as technical milieu is called "associated" because the technical object of which it is the milieu structurally and functionally associates the energies and natural elements composing this milieu, such that nature becomes a function of the technical system. This is the case of the Guimbal turbine, which assigns to saltwater (the natural element) a triple technical function: to furnish energy, to cool the structure of the turbine, and to catalyze the water-proofing of the stages.[38]

The era of digital networked hypomnemata inaugurates the industrial hypomnesic milieu, where the human element of geography is associated with the becoming of the technical milieu. The Internet makes possible a typical participative economy of free software and cooperative technologies—an associated hypomnesic milieu where the receivers are placed in the positions of senders. In that respect, it constitutes a new stage of grammatization that allows us to envisage a new economy of memory supporting an industrial model no longer based on dissociated milieus or on disindividuation. Industrial hypomnesic memory now comprises the very heart of contemporary societies, and it is striking to see objects of daily use become ever more closely linked to media by becoming communicative: iPods, smart phones, GPS navigators, and many other devices using micro- and nanotechnologies—all of these are hypomnesic objects.

Analog mass media imposed an industrial calendarity, with schedules and programs that also served as cardinalities, orienting us in the images of the world through the hierarchization of news and of demographics. The demassification of media brought on by podcasting, personal media, and the suspension of the producer/consumer opposition constitutes a new age of memory in which memory once again becomes transindividual.[39] The catalyst for this new age is the liberation of hypomnesic memory from its industrial function. For if dissociation is what causes the short-circuiting of transindividuation, then the associated hypomnesic milieus of digital networks mark a crucial point of rupture: insofar as they are cooperative and participative, they can reconstitute the circuits necessary for transindividuation. Such a transformation, I want to suggest, requires a change of industrial model, a new economy of hypomnesis and anamnesis that underscores their fundamental complementarity. Cooperative digital technologies can be placed in the service of individuation, but only if the industrial politics of hypomnesis are implemented in the service of a new age of anamnesis. Let us conceive this new age as an ecology of associated hypomnesic milieus.

Notes

1. G. W. F. Hegel, *The Encyclopaedia Logic*, trans. T. F. Geraets, W. A. Suchting, and H. S. Harris (Indianapolis: Hackett, 1991).

2. Gilles Deleuze, "Control and Becoming" and "Postscript on Control Societies," in *Negotiations*, trans. M. Joughin (New York: Columbia University Press, 1995).

3. Gunther Anders, *L'obsolescence de l'homme* (Paris: Encyclopédie des nuisances, 2002).

4. According to Gilbert Simondon's reading of Marx, the passage of our know-how into the machine makes all of us, not simply the working class, proletarians. (Eds.)

5. Jacques Derrida, *Of Grammatology*, trans. Gayatri Chakravorty Spivak (Baltimore: Johns Hopkins University Press, 1998).

6. Jacques Derrida, *Writing and Difference*, trans. Alan Bass (Chicago: University of Chicago Press, 1980).

7. Stiegler's use of the term *reactivatible* is an indirect reference to Husserl's account of hypomnesic memory; the tradition of geometry, according to Husserl (1970), can be "reactivated" by future geometers only because it has been written down. (Eds.)

8. Derrida, *Of Grammatology*, 84.

9. A student of Maurice Merleau-Ponty and Georges Canguilhem, Simondon developed a theory of individuation that spanned processes from the physical through the biological to the psychic and collective. The central insight of his account is the fundamental incompletion of all processes of individuation, which, even as they produce concrete individuals, retain ties to two dimensions of exteriority: the preindividual and the associated milieu. Thus, in Stiegler's reference, we can gloss the associated milieu as an environment in which individuation takes place, a dimension external to the individual undergoing individuation. (Eds.)

10. This concept of grammatization is borrowed from an analysis of the history of language knowledge in Auroux 1992.

11. Walter Benjamin, "The Work of Art in the Age of Mechanical Reproduction," in *Illumina-tions*, ed. Hannah Arendt (New York: Schocken, 1969), 217–52.

12. The fundamentals of a general organology—that is, a theory of the articulation of bodily, artificial, and social organs—are set forth in Bernard Stiegler, *De la misère symbolique*, vol. 2, *La Catastrophè du sensible* (Paris: Galilée, 2004).

13. Adam Smith, *An Inquiry in the Nature and Causes of the Wealth of Nations* (Chicago: University of Chicago Press, 1977).

14. Plato, *Gorgias*, trans. Robin Waterfield (Oxford: Oxford University Press, 1994).

15. Stiegler introduces the term *epiphylogenesis* in *Technics and Time*, vol. 1, *The Fault of Epimetheus* (Stanford: Stanford University Press, 1996), to designate the evolution of (human) life by means other than life, that is, through technical exteriorization. This conception resonates with much contemporary work in the evolutionary cognitive sciences that emphasizes the role of culture in evolutionary processes. (Eds.)

16. On this point, see especially Bernard Stiegler, *Mécréance et discrédit*, vol. 3, *L'esprit perdu du capitalisme* (Paris: Galilée, 2006).

17. The "epiphylogenetic object" would be a technical object that supports epiphylogenesis, or extragenetic evolution. (Eds.)

18. This is particularly clear in Sigmund Freud, *Moses and Monotheism* (New York: Vintage, 1955) and *The Ego and the Id*, trans. James Strachey (New York: W. W. Norton, 1962).

19. Claude Bernard, *Leçons sur les propriétés physiologiques et les altérations pathologiques des liquides de l'organisme* (Paris: Ballière's, 1859).

20. August Weismann, *The Germ-Plasm: A Theory of Heredity* (New York: Scribner's, 1893).

21. Plato, *Meno and Other Dialogues*, trans. Robin Waterfield, (Oxford: Oxford University Press, 2005).

22. Bernard Stiegler, *La technique et le temps*, vol. 3, *Le temps du cinéma et la question du mal-être* (Paris: Galilée, 2001).

23. See Harold Innis, *Empire and Communications* (Lanham, MD: Rowman & Littlefield, 2007). (Eds.)

24. Husserl 1970. See Jacques Derrida, *Edmund Husserl's "Origin of Geometry": An Introduction* (Lincoln: University of Nebraska Press, 1989). (Eds.)

25. Elizabeth Eisenstein, *The Printing Press as Agent of Change: Communications and Cultural Transformations in Early Modern Europe* (New York: Cambridge University Press, 1979).

26. Max Weber, *The Protestant Ethic and the Spirit of Capitalism*, trans. Talcott Parsons (London: Routledge, 2001).

27. Frances Yates, *The Art of Memory* (Chicago: University of Chicago Press, 2001).

28. Theodor Adorno and Max Horkheimer, *The Dialectic of Enlightenment*, ed. Gunzelin Schmid Noerr, trans. Edmund Jephcott (Stanford, CA: Stanford University Press, 2002).

29. See Jean Baudrillard, *The Consumer Society: Myths and Structures* (London: Sage, 1988).

30. The *velocipède*, whose fabrication was entrusted to the Parisian Company of Bicycles, founded in 1867, could not have developed socially without print media. Five specialized journals came out between 1880 and 1900, while *Le Petit Journal*, a daily with a huge readership, ran its own promotional campaign, promoting competitions and finally the Tour de France, which continues to receive extensive media coverage. Before showing performances, the aim of these publications was to show future cyclists that rolling on two wheels without falling down is possible!

31. Ernest Renan, *Qu'est-ce qu'une Nation?* (Toronto: Tapir Press: 1996).

32. "Laurel? —Yeah? —Where did you put the newspaper? —Where it belongs. —You mean? —In the fridge . . . —And why in the fridge? —To have fresh news."

33. Invented by Édouard Belin in 1913, the Belinograph could capture pictures with a photocell and transmit them over regular telephone lines. (Eds.)

34. Jacques Le Goff and Pierre Nora, *Faire de l'histoire 2* (Paris: Gallimard, 1974), 295. Telstar, the first communication satellite to "serve as a relay for the transatlantic exchange of televised programmes," also impressed Heidegger. See his essay "Traditional Language and Technical Language," trans. W. Gregory, *Journal of Philosophical Research* 23 (1998).

35. Jorge Luis Borgès, "Funes the Memorious," *Labyrinths: Selected Stories and Other Writings*, (New York: New Directions, 1964).

36. In *Being and Time* (trans. J. Macquarrie and E. Robinson [New York: HarperOne, 2008]), Heidegger distinguishes *Historie*, which is concerned with the empirical question of occurrence, from *Geschichte*, which, linked to *Geschick* (fate), concerns the deeper significance or directionality of the past toward the future. (Eds.)

37. The terms *retention* and *protention* come from Edmund Husserl's exploration of the structure of time consciousness in *On the Phenomenology of the Consciousness of Internal Time*, trans. J. Brough (Dordrecht: Kluwer Academic Publishers, 1991). Retention names the "just-past" and protention names the "just-to-come," which both belong to the present now, or impression, and constitute it as a thick now. (Eds.)

38. The Guimbal turbine thus exemplifies the complementarity of the process of individuation (here a technical individuation) and the associated milieu of that individuation. Just as its operation renders nature "a function of the technical system," the operation of hypomnesic milieus render anamnesis a part of the larger mnemotechnological system of the Internet. (Eds.)

39. For Simondon, transindividuation comprises a collective individuation that requires first a disindividuation of individual (psychic) individuations and draws directly on the "preindividual," i.e., that which exceeds but nonetheless remains bound to any given process of individuation. Simondon theorizes transindividuation in *L'individuation psychique et collective* and correlates it with the functioning of technical objects in *Du mode d'existence des objets techniques*. Stiegler here suggests that the new digital hypomnesic milieus enable a collective individuation that does not take already individuated individuals as its starting point, but rather directly individuates the collective and sustains the ongoing individuation of this collective. (Eds.)

References and Suggested Readings

Auroux, Sylvain. 1992. *La révolution technologique de la grammatisation*. Liège: Mardaga.

Derrida, Jacques. 1981. "Plato's Pharmacy" [*La pharmacie de Platon*]. In *Dissemination*, trans. Barbara Johnson, 61–171. Chicago: University of Chicago Press.

Foucault, Michel. 1997. "Self Writing" [*L'écriture de soi*]. In *Ethics: Subjectivity and Truth*, ed. Paul Rabinow. New York: New Press.

Husserl, Edmund. 1970. "The Origin of Geometry." In *Crisis of the European Sciences and Transcendental Phenomenology*, trans. David Carr. Evanston: Northwestern University Press.

———. 1991. *On the Phenomenology of the Consciousness of Internal Time*, trans. J. Brough. Dordrecht: Kluwer Academic.

Leroi-Gourhan, André. 1993. *Gesture and Speech* [*Le geste et la parole*]. Trans. Anna Bostock Berger. Cambridge, MA: MIT Press.

Plato. 2003. *Phaedrus*. Trans. Christopher Rowe. New York: Penguin.

Simondon, Gilbert. 1989. *Du mode d'existence des objets techniques*. Paris: Aubier.

———. 2007. *L'individuation psychique et collective*. Paris: Flammarion.

6 :: SENSES CAROLINE JONES

Blueprints and diagrams, regardless of whether they control printing presses or mainframe computers, may yield historical traces of the unknown called the body.

FRIEDRICH KITTLER, *Gramophone, Film, Typewriter*

The senses both constitute our "sense" of unmediated knowledge and are the first medium with which consciousness must contend. Media theorists can argue (as with Kittler) that the senses are an effect of media or (with McLuhan) that mediating technologies are "extensions" of man.[1] These two approaches—technological determinism (the body senses change radically with mediation) versus what we might call naturalization (the senses are grounded in the body and merely "extend" their reach through mediating technologies)—stage the senses in a crucial arena for determining the effects of mediation on understanding.

Consider philosophy, the first secular discipline of knowledge-production. This love-of-knowing created itself by distinguishing between abstract cognition and bodily sensation, beginning with the Greeks' division of mind into *aisthetá kai noetá*—"felt" versus "thought" (a division Kant deemed "quite famous"). Such boundaries between conceptual and physical knowing were sharply articulated in Cartesian doubt, and the border thus formed was an imperial one—mental certainty was to rule the potentially misleading cues sent by eyes, ears, nose, tongue, or sensate skin.[2] Over time, the proximate senses (touch and taste) drifted into ignominy, the acutely animal senses (hearing and smelling) were firmly demoted, and sight—the most distant and far-reaching of our senses—was promoted to proud but unstable preeminence as the crowning metaphor for knowledge itself.[3]

Plato's allegory of the cave (*Republic*, book 7) offers a foundational instance of the anxious primacy of sight. Tropes of seeing function through an overarching set of analogies that link shadows with ignorance, darkness with deception, vision with understanding, and insight with enlightenment. As centuries of commentary reveal, however, these binaries are neither simple nor fixed, nor is the specific architecture of mediation in this most famous of caves clearly mapped. The prisoners are described as being shackled so that they cannot even turn their heads to witness the source of illumination in their shadowy world. In these shadows, they can see shapes they "know" to be objects, animals, and figures, but in truth they are blind to the ideal forms producing what they see—the enduring Platonic entities responsible for those shifting and variable projections. Victims of a woefully partial form of sight, the prisoners represent (we are told) most people's complacent relation to the hidden truths of this world. In Plato's literary rendition, Socrates tells us that the allegory of the cave and its blindered inhabitants will explain the "dividing line" between knowing and mere existence: the prisoners down below in the flickering shadows are merely existing; it is given only to philosophers to exit the cave and apprehend the fully dimensional essence of things as they truly are—*thereby also discovering what has been mediating reality*. Media (the flickering light, the objects, their projected shadows, the rough cave wall) form a system of representation and deception with which the blindered sense of sight colludes. Escaping from the mediumistic cave is the only path to true, free (in)sight.

Yet there is a paradox coded within this parable. Everyday vision for the unreflective prisoners is "blind," and there is no way they can attain higher knowledge unless they become free to *move*, physically and of course philosophically, to see another layer of reality beyond and behind what is before their eyes. Yet before they can achieve *inner* truth, they must become blind again, both to the specters in the cave and to the dazzlement of daylight outside.[4] True vision in this narrative necessarily involves oscillatory movement: turning away from spectacle, or if one cannot turn the whole body, closing one's eyes to the visible world—or its mediated *image*—to question what one sees. Thus there are two tropes of blindness in Plato's narrative: the ignorant blindness of the prisoners and the volitional blindness of the philosopher. From Plato to Paul De Man's deconstructive *Blindness and Insight* (1971) and Derrida's *Memoirs of the Blind* (1993), we have what amounts to a subdisciplinary "focus" on the trope of turning and re-turning to produce this insightful blindness, of moving away from the page to reinvent the text, or looking away from the face in the mirror to limn its visage on the sheet. The pathway from ignorant blindness to philosophical *in*sight leads through the body: its turning and re-turning, its willed shift from retinal sight to mental image. The unspoken proprioceptive sense—the synthesizing viscera that produce orientation, balance, sensory location in space and time—is what permits the targeted blindness that will produce ultimate enlightenment in the unified, "grounded" philosophical subject.

In fact, as classicist Andrea Wilson Nightingale has argued, Plato's apparent paean to abstract reason was anchored in such proprioceptive turnings—cultural practices of actual body knowledge. *Theôria* in its cultural context required the pilgrim in ancient Greece to leave his city of origin and make a ritual journey to an oracular center or religious site, perhaps at a time when it would be animated by a festival honoring a specific cult figure.[5] *Theôria* remained incomplete until one returned to one's city to recount the experience from afar. Plato's diatribe against untutored sight merely internalizes the physical movement of the pilgrim, rendering this sojourn and exposure to others' mediations purely conceptual: "The philosophic *theôros* blinds himself to the human realm in order to see a vision that transforms his soul and gives him a radically different perspective on the world when he returns to it."[6] Plato's parable of the cave thus abnegates the senses in order to arrogate their privileged relation to knowledge. Senses are denied—the blind inhabitants denied sight, the chained bodies denied proprioception—because such sensory occlusion seals the mind in media-driven illusions that must be shattered by intellectual travel and travail.

By restoring the repressed cultural context of pilgrimage to Plato's account, however, we clarify the ways in which intellection is always already haunted by its mediated sensory condition. The work of philosophy must deny the ways in which its knowledge is elaborately constructed from synaptic echoes of sensory processes, and its discipline trains philosophers who can eventually internalize the now "theoretical" journey. Recalling the cultural context of the Greek philosophers is instructive in other ways as well. These leisured males, supported by slave-based economies dependent on military conquest, had the patrician's access to sensual pleasures, but correspondingly became victims of the master's doubt about his mediated relation to the world—a conundrum Hegel would codify as the "Master/Slave dialectic."[7] Only by attending to the Other—the slave, the woman, the animal, the blind, the shackled prisoner in the cave, the foreigner and his cult—could philosophy attain a "theory" that aimed at universal truth. Only by imagining the slave's robust and intuitive relationship to reality could the master break free of sensory delusion.

The oscillations and anxieties I am charting here are systematic; they recur through our histories of grappling with the senses and do not promise to be resolved any time soon. Theories of media often begin with the body, but only to pursue a conceptualization whose task is to hide those tracks. Take "aesthetics," by which we designate the highest form of thinking about how art functions, how a given "medium" becomes "fine art." Originally, by *aesthesis* Plato's student Aristotle meant perception through *all* of the senses, granting an independent cognitive value to sensory ways of knowing (and creating a path for science that Plato had never authorized). Even when Alexander Gottlieb Baumgarten gave "aesthetics" its critical philosophical meaning (in his 1750–58 Latin treatise *Aesthetica*), he was attempting to counter "the shortcomings of rationalism . . . in matters of taste" by celebrating a "sensitive knowledge" that constituted a parallel rational system. Although Kant judged Baumgarten's efforts "futile" because they failed to get at the supposedly a priori laws governing taste, he praised their empirical attempt "to bring our critical judging of the beautiful under rational principles, and to raise the rules for such judging to the level of a lawful science."[8] It was the job of systematic philosophy to privilege the abstract over the empirical, turning the ancients' balance between the integrative and sensory components of cognition into a hierarchy of mastering intellect over the body-as-slave.

In truth the senses are complex cognitive systems in which there is no clear separation between, for example, the "medium" of air, the "message" of sonic information, and the intricate body system that interprets sound waves as language, calculating location on the basis of the skull's own acoustic "shadow" and the microsecond delays between inputs at either ear. (Similarly, the eye is histologically and anatomically an extrusion of the brain, and the nasal smell receptors "recognize" specific chemical isomers emotionally before the brain can express to the mind what they are.) But if the hierarchy of a mastering intellect must continually be restaged and institutionally buttressed, that very process also leaves traces in the medium of its actions—the body. Yielding the modern psychic obsessions with hygiene, ocularity, and abjection of the nonvisual, the presumption that the senses are fundamental and must be "transcended" to achieve reason is itself historical. The dialectic between sense and reason fluctuates over time, and there are moments that favor the slave's physical knowledge over the master's mediated relation to the world.

Enlightenment empiricists, for example, were interested in the slave's perceptions, giving sensory arguments an unprecedented primacy. John Locke's conviction that knowledge was only acquired through sense experience was pushed further by the Anglican bishop George Berkeley, who argued that touch was the "mediate" informer of sight. Perceiving "mediately" meant that one idea was perceived by means of another (we understand the height of a distant tower, for example, because we have been close enough to touch towers in the past and have walked up some of them).[9] The third of this great triumvirate of skeptics was David Hume, who contributed the famous billiard ball example—if we send one ball into contact with another, we "know" that the second will move in a given direction, yet the fact we can imagine anything happening at all shows the force of custom and experience rather than of reason or abstract knowledge. Our delusion that we just "knew" all along that the second billiard ball would move, "that we needed not to have waited for the event, in order to pronounce with certainty concerning it," is merely the force of unreflective habit. "Such is the influence of custom, that, where it is strongest, it not only covers our natural ignorance but even conceals itself, and seems not to take place, merely because it is found in the highest degree."[10]

Such radical empiricism was dicey in its day, since it questioned the divinity of the human mind, the implantation of divine will, predestination, and the availability of a priori knowledge. Those quasi-medieval forms of certainty were replaced with what seemed to some a rubbishy pile of sense data accumulated from living in the world. Such destabilizations of the master/slave (mind/body) hierarchy had definite adherents, who were quick to see its political implications. Encyclopedist Denis Diderot worked hard to popularize such British views in France, using the empirical algebra of blind Oxford mathematician Nicholas Saunderson to argue that the process of human reasoning was clearly a cumulative process that drew on sense data—mediated all the way. Indeed, mediations provide the only conceivable grounds for beginning the process of abstraction:

> But if the imagination of the blind man is no more than the faculty of calling to mind and combining sensations of palpable points; and of a sighted man, the faculty of combining and calling to mind visible or colored points, the person born blind consequently perceives things in a much more abstract manner than we; and in purely speculative questions, he is perhaps less liable to be deceived. For abstraction consists in separating in thought the perceptive qualities of a body, either from one another, or from the body itself in which they are inherent. (Diderot [1749] 1999, 159–60)

For an anticlerical, republican-minded Enlightenment philosopher such as Diderot, the embodied senses stood in living rebuke to the enslaving fantasies of intellect.[11] Death itself proved triumphantly that consciousness is embodied (and it is at his deathbed that Saunderson is ventriloquized by Diderot to protest that he cannot believe in God because he cannot *sense* Him). Senses, and the "mediative" function they were agreed to serve, stood up to be counted—and seemed to threaten the toppling of monarchic and clerical regimes claiming "knowledge" in a higher realm.[12]

Diderot's scandalous position in fact drew on traditions of inquiry that went back to the first moments of the medieval *querelle* between the ancients and the moderns. Senses stand in for the modern, the here-and-now medium of consciousness—and yet consciousness may craft knowledge by selecting among sensory mediations to focus on some "abstract" quality taken from memory of the sensuous encounter. Obtaining knowledge from a swirling sensorium has always been the problem at hand (so to speak). The great medieval thinker William of Ockham articulated the problem with considerable sensory acuity, as this savory quotation shows:

> To abstract is to understand one thing without understanding another at the same time even though in reality the one is not separated from the other, e.g., sometimes the intellect understands the whiteness which is in milk and does not understand the sweetness of milk. Abstraction in this sense can belong even to a sense, for a sense can apprehend one sensible without apprehending another.[13]

Ockham's words are echoed precisely in Diderot's: "abstraction consists in separating . . . the perceptive qualities of a body, either from one another, or from the body itself in which they are inherent." Media studies avant la lettre meant never having to say you're sorry for meditating on mediations—for even as the senses held the capacity for abstraction, the mind itself was a palimpsest of mediations that needed to be sifted for the truth.

Abstraction from the body's senses also allowed for an ideological forgetting of the sensory path to knowledge, and this was the drift of empiricism after the Enlightenment. The senses emerged as a "problem" for the newly reconfigured field of aesthetics, as when Gotthold Ephraim Lessing ([1766] 1962) set out formulae for regulating the genres (painting, poetry, theater) by adjudicating just how appropriately a given art form targeted its particular sense (eyesight, hearing, feeling).[14] This intoxicatingly systematic notion has never ceased being influential, from the early twentieth century, when literary historian Irving Babbit borrowed Lessing's rigor to regulate "priapism of the soul," to the late twentieth and early twenty-first century, when art historian Michael Fried, the era's most gifted purveyor of formalism, demanded that the visual arts avoid stimulating "theatricality" (an embarrassing awareness of one's own body in the gallery) in favor of "presence" (the transcendence of the body through extremely purified visual stimulus).[15] How this worked, how one could use the tradition represented by Lessing to

get from senses to the policing of media under modernism, is exemplified by a 1941 essay by Clement Greenberg, the art writer who most influenced the early Fried:

> Only by . . . excluding from each art whatever is intelligible in the terms
> of any other sense [would the] arts attain the "purity" and self-sufficiency
> which they desired. . . . Purity in art consists in the acceptance, willing
> acceptance, of the limitations of the medium of the specific art. . . . The
> arts, then, have been hunted back to their mediums, and there they have
> been isolated, concentrated and defined. (Greenberg 1986, 304–5)

This elision from the senses (seeing) to medium (painting) is profoundly
important for the course of modernism in the visual arts. It meant that
the same kind of materialist empiricism that was developing "Prussian
blue" and "phthalo green" as pictorial commodities (media) would be
brought to the body itself, in order to purify and regulate the senses.[16]
Criticism and commerce joined philosophy in disaggregating sense from
sensibility, and the "mediative" sensory realm became the subject of systematic investigation in cognitive psychology, physics, medicine, chem-
istry, communication theory, advertising, and entertainment.

But unlike chemical pigments or new casting techniques, the senses
are only and always embodied. (We are only now beginning to achieve
a machine-neuronal interface to replace or supplement retina, cochlea,
skin, and nasal mucosa. At least as of this writing, the body is still all we
have, however amplified and altered by prosthetics.) The senses are, definitionally, *conscious*; to be rendered unconscious is to become "insen-
sate"—to be "knocked senseless." By the same reasoning, the infant in
its womb is "insensible" to the warmth, the muffled sounds, the darkness, and the salty taste of amniotic fluid that constitutes its comfort
zone. Consciousness—and *consciousness of medium*—is born through
friction and difference, through forcible estrangement from the media to
which mammalian senses adapted and evolved. The life-giving medium
of air whistles painfully into the lungs at first cry; that audible cry is generated by and carried on waves of the same medium. The muscles, neurons, ciliated hairs, and follicles relaying the stimulus are themselves media, relying on the forces of push-pull electrical resistance and chemical
differentials to bump and jostle them into the state we call "sensation."

Beyond the neonate and above the neuronal are the complexities of
history and culture, and the two modes of analysis identified at the outset of this essay play their roles in arguing whether we have been irrevocably altered by our chirographic, typographic, and digital technologies, or whether they are mere by-products of the great evolutionary leap
in which throat, brain, and ear participated in the development of lan-

guage (Ong 1967). Marx would seem to have been on the technological-determinist side, advocating that we explore how humans are formed by the senses in contact with technologies and political economies: "The forming of the five senses is a labor of the entire history of the world down to the present."[17] Simmel built on Marx to theorize how modernity produced almost physical changes in urban subjects: "We become not only short-sighted but short-sensed in general; yet at these short distances, we become that much more sensitive" (1997, 119). In this legacy (which at its most extreme yields technodeterminism), theories of media move beyond simple critique (of, say, ocularcentrism or visuality) to a deeper historicization of sensory protocols, and an examination of how such protocols work their way into all aspects of embodied subjectivity. Mid-century modernism, for example, produced subjects in the United States who experienced higher levels of mediation than ever before. Sometimes this involved training (art history courses), sometimes the seduction of a newly accessible medium (ham radio, hi-fi), and sometimes the division into market sectors (perfumed air freshener for the home). Bodies were organized in particular ways that colonized newly specified sensory and bodily functions—bureaucratically enhancing aesthetic relations to those functions, and giving them a commodity address.

Thus, for the short American century (from 1945 to the turn of the millennium), the senses were posited as pure zones of "input" targeted by refined media for maximum effect. Earlier modernists' interests in synesthesia or experiments in derangement were replaced by scientific, medical, and capitalist regimes of intensification and purification: "high fidelity" listening and recording systems, chemically synthesized isomers for perfume and flavoring, even single wavelengths of light (lasers).[18] A passion for purified signals drove the broadest levels of knowledge production in fashion, art, pharmacology, neurology, and other technoscientific realms. The mass medium of the airwaves was divvied up into precisely defined bands—FM and AM radio, television, and soon microwaves. The same drive is discernible in the high-keyed, reduced intensity of Color Field painting and in the new vocabulary training consumers to distinguish "Pine Forest" and "Country Fresh" scents and to demand one or the other in their quest for the hygienic home.

The volatile essences of this kind of modernity could be separated into administrable units that were dominated and hierarchized under sight ("sparkling" clean)—the much-discussed "ocularity" of the modern episteme. Yet at precisely this moment, smell was introduced into modernism's white cube, silence and noise became components of a revolution in music composition, and touch was invoked to counteract instrumentalized sight. These violations of modernist decorum, harking back

Carolee Schneeman, *Meat Joy*, 1964. Judson Church, New York City. Group performance with raw fish, chickens, sausages, wet paint, plastic, rope, and shredded scrap paper. Image courtesy of the artist.

to the practice of the 1910s avant-garde, gained salience precisely as the modernizing segmentation of the senses became most acute. They did so self-consciously, forming a counterhegemonic "underground." John Cage and his students, such as Allan Kaprow; Carolee Schneemann, and feminist performance art in general; Julian Beck and the Living Theater; international artists' groups such as Fluxus, Gutai, Vienna Actionism—these then-marginal transgressives insisted on widening the sensory spectrum of artistic media and radically complicating modernist segmentation. At the same moment, new technologies (videotape, electrostatic copying, facsimile transmission machines) introduced yet further registers of abstraction, speed, and seeming "extension" of the senses.

By 1970 the genre policing conducted by formalism was being radically undermined—both by this countercultural critique and by the interchangeability and extension of the senses that electronic media seemed to offer. Well before digital convergence was an everyday reality, media visionaries embraced a technodeterminism that seems prescient, if slightly overenthusiastic: "The eyes replace the me's and we arrive at a condition where what we show becomes what we say."[19] Gene Youngblood, early anthologist and writer on video as "expanded cinema," described the four hundred million people watching the moon landing on

July 20, 1969, as an aesthetic happening in which the whole globe experienced "the same Warhol movie at the same time": "There's no appreciable difference between four hours of *Empire* and four hours of *LM* [lunar module]." These were "extensions of man" with a vengeance (one can hear McLuhan pulsing in the author's hip and breathless prose):

> No one said how really convenient it was to sit there in your home, looking directly at the moon dust, listening simultaneously to four or five conversations separated by a quarter-million miles, getting metabolic information about the Buzz Armstrongs in a closed-circuit loop that extended humanity's total brain-eye out around the moon and back. Who needs telepathy?[20]

"Looking directly," "sit[ting] there in your home," was technology naturalized: an intact body deliriously magnified by technology ("humanity's total brain-eye") but neither rewired nor obstructed in its access to reality by electronic media themselves. What happened to this heady technodream of unmediated access to zooming and booming information?

Reality hit late capitalism's sagging underbelly in the late 1960s and 1970s, as activist opponents identified technological estrangement of the senses as part of the problem: oil crises, "plastic food," televised war. Suburban banality drove waves of environmentalism, feminism, gay activism, and a capacious "postmodernism" that attempted in the 1980s to bring them all under the same critical wing of the academic establishment. By the 1990s everyday virtuality (in the form of the mobile telephones, wireless Internet, the World Wide Web, streaming media, and the laptop) produced a strong response that might be called the "reformation" of the senses. First came compulsive returns to the object, in a stubborn refusal of the kind of seamlessness offered by "Google image" and the searchable database. "Things" became the focus of Heideggerian analysis and culture studies alike, with scholars nostalgic for the tactile tools that had shaped modernity but were quickly disappearing from everyday electronic interfaces. Second, modernist ocularity was hedged in by two different art world developments: on the one hand, massively tactile and olfactory forms of installation art (piles of coffee, drifts of eucalyptus-heavy water vapor, suspended cow bones, and the like); on the other, a dematerialized but vaguely documentary takeover by video. The reformation countered video's virtual mastery of the art world with "sensory studies," an offshoot of visual and cultural studies concocting a potent brew of *Annales*-school microhistory, Marxian production critique, and feminist "writing the body."[21]

The reformation of the senses has a complex if not impossible task. For in every attempt to reawaken the atrophied or vestigial senses lurks a fantasized return to the whole body—which is thwarted by the very rarefaction, separation, and colonization of the senses entailed by body-building, aromatherapy, radical cuisines, personalized MP3 soundscapes, and other popular aesthetic disciplines. Our yearning for sensory redemption has fueled new genres, such as "sound art" or even "olfactivism" (Jones 2006). It has also spurred the revival of artists especially critical of midcentury modernism's bureaucratization of the senses—such as Hélio Oiticica, a leader of the Brazilian Neoconcretismo movement. Oiticica's fury at the segmentation of aesthetic experience led him to innovate in the 1970s, with Lygia Clark, a set of practices embracing aspects of dance, physical therapy, eroticism, and nonvisual sensory experience in general—epitomized by Clark's spice-laden headgear and Oiticica's elaborate samba costumes (the latter called *parangoles*, or cacophonous happenings). The fact that Oiticica's now-popular works are "exhibited" on white walls next to Do Not Touch signs in our visual mausoleums says much about the fate of reformatory efforts. As long as we insist on searching for these things on the Web or canonizing them as "visual art," we participate in ocular fantasies of unmediated knowledge, still imagining ourselves as free and untethered from the sensory viscera mediating (and thereby producing) our only conceivable relation to the real.

Notes

1. Marshall McLuhan, *Understanding Media: The Extensions of Man* (1964). The 1994 edition (MIT Press) has on its cover the negative image of an eye, with lines of sight stretching out into the universe. McLuhan's febrile extended body was nonetheless human at its core, the technological extensions never reaching back to change tissues and sensory organs themselves. Kittler ([1986] 1999) is not so sure, as he contemplates the German mother whose tongue muscles change with the pronunciations internalized from fascist speech on the radio. The mother becomes a relay in transmission, not an extended and empowered self.

2. Immanuel Kant, *Critique of Pure Reason* (1781), A21, note. Rene Descartes, in *Meditations on First Philosophy* (1641), established a premise of radical doubt in regard to sensory knowledge, leading to the famous precept that abstract thought alone grounds consciousness: *cogito, ergo sum*.

3. Scientists not beholden to such philosophies contested the demotion of the animal senses. Richard Feynman famously demonstrated that if he got within a dog's proximity of a person's hand and sniffed, he could "smell out" which book on a shelf the person had handled.

4. As Socrates tells us: "Any one who has common sense will remember that the bewilderments of the eyes are of two kinds, and arise from two causes, either from coming out of the light or from going into the light, which is true of the mind's eye, quite as much as of the bodily eye" (*Republic*, book 7).

5. Andrea Wilson Nightingale, *Spectacles of Truth in Classical Greek Philosophy: Theoria in Its Cultural Context* (Cambridge: Cambridge University Press, 2004), 40.

6. Ibid., 104–5.

7. "The master relates himself to the thing mediately through the bondsman." Friedrich Hegel, *Phenomenology of Spirit* (1807), #190, online at http://www.marxists.org/reference/archive/hegel/index.htm. Hegel first outlined the concept in his *System of Ethical Life* (1802–3).

8. Peter Osborne, ed., *From an Aesthetic Point of View: Philosophy, Art and the Senses* (London: Serpent's Tail, 2000): 2–3; Kant, *Critique of Pure Reason*.

9. John Locke, *Essay Concerning Human Understanding* (1690); George Berkeley, *An Essay towards a New Theory of Vision* (1709).

10. David Hume, *An Enquiry Concerning Human Understanding* (1772). This excerpt is from the chapter on cause and effect, available online at http://www.marxists.org/reference/subject/philosophy/works/en/hume.htm.

11. As W. J. T. Mitchell pointed out to me, this can also be found in Plato's *Meno*, in which a Pythagorean theorem that cannot be grasped algebraically by the slave is revealed to him by a graphic, geometric demonstration—not unlike Saunderson's materialized geometric peg-boards.

12. This is not to eradicate the tropes of sight and light that were still circulating in French revolutionaries' Enlightenment claims, nor the epithets of unreason hurled by their adversaries. Here, Edmund Burke's description of the French Revolution as a "conquering empire of light and reason" clearly plays to the power of intellection above and beyond the embodied actions of the *clochards,* but I suspect Burke invokes reason quite strategically, rebutting Rousseau in favor of empirical and deliberative reason, not an aristocratic assertion of received knowledge. This ambivalent negotiation with the sense politics of class would surface in Hegel's response to the French Revolution as well; see J. F. Suter, "Burke, Hegel, and the French Revolution," in *Hegel's Political Philosophy—Problems and Perspectives,* ed. Z. A. Pelczynski (Cambridge: Cambridge University Press, 1971).

13. William of Ockham, *Expositio physicorum,* fol. 111c.

14. "The first person to compare painting with poetry was a man of fine feeling who observed that both arts produced a similar effect upon him. . . . A second observer, in attempting to get at the nature of this pleasure, discovered that both proceed from the same source. Beauty. . . . A third, who examined the value and distribution of these general rules, observed that some of them are more predominant in painting, others in poetry. . . . The first was the amateur, the second the philosopher, and the third the critic" (Lessing [1766] 1962, 3).

15. Irving Babbit, *The New Laokoön: An Essay on the Confusion of the Arts* (New York, 1910); Michael Fried, "Art and Objecthood" (1967), in *Art and Objecthood* (Chicago: University of Chicago Press, 1998).

16. Prussian blue, a form of ferrocyanide discovered by accident in 1704–5 by painter Heinrich Diesbach in Berlin (hence its alternate name "Berlin blue"), is considered the first synthetic pigment. Phthalocyanine was discovered, also by accident, around 1907, but its pigment value remained unknown until much later in the twentieth century.

17. Karl Marx, *Economic and Philosophic Manuscripts of 1844 and the Communist Manifesto,* trans. Martin Milligan (Buffalo: Prometheus Books, 1988), 108–9.

18. The countercultures of psychedelia and sensory experimentation arose in the mid- to late 1960s in response to the previous decade's regimes of purification and systematization. The 1962 founding of the Pantone color-matching system, for example, was followed by the "irrational" sensory systems of fluorescent colors, black lights, and bioluminescent paints.
19. Edwin Schlossberg, quoted in an epigraph in Gene Youngblood, *Expanded Cinema* (New York: Dutton, 1970), 257.
20. Gene Youngblood, "Television as a Creative Medium," in ibid.
21. A template for this kind of work might be found in Alain Corbin's pioneering history of smell (1986).

References and Suggested Readings

Corbin, Alain. 1986. *The Foul and the Fragrant: Odor and the French Social Imagination*. Cambridge, MA: Harvard University Press.

Diderot, Denis. [1749] 1999. "Letter on the Blind for the Use of Those Who See," trans. Margaret Jourdain (ca. 1916), in *Thoughts on the Interpretation of Nature and Other Philosophical Works*, 147–201. Manchester: Clinamen Press.

Greenberg, Clement. 1986. "Towards a Newer Laocoön," in *Collected Essays and Criticism*, vol. 1. Chicago: University of Chicago Press.

Jones, Caroline, ed. 2006. *Sensorium: Embodied Experience, Technology, and Contemporary Art*. Cambridge, MA: MIT Press; List Visual Art Center.

Kittler, Friedrich. [1986] 1999. *Gramophone, Film, Typewriter*, trans. Geoffrey Winthrop-Young and Michael Wutz. Stanford, CA: Stanford University Press.

Lessing, Gotthold Ephraim. [1766] 1962. *Laocoon: an Essay on the Limits of Painting and Poetry* [*Laokoon, oder Über die Grenzen der Malerei und Poesie*], trans. Edward Allen McCormick. Indianapolis, IN: Bobbs-Merrill.

Ong, Walter J. 1967. *Presence of the Word*. New Haven: Yale University Press.

Osborne, Peter, ed. 2000. *From an Aesthetic Point of View: Philosophy, Art and the Senses*. London: Serpent's Tail.

Simmel, Georg. 1997. "Sociology of the Senses," in *Simmel on Culture*, ed. David Frisby et al. London: Sage.

7 :: TIME AND SPACE

W.J.T. MITCHELL AND MARK B.N. HANSEN

The concepts of time and space have always played a critical role in the analysis of media. In the arts, some media (painting, sculpture, photography) seem ineluctably spatial, while others (drama, cinema, literature) seem focused on the unfolding of events in time. Spatial arts may indirectly evoke temporal dimensions—the moment captured in a photograph, the historic event recorded in a painting or memorialized by a sculpture—but this is a secondary effect. Similarly, spatial features may appear as minor or secondary elements of temporal media: the stage sets of a play, the settings described in a novel or depicted in a film. In other words, we have a rough intuition that some media are predominantly spatial, others temporal, but no exact idea of what this means. Are time and space merely qualities or characteristics of media, something that arises in the perception of mediated entities? Or are they themselves "master" or "meta" media, highly general frameworks, codes, or environments in which media take shape?

The nature of time and space has been a subject of discussion throughout the history of philosophy. Debates have raged: are they real, substantial things, or merely abstractions from experience? "absolute" dimensions of being (as Newton believed), or relative orders of coexistent objects or sequential events (the position of Leibniz)? Throughout, two conceptions of time and space (and their relationship) have seemed to dominate: objective, mechanical, and mathematical models, in which space and time are measurable quantities, and qualitative, subjective models, in which experiences—memories of the past, perceptions of the present, and imaginings directed at the future—and a sense of place constitute human consciousness. But it also seems clear that these two models are in constant dialogue with one another: technical innovations in the measurement of space and time (clocks and navigational instruments, for instance) have powerful practical effects on the human experience of space-time; and the human craving for mastery over time and space, for increased speed and mobility, for longer life and new sensations, and for access to increasingly remote regions ("space, the final frontier") drive the invention of new technologies. The mediation of time and space by the arts, symbol systems, and technical practices is thus a constantly evolving process, one that is occasionally accelerated by a notable mutation such as the invention of printing or the computer or recording devices. A technology such as writing, for instance, may originate as simply playing with marks or idly scribbling, but it can develop into a medium for the conquest of time and space, making possible records of the past and establishing communication networks that allow the control of vast empires (see Innis 2007).

There is also a strong tradition of setting the two dimensions against one another in an ideological hierarchy. Plato thought space was simply the material world, while time was the habitation of the soul. And Greek aesthetics made it clear that the arts of time were superior. The nine muses, all daughters of Mnemosyne, the goddess of Memory, are the inspirers of time arts: music, poetry, history, dance, song, and so on. There are no muses for painting, sculpture, or architecture. These are practical arts that employ the hands and muscles, in contrast to the intellectual labor of the arts of commemoration, recollection of great events, and the praise of dead heroes. The long-standing rivalry or *paragone* (Leonardo da Vinci's term) between poetry and painting, the verbal and the visual arts, is the source of an enduring dialogue or dialectic between the temporal and spatial arts, with numerous episodes of imitation, borrowing, or renunciation. *Ut pictura poesis* ("as in a painting, so in a poem") was inflated into a synthetic principle in order to elevate the visual arts to parity with literature in the Renaissance.

But the explicit use of space and time as fundamental categories for distinguishing the arts (and, by implication, the media) probably makes its first appearance in the eighteenth century, with Lessing's *Laocoon: An Essay upon the Limits of Painting and Poetry* ([1766] 1984):

> Painting employs wholly different signs or means of imitation from poetry,—the one using forms and colors in space, the other articulate sounds in time,—and if signs must unquestionably stand in convenient relation with the thing signified, then signs arranged side by side can represent only objects existing side by side, or whose parts so exist, while consecutive signs can express only objects which exceed each other, or whose parts succeed each other, in time. (95)

Lessing admits that the distinction between temporal and spatial signs is not absolute. The bodies and objects represented "conveniently" by painting "exist not only in space, but also in time," and their "momentary appearances" in the visual arts can suggest actions, motions, cause and effect, and other temporal characteristics. Phenomena of time such as "actions," similarly, "must always be joined to certain agents" that are necessarily embodied, so that "poetry describes also bodies, but only indirectly through actions," whereas painting can show actions but "only as they are suggested through forms."

Despite these concessions, Lessing is clear about the values involved. Painting's true, natural, or "convenient" vocation is the representation of bodies in space, just as poetry's essential nature is the representation of actions in time. Efforts to overcome this natural difference (descriptive poetry, allegorical or narrative painting) are unnatural, to be condemned as bad taste. Each art should stay in its natural location, in the temporal dimension of language or the spatial dimension of the visual arts:

> Painting and poetry should be like two just and friendly neighbors, neither of whom is allowed to take unseemly liberties in the heart of the other's domain, but who exercise mutual forbearance on the borders, and effect a peaceful settlement for all the petty encroachments which circumstance may compel either to make in haste on the rights of the other. (110)

One of these "just and friendly neighbors," it turns out, is much larger and more powerful than the other. "Poetry has the wider sphere," since it appeals to the imagination; thus, "more is allowed to the poet than to the sculptor or painter." Much as Lessing admires the beauty of classical sculpture, he is firmly committed to the superiority of the temporal and verbal arts, and to the notion that the spatial arts should be confined to the representation of "beautiful bodies" and not aspire to the sublime heights and epic range that poetry achieves.

Lessing's aesthetic norms are reinforced by the metaphysical reflections on time and space by Kant and Hegel, his contemporary and his successor, both of whom emphasize the superiority of time to space. For Kant, both terms designate a priori "forms of intuition," the conditions of sensuous experience as such. Space is the intuitive framework for "outer" appearances, while time is the dimension of "inner" experience. For Hegel, the history of art is governed by a progression from the more primitive and material arts of physical space (architecture and sculpture) to the modern arts of virtual space (painting) and the disembodied, dematerialized arts of time (poetry and music). One can see in these distinctions a consistent pattern of associating time with immaterial, invisible, and spiritual values, and space with the realm of matter, outward sensation, and the body. In traditional media such as theater and performance, which inevitably mix spatial and temporal elements, there was always a strong tendency to privilege the temporal. Aristotle argued that poetry and the plot or "imitation of action" was the "soul of tragedy," while the spectacle was secondary and "incidental to the tragic effect." Ben Jonson railed against the tendency to rely on spectacle, costumes, and "carpentry" rather than poetry, the "soul of the masque." Despite the theoretical parity of space and time as abstract concepts, then, they almost invariably become associated with ideological oppositions when they are used to distinguish the arts and media. For Lessing, the contest between the temporal and spatial arts is linked with national styles; England and Germany are portrayed as literary cultures, while France is denigrated as a culture of painters, "bright eyes," and outward display. Perhaps inspired by Plato's characterization of space as a passive "receptacle" or *chora* where the Demiuge imprints the ideas or forms, William Blake boldly personified these abstractions in terms of the gender stereotypes they so often evoke: "Time and Space are Real Beings. Time is a Man. Space is a Woman."

The categories of time and space in media are radically transformed by the revolutions in media technology that occur in the nineteenth century. The invention of mass media, rapid transportation, and instantaneous communication over large distances makes for a kind of implosion of both time and space. The telegraph, the railroad, and the daily newspaper (and later, air travel, radio, television, and the Internet) seem to *shrink* time and space, or at least to make them highly malleable dimensions of human experience rather than the stable, foundational forms of intuition that they were for Kant. Photography and phonography, as Walter Benjamin (2008) notes, transform the very notion of an artwork's "presence in time and space." The "original" work is wrenched from its natural time-space location and is allowed

> to meet the beholder halfway, be it in the form of a photograph or a phonograph record. The cathedral leaves its locale to be received in the studio of a lover of art; the choral production, performed in an auditorium or in the open air, resounds in the drawing room. (221)

The "natural" distance of objects in historical time and geographical space is shattered, along with the "aura" or sense of uniqueness that characterized traditional works of art. These developments, in Benjamin's view, both feed "the desire of the contemporary masses to bring things 'closer' spatially and humanly," and create the conditions for the emergence of modern mass society as such. The invention of cinema combines the spatial and temporal media in a new synthesis that seems to overcome their distinctiveness altogether. Erwin Panofsky speaks of the "temporalization of space" and the "spatialization of time" in film, as if Lessing's borders between the realms of space and time had now been completely erased.

This does not mean, however, that the traditional categories completely drop by the wayside, as ways of either drawing distinctions between arts and media or reinforcing certain values associated with specific art forms. Art critic Clement Greenberg, for instance, updates Lessing's *Laocoon* for modern art in his classic essay "Towards a Newer Laocoon," making far more radical and stringent claims for the essential "purity" of media than Lessing ever contemplated. Greenberg denounces the "confusion of the arts" imposed on painting and sculpture by the dominance of literature from the seventeenth century onward (24). "It was not realistic imitation" in the visual arts "that did the damage so much as realistic illusion in the service of literature" (27). Greenberg's remedy is not, as in Lessing, to confine the visual arts to the portrayal of beautiful bodies in space, but to banish illusion and imitation altogether. He praises the emergence of "flatness" and abstraction in painting, the frank affirmation of "pure painting" that has no reference to objects in the world, much less their actions in time:

> The arts, then, have been hunted back to their mediums, and there they have been isolated, concentrated and defined. It is by virtue of its medium that each art is unique and strictly itself. To restore the identity of an art the opacity of its medium must be emphasized. For the visual arts the medium is discovered to be physical; hence pure painting and pure sculpture seek above all else to affect the spectator physically. (32–33)

Greenberg in effect eliminates *both* time and space from painting, urging a pure art of self-referentiality that is able "to agitate the consciousness with infinite possibilities by approaching the brink of meaning and yet never falling over it" (33). In a sense, Greenberg seems to return the categories of time and space to their metaphysical and religious limits, the ideas of infinity and eternity, collapsing the very idea of the medium into *immediate* intuitions of sensation and intellect.

It is very difficult, then, to generalize about the effect of modern media innovations on the concepts or perceptions of time and space. From some angles it looks as if the categories have been dissolved into one another, into a "space-time continuum" that is infinitely flexible and malleable. From other standpoints it looks as if radically new notions and experiences of time and space have become available, and that the categories have been reinscribed in new cultural formations. Fredric Jameson argues, for instance, that modernism was dominated by the category of time in its obsession with history and revolutionary change, while postmodernism is a period of space and loss of temporality—the "end of history" forecast by thinkers from Hegel to Francis Fukuyama. These broad-brushed attempts to use time and space as historical master terms need to be supplemented, and probably corrected, by a more nuanced account of twentieth-century innovations in media. Friedrich Kittler argues, for instance, that the three great media inventions of the modern era, cinema, phonography, and the typewriter (or keyboard interface), didn't so much transform the human perceptual world as *analyze* it in a relatively conservative fashion—by attempting to match film and sound editing, say, to the requirements of our natural dispositions toward time and space. Kittler also suggests that, with the invention of the computer and electronic networking, we have reached the end of the age of media, entering into a new posthuman environment in which, presumably, time and space will take on quite new forms.

Kittler's prognosis for the decoupling of computers and media, of machines and human beings, instances one concrete take on a disjunction—between objective, mathematical and qualitative, experiential models of space and time—that has dominated the Western theorization of space and time from Aristotle's systematization onward. Indeed, Aristotle's difficulties in defining time objectively, as the number of movement, without recourse to the numbering (and spatializing) soul furnish eloquent testimony to the imbrication both of these models with one another and of time with space. From Aristotle on, philosophers have grappled with the question of whether time and space can be defined objectively, without recourse to human experience and distinctively human modes of perception and understanding. For Kittler and some other theorists of the digital revolution, the computer provides the medium for precisely such an objectification of time and space. Before turning to an evaluation of the assumptions and merits of this position, let us trace the trajectory of thinking about time and space across the span of the twentieth century.

Against the backdrop of the general acceleration of scientific discovery, and in particular of the revolution in physics around the turn of the century, philosophers became newly concerned with differentiating human experience of time and (to a lesser extent) of space from their merely material, that is, objective existence. In this concern, we witness a strong reassertion of the priority of time over space that characterized modern philosophical models from Descartes and Leibniz to Kant and Hegel. For the two great early-twentieth-century thinkers of time—German phenomenologist Edmund Husserl and French metaphysician Henri Bergson—time is an experiential continuum, while space is a discrete representation of an expanse of time, as if it were detachable from the continuum.

In his first book, *Time and Free Will*, Bergson categorically differentiates the qualitative experience of time (what he calls "duration") from both the quantitative dimension of time and its spatialization or representation as a discrete unit of temporal flux. According to Bergson, between the qualitative experience of duration and the quantitative measurement of time as space, there exists a "difference of kind." Moreover, analyses of time as space—which is to say, most if not all scientific treatments of time—cannot hope to grasp the phenomenon of change, since change occurs in the transitions or passages between the discrete units upon which rests any spatializing analysis. What is necessary to grasp change, to grasp time as change, is a qualitative modification of duration considered as a whole, what Bergson refers to (following German mathematician Bernhard Riemann) as the alteration of a qualitative multiplicity. For the Bergson of *Time and Free Will* (it will later be a question how much his view changes), the capacity to experience such an alteration of the whole of duration is limited to beings endowed with consciousness, which is to say, to human beings.

In his lectures on *The Phenomenology of Internal Time Consciousness*, delivered in 1905 and continuously revised and supplemented during his lifetime, Husserl analyzes the givenness of the world, or rather of appearances, to consciousness. Husserl's interest in time stems from his methodological aim to "return to the things themselves," which is to say, to the conditions on which experiences are constituted. The turn to internal time consciousness—to the analysis of the content of experience constituted by consciousness in time—culminates Husserl's reduction (*epoche*) of the so-called natural attitude. Whereas this generalized reduction, by bracketing out perception of objects in the world, allows attention to be focused on the self-evident, apodictic content of consciousness, attention to the specifically temporal mode of givenness of the content of consciousness allows Husserl to account for the constitution of the lived experiences (*Erlebnis*) of consciousness. This is why, for Husserl, consciousness, or more precisely, internal time consciousness, is not simply constituted but constituting: the temporalization performed by consciousness literally constitutes the content of the experience it generates. Husserl distinguishes between two modes of temporalization: retention and recollection. Focusing on the example of a musical melody, Husserl demonstrates how each impression, or "now moment," is inseparable from a trail of retentions, through which the formerly present now moment gradually becomes past. The impression plus the trail of retentions (and a symmetrical probe of protentions) comprises a thick present—what French phenomenologist Gérard Granel has called the "large now"—and the incessant becoming just-past of each new impression is what supports the ongoing production of new nows, which is to say, the constitution of the temporal continuum itself. Recollection, by contrast, is a voluntary act of consciousness through which a once present lived experience that has become part of the past is represented in a new present. Recollection corresponds to the function of memory as it is typically understood. Concerning space, on the other hand, Husserl says relatively little, other than to assume that temporal constitution requires an extension, which is to say, a concretization in the form of a "temporal object"—say, the musical melody—that is perforce spatial.

Husserl's student Martin Heidegger (who edited the German edition of Husserl's time-consciousness lectures) made the priority of time over space into a matter of principle. In his critical development of Husserl's work on internal time-consciousness (a development that includes a critique of Bergson's conception of duration), Heidegger differentiates between two modes of temporality that are available for the experience of human beings or, in his terminology, *Dasein* (literally "there-being"). On the one hand, there is leveled or fallen, "inauthentic" time, the time of our everyday experience, of clocks and other devices by which means we experience time as a succession of regular, discrete units. (To a great extent, Heidegger's inauthentic time coincides with the spatialization of time repudiated by Bergson.) On the other hand, there is "authentic" time, the time associated with human *Dasein* in its resoluteness or truth to its own inmost possibilities. This time is characterized by ecstasis (the excess of a threefold temporalization over any mere fixation of the present) and the priority of the futural mode. Later in his career, following the so-called turning, Heidegger seeks to decouple time's givenness from any correlation with *Dasein* whatsoever. Like Husserl before him, Heidegger consistently subordinates space to time, although with the turn away from a *Dasein*-centered conception of time, the role of (spatial) things within the givenness of time arguably becomes more central.

At roughly the same time that Heidegger was pursuing his radicalization of time consciousness, his compatriot Theodor Adorno, on his own and in conjunction with colleague Max Horkheimer, was developing a critique of the media—what the German philosophers felicitously dubbed the "culture industry"—that focused on the temporal dimensions of entertainment. According to Adorno and Horkheimer's analysis, the crux of standardized or industrialized entertainment is the homogeneity of its temporality with the time of assembly-line work. To the extent that Hollywood cinema demands a temporal conformism not essentially different from that of the industrial workplace, leisure and work time comprise a false opposition that covers over the reality of domination by a capitalist system adept at colonizing all aspects of life. Notwithstanding their virulent antipathy to the phenomenological tradition (Adorno's *Against Epistemology* indicts Husserlian intentionality, and *The Jargon of Authenticity* is a frontal attack on Heidegger's rhetoric), Adorno and Horkheimer's media theory shares with Bergson, Husserl, and Heidegger a prioritization of time over space. Even when they focus on spatial figure like the bourgeois interior (as does Adorno in his criticism of Kierkegaard) or the public space of mass experience, their thematization of space remains resoundingly negative and unrelentingly surbordinated to the operation of temporal standardization exerted by capitalism in its incipient consumerist phase.

More recently, the unquestioned prioritization of time has become the object of philosophical scrutiny. In his grammatological sublation of Husserlian time-consciousness and Heideggerian onto-theology, French philosopher Jacques Derrida not only exposes the necessity for a quasi-transcendental, nonempirical origin of time and of space (what he enigmatically calls *différance*), but, more directly relevant to our purpose here, demonstrates the theoretical interdependence of time and space, or better, of deferring/differing and spacing. The crux of Derrida's argument—which hearkens back to Kant's need to find a content for inner sense (time) in the representations of outer sense (space) as well as to Husserl's unavoidable recourse to the temporal object as a surrogate for the directly unapprehendable manifold of the temporal flux of consciousness—is that *différance*, its essential reserve or resistance to the empirical notwithstanding, must manifest itself in concrete phenomena, which is to say as a temporalization that occurs in some spatially specified phenomenon.

In the last decade, Derrida's student Bernard Stiegler has developed this condition of Derridean analysis into the basis for a philosophy of technology that returns us directly to the topic of media. For Stiegler, *différance* must always be "technically specified," which is to say, the giving of time and space at any given historical moment is necessarily tied to the technologies that mediate human experience. For Stiegler, the institution of cinema—by which he means global, real-time televisual media—comprises the privileged temporal object through which to reflect on our being in time in the world today. Reprising Adorno and Horkheimer's main theme, Stiegler suggests that today's culture industries exert a stranglehold on our subjectivity through their hyperstandardization; by synchronizing the time of consciousness at the global level, they position commodified memories as the basis for the collective invention of the future (see chapter 5, "Memory"). Leaving aside the throughgoing pessimism of this position, what lies at the heart of Stiegler's work, and what distinguishes his position from Kittler's (as we shall see), is the correlation of human experience and media time: as so many technical exteriorizations of human life, media operate in a time frame that is complementary to the phenomenological time of human living.

This correlation also differentiates Stiegler from, for example, Gilles Deleuze, who, updating Bergson's philosophy of time, develops a very different account of the medium of cinema. What Deleuze calls the cinema of the "time image" directly mediates time, independent of its alleged (phenomenological) configuration with the ratios of human consciousness. According to Deleuze, postwar cinema gives us two varieties of the time image—two configurations through which time is directly presented, without being subordinated to movement through space. These varieties—"peaks of the present" and "sheets of the past"—are, not surprisingly, correlated with the two valences of Bergson's conception of the past as simultaneously past and present. Through the "spiritual automaton" of cinema, time is liberated from its subordination to human consciousness and made available to cognition in its full virtuality.

The conceptual terrain carved out by these divergent configurations of cinema and media becomes particularly salient in relation to computational time, which, in the words of geographer Nigel Thrift, forms the "technological unconscious," the material infrastructure, of experience in the world today. Cultural critical treatments of computational time—those of Jean Baudrillard and Paul Virilio, for instance—tend to emphasize its fundamental antipathy to human experiential time. Baudrillard speaks of the implosion of objects that, not unlike the V-2 bombs as imagined by Pynchon in *Gravity's Rainbow*, strike us in advance of our awareness of them. Virilio, for his part, has built a career on extrapolating the experiential consequences of the military-technological colonization of human functions, not least of which is the monitoring of machines in "real time." At the heart of these and like accounts lies a certain polarization of objective and subjective time. Simply put, the time of the world—and specifically, of computational objects and processes—has become fundamentally disjoined from the time of experience, with the result that we find ourselves facing a new, structurally unprecedented form of alienation: alienation from the flow of information in the world around us.

This splitting of time—into media and computational time—speaks directly to the complex argument advanced by philosopher Paul Ricoeur in his magisterial study *Time and Narrative*. For Ricoeur, Western thinking about time has pursued two trajectories—the phenomenological and the cosmological—which can be found together, for the first and perhaps the last time, in Aristotle's "Treatise on Time" from *Physics IV*. For Aristotle, time can be defined as the number of movement, which is to say, as a physical or cosmological measurement that, so it would appear, remains independent of phenomenology. Yet when he comes to the question of how this numbering is performed, he invokes the soul as the agent. Much ink has been spilled over the logic of Aristotle's argument (including whether his recourse to the soul is necessary), and the division between a physical and a phenomenological time—time as the before and after of movement versus time as differentiated into the three ecstases of past, present, and future—has even captured the attention of analytic philosophers, who, following J. M. E. McTaggart, oppose A-series time (where temporal relations hold only in relation to an act of self-reference) to B-series time (where temporal relations are independent of perspective). In our context, however, what remains most salient about this inauguration of what Ricoeur dubs the fundamental aporia of time is Aristotle's insistence on the irreducibility of measurement: there is no time that is not measured (whether the measuring be explicitly technical or a function of the organic rhythms of the human body), which is equally to say that there is no time in itself, there are only temporalizations, technico-empirical specifications of time.

That these temporalizations invariably suture time to space is a reality recognized by Aristotle himself, and one that has become altogether insistent with the development of technologies based on satellite imaging that allow for unprecedented tracking of bodies, commodities, and information as they move through time and across space. GPS, radio-frequency identification (RFID), and like technologies of ubiquitous computing bring about a concrete suturing of time and space that, in effect, makes Einstein's abstract space-time continuum a practical reality for everyday life. The uniqueness of objects in the world—where uniqueness is tied, first and foremost, to the capacity for surveillance and tracking within global networks of capital flows—stems from their singular, though dynamically evolving, space-time identities. In this context, media can be understood as configurations of space, time, and embodiment. If time is necessarily mediated by its measurement, if it is always both spatial and embodied, then we can assert a correlation among time, space, and media that returns us to our opening question regarding the generality of time and space as conditions for experience: media specify the givenness of time and space, and thereby comprise the very condition of possibility for our experience.

The recent work of Japanese media artist Masaki Fujihata perfectly captures the imbrication of space, time, and embodiment central to our contemporary society of global control and general mediation, but deploys it in the service of self-expression and decelerated negotiation of the border experiences that characterize our highly mobile lives. Fujihata merges various media technologies—the consumer digital video camera, a panoramic lens, the personal digital assistant, and GPS—in order to capture the multivalent information at issue when individuals move through space and across boundaries. In *Landing Home: Geneva* (2005), for example, he asks his subjects—all transplants to the international Swiss city—to walk with him from their homes to a place in the city where they feel at home, while conversing with him about their situations of living across cultures, languages, and geographic and technological boundaries of all sorts. This information is subsequently made available to viewers in installations that allow access not simply according to the linear time line of image registration, but through spatial position data as well. The images literally loom up from a positional "place line" (a trajectory through technically mapped space) as floating signatures of the body's movement through a thoroughly concrete, technically specified space-time. In Fujihata's work, the fine-scaled technological surveillance of movement within highly refined temporal and spatial networks becomes the basis for a meditation on the changing meaning of home and of being at home. Fujihata shows us how, in the midst of a rapidly accelerating surveillance society, we can use the newfound technical precision of space-time mapping as a rich and poignant means of asserting our own existential uniqueness. His media-specific configuration of time, space, and embodiment gives us the opportunity to map global space-time in relation to our own movement through it.

References and Suggested Readings

Benjamin, Walter. 2008. "The Work of Art in the Age of Its Technical Reproducibility." In *The Work of Art in the Age of Its Technological Reproducibility, and Other Writings on Media*, ed. M. Jennings, B. Doherty, and T. Levin. Cambridge, MA: Harvard University Press.

Bergson, Henri. 1998. *Time and Free Will: An Essay on the Immediate Data of Consciousness*, trans. F. L. Pogson. New York: Cosimo Classics.

Deleuze, Gilles. 1989. *Cinema 2: The Time-Image*, trans. H. Tomlinson and R. Galeta. Minneapolis: University of Minnesota Press.

Greenberg, Clement. 1940. "Towards a Newer Laocoon." *Partisan Review* 7, no. 4 (July–August): 296–310.

Husserl, Edmund. 2008. *On the Phenomenology of the Consciousness of Internal Time (1893–1917)*, trans. J. B. Brough. Dordrecht: Kluwer Publishing.

Innis, Harold. 2007. *Empire and Communications*. Lanham, MD: Rowman & Littlefield.

Kant, Immanuel. 1998. *The Critique of Pure Reason*, trans. P. Guyer and A. W. Wood. Cambridge: Cambridge University Press.

Kittler, Friedrich. 1999. *Gramophone, Film, Typewriter*, trans. G. Winthrop-Young and M. Wutz. Stanford, CA: Stanford University Press, 1999.

Lessing, Gottfried. [1766] 1984. *Laocoon: An Essay upon the Limits of Painting and Poetry*, trans. E. A. McCormick. Baltimore: Johns Hopkins University Press.

Stiegler, Bernard. 1998. "The Time of Cinema: On the 'New World' and 'Cultural Exception.'" *Tekhnema* 4: 62–114.

TECHNOLOGY

> > > > > > > > > > > > > > > >

8 :: BIOMEDIA EUGENE THACKER

What Can a Body Do?

Contemporary biotechnologies integrate biology and information in a range of contexts, with effects that are medical, economic, technical, or cultural. On one side are the "life" sciences, which study the phenomena of biological life at many levels—organism, organ system, cell, molecule. On the other side is computer science—including information technologies—which aim to incorporate a technical understanding of information into the concrete tools we use on a daily basis. On the one side, a concern with "life itself"; on the other, with code, message, and information. More often than not, the two endeavors are assumed to be separate and qualitatively different. This presumption has its historical and philosophical roots in the separation of life (*bios*) from technology (*technê*), nature from artifice, the living from the nonliving. Nevertheless, biological life can be approached as technical, open to being designed and engineered at the molecular or genetic level. And information is increasingly seen as having "vital" properties of its own, a capacity to adapt, evolve, and mutate. The two perspectives are never so close as when they take each other as their object. Thus our question: What happens when "life" is understood as being essentially informational? What happens when certain types of information are understood as being indelibly connected to and constitutive of key biological processes?

A wide range of activities falls under the rubric "biotechnology." To begin with, we see a cross-over between biology and information in the way we speak about genetic science and the biotech industry. In the news media, pop science books, and even science fiction, there is constant talk of genetic "codes" and the quest to "crack the code of life." Our technoscientific vocabulary is replete with metaphors, tropes, and figures combining biology and information. But this integration extends also to the artifacts, tools, and technologies that populate the life science research lab: genome sequencing computers and "gene-finding" software, online genome and proteome databases, silicon chips arrayed with DNA fragments, and even "labs on a chip" (bioMEMS). Many of these supplements to the traditional tools of the lab are finding their way into the clinic or doctor's office as well, where they are used as diagnostic tools. Such artifacts also exist in various institutional and disciplinary sites, some of which are quite new. At colleges and universities around the world, established programs in molecular biology have been joined by cross-disciplinary, degree-granting departments of "bioinformatics." The growth of new disciplinary fields has brought with it a demand for new industries to develop and produce new lab technologies. Within the bio-tech industry, some start-ups focus on fields such as genomics or bioin-formatics, others on building the tools for research, and still others on applying the science and the technology to the development of drugs, diagnostics, and therapies.

All of this culminates in "big science" endeavors such as the Human Genome Project, spearheaded by the U.S. National Institutes of Health and the Department of Energy in the late 1980s. By the millennium, however, advances in technology and the rapid growth of the private sector in biotech had changed the playing field. Instead of being a long-term, U.S.-based project rooted in university labs, the effort to map the human genome had become a sort of public-private stand-off. The orig-inal project had expanded to include labs in Europe and Japan, and re-named itself the International Human Genome Sequencing Consor-tium. Meanwhile, the privately funded Celera Corporation had initiated its own genome project. Since that time, it has become apparent that there was a third player in the genome race: high-tech companies such as Perkin-Elmer, which manufacture the genome sequencing computers used by both projects and by many labs worldwide. Many scientists asso-ciated with the genome projects have acknowledged the central role that computer and information technologies have played in mapping the ge-nomes of many species. The effort to map the human genome brings to-gether the language of codes and information (e.g., in media reportage and scientific articles), novel tools and technologies (genome sequencing computers), relations between disciplines and institutions (bioinformat-ics, public-private partnerships), and social and cultural attitudes toward the body, health, and "life itself," manifested, for example, in promises of a "revolution" in medicine, debates on cloning or stem cells, and genetic motifs in popular culture.

"Biology Is Information"

Yet we would be remiss to assume that the transformation brought about by this integration of biology and information is solely due to advances in high technology. It is equally important to ask how the *concept* of a genetic code conditions attitudes toward "life itself" and its attendant scientific, social, technical, and cultural effects. In this sense, there is indeed a history of the genetic code, one characterized by divergence, fits and starts, and conceptual exchanges. I have written on this topic, as have writers as diverse as Richard Doyle, Evelyn Fox Keller, Sarah Franklin, Donna Haraway, Richard Lewontin, Dorothy Nelkin, Hans-Jörg Rheinberger, and Phillip Thurtle.[1] These authors interrogate the concept of a genetic code and the way that such concepts impact our understanding of the relation between the living and nonliving, the natural and the technical.

The most comprehensive historical account is given by Lily Kay in her book *Who Wrote the Book of Life?* (2000), which provides a thorough account of the discursive exchanges that led to the formation of molecular biology as a discipline during and after World War II.[2] Kay considers molecular biology as part of a process of reductionism, in which what is at stake is the search for the basic, essential elements that define "life itself" at the molecular level. Like the historical work of Fox Keller and Rheinberger, Kay's research identifies the influence of technical fields such as cybernetics and information theory as playing a central role in the development of molecular biology as a distinct research field. In particular, she outlines three conceptual stages that characterize molecular biology and biochemistry in the mid-twentieth century: first, a stage in which proteins are thought to hold the key to life at the molecular level, and where the notion of "specificity" (the precise lock-and-key fit between two molecules) is the guiding principle; then a stage in which nucleic acids, and particularly DNA, are understood to contain the "code of life," and where the notion of "information" is central; and finally an overlapping phase in which the effort to decipher the genetic code leads to considerations of its syntax and grammar, a phase where "language" and semantics are the primary concern.

Kay's history covers roughly the period from Erwin Schrödinger's landmark lectures in the 1940s, entitled *What Is Life?*, through the elucidation of DNA's structure in the 1950s by James Watson, Francis Crick, Maurice Wilkins, and Rosalind Franklin, to the "cracking" of the genetic code in the 1960s by Marshall Nirenberg and Heinrich Matthai. Her argument is that the notion of DNA as a genetic code did not develop in a linear, progressive fashion, but that it did and still does contains many discontinuities, fissures, and caesurae. This point has been echoed by others such as Fox Keller and Lewontin. While Schrödinger's lectures did posit a "hereditary code-script" that acted in the organism as "law code and executive power," his speculations were based on the model of physics and not biology. Similarly, while Watson and Crick noted, in their papers on DNA's structure, that "the precise sequence of the bases is the code which carries the genetical information," this in no way meant that there was any consensus on the *way* in which DNA was a code.[3] To state that DNA was a genetic code was only a beginning; the bulk of the work lay in articulating exactly how and in what manner DNA acted like a code.

This was the basis of what Francis Crick dubbed the "coding problem" in the 1950s and 1960s: how did a simple set of four nucleotide bases (adenine, thymine, cytosine, and guanine, commonly abbreviated A, T, C, and G) combine to form a complete informational management system that directed the cell's activities? Kay's history notes the myriad of approaches—some forgotten yet strikingly inventive—in which DNA was theorized as a code. Central to many of these approaches was the influence of technical fields such as cybernetics, information theory, and early computer science. These fields had a decisive influence on molecular biology's formulations of DNA as a genetic code. In his book *Cybernetics, or Control and Communication in the Animal and the Machine*, Norbert Wiener described the cybernetic system as that which maintained itself through the continual regulation of informational flow. Such a system was thus able to modulate itself in response to any internal or external perturbation. Biologists François Jacob and Jacques Monod, for instance, developed their model of "genetic regulatory mechanisms" in the cell based on Wiener's concepts of the informational message and the feedback loop. Their publications contain a number of cybernetic diagrams demonstrating how certain proteins ("repressors," "promoters," "enhancers") act upon DNA, in effect forming a switching mechanism that turns genes on or off in the production of proteins. Jacob and Monod saw DNA as a "cybernetic enzymatics" regulated by the "informational gene" at its core.

Claude Shannon's work in information theory and communications was also important. His emphasis (along with his collaborator Warren Weaver) on the quantitative aspect of information, as well as the information-noise distinction, helped to formalize theories of the genetic code by biologists and biochemists such as Erwin Chargaff, George Gamow, Leslie Orgel, Henry Quastler, and Alexander Rich. John von Neumann's research into the functional organization of the computer— what became known as the "von Neumann architecture"—also had an impact, suggesting to molecular biologists that DNA was not just a code but a code that did things, a code that calculated and computed. It was not just information but part of a computer system, with inputs, outputs, storage, and processing capabilities. During the formation of molecular biology as a discipline, concepts derived from cybernetics, information theory, computer science, and related technical fields thus served to formalize the notion of DNA as genetic code. The picture formed by the end of the 1960s was a varied and mixed set of metaphors for understanding the essence of biological life at the molecular level: DNA as a self-regulating system using informational feedback; DNA as a communication system, sending messages in the form of RNA or proteins; DNA as the core of a computer, complete with storage (chromosomes) and processing algorithms (genes).

As technical as these models seem, it is important to note that what was at stake was not just the promise of a scientific paradigm shift. There was also a philosophical, even theological, dimension to the genetic code. This is attested to in the many popular books written by molecular biologists during the period covered in Kay's history: *Life Itself: Its Origin and Nature* (Crick), *The Language of Life* (George and Muriel Beadle), and so on. Many of these books addressed the same question Schrödinger had posed in the 1940s: "What is life?" More often than not, the answer was "Life is information." Yet, the approaches of such books vary remarkably. Monod's *Chance and Necessity* is highly technical, containing numerous diagrams and emphasizing the mathematical aspects of the genetic code, while Jacob's book *The Logic of Life* is heavily philosophical, beginning with Aristotle and ending with DNA.

The concept of life itself—the unmediated, essential core of biological life—is therefore as much a technical concern of the life sciences as it is a philosophical one. However, "life itself"—as the historian and philosopher of science Georges Canguilhem notes in his many writings on biology, medicine, and the life sciences—is itself always changing. Canguilhem suggests that there have been four major approaches to the question of life itself in the history of Western thought: animation, represented by Aristotle's writings on nature; mechanism, encapsulated in the philosophy of Descartes; organization, developed by the classification systems of Linnaeus, the comparative anatomy studies of Cuvier and Geoffroy, and the microscopic study of cell structure; and finally, information, which emerged from nineteenth-century studies of thermodynamics, gaining precedence in modern, twentieth-century genetics. For Canguilhem, the life sciences often revolve around a paradox: on the one hand, they posit something called "life" that can be scientifically studied, analyzed, and quantified; on the other hand, "life itself" always retains something that is intangible, irreducible, and qualitative. Canguilhem saw this to be the case with modern genetics, the subject matter of which is at once reducible to information and, through processes yet unknown, capable of using that information to generate the complexity of life: "Messages, information, programs, code, instructions, decoding: these are the new concepts of the life sciences."[4]

Biomedia

This historical backdrop to the concept of a genetic code has had significant repercussions in postindustrial, postmodern societies. Numerous social theories have argued that the late twentieth century saw a shift in the dominant modes of production, accompanied by advances in computer and information technologies and the creation of a globalized context that continues to effect exchanges of value, power relations, and the circulation of messages, images, and signs. In this shift, two principles have played an important role in the development of the biotech industry and have influenced the integration of biology and informatics that we have been discussing. The first of these, a *control principle*, is exemplified by the set of techniques known as genetic engineering. The second, a *storage principle*, is exemplified by gene sequencing and the various attempts to map the human genome. With the introduction of genetic engineering techniques in the early 1970s (and the first biotech start-ups in the 1980s), the ability to manipulate DNA and transpose genetic material between organisms became a reality; DNA could be understood as being open to a series of cut-and-paste operations, enabling a more refined control over and intervention into the genetic makeup of any organism. Similarly, the development of computer-based gene sequencing technologies in the 1980s made the quest to map the human genome a feasible reality. Large numbers of DNA fragments could thus be stored, either in bacterial plasmid libraries (*in vivo*) or in computer databases (*in silico*). Taken together, the ability to control precise gene sequences and the capacity to store large amounts of genetic information has meant that, at the molecular and genetic levels, biology is able to be treated as a technology, with biological "life itself" taken as a medium.

Understanding this relationship is the crux of the concept of biomedia. We have seen that, in our contemporary context, there are all sorts of mixtures of biology and information, from artifacts to disciplinary fields to the now-familiar language of genetic "codes." We have also seen that such developments, while seemingly novel, are conditioned by a complicated, discontinuous historical backdrop, one of conceptual and discursive exchanges between cybernetics and genetics, information theory and molecular biology, life science and computer science. Considering this, we can begin to characterize, in a more precise way, the relation between biology and information, "life" and "code," that is at the center of the biomedia concept. *Biomedia entail the informatic recontextualization of biological components and processes, for ends that may be medical or nonmedical (economic, technical), and with effects that are as much cultural, social, and political as they are scientific.* Biomedia can be "things" such as DNA chips or genome databases, but they can also be "acts" such as the sequencing of a DNA sample. In fact, biomedia ask us to consider media things as inseparable from acts of mediation. Biomedia therefore require understanding biological "life itself" as both a medium and as a process of mediation.

There are several important points to make in conjunction with this definition. First, with biomedia the notion of "information" is not immaterial. In other words, biomedia involve not simply the computerization of biology, in which the "wet," material stuff of the biology lab is replaced by the dry, immaterial bits of computers and databases. Instead, biomedia continuously make the dual demand that biology formalize itself as information and that information materialize itself as gene or protein compounds. This point cannot be overstated: biomedia depend upon an understanding of biology as informational but not immaterial.

Second, with biomedia we do not have a split between biology and information, life and code, nature and artifice. Because biomedia are predicated on the concept of a genetic code, a concept that stitches together *bios* and *technê*, there is no primordial, biological life that is subsequently technologized and rendered into genetic code. In molecular biology, the notion of a genetic code implies both a material and an immaterial dimension: the DNA molecule is understood to exist as simultaneously a wet, organic, material compound and a dry, technical, immaterial quantity. In biomedia the genetic code is equally a living compound in the cell, a biological sample in a test tube, and a sequence of code in a database.

Third, biomedia are not computers that simply work on or manipulate biological compounds. Rather, the aim is to provide the right conditions, such that biological life is able to demonstrate or express *itself* in a particular way. In a sense, biomedia do nothing more than to articulate contexts and conditions through which the genetic code appears as such. Biomedia, then, are media in the truest sense of the term, providing the conditions for the biological to exist as biological.

What are these contexts and conditions articulated by biomedia? What makes it possible to refer to the DNA molecule as a genetic code? We can note three necessary conditions: (1) that there is an essential source code, a pattern that can be abstracted from the particular biological substance; (2) that this essential code is tied to but not dependent upon its material substrate (that is, code and substance can be separated); and (3) that this code is mobile and can be transposed across one or more material substrates. Certainly there are great differences between each of these conditions, but they are all recognized as integral to the operation of a genetic code. This enables a wide range of techniques to be performed on DNA as a genetic code: the code can be sequenced, copied or replicated, stored in a plasmid or a database, uploaded, downloaded, mathematically analyzed, visually modeled, and rewritten either in the computer (bioinformatics software) or in the wet lab (genetic engineering). Many of these operations are the cornerstones of molecular biology research, as well as the development of drugs and diagnostics in the biotech industry.

With these techniques, a number of practices are possible. Each such practice foregrounds a specific instance of the correlation of DNA with code. First, the separation of code and material substrate means that DNA is equivalent to its information. For instance, gene sequencing starts with the taking of a biological sample from a patient. The sample is then analyzed and rendered as a linear sequence of A's, T's, C's, and G's in a computer. The patient, at this point, is no longer part of the process, for the code has been extracted and abstracted. The DNA, which exists tightly coiled in chromosomes, themselves densely packed in the nucleus of every living cell, has been transformed into a genetic code. Second, DNA *as code* is portable across different media. DNA can now go from test tube to database and (via gene synthesizers) back into the test tube. This mobility is part and parcel of many research protocols in molecular genetics. Third, the portability of DNA as a code can, in some instances, mean that the code comes to account for the body. The use of genetic diagnostics in the prescription of drugs, reproductive medicine, and genetic screening all involve analysis of DNA as code as a stand-in for the body of the patient. Fourth, DNA as code is generative, producing both more information (in genomics research, for instance) and biological compounds (DNA or proteins, in fields such as regenerative medicine). Although specific scientific fields do differ greatly, what we have been calling biomedia is this ability to create conditions in which biological "life itself" is understood as being informational and yet not necessarily immaterial. The DNA molecule exemplifies this in its equivalency, portability, accountability, and generativity with respect to its existence as a genetic code.

Code, Flesh, and Spirit

Clearly, the question of "what a body can do" with regard to biomedia is wide and varied. But what are the consequences of biomedia, and this notion of DNA as genetic code? Taking the widest possible view, the very idea of a genetic code seems to be everywhere, from science research to science fiction. We can briefly mention four areas in which biomedia have had and will continue to have an impact: medicine, economics, security, and culture.

On the medical front, there have been many pronouncements—perhaps premature—of a coming genetic revolution, involving everything from designer drugs to therapeutic cloning. To date, the integration of biology and information has had its greatest impact in the design of pharmaceuticals, genetic diagnostics, and medical-genetic research. Computer technologies have played a central role here, for they have made possible computerized drug design (pharmacogenomics) as well as advanced diagnostic tools that make use of a patient's genome and "the" human genome database. However, such technical solutions have been far from perfect; the number of adverse reactions to new drugs has not decreased, though industry organizations such as the Pharmaceutical Research Manufacturer's Association continue to promote prescription drugs as the primary way to treat disease.

This leads us to a second area in which biomedia have had an impact, which is economic. In the biotech industry, the merger between bioscience and computer science has spawned a number of subindustries, including those that manufacture tools for research, those offering information services (e.g., database subscriptions), and those that focus on the actual development of new drugs or therapies (the biotech start-ups). In addition, a number of genetically modified organisms have been patented (including microbes, plants, and animals), although questions have been raised as to whether the genetic code itself is public, private, or even "open source." While U.S. patent laws do not permit the patenting of unaltered genetic sequences, this has not prevented the patenting of "derived" sequences or of the techniques for producing them.

While the medical and economic impacts of biomedia have been developing for some time, newer concerns surrounding security and public health have cast the relation between biology and information into a new light. Concerns have grown over bioterrorism and the availability of the knowledge and low-tech means to create a genetically engineered "superplague." At the same time, given the exorbitant cost of "biodefense" and the unreliability of many vaccines, many argue that such programs are as damaging as the threats they purport to deter. Perhaps a greater concern than that of bioterrorism is the prevalence of "emerging infectious diseases," caused by rapidly mutating microbes and transmitted by worldwide networks of transportation and trade. In the United

States and Europe, these threats have prompted new public health measures, which utilize computer and information technologies in a number of ways: to develop real-time "syndromic surveillance" networks to monitor public health, to provide incentives to the biotech industry to develop new vaccines, and to give public health agencies the ability to stockpile and rapidly distribute needed pharmaceuticals.

The integration of biology and information that characterizes biomedia has perhaps had the most visible impact in the cultural domain. While some topics (such as the possibility of a "genetic commons") receive little attention in the mass media, other topics (such as stem cells or cloning) spark intense debate and reveal the social and cultural divisions regarding attitudes toward science, religion, and morality. Of special concern are the popular representations of the genetic code in science fiction literature, films, TV, comics, and video games. In these dramatizations, the traditional motifs of the mad scientist, technology run amok, corporate greed, and the conflict between human and machine are reinvented through the lens of genetics. In this—our postmodern, genetic mythology—DNA is often visually represented using computer graphics, reinforcing the impression of DNA as a code that can be easily manipulated, controlled, and reprogrammed.

Beyond Biomedia?

As we have seen, the concept of biomedia is not limited to a particular use of language, to a particular technology, or to particular disciplines or institutional contexts. It extends beyond the application of computer technology in molecular biology research and does not mean simply the computerization of biology. Biomedia complicate the notion of information as immaterial through their emphasis on biological materiality. Biomedia are neither quite "things" nor "actions" but a process of mediation that enables "life itself" to appear as such. The impact of this orientation can be witnessed not only in bioscience research but in medicine, economics, security, and culture. In this sense, a consideration of biomedia is relevant for media studies, for it brings together biology, technology, and culture in unique ways. *Biomedia present a view not merely of biological life as information, but of biological life that is life precisely because it is information.*

Given this, we may be inclined to ask whether biomedia are "good" or "bad," whether they offer a more complex, innovative understanding of biological life or constitute another form of technical instrumentality. On the one hand, biomedia have brought the biosciences and the computer sciences into a more intimate relationship, in some cases offering new perspectives, such as that of "systems biology," that bypass the pharmaceutical industry's narrow focus on silver-bullet therapies and quick-fix drugs. On the other hand, biomedia have triggered the development of new technologies, technologies that are often developed as economically driven incentives for the biotech industry. Biomedia present us with a complex view of the relation between biology and information that is fraught with limitations. We can summarize a few of these here.

To begin with, any critical assessment of biomedia must begin from the issue of reductionism. Western science is often characterized by the search for an essential core or atomic unit that would describe the complexity of life and the living. A complex whole is understood by being broken down, reduced to its essential parts. As historians of science often note, prior to the discovery of DNA, late-nineteenth- and early-twentieth-century biologists theorized a host of units that could contain the secret of life—Mendelian hereditary factors, pangens, gemmules, genes, and so on. Do our present attempts to understand disease, development, and behavior in genetic terms represent a form of reductionism? The question raised by biomedia is to what extent an informational understanding of biological life is necessarily reductive. Can "life itself" be reduced to number? Or is the problem that our understanding of "number" or the quantitative is itself reductionistic? Do contemporary sciences of complexity and self-organization—themselves based on rigorous mathematical principles—offer a way of understanding biological life as informational and yet not reductive?[5] Biomedia ask us to think outside of the this either-or, qualitative-quantitative dichotomy. Networks, systems, pathways, and swarms may offer alternative models in this sense.

While the critique of reductionism pertains to the history of biology, another critique—that of instrumentality—pertains more to the study of technology. Biomedia present us with a unique instance in which biological "life itself" is at once the tool and the object, the product and the production process. As a way of providing contexts and conditions, biomedia entail life working upon life—a biotechnology in the truest sense. The techniques of genetic engineering, the testing of novel drug targets, and the use of DNA chips all involve DNA working upon DNA, processes (protein synthesis, base-pair binding, gene expression, cellular signaling) that already occur in the living cell. Where exactly do we locate "technology" in this instance? Biomedia are ambiguous on this point. Sometimes there is a clear case of instrumentality (e.g., inserting a foreign gene into a host organism). At other times the split between tool and object is not so clear (e.g., research into self-regenerating tissue). The question raised by biomedia here, in a case where biology *is* the technology, is: What are the limits—if any—to our ability to control and manipulate "life itself"? It is perhaps in this sense that the emphasis on environment, epigenetics, and autopoietic self-regulation have become central in rethinking the technological aspects of biomedia.[6]

The questions regarding reductionism and instrumentality both presume an unproblematic relation between the way we think about "life itself" and the way we talk about it. A more traditional view might argue that the way we talk about something reflects the nature of the thing itself. On this view, the language of codes and information simply reflects the inherent informational structure of DNA, something that has always existed but only recently been unveiled. However our use of language is indelibly connected to our ways of thinking, and our ways of thinking indelibly connected to our understanding of the world "out there." Thus, a more critical viewpoint might argue that the use of certain metaphors (the "book" of life, the "code" of life) influences the kinds of questions asked in scientific research and the consequent production of knowledge. In this case, language precedes and participates in the constitution of knowledge, impacting the way we act in and on the world. In addition, there are many kinds of uses of a single term. The notion of a genetic "code," for instance, may in a biological sense denote a gene, in a technical sense a string of bits in a computer, and in a social or cultural sense something containing a secret. Biomedia ask us to rethink the relation between language and object, metaphor and materiality, as more than a one-way street. The strange, uncanny artifacts that are presented to us as biomedia—DNA computers, nanoprobes, biopathways—are influenced by a prior set of metaphors and challenge us to articulate new ways of using language to comprehend them.

Biomedia ask us to rethink our commonly held views regarding biology, technology, and language, and to do so through critiques of reductionism, instrumentality, and metaphor. We are encouraged to think of biology and technology as inseparable, and to think beyond the nature-artifice paradigm that has long been at the core of Western science and the philosophy of biology. The world presented by biomedia is one in which the age-old question of "life itself" is posed in a new way, presented through a set of artifacts, techniques, and social contexts that are unique to a particular historical moment. Especially when considered alongside artificial intelligence, artificial life, and robotics, biomedia pose questions that ostensibly have to do with *vitalism*: Can life be reduced to a set of mechanical, mathematical, or material principles? What is the difference between the living and the nonliving, the biological and the technological? And how, within these seeming oppositions, is the future of the human (the "posthuman") to be situated?

Notes

1. See Richard Doyle, *On Beyond Living: Rhetorical Transformations in the Life Sciences* (Stanford, CA: Stanford University Press, 1997) and *Wetwares* (Minneapolis: University of Minnesota Press, 2004); Evelyn Fox Keller, *Refiguring Life: Metaphors of Twentieth-Century Biology* (New York: Columbia University Press, 1995) and *The Century of the Gene* (Cambridge, MA: Harvard University Press, 2000); Donna Haraway, *Modest_Witness@Second_Millennium.Fe-maleMan©_Meets_OncoMouse™: Feminism and Technoscience* (New York: Routledge, 1997); Daniel Kevles and Leroy Hood, eds., *The Code of Codes: Scientific and Social Issues in the Human Genome Project* (Cambridge, MA: Harvard University Press, 1992); Richard Lewontin, *Biology as Ideology: The Doctrine of DNA* (New York: Harper Perennial, 1993); Robert Mitchell and Phillip Thurtle, eds., *Data Made Flesh: Embodying Information* (New York: Routledge, 2004); Dorothy Nelkin and Susan Lindee, *The DNA Mystique: The Gene as a Cultural Icon* (New York: W. H. Freeman, 1995); and Hans-Jörg Rheinberger, *Toward a History of Epistemic Things: Synthesizing Proteins in the Test Tube* (Stanford, CA: Stanford University Press, 1997), as well as my books *Biomedia* (Minneapolis: University of Minnesota Press, 2004) and *The Global Genome: Biotechnology, Politics, and Culture* (Cambridge, MA: MIT Press, 2005). There continues to be much historical and theoretical work on the genetic code in the fields of cultural studies, science studies, the sociology and anthropology of science, and the history and philosophy of biology.

2. See also Kay's article "Cybernetics, Information, Life: The Emergence of Scriptural Representations of Heredity," *Configurations* 5, no. 1 (1997): 23–91.

3. James Watson and Francis Crick, "General Implications of the Structure of Deoxyribonucleic Acid," *Nature* 171 (1953): 964–67.

4. Georges Canguilhem, "The Concept of Life," in *A Vital Rationalist*, ed. François Delaporte, trans. Arthur Goldhammer (New York: Zone, 2000), 316.

5. The research of complexity biologist Stuart Kauffman is exemplary in this regard, as is the work on endosymbiosis by Lynn Margulis and the work in developmental systems theory by Susan Oyama.

6. C. H. Waddington's writings on epigenetics are relevant here, as is the work of biologists Humberto Maturana and Francesco Varela on the concept of autopoiesis.

References and Suggested Readings

Canguilhem, Georges. 2008. *Knowledge of Life*. New York: Fordham University Press.

Cooper, Melinda. 2008. *Life as Surplus: Biotechnology and Capitalism in the Neoliberal Era*. Seattle: University of Washington Press.

Doyle, Richard. 2004. *Wetwares: Experiments in Postvital Living*. Minneapolis: University of Minnesota Press.

Jacob, Francois. 1993. *The Logic of Life: A History of Heredity*. Princeton, NJ: Princeton University Press.

Kay, Lily. 2000. *Who Wrote the Book of Life? A History of the Genetic Code*. Stanford, CA: Stanford University Press.

Keller, Evelyn Fox. 1996. *Refiguring Life: Metaphors of Twentieth-Century Biology*. New York: Columbia University Press.

Mitchell, Robert, and Phillip Thurtle, eds. 2004. *Data Made Flesh: Embodying Information*. New York: Routledge.

Parisi, Lucianna. 2004. *Abstract Sex: Philosophy, Biotechnology, and the Mutations of Desire*. New York: Continuum.

Stocker, Gerfried, and Christine Schöpf, eds. 1999. *Ars Electronica: LifeScience*. New York: Springer.

Thacker, Eugene. 2004. *Biomedia*. Minneapolis: University of Minnesota Press.

9 :: COMMUNICATION

BRUCE CLARKE

> She looked down a slope, needing to squint for the sunlight, onto a vast
> sprawl of houses . . . ; and she thought of the time she'd opened a transis-
> tor radio to replace a battery and seen her first printed circuit. . . . There
> were to both outward patterns a hieroglyphic sense of concealed mean-
> ing, of an intent to communicate. (Pynchon 1990, 24)

In this key passage from *The Crying of Lot 49*, through the medium of
light and through the memory of cryptic patterns inscribed on a printed
circuit, the protagonist Oedipa Maas places herself on the receiving end
of an "intent to communicate." Light, hieroglyphic writing, print technologies, telecommunication, meaning: the narration of this transit from
physics to phenomenology, from nature to mind to society, also connects
concepts of media with concepts of communication. Recent discursive
and scholarly developments have registered and reflected upon this link:
as literacy once came as a literal supplement to orality, and grammatology (the science of writing) as a supplement to linguistics (the science
of speech), "media," in the sense that informs media studies has come
alongside the study and theory of communication.

In the usage now current, the term *communication* primarily means
"the imparting, conveying, or exchange of ideas, knowledge, information, etc." (*OED*). The authority for this modern usage is typically attributed to book 3 of John Locke's *An Essay Concerning Human Understanding*
(1690): "To make Words serviceable to the end of Communication" (*OED*;
Kittler 1996). The term derives from the Latin *communicare*, "to impart,
share," literally, "to make common," from *communis*, "in common, public,
general, shared by all or many." Its use to mean the imparting or sharing
of material/energetic or organic characteristics—for instance, the communication of motion from one to another object; the communication
of disease from one to another organism—is now uncommon. But such

uses preserve important connotations still underlying its modern informatic sense:

- the *communality* of communication—its complex multiplicity, its conditionality upon social grounds prior to individual intentions
- the *materiality* of communication—the physical and technical infrastructures necessary for any conveyance of messages or transmission of information

Both of these aspects—social connectivity and material contact—bring communication closer to the concept of media, as that now names the various technologies for the transport or transmission of communications. However, much of the intellectual glamour that now attaches to media is tapped off that of communication.

The conceptual amplification of communication is itself a recent development: only since the mid-nineteenth century "did communication acquire its grandeur and pathos as a concept" (Peters 1999, 5). Yet it did so due to the emergence of the very technologies to which the qualifier *media* is loosely appended: "technologies such as the telegraph and radio refitted the old term 'communication,' once used for any kind of physical transfer or transmission, into a new kind of quasi-physical connection across the obstacles of time and space. Thanks to electricity, communication could now take place regardless of impediments such as distance or embodiment" (Peters 1999, 5). With the expanding capacities of electronic telecommunications systems to dematerialize and multiply the media of messages, communication began its modern career as a master term, its "vogue in the mid to late twentieth century as a 'master discipline'" (Hartley 2002, 32).

In its academic ambition "to assume some of the mantle of philosophy, seeking to explain humanity to itself" (Hartley 2002, 32), the study of communication has appropriated scholarly work on structural linguistics, comparative linguistics, structural anthropology, social science, business, journalism, pubic relations, advertising, media, critical theory, cybernetics, information theory, and computer science. Craig has outlined "seven traditions of communication theory"—rhetorical, semiotic, phenomenological, cybernetic, sociopsychological, sociocultural, and critical—and further indicated how these thematic disciplinary categories are transected by two formal models:

> In the simplistic *transmission model* . . . communication is conceptualized as a process in which meanings, packaged in symbolic messages like bananas in crates, are transported from sender to receiver. Too often the bananas are bruised or spoiled in transport and so we have the ubiqui-

tous problem of *miscommunication*. . . . Communication theorists have recently favored an alternative *constitutive model*. . . . The elements of communication, rather than being fixed in advance, are reflexively constituted within the act of communication itself. (Craig 2001)

According to either model, however, communication and media are tightly bound together. It will be useful to think of them as metonymies—commonly associated concepts for mutually instrumental phenomena—rather than as rival synonyms. "The term 'communication' has had an extensive use in connection with roads and bridges, sea routes, rivers, and canals, even before it became transformed into 'information movement' in the electronic age" (McLuhan 1994, 89). In this context, media are the modes of conveyance. McLuhan continues: "Each form of transport not only carries, but translates and transforms, the sender, the receiver, and the message. The use of any kind of medium or extension of man alters the patterns of interdependence among people, as it alters the ratios among our senses" (90). Here, the interdependence of communication and media echoes the "interdependence among people" communicating through media. And from speech to writing, from writing to printing, from analog to digital media technology, the technological transformations of media have been bound up with the social transformations wrought by changes in the media of communication (Kittler 1999).

What then, broadly considered, distinguishes the topic of communication from the topic of media? The most abstract way to put the distinction is that communication is ultimately a social phenomenon and media technical phenomena. But one cannot assert such a distinction without immediately acknowledging the inextricability of the social and the technological, as Bruno Latour and Donna Haraway have taught us in examining the modern proliferation of hybrids, cyborgs, and quasi-objects—entities that couple the realms of nature and culture, organism and machine, human and nonhuman. Our strategy will be simultaneously to construct and to deconstruct this distinction, to step forward and look through it, but also to step back and look at it. Let us grant for heuristic purposes the basic social/technological distinction, then unfold that distinction further along two main lines:

1. Communication attaches most directly to the sources and destinations of messages, whereas media most directly concern the means by which messages move from one to the other. This distinction can be clarified by reference to the famous diagram of communication presented in Shannon and Weaver's seminal text *The Mathematical Theory of Communication* (1949). Restated in the terms of this diagram, communication ultimately concerns the sociological context, the relations generated

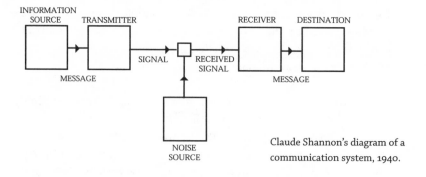

Claude Shannon's diagram of a communication system, 1940.

between the "information source" and the "destination," whereas media occupy the middle of the diagram—the channel—and center on the technological regimes by which transmission devices code messages into signals, which are subjected to medium-specific modes of noise, then decoded by receiving devices for delivery to destinations. Shannon and Weaver abstracted this diagram from a consideration of telephony, but it is obviously generalizable to all media of communication. Filling in the potential complexities of technological mediation often bracketed out of accounts of communicative exchange, it diagrams the indispensability of the media moment to any full consideration of communication.

In 1960 linguist Roman Jakobson, taking his cue from Shannon's diagram, presented an influential translation of communicational into linguistic functions. Jakobson's chief concern was to indicate how developments in communication theory driven from the cybernetic human/machine interface can be productively adapted to traditional linguistic and poetic analyses that presuppose speech or writing as the medium in question. In the process he expanded matters left implicit in Shannon's framework: the "referential" function, for instance, makes explicit the embeddedness of communication within social contexts, as well as implying that semantic reference—the ability of language to signify objects in the world—is itself a function resting on social contracts. Jakobson's "metalingual" function draws attention to language (and other kinds of code) as structures through which signifying intentions must be processed, thereby converting "messages" into "signals" fit for the media at hand. And the "phatic" function marks the media moment per se, orienting "communication" once again to the sense of material connection: even in the most "wireless" communication system imaginable, there still must be, as it were, a real material/energetic string tying the tin cans together.

Jakobson's linguistic intervention in communication theory marks a high point in the discourse of structural linguistics, filling in the middle

REFERENTIAL
CONTEXT

	POETIC		
ADDRESSER_____	MESSAGE_____	_ADDRESSEE	Diagram of com-
EMOTIVE	CONTACT	CONATIVE	municational and
	PHATIC		linguistic functions.
	CODE		Adapted from Jakob-
	METALINGUAL		son (1960, 353, 357).

ground occupied by the structures of mediation implemented by events of communication. If we move from here to a poststructuralist position, a short quote from Jacques Derrida's "Differance" offers a deconstructive perspective on the communication/media distinction: "The use of language or the employment of any code which implies a play of forms . . . also presupposes . . . a spacing and temporalizing, a play of traces. This play must be a sort of inscription prior to writing, a protowriting without a present origin, without an *archē*" (Derrida 1973, 146). Communication (between "source" and "destination," "addresser" and "addressee") is to "the use of language or the employment of any code" as any media technology of transmitted and received signals is to "a spacing and temporalizing, a play of traces." Or, the capacity of a "source" to produce a message is already given by the (linguistic or other) "inscription" of potential forms or distinctions commensurate with the medium available to convey the signals into which messages are transformed in order to be communicated. The medium of signals inevitably feeds back into the form of messages. Hence McLuhan's protodeconstructive pun: "the medium is the massage."

Reconstructing the distinction of communication and media into the realms of the social and the technological, let us unfold it along a second line:

2. Communication factors into issues of synchronous and sequential temporality—"real time," the discrete moments of the origination and reception of messages—whereas media technologies generate "virtual time," processes such as inscription, storage, and retrieval, which suspend or manipulate the time of communication. Here again, communication is to media as speech is to writing. However, this distinction cuts across the previous one from a different, more deconstructive angle. It relocates the communication/media distinction within the realm of media itself, subsuming under "media technologies" a distinction between "communication" and "representation":

Modern media technologies have developed along two distinct trajectories. The first is representational technologies—film, audio, and video magnetic tape, various digital storage formats. The second is real-time communication technologies, that is, everything that begins with *tele*—telegraph, telephone, telex, television, telepresence. Such new twentieth-century cultural forms as radio and, later, television emerge at the intersections of these two trajectories. (Manovich 2001, 162)

Manovich's approach exemplifies the countertendency in new media discussion to bracket the sociological moment of communication in favor of its (media) technological moment. As with our previous distinction, Manovich refers the concept of communication most immediately to the sending and receiving of messages, but he puts the emphasis on medium-specific differences. Communication technologies—gesture, speech, smoke signals, telegraphy, telephony—transmit or broadcast messages without (in the first instance) creating or storing them as media objects. Media technologies per se differ from traditional and modern techniques of communication in that they *inscribe* the information they process: they not only mediate but memorialize—capture and store—their content. Thus, writing, drawing, printing, lithography, photography, phonography, and cinema are some of the forms of media. "New media," then, are figured as the *technological* deconstruction through conglomeration of this very distinction between communication and representation: "computers in principle comprehend all other media" (Kittler 1996). Digital platforms typically transmit and store simultaneously—they mimic or travesty the humanist subject, while doubling once again in binary informatics the prior doubling of the world in communicative representations.

Information and Communication

Kittler's media posthumanism deals a conceptual wild card from the mid-twentieth century that raised the stakes at play between communication and media. Derived from the mathematical-physical treatment of the operation of a communications medium—the telephone system—the discourse of information bid to subsume both communication and media concepts. The primary practical aim of Shannon and Weaver's *Mathematical Theory of Communication* was to quantify the commodity transported by telephonic transmission. Information was detached from qualitative considerations of meaning and rendered as a calculus of signal load (see chapter 11, "Information"). One effect of this abstraction was to carry considerations of communication media away from either sociological specifics or technological infrastructures toward a generalized and imperial notion of cybernetic control. Information theory "may have seemed so exciting because it made something already quite familiar in war, bureaucracy, and everyday life into a concept of science and technology. Information was no longer raw data, military logistics, or phone numbers; it was the principle of the universe's intelligibility" (Peters 1999, 23).

The "decoding" of DNA happened to coincide historically with the unfolding of information theory, and the metaphor of "genetic information" promoted the conviction that information was the skeleton key with which to open up the remaining secrets of matter, energy, and life. The general logic of this position has been articulated as "the informatics of domination," in which "communications sciences and modern biologies are constructed by a common move—the translation of the world into a problem of coding" (Haraway 1991, 164). Restated in the terms we have been examining, to translate the world into "a problem of coding" is to totalize information: one abstracts signals from the material or historical specifics of senders, receivers, and channels, and reorients their communication, away from differential feedback or recursive correction and toward dictatorial one-way flows from agencies of command and control. Haraway goes on: "Information is just that kind of quantifiable element (unit, basis of unity) which allows universal translation, and so unhindered instrumental power (called effective communication). The biggest threat to such power is interruption of communication" (164). This critique suggests that resistance to the informatics of domination depends upon the destruction of control systems. But elsewhere in "A Cyborg Manifesto" Haraway's suggested praxis is more subtle, and "interruption of communication" implies not a breakdown but a redeployment of the informatic tools of communication media, for one, a turn toward *narrative* media for social feedback, countercommunications opening the system up to other possibilities, other constructions.

Although "A Cyborg Manifesto" does not mention him in its countercanon of science fiction authors, Stanislaw Lem's Eastern European perspective on the Soviet cybernetics, bound up by then with Shannon's information theory, was already doing the sort of work Haraway envisioned (see Gerovitch 2002). For instance, in *The Cyberiad: Fables for the Cybernetic Age*, from the mid-1960s, Lem treated the desire for a "translation of the world into a problem of coding." In "The Sixth Sally or How Trurl and Klapaucius Created a Demon of the Second Kind to Defeat the Pirate Pugg," Lem plays on the connection between energy and information mediated by the concept of entropy. His "demon of the second kind" is an informatic retooling of Maxwell's demon, part of an 1870 thought experiment in which the Victorian physicist James Clerk Maxwell attempted to "pick a hole" in the second law of thermodynamics (see Clarke 2001, chap. 4).

Lem capitalizes on the way that Shannon's mathematical theory of communication quantifies information through a calculus of message-probabilities. The "Sixth Sally" satirizes how the cross-over of the entropy concept from energy to information regimes renders the communication of meanings indeterminate, by marking the social variability of observers and the material complexity of media. The cybernetic constructors Trurl and Klapaucius are imprisoned by an Argus-like ogre, the Pirate Pugg, who dwells in a desolate galactic junkyard, the Black Wastes, where he hoards a colossal pile of information: "'I have no use . . . for gold or silver . . . for I collect precious facts, genuine truths, priceless knowledge, and in general, all information of value'" (Lem 1985, 148–49). "'Everything that is, is information,'" Pugg continues, and here Lem draws his oversimplifying overestimation of "information" to a head (150). But as discussed in chapter 11, in information theory, the "value" of a communication varies according to the probabilities specific to particular systems and to the positions from which it is observed. Thus, if "everything is information"—or again, if everything is translatable into a "problem of coding" for no one in particular—then no piece of it is worth any more than another—and thus, all of it is worthless. Without differentiation of probabilities relative to specific clusters of communicators and media channels, the value of information is already wasted. Pressing the excess signification built into Shannon's use of the term *entropy* as the measure of information, Lem's parable humorously refashions the waste energies leading to Victorian thermodynamics' nightmare of "heat death"—the ultimate thermodynamic entropy of the universe—into junk information, a dead universe not of dissipated energies but of useless factoids.

The point I want to make is that information theory is best restated in terms of the constitutive model of communication. Information is not an ontological function with an absolute content or quantity, but is relative to the predispositions of the observer that constitutes it and that observer's position along the total channel through which communications must proceed. As the inclusion of a "noise source" fitted to the media channel in Shannon's diagram implies, the materiality of communication media always determines a potential discrepancy between the message as sent and the message as received. Noise is "anything that arrives as part of a message, but that was not part of the message when sent out." But what is "meaningful signal" and what is "meaningless noise" depends on the position of the observer: "a probabilistic term such as *random* has a relative, not an absolute meaning: the noise is random with respect to the message it muddles, although it may have a perfectly defined and determinate cause in another system" (Paulson 1988, 67). The sense of disorder becomes more complex. It can be valorized negatively in the potential confusion of a sender's selection, or in the deterioration of the message in transit, but given an orientation toward the destination of communication, noise and disorder can also be measured positively, converted from uncertainty into new information depending on the reception it receives.

> In the very copper rigging and secular miracle of communication, untroubled by the dumb voltages flickering their miles, the night long, in the thousands of unheard messages. . . . how many shared Tristero's secret, as well as its exile? . . . Who knew? . . . For it was now like walking among matrices of a great digital computer, the zeroes and ones twinned above, hanging like balanced mobiles right and left, ahead, thick, maybe endless. Behind the hieroglyphic streets there would either be a transcendent meaning, or only the earth. (Pynchon 1990, 180–81)

This situation of uncertain reception is brilliantly configured at the conclusion of *The Crying of Lot 49* (the title of which names an event that occurs only after the novel ends), which leaves Oedipa Maas in a state of uncertainty about the reality of a secret society named the Tristero. The "value" of the information she is about to receive when Lot 49 is cried at auction is left suspended somewhere between zero and infinity. More precisely, Pynchon suspends his reader between the inexhaustible desire for a meaning transported from beyond—one no worldly medium could ever communicate—and the transcendence of that desire for transcendence in an acceptance of the immanent value of our improbable world. Information, its utterance through media, and the meanings placed upon it—all are the affair of observers variously positioned along the social and technological networks of communication. They are all constituted in and constructed by the operation of observing systems.

Society and System

Theories of communication typically work between concepts of the subject and concepts of society. The goal or effect of communication is said to be the creation of a state of commonality or consensus by which individual differences are set aside. "The central challenge facing all communication theories is the question of how individuality is transcended" (Chang 1996, 39). The concept of "intersubjectivity" names the implication that certain kinds of communication effectively render exterior and collective what would otherwise remain interior and private, as the self-knowledge of an individual subject enters the public sphere. Such communications would entail the merger or intermingling of inner and outer, psychological and social events.

Recent conceptions of communication follow what has been termed a "postmetaphysical" trend, away from the traditional philosophical focus on mind, reason, or consciousness as having their source solely in the individual. It is precisely the social aspect of the concept of communication that bids to offer an alternative to "the exhaustion of the paradigm of the philosophy of consciousness" (Habermas 1986, 1:386). The way out of the subjectivist frameworks of idealistic approaches to reason and "the rational subject" becomes "communicative rationality." By this phrase Habermas signifies an account of reason that is constituted through social discourses "oriented to achieving, sustaining and reviewing consensus—and indeed a consensus that rests on the intersubjective recognition of criticizable validity claims" (1:17). Building on Ludwig Wittgenstein's philosophy of language and the speech-act theories of J. L. Austin and John R. Searle, Habermas uses communication theory to move linguistic philosophy toward a social theory of communicative action: "The concept of communicative action presupposes the use of language as the medium for a kind of reaching understanding, in the course of which the participants, through relating to a world, reciprocally raise validity claims that can be accepted or contested" (1:99).

However, Briankle Chang argues cogently that such models of social intersubjectivity do not lead out of but rather reinscribe the identity formations of subjective consciousness: "The conceptualization of communication as the 'transcendence of difference' reflects an implicit subjectivist thesis . . . to which modern communication theories remain heavily mortgaged . . . eventually leading [to an] unquestioned valorization of identity over difference, of the selfsame over alterity" (1996, xi). This is because communication theories built on the concept of intersubjectivity rely on a concept of linguistic *code* (as is Jakobson's "metalingual" function) that smuggles the transmission model of communication back into the theoretical apparatus for the very purpose of providing a medium of social identity that bridges individual differences. In such conceptualizations, "Code is the key to successful communication in that it provides for communicators a standard of translation" (Chang 1996, 58), which in this context implies a mechanism whereby the content of one mind is effectively "translated" or transferred intact to other minds. The problem is not only that the transmission model is untenable, but also that this argument is circular: "Intersubjectivity is the key term in explaining how individuality is transcended, and the concept of code is but one of its theoretical representatives . . . The code can guarantee the successful transmission of messages *precisely because it is intersubjective*" (59). Just as Derrida attended to the play of metaphor in the ostensibly nonmetaphorical texts of philosophy, Chang uncovers a circular play of metaphor in the texts of communication theory, where he locates "a *fundamental analogism*, a principle of substitution between intersubjectivity and mediation," by which they "work as paired metaphors" (64–65).

Chang successfully deconstructs intersubjectivity by eliciting its covert reliance on the transmission model, but where does that leave the social theory of communication? One way beyond this impasse is the work of social systems theorist Niklas Luhmann. "Communication" is also a prime term in his theory of social systems. In Luhmann's theory, the logical circularity Chang uncovers in the intersubjective transmission model is replaced by the *operational* circularity or recursive functionality basic to the model of an "autopoietic" system, a "system that produces and reproduces through the system everything that functions for the system as a unit" (Luhmann 2002, 161). A system, that is, that is the ongoing product of its own production.

From this perspective, the concept of intersubjectivity is incoherent because it blurs the operational boundaries of two distinct kinds of system—social systems and psychic systems. A basic premise of Luhmann's model is the "operational closure" that renders an autopoietic system self-referential. Such systems cannot operate beyond their own boundaries: their closure is the condition of their possibility. The mind (the "subject" of intersubjectivity) is also an autopoietic system: the *psychic* system processes perceptions and (re)produces consciousness. By definition, psyches are also operationally closed, and consciousness as such cannot impinge directly upon its social environment, while at the same time, there is no way for the communications (re)produced by social systems to impinge directly upon the minds in their environment. Rather, they impinge, in the forms properly constituted by the autopoiesis of psychic systems, as internally constructed perceptions and cognitions.

Luhmann's scheme obviously problematizes accounts of social mediation through intersubjective transmission. "A systems-theoretical approach emphasizes the *emergence of communication* itself. Nothing is transferred" (Luhmann 2002, 160); everything is (re)constructed on the fly. Communication obviously occurs, but it is self-constituting and self-perpetuating. "*Only communication can communicate*" (Luhmann 2002, 156), and it does so entirely on the basis of the operational closure of social systems, for which not "subjects" but systems of consciousness, psychic systems, reside in the environment, alongside media systems. In this scheme language and other semiotic codes (and their technological armatures) remain positioned as mediating structures, but not in the mode of substantial transmission across system boundaries (see chapter 16, "Language"). In every instance, autonomous social and psychic systems construct their own meanings out of their own internal elements. To the extent that these processes can be coordinated, this occurs not by the distribution of shared content but by "structural coupling," the fact that psychic and social systems are "coevolutionary" phenomena. Their emergence and maintenance is strictly self-referential, but neither would emerge in the first place without being coupled to the other in their respective environments, and mediated by the medium of meaning.

Luhmann's scheme of epistemological construction specific to social systems represents the strongest extant form of the constitutive model of communication. While Habermas avoids the information-theoretical model we examined previously, Luhmann offers what amounts to a radical extension and complexification of it. Compare Shannon's diagram of the communication system to Luhmann's account of communication as "a synthesis of three different selections, namely the selection of *information*, the selection of the *utterance [Mitteilung]* of this information, and selective *understanding or misunderstanding* of this utterance and its information" (Luhmann 2002, 157). Luhmann's formulation comprehends each aspect of Shannon's model, while stripping "source" and "destination" of subjective or psychological implications and reinscribing them as addresses or "connecting positions" (163) within the recursive network of the social system's autopoiesis. "The system pulsates, so to speak, with the constant generation of excess and selection" (160). With each cycle or pulsation, the system selects information from its memory or its construction of the environment, then selects the mode of its "utterance," that is, the modality of its coding, for further processing.

The entire scheme loops upon itself like this: "Communication . . . takes place only when a difference of utterance and information is first understood. This distinguishes it from a mere perception of others' behavior" (Luhmann 2002, 157). Perception belongs solely to the psychic systems coupled to but apart from the communication system. For instance, such a participating consciousness observes in its environment an arm waving: it can process this as mere perception, random motion, or as information—as a particular gesture or utterance, of greeting or warning or whatever. Understanding must select from its repertoire of possibilities. However, "Understanding is never a mere duplication of the utterance in another consciousness but is, rather, in the system of communication itself, a precondition for connection onto further communication, thus a precondition of the autopoiesis of the social system" (Luhmann 2002, 158). If one waves back, the social system continues.

Luhmann differentiates *communicative* understanding from whatever psychic comprehension participating consciousnesses construct from their interpretation of certain perceptions as communicative. This is why "misunderstanding"—failure of consensus—can as easily spur as impede communication: the understanding of the social system is sufficient as long as it can connect one communication event to another and so continue its autopoiesis. From this perspective, media ecologies are coevolving environmental spin-offs of open-ended social-systematic evolutions. Their transformations significantly impinge upon the changing themes of communication and inflect the forms of social organization, but they do not finally determine how communication will construct its own continuation.

References and Suggested Readings

Chang, Briankle G. 1996. *Deconstructing Communication: Representation, Subject, and Economies of Exchange*. Minneapolis: University of Minnesota Press.

Clarke, Bruce. 2001. *Energy Forms: Allegory and Science in the Era of Classical Thermodynamics*. Ann Arbor: University of Michigan Press.

Clarke, Bruce, and Linda D. Henderson, eds. 2002. *From Energy to Information: Representation in Science and Technology, Art, and Literature*. Stanford, CA: Stanford University Press.

Craig, Robert. 2001. "Communication." In *Encyclopedia of Rhetoric*, ed. Thomas O. Sloane. New York: Oxford University Press.

Derrida, Jacques. 1973. "Differance." In *Speech and Phenomena and Other Essays on Husserl's Theory of Signs*, trans. David B. Allison, 129–60. Evanston, IL: Northwestern University Press.

———. 1984. "Signature Event Context." In *Margins of Philosophy*, trans. Alan Bass, 307–30. Chicago: University of Chicago Press.

Gerovitch, Slava. 2002. *From Newspeak to Cyberspeak: A History of Soviet Cybernetics*. Cambridge, MA: MIT Press.

Gumbrecht, Hans Ulrich, and K. Ludwig Pfeiffer, eds. 1994. *Materialities of Communication*, trans. William Whobrey. Stanford, CA: Stanford University Press.

Habermas, Jürgen. 1986. *The Theory of Communicative Action*, trans. Thomas McCarthy. 2 vols. London: Polity Press.

———. 1995. "Peirce and Communication." In *Peirce and Contemporary Thought: Philosophical Enquiries*, ed. Kenneth L. Ketner, 243–66. New York: Fordham University Press.

Haraway, Donna. 1991. "A Cyborg Manifesto: Science, Technology, and Socialist-Feminism in the Late Twentieth Century." In *Simians, Cyborgs and Women: The Reinvention of Nature*, 149–81. New York: Routledge.

Hartley, John. 2002. *Communication, Cultural and Media Studies: The Key Concepts*. 3rd ed. London: Routledge.

Hayles, N. Katherine. 1990. "Self-Reflexive Metaphors in Maxwell's Demon and Shannon's Choice: Finding the Passages." In *Chaos Bound: Orderly Disorder in Contemporary Literature and Science*, 31–60. Cornell: Cornell University Press.

Jakobson, Roman. 1960. "Linguistics and Poetics." In *Style in Language*, ed. Thomas Sebeok, 350–77. New York: John Wiley & Sons.

Kittler, Friedrich. 1996. "The History of Communication Media." http://www.ctheory.net/articles.aspx?id=45.

———. 1999. *Gramophone, Film, Typewriter*, trans. Geoffrey Winthrop-Young and Michael Wutz. Stanford, CA: Stanford University Press.

Latour, Bruno. 1996. *Aramis or, The Love of Technology*, trans. Catherine Porter. Cambridge, MA: Harvard University Press.

Lem, Stanislaw. 1985. *The Cyberiad: Fables for the Cybernetic Age*, trans. Michael Kandel. New York: Harvest.

Luhmann, Niklas. 2000. "Perception and Communication: The Reproduction of Forms." *Art as a Social System*, trans. Eva M. Knodt, 5–53. Stanford, CA: Stanford University Press.

———. 2002. "What Is Communication?" In *Theories of Distinction: Redescribing the Descriptions of Modernity*, ed. William Rasch, 155–68. Stanford, CA: Stanford University Press.

Manovich, Lev. 2001. *The Language of New Media*. Cambridge, MA: MIT Press.

McLuhan, Marshall. 1994. *Understanding Media: The Extensions of Man*. Cambridge, MA: MIT Press.

Paulson, William R. 1988. *The Noise of Culture: Literary Texts in a World of Information*. Ithaca, NY: Cornell University Press.

Peters, John Durham. 1999. *Speaking into the Air: A History of the Idea of Communication*. Chicago: University of Chicago Press.

Pynchon, Thomas. 1990. *The Crying of Lot 49*. New York: Harper and Row.

Shannon, Claude, and Warren Weaver. 1949. *The Mathematical Theory of Communication*. Urbana: University of Illinois Press.

Weaver, Warren. 1949. "Recent Contributions to the Mathematical Theory of Communication." In Shannon and Weaver (1949, 3–28).

Williams, Raymond, ed. 1981. *Contact: Human Communication and Its History*. London: Thames and Hudson.

Winthrop-Young, Geoffrey. 2000. "Silicon Sociology; or, Two Kings on Hegel's Throne? Kittler, Luhmann, and the Posthuman Merger of German Media Theory." *Yale Journal of Criticism* 13, no. 2: 391–420.

10 :: CYBERNETICS

N. KATHERINE HAYLES

Cybernetics flourished for about thirty years, from about 1940 to 1970, and then all but vanished from the academy as an identifiable discipline. At present there are only a handful of cybernetic departments in the United States and Europe (notably at UCLA and the University of Reading). Yet cybernetics did not disappear altogether; rather, it flowed over a broad alluvial plain of intellectual inquiry, at once everywhere and nowhere. In a sense it is more important than ever, although more for the inspiration it provides and the general framework it pioneered than for contributions as a discrete field of inquiry. For media studies, cybernetics remains a central orientation, represented by approaches that focus on information flows within and between humans and intelligent machines. The connection between media studies and cybernetics is prefigured by Gordon Pask's definition of cybernetics as the field concerned with information flows *in all media*, including biological, mechanical, and even cosmological systems. Now, as information is reimagined within the context of simulations and the computational universe, cybernetics is again surfacing as an area of active debate.

As is well known, the term *cybernetics*, adapted from the Greek word for "steersman," was coined by Norbert Wiener. Feedback mechanisms have been known since antiquity (one such device being Ktesibios's water clock) and are seen also in the eighteenth century (the governor on James Watt's steam engine) and the nineteenth and early twentieth centuries (homeostatic systems within animal physiology). However, cybernetics arguably did not come into existence as such until the traditional notion of the feedback loop was joined with the modern concept of information in the early twentieth century. It took shape as an interdisciplinary field of study during the mid-1930s to 1940s, coming of age in two key papers published in 1943, "Behavior, Purpose and Teleology" by Arturo Rosenblueth, Norbert Wiener, and Julian Bigelow, and "A Logical Calculus of the Ideas Immanent in Nervous Activity" by Warren McCulloch and Warren Pitts. From the beginning, cybernetics was conceived as a field that would create a framework encompassing both biological and mechanical systems; the ambition is clear in Norbert Wiener's 1948 book *Cybernetics, or Control and Communication in the Animal and the Machine.* During the famous Macy Conferences on Cybernetics, held from 1943 to 1952, much of the discussion revolved around the legitimacy of machine-animal-human comparisons. Analogies were drawn between the behavior of relatively simple mechanisms, such as Claude Shannon's electric "rat," William Grey Walter's electric "tortoise," Wiener's "Moth" and "Bedbug," and Ross Ashby's homeostat and that of much more complex animal and human systems.

The model of the neuron presented in McCulloch and Pitts's paper was centrally important in justifying such comparisons. Pitts proved a theorem demonstrating that the neuron model was capable of formulating any proposition that could be proved by a universal Turing machine. That animal and human neurons, acting singly and as a group in neural nets, were capable of performing computational acts was one of the strong justifications for considering both machines and biological organisms as cybernetic entities. Another lynchpin of early cybernetic theory was Claude Shannon's information theory, along with the similar theory developed by Norbert Wiener. Defining information as a function of message probabilities, the Shannon-Wiener approach detached information from context and consequently from meaning. The decontextualization of information was a crucial move in conceptualizing it as a disembodied flow that can move between different substrates and different kinds of embodiment. So powerful was Shannon's theory that it was quickly adopted in fields far removed from electrical engineering, including communication theory, linguistics, and psychology, leading eventually to Hans Moravec's claim that the human brain is nothing but an informational pattern that can be represented in any medium. Hence, Moravec argues, it will possible within the next few decades to upload the human brain into a computer without losing anything essential. Such a view carries into the contemporary period the cybernetic tendency to equate complex biological processes with relatively simple mechanistic ones, now envisioned as ushering in a postbiological era in which humans will shuffle off the mortal coil with which evolution has burdened them and become free to inhabit any kind of computational device they please, as long as it has sufficient storage and processing power.

All along, however, many researchers cautioned that the story is not so simple—that embodiment and context are crucially important factors that cannot be ignored. Donald MacKay, a British neurophysiologist, boldly argued for a theory that defined information relative to the changes it brought about in an embodied and historically situated receiver. The Shannon-Wiener model won out, however, because it produced information as a consistently quantifiable entity, whereas the MacKay model, precisely because it conveyed a richer, more complex sense of information, was intractable to exact quantification.

Indeed, the story of cybernetics as a whole can be seen as a struggle between the simplifications necessary to yield reliable quantitative results and more complex views that yield richer models but thwart robust quantification (see chapter 14, "Technology"). Elsewhere I have suggested that the history of cybernetics can be understood as evolving through three distinct phases; since then, it has become evident that we are well into a fourth phase, and the chronology needs to be updated accordingly. But I am getting ahead of my story; first let us consider the phases as they appeared in 1996, which I formulated as a three-part progression.

In the period from 1943 to 1960, homeostasis, disembodied information, and self-regulation were the central foci of research, and simple mechanisms stood in for much more complex biological organisms. This period is often called first-order cybernetics, because the organism/mechanism was theorized as an entity distinct from the environment in which it was embedded.

In the period from 1960 to 1985, the balance swung away from the simplifications of the first period to encompass the complexity introduced by considering the observer as part of the system. Reflexivity, understood as a shift of focus that brings the framing mechanism into view, was discussed in terms of bringing the observer *inside* the system, rather than assuming an external (and largely unnoticed) observer. This period, concerned both with cybernetic systems and with observers of cybernetic systems, is often referred to as second-order cybernetics. Its characteristic reflexive move is aptly signified by the punning title of Heinz von Foerster's book, *Observing Systems*, which can be taken to mean either that one is observing a system or that one is oneself a system that observes and that can be observed in turn by an observer who can also be observed, ad infinitum.

In autopoietic theory, a theory of the living pioneered by Humberto Maturana and Francisco Varela, the observer is taken into account in a negative way, by making a strong distinction between what an observer perceives and what the system can be understood as producing in its own terms. While an observer may posit causal links between events in the environment and an animal's behavior, autopoietic theory argues that within the living system as such, everything takes place in terms of the system's own organization, which always operates so as continually to produce and reproduce itself. Events outside the system can trigger events within, but no information passes from the environment to the autopoietic system. This premise allows information and meaning to be reconnected, but only as reflexive loops circulating within the system boundaries.

The third phase, as I suggested in 1996, can be understood as virtuality. From the beginning, as we have seen, cybernetics has been concerned with understanding how information, messages, and signals work within systemic boundaries, and with an orientation that implies humans, animals, and machines can all be understood within such a framework. Given this theoretical perspective, media are important primarily for their differential capacities to store, transmit, and process information. The cybernetic perspective implies that human and animal bodies, no less than cybernetic mechanisms, are media because they too have the capacity for storing, transmitting, and processing information. The construction of the body as an informational medium, implicit in the McCulloch-Pitts neuron, in the contemporary period takes the form of bodies tightly coupled with other media, especially computational media such as the Internet and Web. Thus the much-heralded virtuality of cyberspace merits the implicit connection with the history of cybernetics that the prefix *cyber-* invokes.

Today that kind of virtuality is apt to appear as a transition toward a social condition that has once again entangled the frame with the picture, although in a very different way from the second-order reflexive paradigm of autopoiesis. A decade or two ago there was much talk of virtual realms as "cyber" locations distinct from the real world, typified in the 1980s by the Polhemus helmet, which constrained the user within a tangle of wires defining the limits of physical movement. Nowadays that constraining frame is apt to be constituted not by a VR helmet but the Graphical User Interface (GUI) of microcomputers, and it is increasingly giving way to the pervasiveness, flexibility, and robustness of ubiquitous media. Instead of constructing virtual reality as a sphere separate from the real world, today's media have tended to move out of the box and overlay virtual information and functionalities onto physical locations and actual objects. Mobile phones, GPS technology, and RFID (radio frequency identification) tags, along with embedded sensors and actuators, have created environments in which physical and virtual realms merge in fluid and seamless ways. This fourth phase is characterized by an integration of virtuality and actuality that may appropriately be called mixed reality.

Bruce Sterling, in his book *Shaping Things*, proposes the neologism *spime* to denote this condition. Spimes are virtual/actual entities whose trajectories can be tracked through space and time, a capacity that RFID technology makes easily possible. As Sterling conceives the term, however, it implies more than the devices by themselves, connoting the transition from thinking of the object as the primary reality to perceiving it as data in computational environments, through which it is designed, accessed, managed, and recycled into other objects. The object is simply the hard copy output for these integrated processes. The spime is "a set of relationships first and always, and an object now and then" (Sterling 2005, 77); it is "not about the material object, but where it came from, where it is, how long it stays there, when it goes away, and what comes next" (109). Here the information flows *in all media* that Gordon Pask proposed as a definition of cybernetics comes to fruition as data streams processed in pervasive computational environments.

Complementing the move of computational devices out of the box, some researchers have suggested the possibility of a third-order cybernetics. Whereas first-order cybernetics was concerned with the flow of information in a system, and second-order cybernetics with interactions between the observer and the system, third-order cybernetics is concerned with how the observer is constructed within social and linguistic environments. Arnulf Hauan and Jon-Arild Johannessen, for example, see third-order cybernetics as interrogating the construction of the observer located within social networks; Vincent Kenny and Philip Boxer invoke Lacan along with Maturana to explore the linguistic construction of the observer in language communities. Other theorists have associated third-order cybernetics with complex adaptive systems, arguing that the autopoietic model of second-order cybernetics is not sufficiently attentive to the potential of complex systems to evolve and adapt in multiagent, multicausal environments.

From the beginning, the social, cultural, and theoretical impact of cybernetics has been associated with its tendency to reconfigure boundaries. First-order cybernetics, subverting the boundary separating biological organisms and machines, nevertheless implicitly drew a boundary around the system that left the observer outside the frame. Second-order cybernetics redrew the boundary to include the observer as well as the system (or, in the terms that Maturana and Varela develop, the autopoietic, informationally closed system plus the observer looking at the system). Third-order cybernetics redraws the boundary once again to locate both the observer and the system within complex, networked, adaptive, and coevolving environments through which information and data are pervasively flowing, a move catalyzed by the rapid development of ubiquitous technologies and mixed reality systems.

An equally strong tendency within the cybernetic tradition has been the impulse to construct a framework within which animals, humans, and machines can all be located. With the growing importance and increasing power of computational media, this framework has tended to be seen not only as a flow of information but specifically as computational processes. The ultimate boundary-enlarging move is the claim put forward by some scientists, including Stephen Wolfram and Edward Fredkin, that the universe is a giant computer, ceaselessly generating physical reality by means of computational processes that it both embodies and is. The claim has important implications for the nature of reality. In Fredkin's view, for example, it implies that space and time, and indeed all of physical reality, are discrete rather than continuous. The claim also shifts the focus from information flows to computational processes, and this opens the way for a reconceptualization of information.

In a recent presentation, Fredkin suggested that "the meaning of information is given by the processes that interpret it." Although Fredkin did not develop the idea (aside from giving the example of an MP3 player, which interprets digital files to create music), the formulation is solidly within the cybernetic tradition in that it crafts a framework within which the behavior of organisms and machines can be understood in similar terms. At the same time, the formulation goes significantly beyond first- and second-order cybernetics in giving a more enactive and embodied sense of information. Specifically, it breaks new ground by changing the meaning of "interpretation" and of "meaning." Information in this view is inherently processual and contextual, with the context specified by the mechanisms of interpretation. These processes take place not only within consciousness but within subcognitive and noncognitive contexts, both biological and mechanical. A computer, for example, gives information one kind of meaning when voltages are correlated with binary code. Another kind of meaning, much easier for humans to understand than strings of ones and zeros, emerges with high-level programs such as C++, and still another kind when C++ commands are used to generate even more accessible screen displays and behaviors. Human cognition, for its part, arises from contexts that include sensory processing, which interprets information from the environment and gives it meaning within this context. The meaning that emerges from these processes undergoes further interpretation and transformation when it reaches the central nervous system; these meanings are transformed yet again as the CNS interacts with the neocortex, resulting in conscious thoughts.

Donald MacKay, cited earlier as a pioneer in formulating an embodied theory of information, had already envisioned a series of hierarchical and interrelated contexts that included subcognitive processes, anticipating in this respect Fredkin's formulation. MacKay insisted, for example, that the meaning of a message "can be fully represented only in terms of the full basic-symbol complex defined by all the elementary responses evoked. These may include visceral responses and hormonal secretions and what have you" (1969, 42). Fredkin adds to this vision a way of understanding meaning that extends it to mechanical nonhuman processes. Indexed to local subcognitive and noncognitive contexts, "interpretation" ceases to be solely a high-level process that occurs only in consciousness. Rather, it becomes a multilayered distributed activity in which the "aboutness" of intentionality (traditionally used by philosophers as the touchstone of cognition) consists of establishing a relation between some form of input and a transformed output through context-specific local processes. By breaking the overall context of reception into many local contexts, Fredkin's formulation makes the processes at least partially amenable to reliable quantification. Many of these local contexts already have metrics that work: voltages, processing speeds, and bits per second in computers; neural responses, fatigue rates, and the like in humans. The important point is a shift of vision that enables us to see these subcognitive and noncognitive processes not just as contributing to conscious thought but as *themselves* acts of interpretation and meaning.

Fredkin's proposal provides a convenient instance to explore what cybernetics has to contribute to media studies (and vice versa). Although it may seem strange in a book devoted to critical terms for media studies, I want to ask what "media" are. Although references to media are ubiquitous, when I searched a couple of years ago for definitions, I was astonished at the dearth of proposals. It seems everyone knows what media are, but few specify what the term denotes. Ideally I want a definition less broad than McLuhan's ("any extension of ourselves," which includes roads, for example, as well as hammers and language) and not as narrow as most offered by dictionaries (typically along the lines of "anything that stores, transmits, or processes data"). Following a scheme developed by Annagret Heitman, I suggest that media can be understood through four principal levels of analysis, which function, in effect, as a definition through specification: materiality, technology, semiotics, and social contexts. The materiality level specifies what a medium is in its physical composition; for a desktop computer, this would include silicon chips, circuits, display screen, and the like. The technology level specifies how the material object works and functions; in the case of the computer, this includes analyses of hardware and software, their interactions and interconnections. The semiotic level addresses the basic function of media, which I take to be the facilitation of communication; for the computer, this includes binary code, scripting languages, compiled and interpreted languages, and Internet protocols. The social context includes not only the way people use computers but also the corporations that produce hardware and software, the market mechanisms through which they are disseminated into a population, repair and maintenance industries, and so on.

Clearly the computer qualifies as a medium, for even as a stand-alone device with no network capabilities, it facilitates communication for an individual user; moreover, it is never simply a solitary device, for it depends on dense, distributed, and tightly integrated networks of programmers who write the code, software engineers who design the machine, organizations that specify standards for these operations, and many more social, cultural, and technical processes. Add to this network capabilities and the convergence of media into integrated digital devices, and one could plausibly argue that networked and programmable machines (or, as John Cayley prefers to call them, "programmatons") are the most important and pervasive media of the contemporary period.

Returning to the question of cybernetics in relation to media studies, I will focus on the three general contributions: the idea of the feedback loop joined with a quantitative definition of information; the idea of a theoretical framework capable of analyzing control and communication in animals, humans, and machines; and artifacts instantiating these ideas, from the McCulloch-Pitts neuron model to virtual reality platforms such as a CAVE and, more recently, the Internet and Web. The material and technological levels of computational media correspond to cybernetic artifacts, while the semiotic level is routinely understood as information flows, and the social contexts involve myriad feedback loops between humans and computers that continue to reconfigure social, economic, and technological conditions for people throughout the world. In this sense, then, not only do computational media continue the cybernetic tradition; arguably, computational media are the *principal* arenas in which cybernetics and media co-construct each other.

In a move reminiscent of the recursive feedback loops important to cybernetics, we can now cycle back to consider how the computational universe both produces and is produced by cybernetic dynamics. As I have argued elsewhere, the idea of the computational universe is catalyzed by the power and pervasiveness of contemporary programmatons; it is precisely because networked and programmable media have been able to do so much that the analogy between their operations and the natural world becomes compelling. Moreover, the feedback loop circles back into contemporary technologies of computation to authorize computation as the language of nature, displacing the traditional claim of mathematical equations to this role. As Harold Morowitz, among others, has argued, the twenty-first century is witnessing a move away from the study of relatively simple systems that can be modeled by equations with explicit solutions to complex adaptive systems that resist mathematical formalization and can be studied only through computational simulations. What calculus was to the eighteenth and nineteenth centuries, Morowitz argues, simulations are to the twentieth and twenty-first centuries. Feedback loops recursively cycle between and among humans and computers, between autonomous agents in simulations and the environments in which they operate, and between contemporary technologies and theories about the Universal Computer. These feedback loops are simultaneously topics central to media studies and the dynamics through which the most important and central theories of media studies have been constituted.

There is fitting irony in the fact that just as cybernetics disappeared as a discrete field only to reappear in many different areas, so computation, expanded to cosmic scale in the Universal Computer, disappears into the fabric of the universe. Can something still be called a medium when it is the foundation for physical reality, continuously generating the world and everything we know through its computations? Here we come upon another legacy from cybernetics that harbors a subtle paradox, if not a contradiction: artifactual systems, because they are simple enough to be understood in their entirety, reinforce the interpretation of much more complex biological entities as cybernetic systems, while at the same time subverting the distinction that separates the artificial from the natural. If the natural world is itself a giant computer, are not computers the most "natural" objects imaginable? As Bruno Latour has shown, nature/culture hybrids are far from unusual. Cybernetics, in its ambition to create frameworks that apply equally to machines and to bodies, has been one of the forces driving twentieth and twenty-first century thought to interpret the mind/body in computational terms and to think about computers as cognizers capable of evolving in ways that parallel the emergence of humans as thinking beings.

Since computers are also media, considering the body as a medium is a thoroughly cybernetic move. Traditionally, "media" have been understood primarily as artifacts and artifactual systems, but as we have seen, the cybernetic impulse is to erode this distinction. Moreover, the boundary work that would put bodies on one side of a nature/culture divide and media on the other has already been rendered unstable by technologies that penetrate the body's interior and make it available as images through such media devices as ultrasound, MRI, and CT and PET scans. The highly publicized endeavors of the online Visible Human Project and Gunther von Hagen's *Korperwelten* ("Body Worlds") exhibitions have further disseminated the sense of bodies as media into the cultural imaginary. Bernadette Wegenstein's proposal to "reconfigure the discipline of body criticism into one of new media criticism" is a predictable strategy. She argues that "the medium and questions around mediation have literally taken over the space and place of the individual body . . . [and] the body . . . has emerged in place of . . . the very mediation that once represented it for us. The medium, in other words, has become the body" (2006, 121). I differ from her assessment only in cautioning that the feedback loops connecting bodies and computational media should not be allowed to disappear from sight by too easily collapsing bodies and media together, for they form a crucial constellation that reveals yet another way in which the cybernetic project continues to inform contemporary thought.

Understood in evolutionary terms, these recursive feedback loops between culture and computation create a coevolutionary dynamics in which computational media and humans mutually modify, influence, and help to constitute one another in the phenomenon known as technogenesis. What these coevolutionary cycles imply, and where they might be headed, are matters of intense debate. At the extreme end of the spectrum are transhumanist advocates such as Hans Moravec and Ray Kurzweil, who predict that within a few decades, human consciousness will be uploaded into computers, achieving effective immortality. More moderate views, articulated by Rodney Brooks among others, caution that the process will take much longer and may not be possible at all, considering the enormous gap that separates the complexity of the human organism from even the most sophisticated computer. Still others, notably Francis Fukuyama, want the boundary between bodies and cybernetic technologies to be vigorously policed to ensure that human beings will not lose their biological and evolutionary heritages. Mark Hansen stakes out yet another position in acknowledging the importance of technogenesis but arguing that the embodied observer must remain at the center of our understanding of our interactions with digital media.

My own view is that the predictions of Moravec and others that the mid-twenty-first century will witness a "singularity"—a point of transformation so dramatic that the nature of human being will be forever changed—downplays the enormous differences between biological organisms and computers and dehistoricizes what has been a very long process that was already underway when *Homo sapiens* became a distinct species. The emergence of bipedalism, the advent of speech, the escalating complexity and speed of tool invention and use have all irrevocably changed the biology, culture, and cognitions of humans. At the other end of the spectrum, Fukuyama essentializes and indeed fetishizes "human nature" in an equally unhistorical and untenable way. Technogenesis is one of the major forces shaping humans now, as it has been for eons. Important changes have already taken place within the twentieth century, and we can expect the trend to continue with increasing speed and momentum in the twenty-first (assuming, of course, that environmental disasters and cataclysmic events such as nuclear war do not qualitatively change the nature of the game). On my view, responsible theorizing about these changes requires close attention to the materiality of bodies and computational media, a clear understanding of the recursive feedback loops cycling between them, and contextualizations of bodies and machines that reveal how meaning is created through the cascading processes that interpret information.

If we return now to the three major contributions of cybernetics—joining information with feedback, creating a framework in which humans and machines can be understood in similar terms, and creating artifacts that make these ideas materially tangible—we may conclude that contemporary media studies would scarcely be conceivable without the contributions of cybernetics. Friedrich Kittler's aphorism that "media determine our situation," the media archaeology he pioneered and that has been further developed by Bernhard Siegert and others, the technogenesis explored by Mark Hansen and Bernard Stiegler, the hypothesis of the Universal Computer advocated by Stephan Wofram and Edward Fredkin, and the contributions of innumerable others are indebted in both obvious and subtle ways to the ideas that found pioneering expression in the four waves of cybernetics. If cybernetics seems today to have been reduced to a prefix that echoes pervasively across the culture, that is because its essential concepts have been absorbed deeply into the fabric of contemporary thought. Remembering the history of cybernetics reminds us not only of the debt we owe to it but also the necessity to keep its premises in sight so that, in the spirit of the remarkable innovators who launched the cybernetic movement, we can continue to interrogate our assumptions as we search for better ways to envision and create a life-enhancing, life-affirming future.

References and Suggested Readings

Dupuy, Jean-Pierre. 2009. *On the Origins of Cognitive Science: The Mechanization of Mind.* Cambridge, MA: MIT Press.

Haraway, Donna J. 1990. "A Cyborg Manifesto: Science, Technology, and Socialist-Feminism in the Late Twentieth Century." In *Simians, Cyborgs, and Women: The Reinvention of Nature*, 149–82. New York: Routledge.

Hayles, N. Katherine. 1999. *How We Became Posthuman: Virtual Bodies in Cybernetics, Literature, and Informatics.* Chicago: University of Chicago Press.

Heims, Steve J. 1991. *The Cybernetics Group*. Cambridge, MA: MIT Press.

MacKay, Donald. 1969. *Information, Mechanism, and Meaning*. Cambridge, MA: MIT Press.

Maturana, Humberto R., and Francisco J. Varela. 1991. *Autopoiesis and Cognition: The Realization of the Living*. New York: Springer.

Shannon, Claude E., and Warren Weaver. [1948] 1998. *The Mathematical Theory of Communication*. Champaign: University of Illinois Press.

Sterling, Bruce. 2005. *Shaping Things*. Cambridge, MA: MIT Press.

Varela, Francisco J., Evan Thompson, and Eleanor Rosche. 1992. *The Embodied Mind: Cognitive Science and Human Experience*. Cambridge, MA: MIT Press.

Von Foerester, Heinz. 2002. *Understanding Understanding: Essays on Cybernetics and Cognition*. New York: Springer.

Wegenstein, Bernadette. 2006. *Getting under the Skin: Body and Media Theory*. Cambridge, MA: MIT Press.

Wiener, Norbert. 1965. *Cybernetics, or Control and Communication in the Animal and the Machine*. 2nd ed. Cambridge, MA: MIT Press.

Wolfram, Stephen. 2002. *A New Kind of Science*. New York: Wolfram Media.

11 :: INFORMATION BRUCE CLARKE

Everything that is, is information.

Pirate Pugg, in *The Cyberiad* by STANISLAW LEM

The environment contains no information. The environment is as it is.

HEINZ VON FOERSTER

Virtuality

Information is now established as a scientific entity on a par with matter and energy. However, unlike matter and energy, which are reliably conserved under normal physical conditions, information can be created or destroyed at will. And if matter and energy are (more or less) *real* physical quantities, information is *virtual*. This is what Heinz von Foerster means when he says, "The environment contains no information." Information does not exist until an observing system (such as a mind) *constructs* it— renders it as a "virtual reality" for a cognitive process—in response to the *noise* of environmental perturbations. Thus, enthusiastic ontological proclamations, such as Stanislaw Lem put in the mouth of his character Pirate Pugg in *The Cyberiad*, merit satire for the *fallacy of misplaced concreteness* (in Alfred North Whitehead's phrase). Information has no concreteness.

Stated more technically, information is a virtual structure dependent upon distributed coding/decoding regimes within which it can function. As we will detail later, the quantification of information depends upon a set of probabilities that differ relative to the position from which they are observed. That is, the "central explanatory quantity" of cybernetics— information—rests on a shifting measure of "probability," which is "a ratio between quantities which have similar dimensions" but "is itself of zero dimensions" (Bateson 1972, 403). On the plus side, "The advantage of working with information structures is that information has no intrinsic size" (Langton 1989, 39). This means that any *material* thing that can bear and preserve a coded difference, from magnetized molecules to carved granite mountain sides, can serve as a medium for the transmission of information.

Although any medium and its messages can be lost, the scripts borne by traditional media are relatively hard to erase as long as the media themselves are preserved. As a result—and in constant struggle against the entropic drift toward informatic as well as thermal disorganization—geologists, biologists, archaeologists, and historians have been able to salvage and interpret or reconstruct traces of the planetary, evolutionary, and cultural past. In contrast, information preserved in the mediums of printed texts or electromagnetic coding, although equally material, breeds endless copies indistinguishable from any "original," yet if discarded, deleted, or overwritten, leaves no scratch on any surface. But what the virtuality of information loses in place and permanence, it gains in velocity and transformativity.

The implosion of the mode of information within our technoscientific culture has produced a collective effort to bring forth the metaphysics of a new cosmos somewhere off to the side of the prior universe of matter and energy. The nonplace of cyberspace underscores again that the mode of information and the modes of matter and energy are not immediately commensurate. For a practical example, consider as an instance of informatic virtuality the ontology of a hypertext located on the Web: "Deterritorialized, fully present in all its existing versions, copies, and projections, deprived of inertia, ubiquitous inhabitant of cyberspace, hypertext helps produce events of textual actualization, navigation, and reading. Only such events can be said to be truly situated. And although it requires a real physical substrate for its subsistence and actualization, the imponderable hypertext has no place" (Levy 1998, 28).

Language

The canonical popularization of Claude Shannon's information theory, Warren Weaver's "Recent Contributions to the Mathematical Theory of Communication," parallels the canonical presentation of structural linguistics in Ferdinand de Saussure's *Course in General Linguistics*. Saussure already elaborates a *systemic* orientation focusing on the relations between the totality of the linguistic system as a social collectivity (*langue*) and any particular linguistic message (*parole*). The possibility of an individual message in the medium of language bearing significance for its addressee derives from its ability to link its sender and recipient to a collective external structure. Thus, for Saussure, the "integral and concrete object of linguistics," *langue*, "is a system of interdependent terms in which the value of each term results solely from the simultaneous presence of the others" (1966, 7, 114). Compare Weaver: "The concept of information applies not to the individual messages (as the concept of meaning would), but rather to the situation as a whole" (1949, 9). Just as the object of linguistics in its systematic and grammatical dimensions precedes matters of semantics, so information in its practical dimension (in particular, as an electromagnetic signal bearing an increment of message-load carried by a communications system) precedes the matter of *meaning*. Weaver cites Shannon on this point: "the semantic aspects of communication are irrelevant to the engineering aspects" (1949, 8). Information, in Shannon's mathematical treatment, is a matter of quantity—the amount to be transmitted relative to the capacity of a channel—rather than quality.

Similarly, in Shannon as in Saussure, matters of *value* are systemic rather than elemental. Informatic as well as linguistic values derive from "the situation as a whole"—the possibility of making specific selections from finite ensembles of variously probable options—rather than from anything intrinsic to what is selected. Saussure famously remarks, "Signs function . . . not through their intrinsic value but through their relative position. . . . In language there are only differences *without positive terms*" (1966, 118, 120). Compare Weaver (referring to Shannon's diagram, reproduced in chapter 9) on what amounts to informatic *parole* and on the determination of its value: "The *information source* selects a desired *message* out of a set of possible messages. . . . Information is a measure of one's freedom of choice when one selects a message" (1949, 7, 9).

However, just as in language there are finite amounts of paradigmatic difference from which to choose, so in the informatic situation one's "freedom of choice" will be contingent upon the finite statistical structure of a given system. Norbert Wiener clarifies this point in relation to the telegraphic medium: "A pattern which is conceived to convey information . . . is not taken as an isolated phenomenon. To telegraph . . . it is necessary that these dots and dashes be a selection from among a set which contains other possibilities as well" (1950, 4). Our positions as subjects of language, and more broadly, as subjects of information systems, bind our communicative behaviors to ratios of freedom and necessity determined in the first instance by social and technological collectivities: "It is most interesting to note that the redundancy of English is just about 50 per cent, so that about half of the letters or words we choose in writing or speaking are under our free choice, and about half (although we are not ordinarily aware of it) are really controlled by the statistical structure of the language" (Weaver 1949, 13).

Energy and Entropy

To further locate the modern discourse of information and *its* statistical structure, one must consult the history of the science of energy. Shannon quantified information through a calculus of message-probabilities modeled on statistical mechanics, a branch of physics. Statistical mechanics was developed in the late nineteenth century when Ludwig Boltzmann, transferring the mathematics of probabilities James Clerk Maxwell applied in his kinetic theory of gases, produced a measure of the energic disorder, or thermodynamic *entropy*, of physical systems. In all physical processes involving the conversion of energy from one form to another, some of the energy is dissipated in the form of heat: thermodynamic entropy is, at one level of its application, a measure of this "waste" (see Clarke 2002). A famous phrasing of the second law of thermodynamics is: In a closed system, entropy tends to a maximum. That is, observed over time, one can expect a physical or mechanical system—say, a pendulum or a steam engine—to go from order to disorder. Thermodynamically, the more unlikely the energy differentials, the lower the entropy—and so, informatically, the greater the information. Ordered or low-entropy physical systems with highly differentiated energies are relatively improbable; their lesser entropy equates to more information, just as finding a hot cup of coffee on a table in a cool room (a low-entropy scenario) would give you more information about its environment (someone is likely nearby) than the more typical circumstance of finding a cup at room temperature.

Boltzmann's statistical mechanics followed Maxwell in treating energic relations of order and disorder, work and waste, with the mathematics of probability (see Prigogine and Stengers 1984). His innovation was to define the entropy of a physical system as a function of its possible energic complexions—that is, the number of different possible ways to distribute its particles. Ordered complexions are relatively rare. There are many more complexions that yield a random (high-entropy) distribution in which thermal differences are reduced to a minimum. One is more likely to find a system in a state of relative disorder, and disorder is likely to increase over time toward a state of maximum equilibrium in which the evolution of the system slows to a minimum. This, then, is the probabilistic restatement of the second law: In a closed physical system left to itself, molecular disorder is most likely to increase. Boltzmann's quantification of the entropy law is

$S = k \log P.$

As P, the number of possible complexions of a system, increases, so does the likelihood of a random rather than ordered distribution, and so (logarithmically) does the entropy, S.

Explicit attention to Boltzmann's statistical analysis of thermodynamics is writ large in the founding documents of information theory and cybernetics. In 1948 John von Neumann noted, with reference to the mathematical logic of automata, that "thermodynamics, primarily in the form it was received from Boltzmann . . . is that part of theoretical physics which comes nearest in some of its aspects to manipulating and measuring information." (1963, 5:304). Wiener commented that the conceptual alignment of information with the probabilities associated with a set of related informational patterns "was already familiar in the branch of physics known as statistical mechanics, and . . . associated with the famous second law of thermodynamics" (1950, 7). Weaver acknowledged this lineup—to whom he added Claude Shannon—as the set of thinkers most responsible for connecting energy to information, thermodynamics to cybernetics: "Dr. Shannon's work roots back, as von Neumann has pointed out, to Boltzmann's observation, in some of his work on statistical physics (1894), that entropy is related to 'missing information'" (1949, 3).

Informatic Entropy

In order to exploit the link with statistical mechanics, Shannon defined information mathematically on the basis of the probabilistic distribution of a finite ensemble of message elements, arriving at a measure he termed "the entropy of the message." The set of possible messages posits an informatic ensemble analogous to a thermodynamic ensemble having a set of possible complexions with various degrees of probability. Within this framework, information is quantified as a measure of the improbability of a message, specifically, as an inverse function (the negative logarithm) of the probability of a particular message being chosen from a set of finite options. As noted above, "information is a measure of one's freedom of choice when one selects a message." For instance, making a selection from a binary set of choices (yes/no, on/off) yields one bit of information—some but not a great deal—because the options available at the information source are severely constrained. The larger the ensemble of choices, however, the less probable is any particular choice. In this decidedly "liberal" approach to calculating the value of information, the more choices a sender has, the more information the message chosen will contain. Shannon's mathematical formalization of information (H) on the basis of such "probabilities of choice" yielded an "entropy-like expression," analogous to Boltzmann's logarithmic formula for thermodynamic entropy:

$$H = -\sum p_i \log p_i.$$

Information theory translates the ratios or improbable order to probable disorder in physical systems into a distinction between signal and noise, or "useful" and "waste" information, in communication systems. In the development of this transposition, information, or "message-entropy," becomes a variably complex measure of message-probabilities, a measure *dependent upon the position of the observer of the communication system.* The observer can, for instance, assess the value of a message at its source by increase of order, *or* at its destination by decrease of disorder.

To summarize: In physical systems doing work by converting energy from one form to another, the *thermodynamic* entropy of the system is the amount of energy unavailable for further work, or "wasted," usually in the form of heat. In communication systems, the *informatic* entropy of the message is a measure of message-probabilities relative to one of several vantage points:

- at the *source*, where one observes the ratio of *actual* selections to *possible* selections;
- in the *channel*, considering the ratio of *signal* ("useful information") to *noise* ("waste information"); or
- at the *destination*, based on the ratio of *surprise* (improbability) to *expectation* (probability).

At the source, informatic value is a function of the probability or improbability of a message's selection from a repertoire of possible messages: the smaller that ensemble, the fewer the available choices and the less information any given selection will carry. However, selection at the source only initiates a communication event and cannot determine the informatic value of its outcome. For instance, the order of the signal can be lost in transit due to noise in the channel. Finally, the value of information can also be defined by its effect on the receiver: "The amount of information received is the degree to which the receiver's uncertainty . . . has been diminished" (Paulson 1988, 55). Considering matters at the receiving end of informatic transmission underwrites many later twentieth-century developments in reception theory, reader response theory, and cognitive sciences that have focused on the constitutive or constructivist moment for the audience of communications.

Noise

Norbert Wiener channeled information theory toward the science of cybernetics, which he defined as the "study of messages, and in particular of the effective messages of control" (1950, 8). His immediate aim was to advance computer technology by investigating the informatic circuits that allow functional analogies between organisms and machines. Biological nervous systems and modern electronic devices both feed information from certain parts of their structures back into a processing network, and these internal messages enable both the organism and the machine to track and regulate their performance. The transmission of signals through communication channels, whether nerves or phone lines, is analogous to the temporal behavior of closed thermodynamic systems: in each case, disorder tends to increase over time. In informatics this increment of systemic evolution over the time of transmission is called *noise*. "The statistical nature of *messages* is entirely determined by the character of the source. But the statistical character of the *signal* as actually transmitted by a channel, and hence the entropy in the channel, is determined both by what one attempts to feed into the channel and by the capabilities of the channel to handle different signal situations" (Weaver 1949, 17–18).

The amount of "entropy in the channel," as opposed to the entropy of a message before it is sent, is determined by the level of noise—"anything that arrives as part of a message, but that was not part of the message when sent out" (Paulson 1988, 67)—that impinges on the signal. No real-world channel can be made entirely free of random fluctuations that introduce noise, and this introduces another level of uncertainty into the communication process. This is analogous to the emergence of *error* in the process of electronic computation. In both computation and communication, the margin of error is counteracted through *redundancy*. With some sacrifice of efficiency, redundant coding provides a repetition of crucial calculative steps or message elements and so ensures a reliable, if not impeccable, level of integrity at the end of the process.

The concept of noise was at first treated only as a regrettable impediment to perfect efficiency, much as thermodynamic entropy had been a century before. Yet entropy, which had begun as a measure of the loss of "usable energy," is not properly conceived merely as energy's antithesis. Similarly, noise was initially stipulated as a negative or destructive interference, the cause of a loss of "useful information." As Shannon and Weaver appropriated entropy into their informatic vernacular as a *positive* quantity, noise emerged as an ineradicable friction affecting communication. But by the very terms of Shannon's mathematizing of information, noise is not simply "anti-information." Rather, the productive ambiguity of noise emerged from the consideration that it too *is* information—and precisely *unexpected* information, an uncanny increment that rolls the dice of randomness within every communicative and calculative transmission. Much of the most exciting critical work of the past five decades has derived from the informatic integration of the disciplines of knowledge made possible by reversing the sign of noise (see Serres 2007).

The significance of noise for the discourse of information becomes clearer if we switch focus from communications systems (the milieu of Shannon's Bell Labs) to media systems (Manovich's "representational technologies")—that is, from information systems centered on *transmission* (such as the telegraph and telephone) to those centered on *inscription and storage* (the photograph and phonograph and their progeny). Graphic and digital systems do both, of course, but it is important nonetheless to bear in mind this distinction in system functions. We tend to envision information as perpetually in transit, in social circulation, but in equal degree, information accumulates, gets stored, and sits there, in some actual or virtual location, awaiting retrieval. What the inscription and storage of information also allows is its *manipulation*, an opening beyond its utilitarian functions to creative uses. Stored information becomes a medium out of which—by editing, cutting, reframing, resequencing, and so forth—new orders of form can be produced.

From the standpoint of transmission, any such meddling with stored information amounts to the mixing of noise into its signal. But from the standpoint of art forms instantiated in informatic media (aural sounds, visual images, linguistic signs), the noise *is* the art. For instance, the advent of phonography enabled the discovery, within the otherwise "pure" (Pythagorean) tones of an earlier musical acoustics, of noise. Timbre itself is a musical noise derived in the first instance from the material specifics of a given instrument. The noise of timbre does not physically corrupt but, rather, informatically enhances the sound it inhabits (see Kahn 2002), allowing for instrumental differentiations which then become part of the musical orchestration. For another example, with the advent of audiotape, time-axis manipulation (TAM) of the recorded signal became feasible. The Beatles and Jimi Hendrix famously crafted segments of their recordings by replaying pieces of studio tape backward. Media arts remediate information in forms of meaningful noise.

The Informatic and the Material

One of the more problematic legacies of the cybernetic discussion is the pervasive oversimplification of its distinction of information from matter. This is not so much the fault of the original expositors, who made a necessary effort—especially in light of the profound analogies between thermodynamics and informatics—to distinguish the object of cybernetics from the object of physics. Rather, the tendency to set matter and information into dialectical antithesis follows the engrained dualistic trends of Western thought, intellectual habits that persist despite the efforts of key cyberneticists to cultivate new ways of thinking, for instance, about the emergent productions of system/environment ensembles. A case in point is Gregory Bateson's seminal discourse on information, summed up in his famous observation that "what we mean by information—the elementary unit of information—is a *difference which makes a difference*" (1972, 453).

Bateson, who brought about a significant relay of cybernetic discourse from the natural to the social sciences, offers the following comment on "the ancient dichotomy between form and substance" in the context of a protest about the misleading scientism in "the metaphoric use of 'energy' in the behavioral sciences" to schematize psychological events: "The conservative laws for energy and matter concern substance rather than form. But mental process, ideas, communication, organization, differentiation, pattern, and so on, are matters of form rather than substance" (1972, xxv). Bateson's points are entirely congruent with Saussure's "in language there are only differences *without positive terms*": the concept of difference is a formal or relational one. It is *abstract*, in the way that mathematics is an abstraction from the world of things enumerated. But seldom does one find consternation over the "immateriality" of language or the "disembodiment" of mathematics. Bateson's point is precisely that information, under its "cybernetic explanation," crosses the form of linguistic differentiation with the form of mathematical probability.

The tendency, however, has been to read Bateson's *heuristic* exclusion of physical quantities from information theory as an *ontological* exclusion on the mind/nature model that licenses either the pseudo-utopian rhetoric of information as liberation from physical constraints, or alternatively, the materialist counterpolemic against information as a discourse of domination. For a sample of the latter tendency, let us briefly unpack a short passage early in Friedrich Kittler's brilliant work of media discourse theory, *Gramophone, Film, Typewriter*:

The technological differentiation of optics, acoustics, and writing exploded Gutenberg's writing monopoly around 1880. . . . And with this differentiation—and not with steam engines and railroads—a clear division occurs between matter and information, the real and the symbolic. (1999, 16)

Kittler argues provocatively that the "writing monopoly"—print technology as the dominant means of archiving cultural production—broke down in the nineteenth century due to photography and phonography, the new graphic media of that time. In this passage he aligns literature, information, and the (Lacanian) symbolic. All three involve the imposition of a *code* by which the world is rearticulated for storage and transmission—and also by which information about the world is rendered into a coded *signal*. "To record the sound sequences of speech, literature had to arrest them in a system of 26 letters, thereby categorically excluding all noise sequences" (1999, 3)—excluding them, that is, from the *signal*, if not the *channel*. But no such transcriptive process is needed when the phonograph records "the sound sequences of speech" or of anything else; the "continuous undulations recorded by the gramophone and the audiotape" are, in contrast, "signatures of the real" (1999, 118). If the symbolic is pure signal (and so decipherable by definition), the real is pure noise and always already beyond intelligibility, no matter how "recognizable" a particular sound sequence may be.

For Kittler, the arrival of analog media technologies made possible a "reproduction authenticated by the object itself . . . . It refers to the bodily real, which of necessity escapes all symbolic grids" (1999, 12). In this and like remarks Kittler continues the dualistic discussion of information, rendering the "clear division . . . between matter and information, the real and the symbolic," as an absolute opposition on the Lacanian, if not indeed on the Cartesian, model. Here again the crucial analytical distinction between matter and information is reified, with information becoming the technoid signifier for "the *soul* of a new machine"—for immateriality, dematerialization, or disembodiment. In this way, the concept of information remains available for stigmatization by the spectrum of philosophical and political moralizations attached for millennia to ontological disputes over soul, form, essence, spirit, and their sundry historical avatars (see Terranova 2004).

However, if noise is *also* information—noise is a "signature of the real" just as signal is a signature of the symbolic—then the concept of information incorporates the unity of the difference between signal and noise. Signal *or* noise, it's all information. Or again, the bodies of the technological infrastructures of information systems are always part of the message—"the medium is the massage." The student of media can get the kinks out of the concept of information by reentering media environments into the whole picture, whatever transmissions come across the system. This prescription is a restatement of the contextual or "holistic" impetus in the best cybernetic thinking—the imperative always to think "organism plus environment," system *and* environment, message *and* medium. To do so is simply to be methodical about factoring into informatic transactions the matter of their material couplings and their systemic contexts. Bateson goes to the heart of this "relationship between *context* and its content," again with an analogy drawn from linguistics:

> A phoneme exists as such only in combination with other phonemes which make up a word. The word is the *context* of the phoneme. But the word only exists as such—only has "meaning"—in the larger context of the utterance, which again has meaning only in a relationship.

This hierarchy of contexts within contexts is universal for the communicational (or "emic") aspect of phenomena and drives the scientist always to seek for information in the ever larger units. It may (perhaps) be true in physics that the explanation of the macroscopic is to be sought in the microscopic. The opposite is usually true in cybernetics: without context, there is no communication. (1972, 402)

Feedback

The new relations and distinctions forged in the mid-twentieth century between energy and information highlight the crucial difference for systems of all kinds between isolation from, and openness to, their environments. In the cybernetic era the classical thermodynamic emphasis on the tendency of closed systems toward equilibrium shifts to the nonequilibrium operation of open and multiply coupled biotic and metabiotic ensembles. Even given the assumption of a universal drift toward entropy, biological, psychic, and social systems maintain their organizational autonomies through *operational* closure hand in hand with *environmental* openness (see Clarke 2008). For such autopoietic systems worldly perturbations are variously construed as signals or noises—a distinction whose meaning rests on the self-referential binary of meaning/nonmeaning. The point here is that informatic noise always bears "meaning" for the system that construes it, even if for that observer its meaning is to be meaningless, or unintelligble with reference to presently available codes.

If we shift now to an operational orientation, considering the role of information for systems that do not simply store it or transmit it but *use* it to maintain or steer their own functions, we encounter the concept of feedback. As we have noted, information theory defines information mathematically as an inverse function of the probability or predictability of a message. From the receiver's perspective, the less certain a message, the more information it delivers once it arrives. Because the noise of transmission intrudes randomly or unpredictably into signals, the shape it will take in any given communicative situation remains unknown until it is received. By introducing greater uncertainty into the message, noise can thus be thought of not as mere static, a loss of efficiency or clarity, but as a form of information about the media environment, a gain in communicative unpredictability with at least the potential to introduce other information of value into the transmission. As Bateson famously summed up this situation, using "information" as a synecdoche for *signal*: "All that is not information, not redundancy, not form, and not restraints—is noise, the only possible source of *new* patterns" (1972, 410).

The concept of feedback can also be regarded in the light of information theory. At the same moment in the 1940s when electronic computers were first being designed, feedback emerged as a key concept for the science of control mechanisms. In certain systems, output or behavior can be controlled—say, maintained within an effective range—by introducing information about the output back into the system as input. This circle of information, as seen in the figure, is called a feedback loop. In this classical feedback model, the feedback is *negative* if B < 0. The effect of negative feedback is to stabilize the output. This is the desired function in the case of servomechanisms such as thermostats, whose aim is to render the system homeostatic, fixing its operational parameters within an acceptable range. In the case of *positive* feedback, the fed-back signal adds rather than subtracts itself, compounding rather than dampening the output of the system. In either case, when output is fed back as input, the distinction between them breaks down and a looping circularity overtakes a strictly linear flow.

Let's consider feedback within electronic audio amplification in the wider context of its exploitation within popular music. Here the message is a source signal—say, from a guitar pickup—that the audio system registers, codes, decodes, and boosts into speakers. Audio feedback in an amplified circuit is produced when some of the output signal from an amplifier reenters the input signal by way of a microphone or instrument. This can generate unwanted noise, a fraying or distortion of the signal; one common manifestation is the horrible screech of runaway positive feedback that results when a microphone is placed too close to

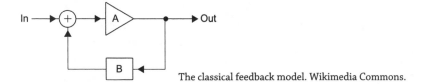

The classical feedback model. Wikimedia Commons.

its speakers. However, when audio feedback is properly calibrated by an operator balancing the amount of output fed back into the system, a kind of harmonic equilibrium can evolve. Sound crystals emerge and condense to reveal the angularities of overtones and chord harmonics. It's a sort of fragile audio homeostasis, an island of order emerging in the chaos of amplified noise. This momentary system effect can itself be modulated within various limits and sustained to form a beam of sound.

Rock feedback is a musical medium created by rodeo-riding a cascade of noise. Emerging full-blown in the mid-1960s, guitar feedback unleashed a new world of previously unheard-of sounds. A natural consequence of pushing an amplifier to fill a room too big for it, feedback was recognized as a sonic resource that could be both tonally and melodically controlled. Its use in rock was anticipated by Chicago-style electrified blues guitarists exploiting the pleasingly gritty sound of overdriven vacuum-tube amplifiers. That electric-blues signature was reprocessed by British guitar heroes such as Eric Clapton, Jeff Beck, and Jimmy Page, who in the mid-1960s found wavery feedback tones effective for signifying the mind-bending effects of pot and LSD. But one performer literally embodies the feedback of feedback—its cultural reentry into the States as the sound of psychedelia. The London-incubated American rocker Jimi Hendrix raised blues-based rock-guitar feedback to an art form, playing feedback like a violin. At the beginning of "Foxey Lady" (1967), for instance, he lays down a classic signature, rattling a string on his Fender Stratocaster into a stack of Marshall amplifiers until it generates enough input/output to loop into a feedback beam.

Hendrix especially perfected the "spacey" feel of psychedelic rock by developing ingenious ways of looping and relayering the noisy feedback signal to produce a sonic density or depth effect. He made guitar feedback sing using, in addition to guitar and amplifiers, a repertoire of newly created effects pedals, especially the fuzztone, which jacked up the volume of the guitar and made sustained feedback tones available at the punch of a floor pedal. To this, Hendrix added the wah-wah pedal, the Octavia octave-splitter, and the Uni-Vibe, which simulated the tremolo effect of the revolving tweeters in the sound box of a Hammond B3 electric organ—giving his feedback sounds a further range of stunning effects.

In "Third Stone from the Sun" (Hendrix 1967), for instance, he comes out of a spacey jam with his band and reasserts the head of the tune by capturing a feedback beam and using it to sing the melody, while rippling the aural solidity of the beam with the guitar's whammy bar. A few years later Hendrix distilled this form of guitar attack in his monumental performance—on New Year's Eve 1969, the night the '60s turned into the '70s—of "Machine Gun" (Hendrix 1970). Here, after the first set of verses, at the beginning of the main instrumental break, the dire horror of jungle warfare is condensed into a long-sustained, perfectly tuned scream of feedback, its octaves split by the Octavia and eerily lashed by the helicopterlike rotations of the Uni-Vibe.

In this example art is formed out of noise by reprocessing not a stored signal but one produced on the fly, in the moment of improvisation. Whereas the pioneers of cybernetics and information theory studied the formal parallels between electronic circuitry and the nervous system, Hendrix showed how to couple the electric guitar and its amplification and sound-processing technologies to the nervous system, communicating his own cybernetic fusion to his live and virtual audiences. Playing on the cutting edge of this human/machine interface, Jimi's rock persona embodied the "Body electric" sighted in the poetic ether a century earlier by America's first rock prophet, Walt Whitman: in Jimi's performance, Whitman's romantic body was transformed into a cybernetic body sustained by the potentially infinite looping of a feedback signal.

References and Suggested Readings

Bateson, Gregory. 1972. *Steps to an Ecology of Mind.* New York: Ballantine.

Clarke, Bruce. 2008. *Posthuman Metamorphosis: Narrative and Systems.* New York: Fordham University Press.

Clarke, Bruce, and Linda D. Henderson, eds. 2002. *From Energy to Information: Representation in Science and Technology, Art, andLiterature.* Stanford, CA: Stanford University Press.

Hansen, Mark B. N. 2006. *Bodies in Code: Interfaces with Digital Media.* New York: Routledge.

Hendrix, Jimi. 1967. *Are You Experienced?* Reprise Records.

———. 1970. *Band of Gypsys.* Capitol Records.

Kahn, Doug. 2002. "Concerning the Line: Music, Noise, and Phonography." In Clarke and Henderson (2002, 178–94).

Kauffman, Louis H. 1987. "Self-Reference and Recursive Forms." *Journal of Social and Biological Structure* 10:53–72.

Kittler, Friedrich. 1999. *Gramophone, Film, Typewriter,* trans. Geoffrey Winthrop-Young and Michael Wutz. Stanford, CA: Stanford University Press.

Krippendorff, Klaus. 1984. "Paradox and Information." In *Progress in Communication Sciences,* vol. 5, ed. Brenda Dervin and Melvin J. Voigt, 45–71. Norwood, NJ: ABLEX Publishing.

Langton, Christopher G. 1989. "Artificial Life." In *Artificial Life*, ed. Christopher G. Langton, 1–47. New York: Addison-Wesley.

Lem, Stanislaw. 1985. *The Cyberiad: Fables for the Cybernetic Age*, trans. Michael Kandel. New York: Harvest.

Lévy, Pierre. 1998. *Becoming Virtual: Reality in the Digital Age*, trans. Robert Bononno. New York: Plenum Trade.

Manovich, Lev. 2001. *The Language of New Media*. Cambridge, MA: MIT Press.

Paulson, William R. 1988. *The Noise of Culture: Literary Texts in a World of Information*. Ithaca: Cornell University Press.

Poster, Mark. 2004. "The Information Empire." *Comparative Literature Studies* 41, no. 3: 317–34.

Prigogine, Ilya, and Isabelle Stengers. 1984. *Order out of Chaos: Man's New Dialogue with Nature*. New York: Bantam.

Saussure, Ferdinand de. [1915] 1966. *Course in General Linguistics*, trans. Wade Baskin. New York: McGraw-Hill.

Serres, Michel. [1982] 2007. *The Parasite*, trans. Lawrence R. Schehr. Minneapolis: University of Minnesota Press.

Shanken, Edward A. 2002. "Cybernetics and Art: Cultural Convergence in the 1960s." In Clarke and Henderson (2002, 255–77).

Terranova, Tiziana. 2004. "Communication beyond Meaning: On the Cultural Politics of Information." *Social Text* 22, no. 3 (Fall): 51–73.

Thurtle, Phillip. 2007. *The Emergence of Genetic Rationality: Space, Time, and Information in American Biological Science, 1870–1920*. Seattle: University of Washington Press.

von Foerster, Heinz. 2003. *Understanding Understanding: Essays on Cybernetics and Cognition*. New York: Springer.

von Neumann, John. 1963. "The General and Logical Theory of Automata" (1948). In *Collected Works*. 6 vols. Ed. A. H. Taub. 5:288–328. New York: Macmillan.

Weaver, Warren. 1949. "Recent Contributions to the Mathematical Theory of Communication." In Warren Weaver and Claude Shannon, *The Mathematical Theory of Communication*, 3–28. Urbana: University of Illinois Press.

Wiener, Norbert. 1950. *The Human Use of Human Beings: Cybernetics and Society*. Boston: Houghton Mifflin.

12 :: NEW MEDIA

MARK B.N. HANSEN

The term *new media* has achieved the kind of widespread cultural dissemination that seems to strip away all specificity. "New" media is everywhere around us, in the gadgets and devices we use to keep organized, to do our work, to play, to access information, and to communicate with friends and acquaintances. At the same time, "old" new media—the zograscope, the optical telegraph, the physiognotrace—have become newly interesting thanks to recent studies of such bypassed technologies. Books have been written on new media as the convergence brought about by digital technology and, at the other extreme, on the newness that accompanies all media at the moment of their introduction. Cutting across these contemporary projects and responsible for their complementarity, if not indeed for their imbrication, is the ambivalent or double case of that central term, *new media*.

At once singular and plural, "new media" would seem to designate both a qualitatively new kind of media and a quality of all media (of every medium) at the point at which they are (it is) introduced into and disseminated across society. The plural face of new media goes hand in hand with the larger dialectic of media innovation that characterizes Western culture from antiquity onward; the singular face suggests that we may, today, have come to a moment of impasse in this very dialectic, a moment in which media may in fact be separated from the technical means by which a culture stores its knowledge and history (see chapter 13, "Hardware/Software/Wetware"). Can it be that, for the first time in our history, media (meaning the storage, dissemination, and transmission of experience) has become distinct from its own technical infrastructure, from the computational networks and machines that undergird most of what we consume as media? And if so, what are the consequences for our understanding of the future prospects for human beings and for the life of our planet? Such are the stakes bound up in the issue of the "newness" of new media.

Both faces of new media—singular and plural—arise on the basis of a common dialectic of media innovation: by changing the conditions for the production of experience, new media destabilize existing patterns of biological, psychical, and collective life even as they furnish new facilities. This convergence of privation and supplementation already informs what many critics hold to be the primal scene of media innovation in Western thought: Plato's meditation on the new medium of writing in the *Phaedrus*. There the issue is writing's status as a *pharmakon*, at once a poison and its antidote, a threat to memory and its extension. This profound ambivalence is clearly expressed in the myth of Theuth, the Egyptian God who invented writing, which Socrates recounts to Phaedrus:

> But when it came to writing Theuth said [to the Egyptian king Thamus], "Here, O king, is a branch of learning that will make the people of Egypt wiser and improve their memories; my discovery provides a recipe for memory and wisdom." But the king answered and said, "O man full of arts, to one it is given to create the things of art, and to another to judge what measure of harm and of profit they have for those that shall employ them. And so it is that you, by reason of your tender regard for the writing that is your offspring, have declared the very opposite of its true effect. If men learn this, it will implant forgetfulness in their souls; they will cease to exercise memory because they rely on that which is written, calling things to remembrance no longer from within themselves, but by means of external marks. What you have discovered is a recipe not for memory, but for reminder. And it is no true wisdom that you offer your disciples, but only its semblance."

Thamus's well-reasoned reserve notwithstanding, this myth captures the fundamental duality that will drive media innovation from the invention of writing onward: to the extent that each new medium operates by exteriorizing some function of human cognition and memory, it involves both gain and loss. In this case, even if writing results in a waning of onboard memory skills, it furnishes an external supplement to internal memory that will become ever more necessary as information proliferates and life becomes more complex.

The fundamental duality that drives media innovation has often taken the form of myth. In the *Protagoras*, Plato himself deploys the Hesiodic myth of Prometheus and Epimetheus as a means of characterizing the singularity of the human, but also of grasping our fundamental dependence on technology. Let us recall the salient details of Plato's account: charged with the task of equipping mortal creatures with suitable powers, Epimetheus makes his distribution following the *principle of compensation*, giving to each creature those capacities that will insure their survival. Not being a particularly clever person, Epimetheus uses all of the available powers on the brute beasts, leaving the human race unprovided for and compelling the famous theft of fire by his perhaps justly more famous brother, Prometheus. Because of our Promethean legacy, so Plato's myth recounts, we humans have "had a share in the portion of the gods" and have distinguished ourselves from all other animals through our use of the arts of fire, which is to say, technologies. This use has resulted in the development of articulate speech and names, the invention of "houses and clothes and shoes and bedding," and the introduction of agriculture. To this Platonic list, we might add the continual development of new technologies and media, which has, in the view of many, led to our ever more powerful domination over nature and now, with the development of genetic engineering, over life itself.

That Prometheus suffered unending punishment for his theft from the Gods should not be forgotten. Indeed, it is this aspect of the myth that reappears throughout our history, at moments of large-scale technological change. To cite only one example, Mary Shelley's *Frankenstein, or the Modern Prometheus* casts Victor Frankenstein as a promethean scientist whose theft of the spark of life leads to disastrous consequences. Leaving aside questions concerning the allegorical scope of Shelley's tale (is it a criticism of industrialism? a plea for proper parenting?), what is important here is its invocation of Prometheus to mark the human engagement with, and ambivalence toward, new technology. Any Promethean step forward is, so it seems, necessarily accompanied by fears that we have overstepped, that we have introduced something detrimental to our "natural" life. One need only recall the anxieties that welled up around cinema at its origin, which stretched the gamut from the physiological (it would hurt our eyesight) to the moral (it would cater to our lowest impulses). Or consider the myriad anxieties that today surround genetic engineering and stem cell research. What the longevity of this mythic kernel would seem to point toward is the dialectic that surrounds adaptation to the new: to the extent that new media introduce modes of experience that challenge the familiar, they are bound to occasion anxiety, resistance, even hostility, as they make their way toward cultural acceptance or "naturalization." The Promethean dimension in this dialectic underscores the fact that such anxiety is not trivial or misguided, but is a constitutive dimension of the human experience of cultural change.

It is this dialectic of media innovation that informs the influential, though much misunderstood, work of pioneering Canadian media scholar Marshall McLuhan. In *Understanding Media* (1964) and various other texts, McLuhan inventoried a broad range of media, from cars to the computer, describing them as *both* extensions of and autoamputations from the human body. For McLuhan, the development of media technology (up to then-contemporary electronic technologies) has operated as an externalization of the nervous system, which in today's terms we might describe as a technical distribution of human cognitive capacities into the environment. Perhaps the most crucial dimension of McLuhan's vision for the topic of new media is his concerted effort to couple media form and media use. Indeed, it is perhaps this dimension that best anticipates current developments in social networking technologies, developments dubbed Web 2.0, that have driven home the profound interdependence of content (use) and form (technology) in the wired age. Far from the technological determinist he has commonly and simplistically been held to be, McLuhan can now be seen as the keen social analyst he always was. In arguing that the "medium is the message," McLuhan certainly did not intend to advance a purely formalistic doctrine; rather, he sought to establish and to foreground the large-scale societal impact of particular media as a phenomenon *distinct from* their concrete deployments by individuals and groups. What McLuhan argues is that the widespread adoption of a particular medium impacts experience at a different (and higher) level of magnitude than its use to convey this or that content. Even though there is and can be no such thing as a medium without content, to reduce the social impact of a medium to the content it conveys is to overlook the profound changes that ensue from revolutions in cultural techniques of information processing and consumption.

In *The Gutenberg Galaxy* (1962), the study immediately preceding *Understanding Media*, McLuhan had focused on the transformational impact of the invention of movable type and the print revolution it catalyzed. While he did analyze the role of knowledge storage and dissemination afforded by the book (hence the title), his central focus was on the altered form of consciousness that emerged in the wake of print. According to McLuhan, the shift from manuscript culture to print culture entailed the dissolution of sensorily distributed and integrated experience in favor of the tyranny of the visual.

Other scholars have eschewed McLuhan's emphasis on the alienation of individual experience in order to concentrate on the profound material effects of the new medium of print. In her important study, *The Printing Press as an Agent of Change* (1979), Elizabeth Eisenstein analyzed the social and political impact of print; specifically, she studied the printing press as a form of standardization that afforded unprecedented capacities for storage and dissemination of information. Using empirical methods, Eisenstein convincingly demonstrated that the invention of movable type and the print revolution played an important role in the

Protestant Reformation, the Renaissance, and the Scientific Revolution. In a sense, Eisenstein's stress on the standardization of linguistic marks that lies at the heart of the printing press anticipates the media revolution of the nineteenth century as analyzed by German media scientist Friedrich Kittler. For Kittler, the triad of gramophone, film, and typewriter differentiated the inscription, storage, and dissemination of the various sensory fluxes—aural, visual, and linguistic—in a way that expands the standardization of print to other experiential registers. Interestingly enough, for all of these scholars, otherwise so different in their metholodgies and commitments, the advent of digital technology promises some form of experiential reunification, whether utopian (McLuhan) or dystopian (Kittler).

In *Technics and Time: The Fault of Epimetheus*, French philosopher Bernard Stiegler transforms McLuhan's vision of media into a full-fledged philosophy of technical evolution. At the heart of Stiegler's thought is the understanding that human beings, from the very origin of the species, have always been technically mediated. Stiegler's effort to overturn the repression of technics in Western philosophy follows in the wake of efforts by his teacher and mentor, Jacques Derrida, to deconstruct the metaphysics of presence by way of the *essential* technicity of writing and other technologies of *différance*. As Derrida has shown, in studies on topics ranging from the Platonic myth of writing to the logic of the supplement in Jean-Jacques Rousseau, the antecedence of writing (here understood as "arche-writing," the iterability of the mark or *grammé*) in relation to speech and concrete writing systems means that the origin of meaning is always given through *différance*, which is to say, as differing and deferred. In his own take on Derrida's crucial concept of arche-writing, Stiegler insists on the necessity of thinking a history of the supplement, such that the operation of *différance* is put into a functional relation with concrete technologies of storage and transmission (see Stiegler, "Derrida and Technology"). With this move, Stiegler relativizes what he calls the "quasi-transcendental" field of *différance* or arche-writing in relation to the material infrastructure of its appearance and efficacy in the world at any given moment in time. Thus the paradoxical anteriority or withdrawal of any moment of origin (presence) becomes tightly bound up with the technical conditions of its belated appearance.

As the subtitle of the first volume of his study *Technics and Time* indicates, Stiegler routes his own negotiation with the figure of paradoxical origin through the crucial but neglected figure of Epimetheus in the Hesiodic myth and its legacy. In a compelling argument, he insists that the figure of Prometheus, and the dialectic of technological change it expresses, would have no meaning without the "fault" of Epimetheus—

the originary act of forgetting that left the "natural" human being naked and unprotected, in need of technical supplementation. In Stiegler's reading, what the myth expresses is the "originary technicity" of the human, the fact that human beings have always depended on and coevolved with technologies. Drawing on paleontological studies of early flint tools, Stiegler foregrounds the fundamental correlation of the organic *cortex* with the inorganic *silex* as the basic characteristic of the human: from the outset, human beings have evolved not simply genetically but culturally, which is to say, by exteriorizing their know-how and collective memory in the form of cultural artifacts and objective memory supports. This means, of course, that the evolution of the human can be characterized in terms of a long series of "new media" revolutions: what our material history teaches us is that human beings evolve in correlation with the evolution of technics; the long line of once-new new media would simply be the index of this coevolution. In light of the complex form of human evolution ensuing from our coupling to technics (a form Stiegler dubs "epiphylogenesis," meaning evolution by means other than life), it follows—and this is Stiegler's thesis—that human beings, in their developmental and genetic evolution, are "essentially" correlated with technical media. Understood broadly as the objective or exterior support for human life in its diverse sensory, perceptual, cognitive, and collective modalities, technical media on this picture are nothing less than the necessary correlates of human beings. Contemporary cognitive scientists speak of "cognitive distribution" to describe the significance of this exteriorization of know-how and memory into media, but what their claims really underscore, when viewed through the lens of media studies, is how mediation forms the very basis of human existence. Human beings literally exist in the medium of the world, which is to say, in a medium that has always been technical.

Lest this sound overly anthropocentric, as if media existed exclusively to support human evolutionary and developmental processes, it should be pointed out that media have increasingly converged with technical forms of inscription of experience and of time; as a result, they now participate in processes of technological evolution and development that, at least since the Industrial Revolution, can lay claim to some sort of qualified autonomy. More than any other critical corpus, the work of Friedrich Kittler has drawn attention to this sobering reality. In *Discourse Networks 1800/1900* and in *Gramophone, Film, Typewriter*, Kittler has articulated a history of media that moves from the monopoly on storage long exercised by the alphabet to the media differentiation of the nineteenth century and finally to the contemporary convergence of media in the form of digital code and computer processing. At the core of his media history is an appreciation for technics as a material production (a production of the real) that is not preadapted to or constrained by the sensory and perceptual thresholds of human experience (see chapter 14, "Technology").

A glimpse of this qualified autonomy of technics can be found in techniques for sound analysis that developed out of the phonographic revolution, which is to say, in the wake of the new medium of the gramophone. While the dominant uses of the gramophone, from its invention until its recent obsolescence (and now, of course, in its afterlife), invest almost wholly in the synchrony of technical recording and human sense perception (meaning that they involve the recording and replaying of sound for human consumption), the capacity of technical sound recording to inscribe frequencies outside the range of human hearing allows for an inscription (or "symbolization") of the flux of the real that is not narrowly bound to human modes of symbolization. Sound inscription thus instances the break with natural language and alphabetic writing that characterizes technical recording as such; whereas the inscription of natural language operates on the discrete ordering of the alphabet, the inscription of sound operates on a far more fine-grained discretization of the sonic flux. One technique for such discretization, Fourier analysis, symbolizes the raw flux of sound by means of intervals that periodize nonperiodic, innumerable frequency series. According to Kittler, what is most important about these so-called Fourier intervals—and what makes them exemplary of digital signal processing per se—is the recourse to real number analysis (a mathematical technique encompassing the continua between whole numbers) they make necessary. Generalizing from the technicalities of Kittler's discussion, we can say that high-frequency analysis "symbolizes" the flux of the real on the matrix of real numbers (whereas the alphabet does it on the matrix of natural language). To say this is to suggest that the technical inscription of sound symbolizes the real for systems other than human sense perception, and indeed this is what, for Kittler, makes it exemplary of the operation of the computer as such. It is the reason why computers, as Kittler puts it, are "becoming ever more necessary" while people "are becoming ever more contingent."

As the generalization of an operation (machinic symbolization) that could (and did) remain marginal until its widespread social proliferation, the computer marks a certain dissociation of media from technics. Arguably for the first time in history, the technical infrastructure of media is no longer homologous with its surface appearance. As distinct from phonography, where the grooves of a record graphically reproduce the frequency ranges of humanly perceivable sound, and from film, where the inscription of light on a sensitive surface reproduces what is visible to the human eye, properly computational media involve no direct correlation between technical storage and human sense perception. What we see on the computer screen (or other interface) and hear on the digital player is not related by visible or sonic analogy to the data that is processed in the computer or digital device. Indeed, as the work of some digital media artists has shown, the same digital data can be output in different registers, yielding very different media experiences. Pioneering new media theorist Lev Manovich has described this unique situation in terms of a divide between the media surface and the underlying code:

> New media in general can be thought of as consisting of two distinct layers—the "cultural layer" and the "computer layer." . . . Because new media is created on computers, distributed via computers, and stored and archived on computers, the logic of a computer can be expected to significantly influence the traditional cultural logic of media; that is, . . . the computer layer will affect the cultural layer. The ways in which the computer models the world, represents data, and allows us to operate on it; the key operations behind all computer programs (such as search, match, sort, and filter); the conventions of HCI [human-computer interface]— in short, what can be called the computer's ontology, epistemology, and pragmatics—influence the cultural layer of new media, its organization, its emerging genres, its contents. (2002, 46)

Manovich situates the conjunction in computational media of surface and code as the legacy of two converging yet hitherto distinct cultural traditions: media and computation. In his telling (and it must be stressed that his *Language of New Media* first appeared in 1999), these two traditions are held together by the cultural dominance of the cinematic metaphor, which has largely dictated how digital data have been transposed into readily consumable media forms (one need only think of the role of cut scenes in video games or introductory pages on Web sites circa, say, 2004).

While this may be (or may have been) an appropriate analysis of the empirical deployment of computational media, it doesn't begin to tap the potential that the computer holds for fundamentally remapping our experience of space and time (see Hansen 2004). Taking stock of the expansive role played by computational processes in creating the infrastructure for experience today, it becomes difficult to ignore the reality that we depend on regimes of technical mediation, what geographer Nigel Thrift has called the "technological unconscious," that not only exceed our attention but remain fundamentally unfathomable by us. Put another way, the forms of media—visual, aural, tactile—through which we interface with our informational universe are no longer homologous with the actual materialites, the temporal fluxes, that they mediate. While these media forms may still adequately capture the flux of our experience (although recent studies in the fine-scale temporal processes of cognition suggest that they may not), they, like the experiences they inscribe, are only indirectly coupled to the underlying computational processes supporting them. In light of the disjunction of technics and media, we must differentiate and hold separate two distinct functions of media: on one hand, to exteriorize human experience in durable, repeatable, and hence transmissible form; on the other, to mediate for human experience the non- (or proto-) phenomenological, fine-scale temporal computational processes that increasingly make up the infrastructure conditioning all experience in our world today. What is mediated in both cases is, to be sure, human experience, but according to two distinct programs: for whereas media in the first, traditional sense mediates human experience itself (its content is that experience), media in the second sense mediates the technical conditions that make possible such experience—the "transcendental technicity" underlying real experience in our world today.

What has been termed Web 2.0—a blanket term encompassing the host of social networking sites and collectively produced archives (wikis) that developed in the wake of the dot-com crash of 2001—perfectly illustrates this bifurcation in the function of media, and in the process demonstrates the thoroughly social and collective dimension of "transcendental technicity." By taking full advantage of the many-to-many connectivity facilitated by the Internet, the explosion of user-generated digital "content" (blogs, discussion forums, photo-sharing, video animation, and so on) has refocused the function of computational media from storage to production, from the archiving of individual experience to the generation of collective presence and of connectivity itself. By now (2009), this refocusing has itself been commodified by a myriad of companies created to host this content, including platforms like MySpace, Flickr, Facebook, and YouTube. As attested by the massive popularity of these and similar social networking sites, what is mediated by Web 2.0 is less the content that users upload than the sheer connectivity, the simple capacity to reach myriad like-minded users, that is afforded by that act of uploading content. What is mediated here, in other words, is the technical capacity to connect on a massive, many-to-many scale, which is to say (although this dimension need not, and perhaps rarely does, come to the fore), the entire computational system that facilitates this new scale of connectivity. This is a truly McLuhanesque moment in the precise sense that, over and above any content that happens to be transmitted, what is involved in Web 2.0 is a widespread mediatic regime change—nothing less, I would suggest, than a change in the vocation of media and mediation themselves.

If new media can be held to be "new" in a new way—if digital computational media are distinctive in a qualitatively different sense than were all previous forms of media at the moment of their introduction—it is precisely because of this new vocation assumed by media in the age of networked computation. In addition to storing experience, as it has always done, media today mediates the conditions of mediation, which is to say, it brokers the experiential impact of the new computational networks that comprise today's "technological unconscious." Beyond mediating individual users' stored experience, the transmission of media—of photos on Flickr or videos on YouTube—itself mediates the situation of the user in the regime of networked computation. It mediates, in short, the new capacities for making contact that individuals acquire simply by distributing (traces of) themselves on many-to-many computational networks. To the extent that commercialized Web 2.0 technologies channel this impact exclusively toward the ends of human social networking, the "total" significance of this bifurcation, of this new vocation of media, remains obscured. For the basic reality is that the "social" or networked transmission of media by Web 2.0 sites is built atop a technical infrastructure that is and must be structurally dissociated from the form of that media. The experiences afforded by social media sites are made possible on the basis of a technical logic that operates at a temporal scale far finer than that of human sense perception (and its mediation) and with a level of complexity that defies capture in the form of (traditional) media. That the fundamental disjunction between media output and technical basis can be (and has been) sutured bears witness, as Kittler has astutely noted, to the power of economics: Web 2.0 perfectly expresses the reality that money can be made by using computation to offer connectivity. With this in mind, perhaps we could say that the commercialized Web 2.0 technologies operate precisely by collapsing the dissociation between media and technics: they give us a new functionality—massive connectivity—by transmitting familiar media forms *in ways that avoid drawing attention to* the new "transcendental technicity" of computational networks.

That a new technicity is nonetheless at stake in social media appears obliquely here to the precise extent that connectivity emerges as an end in itself, distinct from the actual sharing of the (traditional) media content transmitted in these networks. This disjunction of connectivity from the sharing of content provides evidence of some minimal embrace of the technical logic underlying Web 2.0 as the ground for human experience. Indeed, to the extent that massive connectivity is a new capacity for human beings, its emergence here attests to our willingness to let our experience be organized in ways that cut against the grain of what we've known hitherto and, specifically, of the function of those media forms we have developed up to this point in our history. Given the tension that exists between such emergence and the commercial profitability of social media, it is fitting that one key source of insight into the revolutionary promise of Web 2.0's technical logic would come by way of aesthetic transformations of paradigmatic social media sites. An exemplary series of such transformations can be found in artist Mario Klingemann's Flickr.com–based works: *Flickeur*, *Clockr*, *Tagnautica*, *Picturedisco*, *Islands of Consciousness*, and *The Stake*. Despite their differences, all of these works involve an effort to exploit for aesthetic ends the technical processes of massive-scale data organization and retrieval that underlie social media sites. In so doing, these works raise the possibility that the new vocation of media—to mediate our indirect relation with computational networks—might in fact go hand in hand with a new aesthetics of experience.

The first of Klingemann's transformations, *Flickeur* is, as its name hints, a voyeuristic appropriation of the photo-sharing site Flickr.com. When loaded onto a browser, *Flickeur* grabs images randomly from Flickr and strings them together using randomly selected transitions from the grammar of cinema (fade-ins and -outs, pans, jump cuts, etc.) to the accompaniment a looping soundtrack. What results, as *Flickeur* continues to grab new images, is an "infinite" film that, in addition to being open onto the indeterminate future, has no internal principle of composition. The principle governing the images' selection is not the aesthetics of the human audiovisual flux (as is the case with cinema and all previous audiovisual media) but rather the capacities embedded in the computational algorithms themselves. What the human viewer encounters is, accordingly, less an internally coherent sequence than a proliferating series of discrete audiovisual events, bounded by the temporal cycling of the computer networks carrying out Klingemann's algorithms for image selection and combination. The work does not yield any stable objects and indeed, *every instance is unique*: if two computers download the site simultaneously, they will grab different images and assemble them in different ways. In the place of the linear, cinematic flux of images, *Flickeur* engages a virtual matrix of potential image combinations that will never come close to being completely actualized, no matter how many users download the site at any given time.

The work's aesthetic interest does not lie in its ordering of images; discrete juxtapositions may be startling or otherwise interesting juxtapositions, but the flux is by no means cinematic. What does become interesting, however, is the way in which the work mediates for the human perceiver the technical logic of computational networks: these discrete, randomly associated images (random, that is, from our perspective) furnish aesthetic analogs of discrete computational processes and thereby give some degree of experiential, aesthetic access to the technical logic of computation. In this way, *Flickeur* exposes what remains obscure in the predominant use of social networking sites for sharing media and connecting with other users: namely, the fact that the underlying organizational principles are anything but homologous with the associational networks of human cognition. But *Flickeur*—and this is what makes it exemplary—does more than simply expose a technicist logic; it takes seriously the idea that this logic could have affirmative aesthetic consequences. Thus at the same time that the aesthetic experience afforded by *Flickeur* mediates the technical processes that produce its random image transitions, the work also asks whether the technicist organization of information might not furnish new, specifically *noncinematic* principles for experiential synthesis. Taken seriously, *Flickeur* calls on us to ask what it would be like to live time, and the aesthetic content that necessarily fills time, from the standpoint of its discreteness.

In this way, *Flickeur* argues against any move to identify media (and mediation) narrowly with the technical. Far from being a direct consequence of a specific technology (networked computation), the medium that is *Flickeur* is an invention on the basis of a new technical "automatism" (Stanley Cavell). And while the specific materiality of the latter's technical logic is central here, what makes it a medium is the interface of this logic with human aesthetic experience. Nonetheless, there does seem to be something *new* involved in this media invention, which is precisely the opening of human experience to a form of storage and transmission that occurs in a form of embodiment (networked computation) and at a level of temporal processing radically discontinuous with human embodiment and the temporal range characteristic of media. So perhaps "new media," far from designating either one more new medium or some blanket postmedium condition, should be thought of as an expression for this newness, which is to say, an expression that indexes the changing vocation of media itself. Not simply the direct, *technical* consequence of digital computation, new media nonetheless concerns what is new about the widespread role of computation in our world: new technicist logics of informational organization that might also prove fruitful for our self-understanding and our understanding of (the role of) media. From this standpoint, the sheer breadth of what falls under the term "new media" might begin to make sense. And so too might the retreat from an effort to find a technical core for each new medium. For if "new media" today

names a range of contemporary technical, aesthetic, and social developments, what holds them all together is not a common technical basis so
much as an effort to interface the technicist logic of computation with
human experience. Isn't this, ultimately, why new media can encompass
new inflections of mass media (the Net and the blogosphere, transformations in the form and transmission of the news), new gadgets (iPods,
digital television, Web-accessible cellular phones, GPS instruments), and
new experiments with the effects of these inflections and gadgets on the
senses, emotions, and perceptual, social, and imaginary experience (artworks, new forms of community, transitory and highly responsive political affiliations, cultural metaphors)?

What is *new* here is new in a different sense from the newness that
accompanied prior media upon their introduction. To see this, we need
only invoke German media theorist Wolfgang Ernst's discussion of computer emulation of other media, and specifically the example of Erich
von Hornbostel's Berliner Phonogramm-Archiv, whose collection of wax-
cylinder recordings of peoples threatened by extinction can be experienced by us today only because of the computer, or more specifically,
because of endoscopic recording devices that can "read" the wax sound
traces graphically, "re-translating them into audible sound by algorithmically transforming visual data into sound." A lost "old new medium" is
thus revivified precisely because of the computer's difference from older
media, which is to say, its indifference to the aesthetic and medial differences between audio and visual data; it is, specifically, this indifference
to medial difference that allows the digital computer to emulate one interface through another. Again, we see clearly how media and mediation have changed vocation; no longer directed primarily toward or operating primarily at the level of human sense experience, the computer's
emulation of Hornbostel's wax-cylinder recordings quite literally mediates an old new medium. That it emulates it for our sense perception,
however, announces the noncontingent role of the human. Indeed, the
interface to human experience is precisely what—notwithstanding its
materialist indifference to medial differences— makes it media in the
first place.

References and Suggested Readings

Derrida, Jacques. 1998. *Of Grammatology*, trans. G. Spivak. Baltimore: Johns Hopkins University Press.
Eisenstein, Elizabeth. 1979. *The Printing Press as an Agent of Change*. Cambridge: Cambridge University Press.
Ernst, Wolfgang. 2006. "Dis/continuities: Does the Archive Become Metaphorical in Multi-

Media Space?" In *New Media/Old Media: A History and Theory Reader*, ed. W. Chun and T. Keenan, 105–24. New York: Routledge.

Hansen, Mark. 2004. *New Philosophy for New Media*. Cambridge, MA: MIT Press.

Kittler, Friedrich. 1999. *Gramophone, Film, Typewriter*, trans. G. Winthrop-Young and M. Wutz. Stanford, CA: Stanford University Press.

Klingemann, Mario. "Quasimondo." http://www.quasimondo.com.

Manovich, Lev. 2002. *The Language of New Media*. Cambridge, MA: MIT Press.

McLuhan, Marshall. 1994. *Understanding Media: the Extensions of Man*, ed. L. H. Lapham. Cambridge, MA: MIT Press.

Plato. 2005. *Phaedrus*, trans. C. Rowe. New York: Penguin.

Stiegler, Bernard. 1998. *Technics and Time*. Vol. 1, *The Fault of Epimetheus*, trans. R. Beardsworth and G. Collins. Stanford: Stanford University Press.

———. 2002. "Derrida and Technology: Fidelity at the Limits of Deconstruction and the Prosthesis of Faith." In *Derrida and the Humanities: A Critical Reader*, 238–70. Cambridge: Cambridge University Press.

13 :: HARDWARE/ SOFTWARE/WETWARE

GEOFFREY WINTHROP-YOUNG

Things of Theory

Computers are puzzling things. Admittedly, *thing* is not a very inspired term for such an impressive—well, what?—tool? machine? medium? None of the labels fit. The computer is not a tool because that term implies a context-oriented handiness or Heideggerian *Zuhandenheit* that is said to be at odds with the computer's versatility. Neither can computers be called machines, unless the term is preceded by a qualifier such as "nonlinear" or "nontrivial." Computers do not rely exclusively on history-independent, linear operations to produce completely predictable results; rather, they use recursive routines to present previously unknown information. And—to anticipate a point we shall return to—it is highly questionable whether a computer is a medium, given the ways in which it violates, annuls, or supersedes notions of communication, remediation, and intermediality that are presupposed by most conventional definitions of medium.

The computer's unwillingness to submit to customary conceptual frameworks is exacerbated by its seamless integration into everyday life. Computers are so puzzling precisely because they are so compliant. Like all other media (in this particular context, the label fits), computers are most powerful when least noticed; and they are least noticed when most empowering. In his optimistically titled *Understanding Media*, Marshall McLuhan linked human narcissism to media-induced narcosis: Media that appear to directly extend our body and mind serve to mirror us in comforting, narcotic ways that can only be dispelled by what appears to be an import into media theory of notions of defamiliarization, *ostranenie*, and *Verfremdung* first developed in the context of artistic innovation. No wonder, then, that a lot of contemporary media theory is as much about understanding computers as it is about understanding why exactly we have to understand them, and no wonder that many approaches (including McLuhan's) originated in literary scholarship. The issues, no doubt, are crucially important. In what ways does the computer redraw the boundaries between humans and technology? How do digital machines impact individual agency and social structure? How and why do they affect media-theoretical concepts such as communication, information, materiality, body, image, and writing? In short, what new conceptual frameworks does media theory have to develop in order to integrate the computer? All these questions, however, presuppose that media theory is a sufficiently well-established body of work to be capable of evaluating and integrating the digital newcomer, even if it involves changing fundamental media-theoretical assumptions. But was there really media theory before the computer? In a strictly institutional sense, no. Universities did not offer courses in "media studies" or "media theory" until quite recently; indeed, it may well have been the introduction of affordable personal computers and the concomitant explosion of the private software sector in the 1980s that triggered the institutionalization of media theory. The automatic response, of course, is to point out that media theory was around much earlier, if under different names. Surely, most of the canonical founding documents of modern media theory—from Walter Benjamin's essay on mechanical reproduction and the "Fragments on the Culture Industry" in Horkheimer and Adorno's *Dialectics of Enlightenment* to key texts from prewar U.S. communications studies and the work of Harold Innis—predate the first working computers. But at the risk of imputing a teleological perspective to media theory (as if it had since its inception been headed toward the computer), it is worth pointing that a number of important features later implemented by the computer were haunting early media theory.

Media theory arose from the growing preoccupation with the technological, aesthetic, and social impact of new storage and communications technologies, which from the very beginning involved a sustained attention to the estrangement of human experience and sense perception by technology. The exploration of technologies and of the psychic apparatus went hand in hand, frequently involving mutual mapping procedures in which media were modeled on senses and vice versa. If dates must be assigned, the crucial time period would have to be the 1920s, when widespread literary, essayistic, or anecdotal accounts gradually crystallized into the first attempts to provide a theoretical framework for the new media, with basic key terms, analytic propositions, and at least a rudimentary degree of historical perspective. There are many ways of classifying the various strands of media theory, depending on place of origin, technological focus, ideological indebtedness, disciplinary background, and so on, but one of the most basic and fruitful distinctions is to plot two trajectories that dominated the field from the outset: a bias toward *communication* and a bias toward *mediality*. The former was especially prominent in the United States. Its basic aspiration is best summarized by the motto of the U.S. Signal Corps: Get the Message Through (see Schüttpelz 2005). Ultimately, it was less concerned with analyzing the specific medial qualities of a given channel than with evaluating and designing procedures that would facilitate desirable (or impede undesirable) communications. In many ways its culmination was Claude Shannon's mathematical theory of communication with its rigorous abstraction from the particular qualities of distinct media. And this is precisely what the computer performs on a technological level. Shannon's communication theory is as much a "universal" theory as the computer is, in Alan Turing's sense, a "universal" machine. The former's mathematical apparatus corresponds to an *über*-medium that implements the underlying bias of communications-oriented media theory (see chapter 11, "Information").[1]

The focus on mediality was more prominently developed in Continental and Canadian media theory. Its quintessential maxim, Marshall McLuhan's mantra "the medium is the message," marks the culmination of a longstanding interest in the analysis of how individual media technologies operate. As is often the case with McLuhan, the seemingly most trivial proposals are the most important. Obviously, the focus on the distinctive features of any one media technology can only take place against a background of other medial experiences. Mediality is always already intermediality. As a result, one of the overriding trends of this bias in media theory has been to make explicit the underlying intermedial premises—be it by carefully probing the commonalities that allow for intermedial distinctions in the first place, or by more actively arguing for a (re)integration of differing media formats. McLuhan's focus on the synthesis of fractured media and senses in the new electronic universe is the most prominent example of the latter. But earlier theories were already pointing in that direction: Benjamin's emphasis on reproducibility and the destruction of an alleged aura, Horkheimer and Adorno's grim reflection on standardization, and Innis's utopian vista of a socially beneficial balance between time- and space-biased technologies are early attempts to organize a diverse media ecology around general media-based features and effects—all of them pointing toward an attempt to delineate general media ontologies that straddle intermedial divides. This, too, brings to mind the computer. In the case of the computer, however, it is not a matter of one technology remediating another. The computer tells us something about the construction of *all* the media formats it simulates. And this is at the core of the problems mentioned at the outset. It is one thing to conceptualize one new media technology; it is something altogether different to conceptualize a technology that is recasting all its predecessors, especially if the latter were already pointing toward it before it was fully realized. Every new media technology rewrites the history of its predecessor, but the computer is on the verge of rewriting the entire history of media technology—and hence of media theory (see chapter 12, "New Media"). In order to shed some light on these vexing issues, it is helpful to reverse Occam's razor and increase rather than reduce the number of words and things by replacing *computer* with *hardware*, *software*, and *wetware*.

A Troublesome Trinity

What is software? The *Computer Desktop Encyclopedia* defines it as "instructions for the computer." The *Dictionary of Information Technology* and the *Dictionary of Personal Computing and the Internet* specify that it comprises "any program or group of programs which instructs the hardware on how it should perform." The *American Heritage Dictionary* refers to "the program, routines, and symbolic languages that control the functioning of the hardware and direct its operation," while the *Oxford English Dictionary* speaks of "programs and procedures required to enable a computer to perform a specific task, as opposed to the physical components." The *Encyclopaedia Britannica*, surprisingly, gets straight to the point: "Software" denotes "instructions that tell a computer what to do." No matter how pithy, these definitions are far from innocent. Some center on the relation between *software and computer* while others focus on the binary comprising *software and hardware*. In the former case, software appears as immaterial agent that—to quote the *Random House Personal Computer Dictionary*—"has no substance" but sends out directions to "objects you can actually touch, like disks, disk drives, display screens, keyboards, printers, boards, and chips." It is not too difficult to discern echoes of the insubstantial entity called soul, mind, or consciousness and its relation to the corporeal entity it inhabits and animates. The computer/software binary restages the old boundary disputes between body and spirit. Definitions centered on the strictly relational aspects of the terms *hardware* and *software*, by contrast, appear better aligned with more recent notions of embodiment or embodied practices that endeavor to overcome the mind/body dualism by insisting that the performance and identity of (biological and electronic) agents emerge from the mutually constitutive interactions between no longer categorically differentiated corporeal and incorporeal components. Humans are not composed of an autonomous mind animating a reified body; they emerge from a sequence of context-specific *embodiments* in which mental and affective processes on the one hand and material and physiological conditions on the other shape each other (see Hayles 1999). As the *Computer Desktop Encyclopedia* states with military briskness: "In operation, a computer is both hardware and software. One is useless without the other. The hardware design specifies the commands it can follow, and the instructions tell it what to do."

The computer-related usage of the word *software* is commonly attributed to John W. Tukey (1915–2000). The word, of course, is older and not exclusively tied to the digital domain. Originating in the mid-nineteenth century, "software" first referred to woolen or cotton fabric and more generally to perishable consumer goods. In television slang it indicates program fillers such as cheap reruns. (No doubt the negative connotations inherent in this semantic spectrum, from fluffy fashion to broadcast fluff, are still at work in the more critical assessments of software products by particularly Puritan observers.) Tukey introduced the modern meaning in a 1958 issue of the *American Mathematical Monthly*: "Today the 'software' comprising the carefully planned interpretive routines, compilers, and other aspects of automotive programming are at least as important to the modern electronic calculator as its 'hardware' of tubes, transistors, wires, tapes and the like" (2). Note the blending of quaint grammar—"'software' . . . are"—with quaint technology (tubes, transistors, tapes) and the equally quaint assertion that software is "at least as" important as hardware. Initially, Tukey's term was an unstable neologism, a tentative terminological innovation used by a small in-group. Its rise to stable status and subsequent promotion to epistemological cliché (nowadays all kinds of coded or institutionalized forms of knowledge processing, from running Mesopotamian city-states to telling stories Hollywood-style, are known as "software") was no doubt fueled by the high profile and cultural cachet of increasingly specialized interactive applications that claim to provide consumers with powers of access, manipulation, computation, and presentation far exceeding the capabilities of older media. To be sure, nothing is easier than debunking computer hype. Probably only computers are powerful enough to calculate the number of promises they thus far have failed to keep, from the paperless office to sex with holograms. Yet even Luddites must admit that the combination of sufficiently strong storage power and sufficiently complex software design offers experiences of simulated immersion and mediated immediacy that come close to the dreams of complete immersion and pure immediacy that haunt the history of media and communication.

The flip side of the computer's wondrous compliance is the fact that all of these user-friendly applications are merely the most visible part of a bewildering edifice made up of control programs and operating systems that for the vast majority of users remain out of sight. An increasingly complex software architecture responsible for the functioning of the computer and its peripherals interposes itself between the user and the basic operation of the servile tool. To some critics, this discrepancy between empowerment and marginalization—I can do so much *with* the computer because I can do little *to* it—is the core issue of the human/machine relationship, and it serves to introduce our third term, which is as glib and flippant as it is problematic.

The term *wetware* is attributed to the writer-mathematician (and descendant of the philosopher Hegel) Rudy Rucker. Whether referring to the human brain (a.k.a. grayware), the human body (a.k.a. meatware), or any other feature of human physiology, "wetware" should—like hardware and software—be regarded as a strictly relational term: It constructs the human factor only insofar as it relates to computing. An underlying bias, however, appears to be that, in comparison to hardware and software, wetware is a somewhat dysfunctional component, first and foremost a source of error. The term is a tongue-in-cheek reminder that humans fall behind their digital technology, that they are too slow, too flesh-and-carbon-bound, too nonprogrammable to flourish in a world of clicks and codes. But things are more complex, for its precisely this obstinate inferiority that renders humans unique. In E. T. A. Hoffmann's famous story "The Sandman," the inhabitants of a small town in which a young woman has been exposed as a mindless automaton start behaving in erratic, impulsive fashion in order to prove that they are not artificial. By adopting behavior patterns that programmed hardware cannot emulate, they emphasize their idiosyncratic wetware features so as not to be mistaken for robots. Starting in the age of Romanticism it has been our nonlinear idiosyncrasy rather than—as the Enlightenment had decreed—our rationality and reasoning power (which is allegedly most fully realized in the computer) that emerges as humanity's distinguishing feature. Wetware, then, may be blatantly inferior, but some of its inferior aspects are—still—unattainable to hardware and software. Wetware designates human insufficiency but also marks the embattled area that the computer must yet master in order to render humans obsolete. The result will be something that exceeds both humans and computers because it retains and rejects elements of both. In short, wetware is—to activate a sleeper term that went into hiding a few decades ago—a truly dialectical concept.

Ultimately, hardware/software/wetware is a troublesome trinity with limited critical purchase. The three terms originiated at different times, they operate on different levels, and they reveal different attitudes of seriousness. When scrutinized more closely, the neat tripartition gives way to mutual disdain. As we shall see, the relationship between hardware and software, in particular, brings to mind the image of porcupines in winter: In order to avoid freezing they must move together, but they can only do so at the risk of impaling each other. It is precisely this fractious boundary dispute that will allow to us to revisit and further investigate the questions posed at the beginning.

No Software. No Hardware. And Ultimately No Media?

Let us return to the blissful ignorance of computer-attached wetware. As some of the more disgruntled experts keep emphasizing, very few users make full use of their computers (another parallel, it seems, between the computer and the human brain). As long as our PC does what it promises to do, we are content to contract out the exploration of its technological and aesthetic mysteries to engineers and artists. And why not? Why should the average driver study the intricacies of the combustion engine when there are qualified mechanics? This mixture of obliviousness and trust in specialization was at the core of the famous streetcar example in Max Weber's "Science as a Vocation," which linked modernity's disenchantment of the world to potential explainability rather than to actual explainedness:

> Unless he is a physicist, one who rides on the streetcar has no idea how the car happened to get into motion. And he does not need to know. He is satisfied that he may "count" on the behavior of the streetcar, and he orients his conduct according to this expectation; but he knows nothing about what it takes to produce such a car so that it can move. . . . The increasing intellectualization and rationalization do not, therefore, indicate an increased and general knowledge of the conditions under which one lives. It means something else, namely, the knowledge or belief that if one but wished one *could* learn it at any time. Hence, it means that principally there are no mysterious incalculable forces that come into play, but rather that one can, in principle, master all things by calculation. This means that the world is disenchanted. (Weber 1994, 286)

Of course there are a number of differences between a streetcar and a computer. We do not ask the streetcar itself how it operates. Inquiries about computers, however, are increasingly addressed to computers. More importantly, while we may wonder how a streetcar operates there is no doubt that this act of moving itself and its load from A to B is its principal intended function. In the case of the multifunctional computer, however, it is more difficult to come up with the right question. More than any other technological accomplishment, the computer supports the charge articulated by Günther Anders, Martin Heidegger's most irascible student, that technological advances have turned us into "inverted utopians." A utopian conceives of more than the world is currently capable of, and that, Anders argues, is precisely what we are no longer capable of: "While utopians cannot produce what they imagine, we can no longer imagine what we produce" (Anders 1981, 96). It is not a matter of not knowing how a computer works but of not even grasping what it could do because its capabilities outstrip our imagination.

Yet amid all this apocalyptic technophobia, computers are still predominantly viewed as compliant tools or human extensions that perform at our beck and call. But—to draw upon the work of Friedrich Kittler—this is a delusion perpetuated by software. To be sure, this take on hardware/software is as problematic as it is extreme, but in the case of the computer the road to wisdom may well be paved with exaggerations. Kittler's main thesis is already contained in the title of his notorious essay, "There Is No Software" (1997, 147–55). All software operations, he asserts, can be reduced to basic hardware operations:

> Not only no program, but also no underlying microprocessor system could ever start without the rather incredible autobooting faculty of some elementary functions that, for safety's sake, are burnt into silicon and thus form part of the hardware. . . . Any transformation from entropy into information, from a million sleeping transistors into differences between electronic potentials, necessarily presupposes a material event called reset. . . . All code operations . . . come down to absolutely local string manipulations, that is, I am afraid, *to signifiers of voltage differences.* (150; emphasis in original)

As with the straightforward definitions quoted above, this reduction of software to hardware is rife with older boundary conflicts. Kittler is debunking software in much the same way as nineteenth-century science pried apart the human mind by examining how the brain works. Ultimately, there is no software for the same reason that there is no higher faculty known as mind or spirit: Both are no more than fleeting configurations that can be reduced to the switching on and off of countless tiny circuits routed through hollow containers made of tin, bone, or plastic.

But much to Kittler's chagrin, the fact that this "postmodern Tower of Babel" is at base a hardware configuration has been "explicitly contrived to evade our perception" (1997, 148). This is where the argument moves from technological reductionism to a technologically evolved version of ideology criticism. Operating systems, especially those that with names like Windows promise unobstructed transparency, are in fact one-way mirrors. Like invisible police investigators examining a suspect, the computer sees us; looking at the computer, we only see ourselves. We are, quite literally, screened off from our computers. The result of our software's ability to "to understand our desires, to anticipate our needs, to foresee consequences, to make connections, to handle routine chores without being asked, to remind us of what we ought to be reminded of while filtering out noise" (Stephenson 62), is to perpetuate our self-understanding as masters of our machines. Tool-faking computers allow their users to see themselves as their tool-making masters, that is, as humans. "Through the use of keywords like user-interface, user-friendliness or even data projection, the industry has damned humanity to remain human" (Kittler 1997, 157). And just as the definitions quoted above still bear the scars of the ongoing psychophysical boundary conflicts between materiality and spirituality, this type of software critique reverberates with old political struggles: Software is condemned as the new opium for the people; it is dispensed by forces that are bent on keeping the untrusted user masses from taking over the digital means of production. (Microsoft, in other words, is behaving much like the old Catholic church when it was bent on preventing its flock from gaining direct access to its holy texts). Hence we should discard those fancy operating systems and resort to the text-based teletype interface that prevailed in the early days of computing. While this will not result in any mastery over digital machines, it will ensure that our interactions with the supermedium take place on the computer's basic operating level. At least we will be eye to eye (or signal to signal) with that which is on the verge of leaving us behind.

So totalizing is this argument that it can easily be turned on its head. Consider, once again, the popular notion that media history is essentially a sequence a remediations in the course of which an old medium becomes the content of a new one. As already mentioned, digital technology supercharges this remediation effect because it involves universal machines capable of simulating all of their predecessors. But as Arjen Mulder points out, media do not merely remediate, they hybridize the old and the new into something unprecedented. And this is crucial for the emulation practices of the computer:

> Emulation is the translation of hardware into software. Emulation makes it possible to run not only very old and yet-to-be-developed PC programs on the average computer . . . —in short, all the hardware of every time and everything it ever was, and will be capable of doing. Because the entire digital universe is made up of ones and zeros, it can be called forth on a single machine. The fact that there are different types of hardware

is an expression of the economic boundaries between the different computer companies. These economic boundaries are a consequence not of the traits of the computer medium but of historical circumstances. (Mulder 2006, 295)

By collapsing all digital operations into "signifiers of voltage differences" Kittler collapses software into hardware; by emphasizing that the digital universe is made up of ones and zeros, Mulder demotes hardware to secondary status. But regardless of whether the emphasis is on electrophysical properties or on the basic code of flickering signifiers, the end result is to move *beyond media*. For theorists like Kittler, the fact that any medium can be translated into another because formerly distinct data streams (sights, sounds, and word) have been converted into digitized numbers, signals that the concept of medium has become obsolete. "With numbers, everything goes. Modulation, transformation, synchronization; delay, storage, transposition; scrambling, scanning, mapping— a total media link on a digital basis will erase the very concept of medium." (Kittler 1999, 2). For theorists like Mulder, the fact that everything can be converted into software leads to the very same conclusion: "If it is true that even a computer's hardware can be converted into software, and other 'media' remediated on computers are nothing more than software packages, then there is no longer any point in speaking of media when we talk about computers." (296). We are left with a vexing conclusion: If the computer was indeed inscribed into the beginnings of media theory, then we are dealing with a body of theory that grew out of the anticipation of that which renders its object obsolete. No wonder then, that those who voice such diagnoses are in search of alternate research programs. No longer calling himself a "media theorist," Kittler has moved into a Heidegger-inspired history of the alphanumerical codes, while Mulder claims that "what the computer age needs is a unified software theory. That is beyond the reach of media theory." (296)

Postscript: Giving Humans a Hand

Yes, at least in the eyes of theorists computers are indeed very puzzling things. The term, incidentally, is less sloppy than it appears. From Martin Heidegger to Bruno Latour, philosophers have delighted in teasing out the fact that *thing/Ding* originally (as in the Icelandic *Allthing*) referred to a gathering or coming-together (see Latour 2005). The remarkable semantic migration from gathering to that which is discussed and contested at a gathering and, finally, to generic object is, quite literally, a reification: turning something living—something that brought together and divided—into an inanimate object removed from the subject. And that, of course, is the basic paradigm underlying most conceptualizations of technology, including media technology. But whether we assume that technology is an assortment of tools, from choppers to chips, manufactured by humans, or inverting the power relationship, that humans have lost control and are being ousted by their former machine slaves, we continue to see humans and technology as completely separate entities. This, ultimately, is an artifactual fallacy that falls short of evolutionary insights. Take the most obvious example: It is highly doubtful that humans *first* developed basic traits such as articulated speech, opposable thumbs, bipedalism, and the ability to consciously plan their interactions with their environment, and *then* started making tools. Rather, as André Leroi-Gourhan has argued, an ongoing feedback between changing bodies and changing artifacts freed the mouth, righted the posture, and refunctionalized the hand. Humans, then, are neither tool makers nor made by tools. Literally and metaphorically, emerging technologies gave emerging humans a hand.[2] Just as there was no fully developed media theory before (or without) the computer, there was no fully developed human before (or without) technology.

Indeed, some of the most interesting recent media-theoretical advances—by Bernard Stiegler in France, Mark Hansen in the United States, Frank Hartmann in Austria—have taken their cue either from Leroi-Gourhan, Heidegger, or Ernst Kapp (the still frequently misunderstood originator of the organ projection hypothesis) and have focused on technology as an "ontological condition of humanization" (Hansen 2006, 300). Just as the institutionalization of media theory was triggered by the dissemination of digital technology, these new adventures in theory grow out of the amazement over the ongoing internalization of the computer, the ontologically unruly cross between machine and environment that gathers or wires together props, programs, and people.

The most up-to-date technology, then, has become instrumental in highlighting the originary coupling of humans and technology. But how could it do so? Look, for example, at the way in which the computer is implicit in recent elaborations of one our alpha-terms, communication. It is no coincidence that the rise of the computer parallels the rise of system theory, the more advanced variants of which claim that consciousness is a psychic system that does not simply accept incoming messages. Rather, it processes external stimulations strictly on its own, internal terms; and it is precisely this closing-off that allows for the emergence of high internal complexity. There is no direct communication between minds (see chapter 9, "Communication"). Similarly, the computer is such an extremely powerful "tool" precisely because it closes itself off from its user, though it has evolved extensive software features that allow users to believe communication is still going on.[3] To misapply psychological terms, the computer is both very social and irredeemably autistic—fitting for our age. But it is not enough to say that human communication is modeled on the computer. The computer also exteriorizes and participates in the ongoing evolution of communication in much the same way as primeval tools both externalized and shaped human body dynamics. The computer, then, is simultaneously model, external structure, and an integral part of our evolution, and the boundary conflicts between hardware, software, and wetware are both indicative of, and complicit in, the constant reshaping of the fluid boundaries between technological properties, signifying practices, and human bodies, none of which predated the shifting alignments between the three. Media theory, finally, will have to realize the extent to which it has been itself inscribed by this coevolution of humans and machines.

Notes

1. Alan Turing's 1937 paper "On Computable Numbers with an Application to the Entscheidungsproblem," in which he worked out the mathematical details of a universal computing machine that could simulate the workings of all other machines, illustrates the degree to which the computer, more than any other "media" technology, is preceded by theory. Turing's paper amounts to nothing less than an inversion of Cato the Elder's proverb *rem tene, verba sequentur*—stick to things, the words will follow. Its motto, if summarized in Latin, would be *numeros tene, res sequentur*—stick to numbers and (all) things will follow.

2. A note of warning: Stressing the coevolution of humans and technics does not automatically invalidate the grim vision of human subjection to technology. One can well argue for the orginary part technology played in human technogenesis and then, as Kittler sometimes does, paint a techno-Hegelian scenario in which humans—that is, always already technologized humans—were just a temporary aide, discardable skyhooks in the growth of transhuman macrostructures (on this trans-, post-, and allegedly antihumanist scenario, see Winthrop-Young 2006).

3. The basic idea is not new. It was first spelled out by the philosopher Leibniz, who—not coincidentally—introduced the binary system while indulging in diplomatic activism to enhance communication in a Europe torn apart by wars and confessions. Leibniz spoke of monads that do not interact or even causally affect each other. The fact that we nonetheless seem to do so Leibniz attributed to a preestablished harmony: God has programmed the monads to act thus. Michael Heim updated this idea by comparing monads to computer terminals: We are completely shut off from each other and experience the world and its incoming messages only in terms of how they are represented on our screen. God is the "Central System Operator (sysop), who harmonizes all the infinite monadic units"; without him, "no one could get online to reality" (1993, 99). In other words, preestablished harmony is guaranteed by basic network software. Much like the nineteenth-century ether, network software is an indispensable prerequisite for communication, a pseudomaterial substance that facilitates the cause and effect of mutual exchange.

References and Suggested Readings

Agar, Jon. 2003. *The Government Machine: A Revolutionary History of the Computer*. Cambridge, MA: MIT Press.

Anders, Günther. 1981. *Die atomare Drohung: Radikale Überlegungen*. Munich: Beck.

Brooks, Frederick P. 1995. *The Mythical Man-Month: Essays on Software Engineering*. Reading: Addison-Wesley.

Campbell-Kelly, Martin. 2003. *From Airline Reservations to Sonic the Hedgehog: A History of the Software Industry*. Cambridge, MA: MIT Press.

Ceruzzi, Paul E. 2004. *A History of Modern Computing*. Cambridge, MA: MIT Press.

Doyle, Richard. 2003. *Wetwares: Experiments in Postvital Living*. Minneapolis: University of Minnesota Press.

Hansen, Mark B. N. 2006. "Media Theory." *Theory, Culture and Society* 23, nos. 2–3: 297–306.

Hayles, N. Katherine. 1999. *How We Became Posthuman: Virtual Bodies in Cybernetics, Literature, and Informatics*. Chicago: University of Chicago Press.

Heim, Michael. 1993. *The Metaphysics of Virtual Reality*. New York: Oxford University Press.

Kittler, Friedrich. 1997. *Literature, Media, Information Systems*, ed. John Johnston. Amsterdam: Overseas Publishers Association.

———. 1999. *Gramophone, Film, Typewriter*. Stanford, CA: Stanford University Press.

Latour, Bruno. 2005. "From Realpolitik to Dingpolitik." In *Making Things Public: Atmospheres of Democracy*, ed. Bruno Latour and Peter Weibel. Cambridge, MA: MIT Press.

Mulder, Arjen. 2006. "Media." *Theory, Culture and Society* 23, nos. 1–2: 289–96.

Parikka, Jussi. 2007. *Digital Contagions: A Media Archaeology of Computer Viruses*. New York: Peter Lang.

Schüttpelz, Erhard. 2005. "Von der Kommunikation zu den Medien/In Krieg und Frieden (1943–1960)." In *Gelehrte Kommunikation. Wissenschaft und Medium zwischen dem 16. und 20. Jahrhundert*, ed. Jürgen Fohrmann, 483–552. Vienna: Böhlau.

Stephenson, Neal. 1999. *In the Beginning Was the Command Line*. New York: Avon.

Tukey, John W. 1958. "The Teaching of Concrete Mathematics." *American Mathematical Monthly* 65, no. 1: 1–9.

Weber, Max. 1994. "Science as a Vocation." In *Sociological Writings*, ed. Wolf Heydebrand, 276–303. New York: Continuum.

Winthrop-Young, Geoffrey. 2006. "Cultural Studies and German Media Theory." *New Cultural Studies: Adventures in Theory*, ed. Gary Hall and Clare Birchall, 88–104. Edinburgh: Edinburgh University Press.

14 :: TECHNOLOGY

JOHN JOHNSTON

Historians of technology typically distinguish between the simple machines known in antiquity (wheel, axle, lever, pulley, wedge, screw) and the power-driven machines that characterize modernity (windmill, turbine, steam and combustion engines). However, with the invention of the computer, a fundamentally new type of machine appeared. Whereas the two earlier types transmit force or energy, this third type processes information. But what exactly is "information," and what does "processing" it entail? For the first modern computers, built in the late 1940s and early 1950s, "information" meant numbers (or numerical data) and processing was basically calculation—what we today call "number crunching." These early computers were designed to replace the human computers (as they were called), who during World War II were mostly women calculating by hand the trajectories of artillery and bombs, laboring to break codes, and performing other computations necessary for highly technical warfare.

The popular press, however, was more farsighted and portrayed these new machines not as high-speed automatic calculators but "electronic brains." Indeed, with the development of electronic, stored-program computers (the first was ENIAC, which became operational just after the war), much more complex tasks could be performed, based on conditional instructions (if result = x, do A; if not, do B) and systematic searches of large databases. It was the stored program that gave this new machine its multifunctionality. Not surprisingly, the question of whether these electronic brains could "think" soon spawned a new science, artificial intelligence, largely inspired by programs like Herbert Simon and Alan Newell's Logic Theorist (1956), which could prove new theorems in symbolic logic. As computer technology rapidly developed, so did the functionality and applicability of the information these new machines were said to process. Having started off as a calculator, the computer first became a general symbol manipulator, and then—through rapid improvements in processing chips, circuit design, digital data storage, programming languages, and networking—a universal media machine in which "information" was any content expressible in a language of discrete elements that could be "processed" algorithmically, that is, in coded instructions that could be written, read, and carried out automatically by a machine.

Although the computer ushered in the Information Age, the term *information* was never restricted to these new machines. This is evident in its first significant use in the formulations of cybernetics and the first formal theory of communication, both developed just after World War II (see chapter 10, "Cybernetics"). In *Cybernetics, or Control and Communication in the Animal and the Machine* (1948), Norbert Wiener signals a critical shift in the understanding of the living organism, which in the nineteenth century was understood as "a heat engine" burning glucose, fats, and proteins. Wiener and his contemporaries realized that while the organic body "is very far from a conservative system" (1948, 42), extracting and expending a great deal of energy from and into the environment, the nervous system and organs responsible for the body's regulation actually require very little energy.

As Wiener puts it, "the bookkeeping which is most essential to describe their function is not one of energy" (42). Rather, it is accomplished by regulating the passage of information, like a vacuum tube does in an electronic circuit, from the body's sense organs to effectors that perform actions in the environment. Accordingly, "the newer study of automata [the central topic of cybernetics], whether in the metal or in the flesh, is a branch of communication engineering, and its cardinal notions are those of message, amount of disturbance or 'noise'—a term taken over from the telephone engineer—quantity of information, coding technique, and so on" (42). In short, both living creatures and the new machines operate primarily by means of self-control and regulation, which is achieved by means of the communication and feedback of electrochemical or electronic signals now referred to as information. As Wiener emphasizes, an important consequence is that the "theory of sensitive automata" (by which he means automata that receive sensory stimulation from the environment and transfer that information through the equivalent of a nervous system to effectors that perform actions) will have to be based on statistics:

We are scarcely ever interested in the performance of a communication-engineering machine for a single input. To function adequately, it must give a satisfactory performance for a whole class of inputs, and this means a statistically satisfactory performance for the class of input which it is statistically expected to receive. Thus its theory belongs to the Gibbsian statistical mechanics rather than to the classical Newtonian mechanics. (44)

Wiener's valorization of information in feedback circuits as a means of control and regulation was reinforced by Claude Shannon's quantitative theory of information, published in the same year as Wiener's *Cybernetics*.[1] Although intended to overcome engineering problems in electronic communications—specifically to reduce noise in telephone lines—Shannon's theory was a formal theory that could be applied to the communication of information in any medium. Like Wiener, Shannon defined information in statistical terms, explicitly basing his formula for the quantity of information transmitted in a message on Ludwig Boltzmann's famous formula for computing the entropy (or amount of randomness) in a thermodynamic system. Given the uncertainty of molecular states, Boltzmann proposed a measure based on their statistical distribution. He even thought of our incomplete knowledge of these states as "missing information." For Shannon, on the other hand, the uncertainty of a message depends on how much choice or freedom the sender has in selecting a particular message (or the set of symbols constituting a message). The greater the number of possible messages, the greater the uncertainty and hence the greater the amount of information contained in a single selected message or symbol. In addition to this initial uncertainty, there is also the uncertainty generated by the presence of "noise" in the communication channel. In Shannon's theory noise acquires a paradoxical complexity, since it appears to be both what impedes the transmission of information and what is not yet coded as information. Curiously, because of noise the amount of information received can be *greater* than the amount transmitted. This is simply because the received message is selected out of a greater set of possibilities than the transmitted message (see chapter 11, "Information").

This and other paradoxes notwithstanding, Shannon's theory was at bottom directed toward solving a very practical problem: How to encode a message in such a way that its transmission rate through a noisy channel (in bits per second) could be maximized and the error rate minimized. Using Boltzmann's formula to define the entropy both of an information source, or input to a communication channel, and of the received signal, or output, Shannon was able to give a very precise definition of "channel capacity": it is the maximum of the "mutual information" between source and receiver computed over the whole range of possible messages. Mutual information thus measures the reduction in the uncertainty that results from receiving a message from a sender (see Cover and Thomas 1991). On this basis, Shannon was able to establish a fundamental theorem for the maximum rate of symbol transmission for a particular channel. Previously it had been assumed that noise could be overcome simply by repeating the message or adding redundancies to the code, at an obvious cost in transmission capacity. Shannon's theorem demonstrated that, to the contrary, there were inherent, insurmountable limits. At the same time, it suggested unexpected ways to encode a message to take advantage of the statistical properties of a particular channel, resulting in a more efficient signal-to-noise ratio and pointing to more efficient methods of error detection and correction. Indeed, these discoveries are actually what made modern digital communications possible

To be sure, Shannon's elimination of meaning from the definition of information makes for difficulties when the idea of information is evoked in other contexts—as inevitably it is.[2] Even between Shannon and Wiener, differences of interpretation come into play; whereas for Shannon information measures the uncertainty or entropy of the message, for Wiener it measures a gain in certainty.[3] Wiener, therefore, considered information to be a measure of negative entropy, or "negentropy." This "positive" definition, as well as Wiener's emphasis on continuous (analog) rather than discrete (digital) modes of information transfer, may have reflected his greater interest in living organisms. In *The Human Use of Human Beings: Cybernetics and Society* (1950), a popular version of his theory of cybernetics, he explains how the process of cybernetic feedback made possible systems and forms of organization that ran counter to nature's statistical tendency to disorder and increasing entropy. Only in these pockets of negentropy, he argued, could something like biological life arise; indeed, it was precisely by regulating changes in a life-form's internal states and relationship with the environment that information processing made life possible. In 1953 Watson and Crick's discovery of how the DNA code functioned in the reproduction of life further extended and consolidated the application of information processing to biology, though dissenting biologists like Humberto Maturana and Francisco Varela (1980) would later contest its primacy in the definition and understanding of life.[4]

The parallel or even general equivalence postulated in cybernetics between natural and artificial (human-constructed) information processing machines has an interesting and complicated history. But from the perspective of the further development of what became standard computer technology, its importance quickly receded. Nevertheless, in what no longer seem to be peripheral developments—like neural networks as recognition devices, new computer-based sciences like artificial intelligence, artificial life, and bioinformatics, and interest in parallel processing and network models of distributed agents— instances of natural computation have played an essential role as a source of ideas, techniques, and models. For the moment, however, let us focus on the computer as a specific type of human-made machine, and take up biological models of information processing and computation—what we now think of as wetware— when they become necessary.

Curiously, the first modern computer was never built. It was an entirely abstract, hypothetical machine conceived in 1935 by the British mathematician Alan Turing as part of a proof about the computability of numbers. Of course, we might simply say that the Turing machine, as it came to be known, was the conceptual forerunner of the modern computer, except for the inconvenient fact that all modern computers *are* Turing machines. That is to say, they possess a central defining feature first captured by Turing's abstract machine: they are universally computational by virtue of their capacity to simulate any other computational machine. This singularity is worth examining in some detail.

Turing's foundational paper (1936) addresses the problem of computability—whether a number or function can be computed— and thus the larger question of whether a mathematical problem can be solved. Turing proposed that if the problem can be expressed as an algorithm, that is, a precise set of formal instructions for arriving at the specified solution, then it can be computed mechanically by a machine. The question then becomes: Is there any way to know in advance whether this machine will "halt" with a finite answer when instructed to compute a specific number or instead churn on endlessly? As Turing describes it, the machine would consist of three parts: a reading/writing "head," an infinitely long "tape" divided into square cells that passes through the head, and a table of instructions that tell the "head" what to do. The head would scan the tape square by square and, depending on the head's current "state" and whether a mark was present or absent in a particular square, either enter a mark, erase a mark, or leave the square as it is, then move to another square. Since at any moment the reading/writing head could be in only one of a finite number of internal "states" defined by the table of instructions (known as its state-transition table), it was considered to be a finite-state machine or automaton.[5]

With this simple device two things could be accomplished. Data could be entered in the form of a string of symbols—for example, binary numbers (one or zero) could be encoded as the presence or absence of the mark. And operations could be performed according to the table of instructions given to the head (for instance: if no mark, enter a mark and move to the square on the left; if a mark, move to the square on the right). These instructions and the memory constituted by the tape allow the head to manipulate the marks or symbols in various ways, thereby performing mathematical operations. However, what makes this finite-state machine a Turing machine is its auxiliary memory—the infinite tape—for it is this memory capacity that enables it to perform a range of different computations.[6] A simple finite-state machine, for example, cannot multiply large numbers, because it has no way to store and bring forward the results of previous stages of calculations as it advances. From this simple fact we can grasp the importance of memory—not only how much but from where (i.e., what "state") it can be accessed—in defining a machine's computational capacity.

Turing's thesis, subsequently accepted by virtually all mathematicians, states that every computation expressible as an algorithm, or every determinate procedure in a formal system, has its equivalent in a Turing machine. For complex computations these machines could be combined, the output of one becoming the input of another, and so on. More important, Turing further postulated the existence of a universal machine (now known as a Universal Turing Machine), which could emulate the behavior of any specific Turing machine. A universal computing machine would therefore be one that, given any table of instructions that defined a Turing machine, could carry out those instructions; it would, in short, be "programmable." Recall that Turing's ultimate objective was to prove that there is no way to determine in advance whether certain numbers *are* computable, that is, whether the machine set up to compute them will ever "halt." Invented as part of the proof, his notion of the Turing machine would eventually provide a formal basis for the modern computer, in which different sets of instructions or programs—for computation, data processing, sending and receiving data, and so on—allow the same machine to do a variety of tasks. Defined by a set of logical and mathematical functions rather than a material structure, the computer is thus a fundamentally new *type* of machine. It is an abstract, second-order machine in which the logical form of many different kinds of machines is abstracted and made equivalent to a set of algorithms.

Although today's desktop computers are usually made of silicon and copper wire encased in plastic and metal, in principle they could be constructed out of a wide variety of materials. As abstract machines, their functions are not defined by the behavior of the materials from which they are constructed; rather, this behavior is used to physically instantiate a symbol system that operates according to its own formal rules and syntax. Independent of its material substrate, a Turing machine, like information, is a technical abstraction; yet, also like information, it has applicability however it is instantiated. Ironically, perhaps, it was the inventor of information theory who discovered the most efficient way to materially implement the modern digital computer's most fundamental component: its logic circuits. Only a year after Turing's 1936 essay, Claude Shannon demonstrated in his master's degree essay that arrays of on-off switches in an electrical circuit could be used to instantiate all the operations of symbolic logic. While logic circuits can be and have been constructed out of gear assemblies, water pipes, and Tinker Toys, it turns out that minute electrical voltage differences carried on copper lines etched on silicon chips are by far the fastest and most efficient material instantiations.[7]

Not surprisingly, the efforts required to construct real material computers have been immense, involving extensive collaboration among large numbers of mathematicians, scientists, and engineers. One key story in this effort, the building of ENIAC and its successor EDVAC, is worth briefly repeating because of a conflict between "the engineers and the logicians" over issues of design and implementation that bears on the fundamental distinction between the early high-speed electronic calculators and the first fully modern computers.[8] Constructed between 1943 and 1946 at the Moore School of Electrical Engineering at the University of Pennsylvania, ENIAC occupied an entire large room. The logic circuits were built of some 17,500 vacuum tubes. Since these tubes would frequently burn out, one problem was how to keep them all going long enough to complete a computational cycle. Input was achieved with large stacks of IBM punch cards, and information was stored in long tubes filled with mercury called "delay lines." (Later these were replaced with magnetic drums.) Though the chief engineers, J. Presper Eckert and John Mauchly, had discussed the advantages of stored programs, they ultimately decided on a technological, rather than a logical, solution. Essentially, changing the setup so that ENIAC could perform different kinds of calculations entailed reconnecting hundreds of cables into large plugboards and resetting vast arrays of switches (which numbered over four thousand). In short, changing the "program" literally meant rewiring the computer. Furthermore, although ENIAC was a digital device it was modeled on the older differential analyzers, as the analog computers built in the 1930s were called. As a result, its arithmetic operations were still represented in decimal digits and required modules for conversion to binary notation.

In 1944 Herman Goldstine, a physicist and U.S. Army officer who was the government liaison for the project (ENIAC's primary purpose would be to calculate artillery firing tables), brought in the renowned mathematician John von Neumann as an adviser. Von Neumann had become very interested in computers as a consequence of his role as a science consultant in the building of weapons during the war, most notably the first atomic bomb at Los Alamos. His involvement in the project was greatly appreciated, especially his theoretical insights into ENIAC's limitations, which the group sought to rectify in its successor EDVAC. Without consulting the other members, however, in June 1945 von Neumann wrote and circulated the "First Draft of a Report on the EDVAC," in which he proposed a completely new design that became the standard for most computers built for the next fifty years. Known as the von Neumann architecture, it did not see any rivals until massively parallel processing computers began to appear in the 1990s.[9]

Like many of the engineers and technicians working on these early computational machines, Eckert and Mauchly hadn't read Turing's paper but simply saw the huge practical advantages of stored programs. Von Neumann, on the other hand, had known and worked with Turing and saw the stored program as a necessary aspect of a more tightly logical design modeled on Turing's concept of the universal machine. In addition, von Neumann's approach to computing was greatly informed by a keen interest in biological information processing. He was especially influenced by McCulloch and Pitts's paper on the computational properties of neurons in "neural nets," and he would later write a short book (unpublished in his lifetime) titled *The Computer and the Brain*.[10] In his paper on EDVAC von Neumann proposed that the new machine be comprised of five functional units: a central arithmetic unit (to perform the computations, based on Boolean algebra and using binary arithmetic), a logical control unit (to regulate the sequencing of the machine's operations), a storage unit (which von Neumann called "memory," to store all data and instructions), and finally, input and output units. These units, or "organs" as he sometimes called them, were to be connected by communicating pathways, later known as "buses," along which information—encoded as voltage differences in electrical current and thus easily represented in binary notation—would be communicated. The storing of data and program instructions in the same location (at different addresses, of course) was central to the design. First, it allowed for what is now called "random access memory" (RAM), which meant that any data or instructions stored in memory could be accessed from any point in a program. ("Stack" memory, in contrast, operates on a "last in, first out" principle.) But above all, storing data and instructions together made it possible to think of the relation between them in more fluid, relational terms: since programs were stored as data, it also became possible to think of programs that treat other programs *as* data. Programs could thus be made that process other programs or even themselves; indeed, programming itself became possible as a concept.

This concept inevitably brings us back to Turing's two core ideas: simulation and universality, which we now usually think about in terms of hardware and software. What makes a computer a universal machine is its ability to emulate any other Turing machine. That is, a computer is said to be universal or Turing equivalent if, given enough time and memory, it can perform any computation that a Turing machine can perform. The memory tape on Turing's original machine is infinitely long, and storage capacity on actualized Turing machines is assumed to be large and indefinitely extensible. In practice such a universal machine simply possesses a core instruction set and enough memory to be able to perform a core set of mathematical and logical functions.[11] What we think of as the computer is such a machine, but defined rather by its capacity to run any number of programs that do different things—word processors, spreadsheets and databases, games, e-mail programs, Internet browsers, accounting applications, and so on. These various software programs rely on a larger software program, the computer's operating system—Unix, Windows XP, Mac OS X and Linux are currently the most common—that in turn runs on the hardware "beneath." This layering tends to obscure the fact that hardware and software are mutually interdependent, doing what they do only thanks to each other. In fact, only at a fairly advanced stage of the computer's historical evolution did they begin to be developed separately (see chapter 13, "Hardware/Software/Wetware").

A strong incentive for development has been the bottleneck inherent in the von Neumann architecture, where information processing is performed by a central processing unit (CPU) in a step-by-step, linear fashion. First, a program is loaded into memory.[12] Then, in a series of carefully timed operations, instructions and the necessary data are brought to the processor, the computation performed, and the results stored in registers for the next operation or written to memory. This "fetch and execute" cycle was speeded up considerably by the development of "pipelining" techniques that cut down on the time the processor sits idle, waiting for new instructions or data, but the bottleneck itself could only be alleviated, mainly by building faster processors with increasingly large temporary memory "caches" located directly on the chip to reduce retrieval time. Memory also became larger and cheaper and the buses got faster. One fairly recent solution is the multicore processor, which divvies up the computational load among several subprocessing units. However, writing software that can break down the computational tasks in various software applications for different processors (which may either share memory or each possess its own memory) poses a variety of difficult problems. Nevertheless, the current trend in developing computer technology is to seek alternatives to the now sixty-year-old von Neumann architecture.

Von Neumann himself was, of course, aware of the most obvious alternative model: the human brain itself, in which billions of neurons in elaborate networks process many information streams simultaneously in a massively parallel manner. Again, however, because of the difficulty writing the software, very few parallel processing computers were built in the 1960s and 1970s. In the 1980s that began to change.[13] A notable instance was Danny Hillis's "Connection Machine," which integrated some 65,536 processors, each with its own RAM, all arranged as a hypercube. These were simple, minimalist processors set up in a configuration known as SIMD (single instruction, multiple data), suited to experimental computation in the field of artificial intelligence. Later Connection Machines, built in MIMD configurations (multiple instruction, multiple data), were found to have commercial applications. The differences in the way processors and memory are set up mostly depends on the computational tasks for which particular computers are designed. Generally, parallel computing machines are more suitable than von Neumann machines when there is a large amount of data to be processed and/or the computations to be performed can be manageably decomposed into many small tasks.[14] Early in the development of parallel processing Gene Amdahl proposed a formula for calculating the limits to the speed-up that could be obtained by using multiple processors, but Hillis has disputed the law. And although Amdahl's law is still taught in computer science classes, history seems to be on Hillis's side. Since about 1995 almost all supercomputers have been massively parallel processing machines. Currently the fastest of these machines are the IBM Blue Genes, which regularly attain performance speeds of 280 teraflops, or 280 million million computations per second.[15] This is unimaginably fast, but such speeds are necessary for the "real-time" computation involved in, to cite only a few examples, scientific simulations of weather systems (and the effects of global warming), tracking the transactions of global financial markets, and recording and decrypting the e-mail and phone calls of Americans by the National Security Agency.

But whether we are speaking of high-end, special-purpose supercomputers, the desktops, laptops, and workstations used by individuals and businesses, or the low-end integrated circuits used to control and regulate machines in industrial plants and the everyday household, the development of information-processing technology has been nothing short of spectacular. For over twenty-five years, not only have faster, more powerful (and smaller, more portable) machines been steadily produced, but new applications and new markets as well. Indeed, as is well known, the increase in computational power and speed (and concomitant decrease in per unit cost) has been literally exponential for over thirty years.[16] With the more recent mushrooming growth of the Internet the pressure has mounted to develop more (and new types of) networked information processing systems that operate on local, national, and global levels simultaneously. But this new phase of development in information processing only makes glaringly obvious what has always been true: that information processing is at the heart of a new and specific kind of technical system, and that instead of focusing on individual types of machines we need to be aware of both the multiplicity of computational assemblages that define this new system and the dynamic of forces impelling both its historical development and evolution.

Let us first briefly consider the notion of a technical system as developed by Bernard Steigler. Very generally, a technical system forms when a technical evolution stabilizes around a point of equilibrium concretized by a particular technology, "enabling a whole play of stable interdependencies at a given time or epoch" (1998, 26). Tracking the concept from its origins in the writings of Bertrand Gille and development in those of André Leroi-Gourhan and Gilbert Simondon, Stiegler shows that what is at stake is the extent to which the biological concept of evolution can be applied to the technical system. For example, in *Le mode d'existence des objets techniques* (1958), Simondon argues that with the Industrial Revolution a new kind of "technical object," distinguished by a quasi-biological dynamic, is born. Strongly influenced by cybernetics, Simondon understands this "becoming-organic" of the technical object as a tendency among the systems and subsystems that comprise it toward a unity, a constant adaptation to itself and to the changing conditions it brings about. Meanwhile, the human role in this process devolves from that of an active subject whose intentionality directs this dynamic to that of an operator who functions as part of a larger system.

It seems hardly necessary to point out that the contemporary technical system centers on the new technology of the computer. The computer's transformative power has left almost no sector of the first or developed world—in industry, the sciences, communications, medical and military technology, art, the entertainment industry, or consumer society—untouched. Furthermore, if this transformation and exponential growth is the result of a "quasi-biological dynamic," as Simondon suggests is true of technological growth since the Industrial Revolution, then there are larger questions that must be addressed about the relation of technology (and computer or information processing technology in particular) to biological evolution. In my concluding remarks I shall focus on two such larger questions: First, why, and to what extent, is biological evolution applicable to the evolution of technology? (Is it, for example, simply a metaphor?) Second, what is it about information processing in particular that enables and even accelerates this quasi-biological dynamic, visible in the increasing tendency to mimic and reverse-engineer natural instances of information processing, and leading to a transformation of the "machine" from something solid, isolated, mechanical, determinate, and inflexible to soft systems that are fluid, pervasive, and increasingly adaptable?

As John Ziman frames it, the transformation of an evocative metaphor like "technological evolution" into a well-formed model requires several steps.[17] The first is to address the problem posed by "disanalogies," foremost among which is that technological innovation exhibits certain Lamarckian features normally forbidden in modern biology. At first glance a Lamarckian model would indeed seem more directly applicable to the evolutionary tendencies of machines and technical systems than Darwinian theory. (A precursor of Darwin, Jean-Baptiste Lamarck believed that *acquired* traits are passed down to subsequent generations through hereditary mechanisms.) For Ziman, however, the real question is not Darwin versus Lamarck but whether modern technology as a process guided by design and explicit human intention can be reconciled with evolution, "which both Darwin and Lamarck explained as a process through which complex adaptive systems emerge *in the absence of design*" (2000, 6). "We may well agree that technological change is driven by variation and selection," he continues, "but these are clearly not 'blind' or 'natural.'" Yet despite these reservations Ziman believes that an evolutionary model can incorporate the factors of human intentionality, since human cognition is itself the product of natural selection and takes place, as he puts it, "in lower level neural events whose causes might as well be considered random for all that we can find out about them" (7). Thus, the process as a whole can be said to operate blindly. Actually, the process need not even be blind in the way that mutations in DNA are blind; rather, all that is required is that "there should be a stochastic element in what is actually produced, chosen and put to the test of use" (7). Given that there are no universally agreed upon criteria that determine which technological innovations are selected, and that "artifacts with similar purposes may be designed to very different specifications and chosen for very different reasons," Ziman concludes that "there is usually enough diversity and *relatively* blind variation in a population of technological entities to sustain an evolutionary process" (7). Finally, in a not altogether unanticipated move, he suggests that, instead of lumping technology and biology together, we should treat them as "distinct entities of a larger genus of *complex systems*." Essentially this means that instead of worrying about whether evolutionary processes conform to strictly Darwinian or neo-Darwinian principles, we should be exploring the properties of "a more general *selectionist* paradigm" (11).

In biological evolution a trait is selected because it contributes to the survival rate of the organisms that possess it, whereas in technological evolution a particular technology or part of a technological system is selected for fairly obvious reasons—for instance, it's useful, easy, and cheap to produce, or it fills a niche and is therefore profitable. But often there are contingent factors, like the lucky alignment of market forces for the company that produces one version of a technology, even if it is not necessarily the best, as in the instance of Betamax and VHS. What contemporary theorists of technology stress are not so much such individual instances and their obvious differences as a larger trajectory involving the internalization of the evolutionary dynamic into the human environment. The scenario goes something like this: For the last two hundred thousand years or so *Homo sapiens sapiens* has evolved hardly at all; instead, the evolutionary dynamic has passed into the human environment, that is, into the development of human technology. In other words, as far as human being is concerned, the development of technology *is* evolution under different conditions and by different means. Furthermore, within this larger trajectory there is an internal repetition: the acceleration of the evolutionary process itself. Just as, in the history of the earth, it took several billion years for single-celled organisms to appear, but then less time for multicelled organisms to arise, and then much less time (even taking into account several sweeping extinction events) for the differentiation and multiplication of species, so in the evolution of technology we witness an acceleration from the appearance of simple weapons and farming tools to the printing press and the Industrial Revolution and the recent explosive development of information technology. Although there are obvious differences between the two processes, what is important—and largely accounts for the exponential acceleration—is that both build on previous achievements, leading to what has been called a "law of accelerating returns." In fact, many theorists now see the evolution of life and the recent accelerated development of technology in the same terms: as the evolution of information processing itself.

Notes

1. Originally published in the *Bell System Technical Journal* 27, no. 3 (1948), Shannon's theory subsequently appeared, with a long introduction by Warren Weaver, as Shannon and Weaver (1949).

2. An early alternative definition, proposed by Donald McKay (1969), takes into account the specific context in which the act of selection (by which information is defined) occurs. Another alternative, which still enjoys a certain currency, is Gregory Bateson's aphoristic observation that information is simply "a difference that makes a difference."

3. Apparently Shannon believed that this difference was complementary, rather than contradictory, and merely reflected a difference in his and Wiener's points of view. At least this is what he states in a letter to Wiener dated October 13, 1948 (Wiener papers, Box 2.85).

4. For a critique of the "writing" of DNA reproduction and protein synthesis in information theoretic terms, see Kay (2000).

5. A familiar example of a finite-state automaton is a two-way traffic light set to flash green, yellow, and red in a sequence that allows traffic to pass safely at an intersection.

6. For a discussion of the difference between finite-state machines and Turing machines, see Minsky 1967.

7. See the chapter "Nuts and Bolts" in Hillis (1998).

8. A version of this story is recounted in almost every history of the computer. For one that is succinctly focused on the theoretical issue, see Davis (2000).

9. The appearance of the report particularly irritated Eckert and Mauchly, who felt they hadn't received proper credit for their role in developing the first stored-program computer; the dispute later turned acrimonious when their patent claims were thrown out of court. Whereas Eckert was motivated by the computer's new commercial possibilities, von Neumann's primary concern was that the new ideas be disseminated as quickly as possible for use in new scientific and military applications—a conflict that would recur throughout the history of the computer's development.

10. Warren McCulloch and Walter Pitts, a neurophysiologist and logician respectively, were probably the first to apply Turing's ideas to biological information processing. In their essay "A Logical Calculus of the Ideas Immanent in Nervous Activity" (1943), they demonstrated how networks of interconnected brain cells or neurons could perform logical operations and claimed that these "neural nets" thus instantiated the formal equivalent of a Turing machine. In "Intelligent Machinery" (1948), a prophetic later essay published posthumously, Turing himself had introduced what he called "unorganized machines" composed of randomly connected neuronlike elements. By training these machines to modify their own structures, one could teach them new computational tasks; in short, they could be taught to learn. Turing thus anticipated the development of neural net theory, which in the 1980s flowered under the banner of connectionism.

11. Computational universality can also be defined in formal language theory, in terms of the machine's ability to generate and recognize complex languages defined by set theory. Of course, there are many useful information processing machines and devices that are *not* universal or Turing equivalent, and have no need to be, since they are dedicated to specific tasks like control and regulation of other machines. An increasing number of machines and appliances today have embedded microchips that perform such functions; they process information but are not universal computers.

12. In modern computers RAM is distinguished from storage devices (like hard disks) that are nonvolatile, meaning the data and instructions stored there do not disappear when the power is turned off. This difference raises the question of how a computer can be turned on (or "booted up"), that is, how control of the machine can be passed from hardware to software (the operating system). The answer is that boot instructions are hardwired on a special chip that, when activated, loads the operating system into memory, thereby making the machine accessible.

13. Resnick (1994) discusses the upsurge of interest in parallelism in relation to the wider cultural interest in decentralization.

14. Parallel processing is also accomplished by networked computers, a practice more commonly known as distributed computing. One of the best known examples is SETI (Search for Extraterrestrial Intelligence), which uses idling computers connected to the Internet to process vast amounts of information gathered from radio telescopes.

15. "Flop" is short for "floating point operation per second," meaning a computation with floating point numbers (real numbers rather than simple integers). A teraflop is 10^{12} operations per second.

16. The most often cited formulation, known as Moore's law (after Gordon E. Moore, cofounder of the chip manufacturer Intel), states that the number of transistors on an integrated circuit has doubled every two years since about 1970.

17. See Ziman (2000), particularly the chapters contributed by Ziman: "Evolutionary Models for Technological Change" and "Selectionism and Complexity."

References and Suggested Readings

Cover, Thomas M., and Joy A. Thomas. 1991. *Elements of Information Theory*. New York: John Wiley & Sons.

Davis, Martin. 2000. *The Universal Computer*. New York: W. W. Norton.

Hillis, Daniel. 1998. *The Pattern on the Stone*. New York: Basic Books.

Kay, Lily E. 2000. *Who Wrote the Book of Life?* Stanford, CA: Stanford University Press.

Maturana, Humberto R., and Franciso J. Varela. 1980. *Autopoiesis and Cognition: The Realization of the Living*. Boston: D. Reidel.

McKay, Donald. 1969. *Information, Mechanism, Meaning*. Cambridge, MA: MIT Press.

Minsky, Marvin L. 1967. *Computation: Finite and Infinite Machines*. Englewood Cliffs, NJ: Prentice-Hall.

Resnick, Mitchel. 1994. *Turtles, Termites and Traffic Jams: Explorations in Massively Parallel Microworlds*. Cambridge, MA: MIT Press.

Shannon, Claude, and Warren Weaver. 1949. *The Mathematical Theory of Communication*. Urbana: University of Illinois Press.

Stiegler, Bernard. 1998. *Technics and Time*. Vol. 1, *The Fault of Epimetheus*. Stanford, CA: Stanford University Press.

Turing, A. M. 1936. "On Computable Numbers, with an Application to the *Entscheidung-*

sproblem." *Proceedings of the London Mathematical Society*, 42 (ser. 2): 230–65. Reprinted in *The Essential Turing*, ed. B. Jack Copeland, 58–90 (Oxford: Oxford University Press, 2004).

Wiener, Norbert. 1948. *Cybernetics, or Control and Communication in the Animal and the Machine*. Cambridge, MA: MIT Press.

———. 1950. *The Human Use of Human Beings: Cybernetics and Society*. New York: Houghton Mifflin.

Ziman, John, ed. 2000. *Technological Evolution as an Evolutionary Process*. Cambridge: Cambridge University Press.

SOCIETY
* * * * * * * * * * * *

15 :: EXCHANGE   DAVID GRAEBER

We commonly speak of people "exchanging insults" or "exchanging ad-dresses." One can also speak of exchanges of letters, prisoners, ideas, or gunfire. These examples appear to have only one thing in common. They are all governed by a principle of reciprocity: there are two parties, each of whom gives and gets the same thing in roughly equal measure. Indeed, the primary definition for *exchange* in the *Oxford English Dictionary* is "the action, or an act, of reciprocal giving and receiving."

When we use the term in the abstract, however, we are usually talk-ing about economic transactions, the kind regulated, for example, by the Securities and Exchange Commission. Here is the definition on one Wall Street Web page:

> Exchange: to provide goods and services and receive goods or services of approximately equal value in return; here, also called barter.[1]

We are speaking here of a voluntary transaction. Two parties each agree to transfer something in their possession to the other—presumably be-cause at that moment what they are getting is worth more to them than what they are giving up. For economists, voluntary exchanges of this sort are the basic building blocks of any market system—which is why many see the market as the very incarnation of human freedom.

In each of these examples whatever it is that passes back and forth can be referred to as the "medium" of the exchange. Economic transac-tions, however, are somewhat different than the others. Those who ex-change greetings, or gunfire, are giving and taking more or less exactly the same kind of thing. But no one would normally exchange one tube of toothpaste for another tube of toothpaste. What would be the point? The point of economic exchange is to get one's hands on something one does *not* already have. In fact, in a market economy, whether one is sell-ing a house or buying a candy bar, most commodities are not exchanged for other commodities at all but for a symbolic substance, which may or may not take material form, referred to as *money*. Money is thus treated as the ultimate "medium of exchange," a universal equivalent.

In order to explain how this situation came about, economists like to tell a story. It goes back at least to Adam Smith and to this day can be found in just about any economic textbook. In primitive times, the story goes, people did indeed exchange things directly with one another. Say someone had a large number of chickens and wished to acquire a cow. He would seek out someone with an extra cow who needed chickens and strike a deal. Obviously this was not the most efficient way to go about things (what if he couldn't find such a person?). So, the story continues, eventually people began to stockpile certain commodities that were in general demand—perhaps cows at first; later, gold and silver—and these came to be used as a medium of exchange. Once gold, say, came to be used this way, it also became an abstract measure of value—one could calculate the price of anything in gold—and provided a means to store up wealth. This was money. Gradually, governments began to issue pieces of gold and silver in uniform sizes, and one saw the emergence of complex systems of banking, credit, and, eventually, futures markets. At the same time, most economists (e.g., Samuelson 1948) insist that all of this is largely froth, that ultimately all economies are just elaborate systems of barter.

We will examine these premises in a moment (they are almost entirely false). For now let me stress that, just as economists argue that all economic life is founded on barter, many social scientists have held that social life in general is founded on exchange. This position was particularly popular in the mid-twentieth century. In the 1960s, for example, Claude Lévi-Strauss (1963, 296) made a famous argument that not only was reciprocity the organizing principle of all social life, but that all societies could be said to be organized around three fundamental forms of exchange, each distinguished by its principle medium:

- the economy (the exchange of goods),
- kinship (the exchange of women), and
- language (the exchange of words).

While this was always considered an extreme position, it raises telling questions. Even if we put aside Lévi-Strauss's notoriously controversial argument that society is founded on the incest taboo, whereby men "renounce their sisters to exchange them against the sisters of others," in what way is trading fish for plantains, or buying an umbrella, really analogous to conducting a conversation? Are the participants in a conversation necessarily trying to acquire something—information, perhaps, or ideas? If so, in what way does the logic resemble that of a financial transaction? One could make a case. Certain types of information, for example, might be considered scarce resources; one might not wish to give up a piece of such information except in exchange for another piece (or something else) that one considers to be of equal value. Ideas, on the other hand, often work on exactly the opposite principle: the more people know you have such a good idea, the greater its value. Or does "exchange" here simply refer to any sort of interaction conducted on a fairly equal basis?

"Exchange theory" of this sort has largely faded away. More prevalent nowadays is what has come to be referred to as "rational choice theory," an approach that takes the logic of the market—self-interested economic exchange—and applies it just about every human relation, even those that do not involve money or material goods. The emphasis here is not on reciprocity but on the fact that, in market transactions, each party is normally trying to gain an advantage over the other. The assumption, inspired by neoclassical economics, is that there are only so many good things in the world and all of us go about life calculating how we can get the most of them for the least effort or sacrifice; thus, when two people interact, one can expect that each will be calculating how to maximize his or her own advantage. In this sense, absolutely everything, from smiles and compliments to honor and faith can be considered, like so many cans of sardines or tractor-trailers, as media for an endless series of self-interested exchanges—this being the basic business of human life.

The legacy of such theories makes it very difficult to talk about exchange in the abstract, since the subject quickly comes to encompass everything. What's more, the ideology of exchange has become so central to our culture that an essay like this must always begin by puncturing assumptions. Let me do so. In reality, market exchange—or reciprocal exchange of any sort—cannot provide a model for all human activity. Outside of market contexts, moreover, valuable objects tend to become the media not of exchange, but of human relationships, which are often anything but reciprocal in nature. On the other hand, this means that they are extremely important; since human beings are, after all, largely the sum and internalization of their relationships with others, this makes such objects the material media through which we become who we are.

The Myth of Barter and Varieties of Noncommercial Exchange

Around a century ago anthropologists began to test economists' assumptions by examining economic systems in Melanesia, Africa, Southeast Asia, and the Americas that operated without commercial markets. They soon discovered the economists were simply wrong. They were unable to find a single society where economic life was based on barter of the "I'll give you twenty chickens for that cow" variety. Where barter did occur, it occurred between societies: that is, between strangers who would just as happily have stolen the goods had it been more convenient. Transactions within societies, that is, between those to whom people felt any sort of moral commitment, tended to take a very different form. They more closely resembled the way people in our own societies act outside the impersonal sphere of the market, when dealing with family, lovers, friends, or enemies. What really mattered were the personal relationships. As a result, the last thing anyone was interested in was barter, a simple tit for tat that created no further mutual obligations. Even when people were mainly interested in the goods, they would pretend otherwise. Accounts were almost never kept, and insofar as there was overt competition, it was likely to take the form of people vying to outdo one another in grand shows of generosity. As a result, French anthropologist Marcel Mauss (1925) dubbed these "gift economies."

This is a useful phrase, but it can be slightly deceptive. First of all, "gifts" of this sort have nothing to do with altruism or charity—concepts that really emerge only with the rise of the market, as its complementary mirror image. Rather, a gift economy is one in which wealth is the medium for defining and expressing human relationships (Gregory 1982). Second, people have an unfortunate tendency to talk about "the gift" as if it were just one thing, lumping together what are in fact a wide variety of different kinds of noncommercial transaction that operate according to very different principles. Here is a very simplified typology:

COMMUNISTIC RELATIONS

I use "communistic" in the sense of relations that operate on Louis Blanc's famous principle "from each according to his abilities, to each according to his needs." While there has almost certainly never been a society in which everyone interacts on this basis in every context, there is in any social system always a certain baseline communism, at least for certain basic needs (e.g., one freely offers directions to strangers, assuming that any stranger would do likewise; and in some societies, no one would normally refuse a request for food) or in certain circumstances (such as dire emergencies). Sometimes communistic relations are institutionalized: two clans might each have responsibility for, say, burying the other's dead. In such cases the responsibilities are rigorously specified, but no accounts are kept. In relations between very close kin, close friends, "blood brothers," and the like, the range of responsibilities can become so wide as to encompass almost anything; hence, Mauss suggested that most societies can be seen as threaded with relations of what he called "individualistic communism" (1947, 106).

Communistic relations are reciprocal only in the sense that both sides are equally disposed to help one another; there is no feeling that accounts ought to balance out at any given moment—in part, because there's no assumption such relations will ever end.

RECIPROCAL EXCHANGE

Here falls the exchange of compliments or favors or rounds of drinks. Such relationships can be broken off after any given round because the return is considered a more or less exact equivalent to the initial gift. Often relations are kept up by delaying the response in time (if I buy dinner for a friend, he will likely feel in my debt until he is able to reciprocate). Or people make a point of ensuring the response is not quite an equivalent (if he buys me a much more expensive dinner, or a much cheaper one, the feelings of debt do not quite cancel out). There are numerous variations here, ways of testing the limits.[2] The critical thing is that unlike communistic relations, these are not assumed to be permanent. Reciprocity of this sort is about maintaining one's personal autonomy in a relatively equal relationship.

HIERARCHICAL RELATIONS

Relations between masters and slaves, patrons and clients, parents and children, and so on do not tend to operate in terms of reciprocity but rather by a logic of precedent. If one gives money to a beggar (or to a charity fund) the recipient will almost certainly not feel obliged to return something of equal value but instead will be more likely to ask for more. Similarly, if parents allow a child an indulgence the child is likely to expect the same in the future. The converse is equally true: if a medieval serf or vassal presented a gift to a feudal superior, it was likely to be treated as a precedent, added to the web of custom, and thus transformed into an obligation for the future.[3] There are endless variations here too—from institutionalized plunder or ritualized theft to redistribution, inheritance, or other gifts that pass one's superior status to former inferiors—but except for the last, all presume a permanent or at least ongoing relation that has nothing to do with reciprocal exchange because it is not assumed to have anything to do with equality.

Tit-for-tat exchange can also mount into contests of one-upmanship, where each party tries to present a gift or countergift so lavish that their rival cannot reciprocate. In these situations the equal standing of the parties is up for grabs at any moment, with the danger that the relation might degenerate at any moment—at least symbolically—into subordination and hierarchy. "Gifts make slaves," the Inuit saying goes, "as whips make dogs." This is the sort of gift exchange that has tended to attract the most attention in the literature on the subject, but it only really becomes a dominant social form in stateless aristocratic societies like Homeric Greece, Vedic India, early Celtic or Germanic societies, or the indigenous societies of the Pacific Northwest.

+   +   +

As should be clear, none of these modes are peculiar to "gift economies." We are all communists with our closest friends and feudal lords when interacting with small children. What varies is how they knit together with the more impersonal relations of the market. It's also clear that such transactions are by no means uniformly governed by principles of reciprocity: those involved in agonistic exchange do not wish the outcome to be reciprocal, and communistic and hierarchical relations are not really even forms of exchange.

This is important because there is a widespread assumption that societies are, in some sense, systems of reciprocal exchange in which accounts ultimately balance out. This is simply not the case. In fact it is so obviously not the case that one might well ask why it is even possible to imagine such a thing. Probably the reason is that reciprocity seems, everywhere, essential to conceptions of justice; therefore, when attempting to describe extremely hierarchical systems in the abstract, people will fall back on lines like "this is how we repay our parents for having raised us" or "the peasants provide food and the lords provide protection"—even though the logic of practice is utterly different. The very idea of "the market," in which all exchanges balance out, is just such an imaginary projection; it comes down to little more than the faith that ultimately, somehow, everything will always balance out. One could well argue that the very idea that we all live in bounded objects called "societies" (an idea that almost always dissolves away when you try to define its borders) is a similar imaginary totality.

In almost all of these cases, the material medium of exchange can be said to take on some of the qualities of the relationship. Schieffelin (1980, 509) provides a simple example: among the Kaluli in Papua New

Guinea, two friends who eat a bird together will henceforth refer to each other as "my bird." This sort of thing is actually quite common in communistic relations. Hierarchical transactions tend to be more complicated. The Kwakiutl and other First Nations of the Northwest Coast of North America are famous for ceremonies called potlatches, communal feasts that aristocrats would sponsor in order to "fasten on" a title they had received. Such titles were embodied in material objects: masks and other regalia, ownership of which carried with it the rights to perform certain roles in dramatic rituals, to gather berries along a river, and so on. If the holder of such a title gave it, with its accompanying paraphernalia, to someone else, the recipient would become the person the giver used to be (much as if one granted title to a dukedom). In order to be recognized in that new title, however, the new holder was expected to appeal to his clan and allies to amass vast sums of wealth in blankets, bracelets, fish oil, and so on, in order to hold a potlatch in which he would shower this wealth on members of rival clans. These goods were, in turn, called "bad things," since the point was to show how contemptuous the title holder was of such trifles, and handing them out was a way of belittling the recipients. Occasionally, when two aristocrats laid claim to the same title, one chief would actually destroy some object of great value, pass the remains to his rival, and challenge him to reciprocate. Almost always, in Kwakiutl exchange, the medium served to define the recipient—it ennobled or degraded. In other systems—say, a caste system where different orders of society are defined as "smiths" or "fishermen" on the basis of what products or services they provide to the king (Hocart 1968)—the medium defines the giver. Always, though, it is human qualities that are at stake.

On the Origins of Currency

What, then, were the real origins of money? Many societies without commercial markets did have something that resembled money—what used to be referred to as "primitive currencies": shell moneys, feather moneys, wampum, trade beads, whale's teeth, and the like. In just about every case, they were used primarily not to acquire wealth but to rearrange relations among people. Tellingly, the objects themselves rarely consisted of what an economist would consider "useful commodities"—food, tools, or the like—but rather things that were otherwise used mainly as forms of personal adornment. Like gold and silver, beads, shell necklaces, and the like exist primarily to be seen, and in being seen, to establish the beauty, rank, or significance of the bearer. These are visual media, then, used to define the value of persons, that have become detached, as it were, and serve as the media of exchange between them (Graeber 1996).

The most common use of such currencies is for paying what anthropologists call "bridewealth": a man's parents will present them to the family that provides him with their daughter in marriage. Usually the payment establishes their rights to the woman's fertility, that is, to claim the offspring of the union as members of their own lineage or clan. The French anthropologist Pierre Rospabé (1995) makes a compelling argument that these are not even, strictly speaking, payments; most societies with bridewealth recognize that the only way to really reciprocate the gift of a sister in marriage is to give one's own sister. In societies that do practice sister exchange, bridewealth is only presented when that option is not available or when the return is to be delayed to later generations. Similarly with the second most important use of primitive currencies, the payment of "bloodwealth," or compensation for wrongful death, a taking rather than a giving of life. Material wealth cannot truly compensate for the death of a loved one, and no one pretends that it can. At best, it can be used to acquire a wife for one of the victim's relatives (or even for his ghost), whose offspring will in some sense replace him. In either case, money originates as a token of recognition of a debt that *cannot* ever be repaid.

How then can such a token become its opposite: a means of payment and medium of exchange—a way of canceling debts? There are a variety of possible explanations. Once such tokens exist, they tend to take on a kind of power in and of themselves. What begins as a pure medium of expression of the importance of certain social relations—particularly those of creating or destroying life—comes to be seen as possessing a vital power in and of itself, even as the origin of the very value it represents. Thus it becomes a way of creating new social relations. The Iroquois, for instance, never used wampum to buy or sell things to each other, but they did use it to create treaties and agreements. Often bloodwealth systems develop into elaborate systems of fines and penalties for all sorts of offenses; some (see, e.g., Grierson 1977) have suggested these might be the origins of "general purpose" currency.[4] However this may be, the historical record makes one thing quite clear: wherever tokens that were once used mainly to regulate sexual or domestic affairs transform themselves into full-blown commodity money, allowing the definitive transfer or alienation of what is bought and sold, the result is a moral crisis. New and scandalous possibilities arise, such as commercial prostitution and slavery. This often sparks frantic efforts by the wealthy to insulate their own families from such possibilities and to relegate them exclusively to the poor. The results for the situation of women of all classes are often devastating. To chose just two notorious examples: the Mediterranean "honor complex" with its sequestration of women appears to trace back to aristocratic reactions to the market in ancient Greece (e.g., Kurke 2002), and the practice of veiling in the Near East appears to have originated as a way of marking off "respectable" women from slaves and prostitutes, whose bodies could be bought and sold (Lerner 1986).

A Very Brief History of the World in Terms of Media of Exchange

Current research has revealed that the economists' original assumptions—that first there was barter, then money, then finally complex systems of credit—gets the order precisely backward. Credit money came first. The earliest forms of money, in ancient Mesopotamia and Egypt, were, as we would now put it, virtual; banking, interest, and even the equivalent of expense accounts all existed long before the invention of actual coined money. For two thousand years, then, the "media of exchange" were records kept on cuneiform tablets. Conversely, genuine barter, when it does occur, seems to emerge—as quite recently in Russia and Argentina—in places where currency systems once existed but have (at least temporarily) broken down (Servet 1978).

The story is too long to tell in any great detail but one might sketch an outline of Eurasian history along the following lines.

AGE OF THE FIRST AGRARIAN EMPIRES (3500–800 BCE)
DOMINANT FORM: VIRTUAL CREDIT MONEY

Our best information on the origins of money goes back to ancient Mesopotamia, but there seems no particular reason to believe matters were radically different in Pharaonic Egypt, Bronze Age China, or the Indus Valley. The economy was dominated by large public institutions (temples and palaces) whose bureaucratic administrators essentially created money of account by establishing a fixed equivalent between silver and the staple crop, barley. Debts were calculated in silver, but silver was rarely used in transactions; payments were instead made in barley or anything else that happened to be handy and acceptable. Major debts were recorded on cuneiform tablets kept as sureties by both parties to the transaction.

Markets, certainly, did exist. Prices of certain commodities that were not produced within temple or palace holdings, and thus subject to administered price schedules, tended to fluctuate according to the vagaries of supply and demand. Even here, though, such evidence as we have (e.g., Hudson 2002, 25; 2004, 114) suggests that everyday purchases, such as beer advanced by "ale women," or local innkeepers, appear to have been on credit, with tabs accumulating to be paid, typically, at harvest time.

Interest rates, fixed at 20 percent, remained stable for two thousand years. This was not a sign of government control of the market; at this stage, such institutions were what made markets possible. Insofar as governments did intervene, it was to deal with the effects of debt. In bad years the poor tended to become hopelessly indebted to the rich and would often have to surrender their lands, and ultimately, family members, into debt peonage. Hence, it became customary for each new ruler to wipe the slate clean, cancel debts, and return bonded laborers to their families.

AXIAL AGE (800 BCE–600 CE)
DOMINANT FORM: COINAGE AND METAL BULLION

This is the age that saw the emergence of coinage, as well as the birth, in China, India, and the Middle East, of all of the major world religions.[5] It was a time of spectacular creativity and, in much of the world, almost equally spectacular violence, from the Warring States in China and fragmentation in India to the carnage and mass enslavement that accompanied the expansion (and later, the dissolution) of the Roman Empire.

Coined money, the actual use of gold and silver as a medium of exchange, allowed markets in the now more familiar, impersonal sense of the term. Precious metals were also far more appropriate for an age of generalized warfare, for the obvious reason that they can be stolen. Coinage, certainly, was not invented to facilitate trade (the Phoenicians, the consummate traders of the ancient world, were among the last to adopt it). It appears to have first been invented to pay soldiers.

Throughout antiquity one can continue to speak of what Ingham (2004, 99) has dubbed the "military-coinage complex." He might better have called it a "military-coinage-slavery complex," since the diffusion of new military technologies (Greek hoplites, Roman legions) was closely tied to the capture and marketing of slaves. The other major source of slaves was debt; now that states no longer periodically wiped the slates clean, those not lucky enough to be citizens of the major military city-states were fair game. The credit systems of the Near East did not crumble under commercial competition; they were destroyed by Alexander's armies—armies that required half a ton of silver bullion per day in wages. The tax systems of the Hellenistic and Roman empires, which demanded payment in coins the state itself had mined and minted, were designed to force their subjects to abandon other modes of circulation and enter into market relations, so that soldiers (and government officials) would be able to buy things with that money. The effects of the constant wars conducted by those legions, in turn, guaranteed that much of the consequent trade was in fact in human beings, or in the products of slave labor.

However tawdry the origins of coinage, the creation of new media of exchange appears to have had profound intellectual effects. Some (Shell 1978, 1982; Seaford 2004) have even argued that early Greek philosophy became possible only because of conceptual innovations introduced by the technology of coinage. Certainly, it seems significant that the emergence of so many major philosophical trends and world religions coincided almost exactly with that of coined money. While the precise links are yet to be fully explored, one thing is clear. The ideals of charity, altruism, and selfless giving typically promoted within the new religions appear to have arisen in direct reaction to the logic of the market. As Mauss liked to point out, in a gift economy pure selfishness, or pure selflessness, would be almost inconceivable. To put the matter crudely: it would seem that, once a certain social space is dedicated simply to the selfish acquisition of material things, it becomes almost inevitable that another domain will be set aside to preach, from the perspective of ultimate values, the unimportance of material things and the illusory nature of selfishness—or even of the self. The fact that these markets were, in fact, based on coinage, which allowed for far more impersonal and, hence, potentially violent forms of market behavior than earlier credit relations presumably made the distinction all the more compelling.

THE MIDDLE AGES (600 CE–1500 CE)
THE RETURN OF VIRTUAL CREDIT-MONEY

If the Axial Age saw the emergence of complementary ideals of egoism and altruism, commodity markets and universal world religions, the Middle Ages was the period in which those two institutions began to merge and monetary transactions increasingly came to be carried out through social networks defined and regulated by those same religions.[6] This in turn occasioned a return, throughout the world, of various forms of virtual credit-money.

In Europe, where all this took place under the aegis of Christendom, coinage was only sporadically, and unevenly, available. Prices after 800 CE were calculated largely in terms of an old Carolingian currency that no longer existed (it was referred to even then as "imaginary money"), but day-to-day buying and selling was mainly carried out with tally-sticks, notched pieces of wood that were broken in two as records of debt—one half being kept by the creditor, the other by the debtor. Such tally-sticks remained in common use in much of England well into the sixteenth century (Innes 1913, 1914). Larger transactions were handled through bills of exchange, with the great commercial fairs serving as clearinghouses. The church, meanwhile, provided a legal framework, enforcing strict controls on the lending of money at interest and prohibitions on debt bondage.

The real nerve center of the medieval world economy, however, was the Indian Ocean, which along with the central Asian caravan routes, connected the great civilizations of India, China, and the Middle East. Here trade was conducted through the framework of Islam, which not only provided a legal structure highly conducive to mercantile activities (notwithstanding an absolute prohibition on the lending of money at interest) but allowed for peaceful relations between merchants over a remarkably large part of the globe, fostering the creation of a variety of sophisticated credit instruments. In China this same period saw the rapid spread of Buddhism, the invention of paper money, and the development of even more complex forms of credit and finance.

Like the Axial Age, this period saw its share of carnage and plunder (particularly during the great nomadic invasions), and coinage remained an important medium of exchange in many times and places. Still, what really characterizes the Middle Ages appears to be a movement in the other direction. Money, during most of the medieval period, was largely delinked from coercive institutions. Money changers, one might say, were invited back into the temples, where they could be monitored. The result was a flowering of institutions premised on a much higher degree of social trust.

AGE OF EUROPEAN EMPIRES (1500–1971)
RETURN OF PRECIOUS METALS

With the advent of the great European empires—Iberian, then North Atlantic—the world saw a reversion to the use of chattel slavery, plunder, and wars of destruction, and the consequent rapid return of gold and silver bullion as the main form of currency. Historical investigation will probably demonstrate that the origin of these transformations were more complicated than we ordinarily assume. Among the main factors prompting the movement back to bullion, for example, were popular movements during the early Ming dynasty, in the fifteenth and sixteenth centuries, that ultimately forced the Chinese government to abandon not only paper money but any attempt to impose its own currency. This led to a reversion in the vast Chinese market to an uncoined silver standard. Since taxes were also gradually commuted into silver, it soon became the more or less official Chinese policy to bring as much silver into the country as possible, so as to keep taxes low and prevent new outbreaks of social unrest. This sudden enormous demand for silver had effects across the world. Most of the precious metals looted by the conquistadors, and later extracted by the Spanish from the mines of Mexico and Potosi (at almost unimaginable cost in human lives), ended up in China. These new global-scale connections have, of course, been documented in great detail. Crucial here is the delinking of money from religious institutions, and its relinking with coercive ones (especially the state), accompanied here by an ideological reversion to "metallism."[7] Credit, in this context, was increasingly an affair of states, which themselves ran largely by deficit financing, a form of credit that was, in turn, largely invented to finance increasingly expensive wars. Internationally, the British Empire was steadfast in maintaining the gold standard even through the nineteenth and early twentieth centuries.

CURRENT ERA (1971 AND ON)
THE EMPIRE OF DEBT

The current era might be said to have been initiated on August 15, 1971, when President Richard Nixon officially suspended the convertibility of the U.S. dollar into gold and effectively created the present floating currency regimes (Gregory 1997). We have returned, then, to an age of virtual money, in which consumer purchases in wealthy countries rarely involve even paper money, and national economies are driven largely by consumer debt. All of this has been accompanied by what's often called a "financialization" of capital, with speculation in currencies and financial instruments becoming a domain unto itself, detached from any immediate relation with production or even commerce (see, e.g., Arrighi 1994; Harvey 2005). What remains to be seen is whether, as in previous ages dominated by virtual credit money, there will arise overarching institutions prepared to impose some sort of social control over the human consequences of spiraling debt. So far, the trend has been the opposite: such overarching institutions as have emerged—for instance, the International Monetary Fund and the World Bank—have been more concerned with enforcing debts, leaving poorer nations locked in a kind of permanent debt peonage. But the period has just begun.

A Final Word on Media of Value

Two themes stand out for anyone concerned with the nature of media. The first is the tendency for media of exchange, and of value more generally, to take on lives of their own—and ultimately, to come to seem the origin of the very powers they appear to represent. "Primitive currencies" that initially represent powers of creation—the power to create human life and human relations—end up invested with creative power in their own right. In a similar way Marx argued that, under capitalism, money really represents the value of labor power—the human capacity to bring new things into being—but that, since in a wage labor system workers actually produce things only to get money, money becomes a representation that, in any given context, brings into being the very thing it represents. This, he argues, is what makes it possible to see money, or wealth, as somehow productive in itself. The "financialization of capital" is only the ultimate form—but these processes are not limited to capital. Something similar happens with media of value of any sort (Graeber 2001).

The second theme is the intimate relations between media of exchange, and visual media. These can be remarkably subtle and complex. Consider the phenomenon of a hoard of gold. Gold has value almost entirely because it's pleasant to look at. Yet the first thing that seems to happen when it becomes a medium of exchange is that people begin to hide it, to put it intentionally out of sight. As adornment to the person, it becomes—like beads or shells—a way of defining who one is, one's public, visible persona. As a source of power—money, giving the bearer the ability to acquire and, often, to do almost anything—it is hidden away, identified with the bearer's inner, vital powers, that very quality that can be represented only by not being represented, since it is the sheer potential to act or create. Both phenomena—the display of wealth and money as hidden power—are obviously very much still with us. Despite all the tendency for media of exchange to break free and take on autonomous lives of their own, it would seem they cannot completely detach themselves from their origins as aspects of human being.

Notes

1. http://www.investorwords.com/1797/exchange.html (accessed July 26, 2006).

2. Sometimes people test the limits of ostensibly communistic relations through what might be called "contests of outrageous demand." Take, for instance, blood brothers in Madagascar, who in theory can refuse each other nothing; one might demand his partner's favorite pet, or the right to sleep with his wife—but only in the knowledge that the other has the right to reply in kind. This can ultimately shade into something very much like barter.

3. "In the ninth century, when one day there was a shortage of wine in the royal cellars at Ver, the monks of Saint-Denis were asked to supply the two hundred hogs-heads required. This contribution was thenceforth claimed from them as of right every year, and it required an imperial charter to abolish it. At Ardres, we are told, there was once a bear, the property of the local lord. The inhabitants, who loved to watch it fight with dogs, undertook to

feed it. The beast eventually died, but the lord continued to exact the loaves of bread" (Bloch 1961:114).

4. Hence the fact that in most European languages, the words for *sin*, *fault*, and *price* are often etymologically related; similarly, "to pay" is originally the same as "to appease."

5. The phrase "Axial Age" was coined by Karl Jaspers to describe the period between 800 and 200 BCE, during which, he believed, almost all of the main philosophical traditions we are familiar with today arose in China, India, and the Eastern Mediterranean. I am following Lewis Mumford in extending its scope from roughly the time of Zoroaster to that of Mohammed.

6. I am here relegating most of what is generally called the "Dark Ages" in Europe to the earlier period, characterized by predatory militarism and the consequent importance of bullion. The Viking raids, and the famous extraction of *danegeld* from England, might be seen as one of the last manifestations of that age.

7. The myth of barter and commodity theories of money were of course developed precisely in this period.

References and Suggested Readings

Arrighi, Giovanni. 1994. *The Long Twentieth Century: Money, Power, and the Origins of Our Times*. London: Verso.

Graeber, David. 1996. "Beads and Money: Notes toward a Theory of Wealth and Power." *American Ethnologist* 23, no. 1.

———. 2001. *Toward an Anthropological Theory of Value: The False Coin of Our Own Dreams*. New York: Palgrave.

Gregory, Chris A. 1982. *Gifts and Commodities*. New York: Academic Press.

———. 1997. *Savage Money: The Anthropology and Politics of Commodity Exchange*. Amsterdam: Harwood Academic.

Grierson, Phillip. 1977. *The Origins of Money*. London: Athlone Press.

Hart, Keith. 1986. "Heads or Tails? Two Sides of the Coin." *Man* (n.s.) 21:637–56.

———. 1999. *The Memory Bank: Money in an Unequal World*. London: Perpetua Books.

Harvey, David. 2005. *A Brief History of Neoliberalism*. New York: Oxford University Press.

Hocart, A. M. 1968. *Caste: A Comparative Study*. New York: Russel & Russel.

Hudson, Michael. 2002. "Reconstructing the Origins of Interest-Bearing Debt and the Logic of Clean Slates." In *Debt and Economic Renewal in the Ancient Near East*, ed. Michael Hudson and Marc Van de Mieroop, 7–58. Bethesda: CDL.

———. 2004 "The Archeology of Money: Debt vs. Barter Theories of Money." In *Credit and State Theories of Money*, ed. Randall Wray, 99–127. Cheltenham: Edward Elgar.

Ingham, Geoffrey. 2004. *The Nature of Money*. Cambridge: Polity Press.

Innes, A. Mitchell. 1913. "What Is Money?" *Banking Law Journal*, May, 377–408.

———. 1914. "The Credit Theory of Money." *Banking Law Journal*, January, 151–68.

Kurke, Leslie. 2002. *Coins, Bodies, Games, and Gold: The Politics of Meaning in Archaic Greece*. Princeton, NJ : Princeton University Press.

Lerner, Gerda. 1986. "The Origin of Prostitution in Ancient Mesopotamia." *Signs* 11, no. 2: 236–54.

Lévi-Strauss, Claude. 1963. *Structural Anthropology*. New York: Basic Books.

Mauss, Marcel. 1925. "Essai sur le don: Forme et raison de l'échange dans les sociétés ar-chaïques." *Annee sociologique* (series 2) 1:30–186.

——. 1947. *Manuel d'ethnographie*. Paris: Payot.

Rospabé, Philippe. 1995. *La Dette de Vie: Aux origines de la monnaie sauvage*. Paris: Editions la Découverte/MAUSS.

Sahlins, Marshall. 1972. *Stone Age Economics*. Chicago: Aldine.

Samuelson, Paul A. 1948. *Economics*. New York: McGraw Hill.

Schieffelin, Edward L. 1980. "Reciprocity and the Construction of Reality." *Man* 15:502–17.

Seaford, Richard. 2004. *Money and the Early Greek Mind: Homer, Philosophy, Tragedy*. Cam-bridge: Cambridge University Press.

Servet, Jean-Michel. 1978. "Primitive Order and Archaic Trade. Part I." *Economy and Soci-ety* 10, no. 4: 423–50.

——. 1979. "Primitive Order and Archaic Trade. Part II." *Economy and Society* 11, no. 1: 22–59.

Shell, Marc. 1978. *Economy of Literature*. Baltimore: Johns Hopkins University Press.

——. 1982. *Money, Language, and Thought*. Baltimore: Johns Hopkins University Press.

16 :: LANGUAGE   CARY WOLFE

"However the topic is considered, the *problem of language* has never been simply one problem among others." So begins one of the most influential discussions of language in contemporary critical theory and philosophy, Jacques Derrida's *Of Grammatology* (published in French in 1967, in English in 1974). Indeed, the topic of language is so vast, its implications so far-reaching, that any serious discussion of it leads very quickly to questions that are obviously ontological (questions of being), phenomenological (questions of experience), and ethical (questions of the good and the just). Thinkers in a range of disciplines, from philosophy to contemporary cognitive science to anthropology, have often argued that language fundamentally separates the human from all other forms of sentient life; it is language that makes us different, not just in degree, but in kind. Language makes the world cognitively available to us in a way that is impossible for other forms of life, and it thus establishes the ontological domain of what we call the specifically "human." In the first half of the twentieth century, for example, philosophers as vastly different as Ludwig Wittgenstein and Martin Heidegger (both key figures in what has often been called the "linguistic turn" in twentieth-century philosophy) argued that language establishes a sort of world-within-the-world—a world of abstract meaning and concepts—that is unavailable to nonlanguaging beings. And it is from that fact that the essential ontological nature and special ethical standing of the human derives.

It is just this set of presuppositions that Derrida's work is calculated to "deconstruct" (to use a term often associated with his writings). In *Of Grammatology* and other early works, Derrida returns to what is arguably the single most important text of the twentieth century on the topic of language in the more limited, strictly linguistic sense: Ferdinand de Saussure's *Course in General Linguistics* (compiled from seminar notes taken by his students at the University of Geneva between 1906 and 1911). Saussure's decisive methodological innovation was to analytically delimit his field of investigation, the better to understand the general formal dynamics of the linguistic system. He recognized that language is made up of two fundamental dimensions: the abstract system of rules that constitutes any language system at a given moment in time (*langue*), and the heterogeneous utterances and speech acts in which individual speakers engage (*parole*) ([1915] 1959, 9–17). On the one hand, the linguistic system is, over time, built up out of, and only exists by virtue of, concrete instances of *parole*; on the other hand, those individual speech acts are meaningful only within the larger system of *langue*. As Saussure put it, *langue* is thus "both a social product of the faculty of speech and a collection of necessary conventions that have been adopted by a social body to permit individuals to exercise that faculty" (9). Saussure chose to focus his investigations upon *langue* because, as he observed, "language is not complete in any speaker," nor is it, strictly speaking, "a function of the speaker." His focus is therefore intended not only to separate "what is social from what is individual," "what is essential from what is accessory and more or less accidental" (14), but to underscore the fact that only *langue* can serve "*as the norm of all other manifestations of speech.*" Once we give *langue* "first place among the facts of speech, we introduce a natural order into a mass that lends itself to no other classification" (9).

With these important methodological distinctions in hand, Saussure's first move was to reject an object-centered view of language (which would see the linguistic features of words as somehow causally derived from their referents). "If words stood for pre-existing concepts," he pointed out, "they would all have exact equivalents in meaning from one language to the next; but this is not true" (116). Instead, he proposed a relational and "diacritical" understanding of language as a system based not on any natural or anthropological ground, but rather as established by social convention alone. "The linguistic sign unites, not a thing and a name," he wrote, "but a concept and a sound-image," a "signified" and a "signifier." Moreover—and this is perhaps his most crucial point—"the bond between the signifier and the signified is arbitrary" (66–67).

Saussure used an analogy to make his point: "Just as the game of chess is entirely in the combination of the different chesspieces, language is characterized as a system based entirely on the opposition of its concrete units" (107). A chess piece—a knight, say—is not, by itself, an element of the game, "for by its material make-up—outside its square and the other conditions of the game—it means nothing to the player; it becomes a real, concrete element" only when assigned a specific value within the game, "where elements hold each other in equilibrium in accordance with fixed rules" (110). As Saussure summarized it—in a crucial passage that frames many of the key assumptions of what will later in the century be called semiotics or semiology (the study of sign systems):

> Everything that has been said up to this point boils down to this: in language there are only differences. Even more important: a difference generally implies positive terms between which the difference is set up; but in language there are only differences *without positive terms*. Whether we take the signified or the signifier, language has neither ideas nor sounds that existed before the linguistic system, but only conceptual and phonic differences that have issued from the system. . . . But the statement that everything in language is negative is true only if the signified and the signifier are considered separately; when we consider the sign in its totality, we have something that is positive in its own class. . . . Although both the signified and the signifier are purely differential and negative when considered separately, their combination is a positive fact; it is even the sole type of facts that language has, for maintaining the parallelism between the two classes of differences is the distinctive function of the linguistic institution. (120–21)

A few points are worth emphasizing here. First, there is the apparently rather limited observation that language is a "differential and negative" system. What this means, however—to use systems theorist Gregory Bateson's terminology—is that language is not an *analogue* system of communication and representation, in which real "magnitudes" of physical properties have a direct and causal link to the signs used to express them (as in, for example, the readings on a mercury-filled thermometer that correspond in a linear way to real changes in body temperature). Rather, in a *digital* system such as human language (or mathematics), signs have no "correspondence of magnitude" with what they stand for. "The word 'big' is not bigger than the word 'little,'" Bateson points out, "and in general there is nothing in the pattern (i.e., the system of interrelated magnitudes) in the word 'table' which corresponds to the system of interrelated magnitudes in the object denoted" (1972, 373).

Even on this most elementary level, however, "difference" (say, the difference between the words "big" and "little") is far from a one-dimensional matter, since it is not a question of difference pure and simple, but rather—to use Bateson's winning formulation—of "*a difference which makes a difference*" (453): a difference whose meaning can only be determined by reference to the larger system of rules within which that difference functions. For example, Bateson points out, the differences between letters in the English language are not all exactly the *same* difference; in fact (as devotees of the board game Scrabble will appreciate), information theory has calculated mathematically the informational value of each letter in the alphabet of a given language, based on the statistical frequency of that letter's appearance (402). Moreover (as fans of the television show *Wheel of Fortune* would be the first to glean), if I show you a word in English whose elements are all masked except for the letter Q, you will be able to guess with far better than random success that the following letter is *U*.

Notice that the information thus communicated is not, strictly speaking, contained "in" the individual element in question. But neither is it wholly "outside" that element. Yet somehow it cannot be "squeezed" between the element and some aspect of the context in which it appears, because, as Bateson points out, "'information' and 'form' resemble contrast, frequency, symmetry, correspondence, congruence, conformity, and the like in being of zero dimensions"; unlike "quantities of real dimensions (mass, length, time) and their derivatives (force, energy, etc.)" (403), information and form "are not to be located" (408). What this means is that the meaning of any signifier cannot, strictly speaking, be fixed and located *anywhere*, since what it *is* is also a product of what it is *not* (i.e., other elements and rules in the system). The "presence" of the signifier's meaning is therefore quite literally predicated upon an "absence." What Derrida calls the *grammé*, to be studied by "grammatology" (and here we should recall Bateson once more), names this notion of the sign as irreducible relationality, this "element without simplicity" — an element at work not just in linguistic systems, but also, Derrida argues, in the notion of "program" in the informational and biological sciences (1974, 9).

Moreover, when we remember that Saussure's description of this dynamic covers not just signifiers but also signifieds ("concepts") — "language has neither *ideas* nor sounds that existed before the linguistic system, but only *conceptual* and phonic differences that have issued from the system," he writes — then the wide-ranging implications of his discovery come fully into view. For what this means, as Derrida puts it, is that the

> concept is never present in and of itself, in a sufficient presence that would refer only to itself. Essentially and lawfully, every concept is inscribed in a chain or in a system within which it refers to the other, to other concepts, by means of the systematic play of differences. Such a play, *différance*, is thus no longer simply a concept, but rather the possibility of conceptuality. (1982, 11)

But, given everything we have just said, this means that the conditions of possibility for a concept are at one and the same time the conditions of its *impossibility*—and it is that undigestible paradox (undigestible, at least, for the philosophical tradition Derrida is at pains to deconstruct) that Derrida's substitution of the *a* for *e* in his neologism *différance* is meant to mark.

It is just these implications, however, that Saussure's work finally sidesteps in its specific formulation of the theory of the sign. In so doing, Saussure attempts—either consciously or unconsciously—to push the genie of *différance* back into the bottle of what Derrida calls "the metaphysics of presence." The two primary symptoms of this failure in Saussure's work, according to Derrida, lay, first, in the details of Saussure's theory of the linguistic sign itself and, second, in his elevation of speech above writing. As for the first, Derrida observes that Saussure's "essential and juridical distinction" between the signifier and the signified "inherently leaves open the possibility of thinking *a concept signified in and of itself*, a concept simply present for thought, independent of a relationship to . . . a system of signifiers." Saussure thus reintroduces the very thing his theory had rightly meant to reject: the possibility of what Derrida calls a "transcendental signified" that would "exceed the chain of signs" (1981, 19–20). As for the second, Saussure's privileging of what Derrida calls "phonic substance" (21)—as in Saussure's insistence that "the linguistic sign unites, not a thing and a name, but a concept and a *sound-image*"—makes it possible to think of an intimate, unmediated relationship between consciousness and conceptuality, of consciousness expressing itself in and through "a signifier that does not fall into the world, a signifier that I hear as soon as I emit it, that seems to depend upon my pure and free spontaneity, requiring the use of no instrument, no accessory, no force taken from the world" (22). "To reduce the exteriority of the signifier," Derrida continues, "is to exclude everything in semiotic practice that is not psychic" (22)—which is exactly, of course, what Saussure set out *not* to do. It is also, at the same stroke, to reintroduce a notion of *communication* that "implies a *transmission charged with making pass, from one subject to another, the identity* of a *signified* object, of a *meaning* or of a *concept* rightfully separable from the process of passage and from the signifying operation" (23).

What is needed, then, is a theory of language that takes account of the fundamental *difference* between the psychological and the communicational dimensions, even as we need to be able to explain their obvious interactions and interrelations in and through language (see chapter 9, "Communication"). Here, the work of contemporary systems theorists such as Humberto Maturana, Francisco Varela, and Niklas Luhmann has proved valuable in developing in far more detail the observations of earlier systems theorists such as Bateson, and also in taking up the questions that occupy Derrida. In contemporary systems theory's handling of this problem, there is no better place to begin, perhaps, than with Luhmann's audacious assertion that "humans can't communicate. Not even their brains can communicate; not even their conscious minds can communicate. Only communication can communicate" (1994, 371). This may seem counterintuitive (to say the least), but in a sense Luhmann is simply inheriting and developing two key points from Saussure as radicalized by Derrida's deconstruction: the insistence that communication is above all a *social* (and not a "personal" or "psychological") fact, and the related suggestion that we might develop a "general semiology" (of which the analysis of specific linguistic systems might be only a part). In Luhmann's work, this project will be undertaken on the basis of two key theoretical commitments: first, his distinction between social systems (whose fundamental medium is *communication*) and psychic or psychological systems (whose fundamental medium is *consciousness*) and, second, his theoretical account of the formal dynamics of *meaning*, which both types of systems use to sustain themselves and carry out their "autopoiesis" (literally, "self-making"). Only within this antecedent theoretical framework does the question of *language* per se arise as a specific, second-order evolutionary development in the history of psychic and social systems.

The fundamental theoretical postulate of Luhmann's system theory (and of systems theory generally) is that once we have replaced the ontological distinctions familiar to us from the tradition of metaphysical philosophy (spirit/matter, mind/body, culture/nature, and so on) with the *functional* distinction system/environment, we must understand that the system/environment distinction is in an important sense asymmetrical, because the environment of any system is always already more complex than any single system can be. Because it is obviously impossible for any system—whether psychic or social—to establish point-for-point correspondences between its own internal states and the entirety of its environment, systems must find a way to deal with the problem of overwhelming environmental complexity. They do so, Luhmann argues, by deploying a self-referential code that provides a principle of selectivity for processing and responding to environmental changes, thus reducing environmental complexity to a degree that the system can manage. Moreover, under constant adaptive pressure, systems increase their selectivity—they make their environmental filters more finely textured, if you like—by building up their own *internal* complexity in a process that involves what Luhmann calls the "re-entry" of the system/environment distinction *within* the system itself.

Take, for example, the development of digital reproduction and the dissemination of its effects. The legal system need not (and cannot) respond to all of the technological, economic, and cultural factors that have caused this massive change in its environment. Rather, it reduces that complexity, responding *selectively* on the basis of the self-referential code "legal/illegal," which determines the relevance of some environmental factors and not others. For example, the technological differences between second- and third-generation Apple iPods (though they are indeed real changes in the environment and, in some contexts— marketing, say—immensely important) would be relevant for the legal system only to the extent that they bear upon the question of illegal file-sharing. The legal system responds to those environmental changes by building up its own internal complexity via the process of "re-entry." The system itself becomes the environment for the increasing complexity of the internal subsystem known (in this example) as "copyright law," for which, in turn, certain areas of its legal environment are relevant (issues of ownership and contract, say) and others (traffic laws) are not.

It is within this context that the development of "meaning" as a form has a key evolutionary and adaptive role to play for both psychic and social systems. Meaning provides for systems a form in which the "actual" and the "possible" can appear simultaneously; this is of obvious adaptive advantage because it provides a kind of modeling of environmental complexity for the system, thus enhancing the system's strategic options and range of choices (Luhmann 1995, 63). This "virtualization" of the environment via the form of meaning is put to good evolutionary use by both psychic and social systems, providing them with a more complex and flexible way of mapping and responding to the world around them. Indeed, in the coevolution of psychic and social systems, "meaning," Luhmann argues, "is the true 'substance' of this emergent evolutionary level. It is therefore false (or more gently, it is falsely chosen anthropocentrism) to assign the psychic . . . ontological priority over the social. It is impossible to find a 'supporting substance' for meaning. Meaning supports itself in that it enables its own self-referential reproduction. *And only the forms of this reproduction differentiate psychic and social structures*"—namely, "whether consciousness [in the case of psychic systems] or communication [social systems] is chosen as the form of operation" (98).

Here, of course, we find Luhmann's version of Derrida's critique of the assumption that writing or communication can be referred for its efficacy or validity to the ontological substrate of consciousness; in fact, it is the ontologically unsupported dynamic of writing-as-*différance* (Derrida) or "meaning" (Luhmann) that is fundamental. "The difficulty in seeing this," Luhmann writes (in a disarmingly commonsensical moment),

> lies in that every consciousness that tries to do so . . . cannot get outside of consciousness. For consciousness, even communication can only be conducted consciously and is invested in further possible consciousness. *But for communication this is not so.* Communication is only possible as an event that transcends the closure of consciousness: as the synthesis of more than the content of just one consciousness. (99)

Meaning, then, "enables psychic and social systems to interpenetrate, while protecting their autopoiesis" (219).

But meaning, of course, is a *form* and not a medium, so how is this "interpenetration" to take place, given Luhmann's insistence on the separation of consciousness and communication? It takes place, he contends, through the all-important medium of *language*. For Luhmann, language is not constitutive of either psychic or social systems, both of which can and do regularly engage in communication *without* using language per se. Rather, language is a very specific, second-order development in the evolution of human societies, a type of "*symbolically generalized communication media*" (161). After all, "communication is also possible without language" and may take place in all sorts of nonlinguistic ways, "perhaps through laughing, through questioning looks, through dress" (150). Even in the case of face-to-face communication between speakers who share the same language, we are better off thinking of the linguistic component of their communication as simply one element among many in a complex and often discontinuous ensemble that includes kinesics, gestures, and other performative elements, all of which communicate without words (the absence of these sorts of dampening and contextualizing elements may explain why many people find e-mail to be such a brittle and incendiary form of communication). Indeed, as Bateson points out, "when boy says to girl, 'I love you,' he is using words to convey that which is more convincingly conveyed by his tone of voice and his movements; and the girl, if she has any sense, will pay more attention to those accompanying signs than to the words" (1972, 412).

Language, then, may be "a medium distinguished by the use of signs"—one capable of "*extending* the repertoire of understandable communication *almost indefinitely in practice*," an achievement whose significance "can hardly be overestimated"—but "one must also keep its boundaries in view" (Luhmann 1995, 160). This disarticulation of language per se from meaning in a more general sense is crucial to understanding the specificity of art—and language's function as a medium within it. In fact, Luhmann argues, works of art use the *difference* between perception and communication in two fundamental ways: on the one hand, they use perceptual elements to stimulate communication about the artwork's meaning; on the other hand, they dramatize how the meaning of the work cannot be reduced to just its perceptual substrate or its medium alone (think here, for example, of Marcel Duchamp's urinal and snow shovel) (2000, 22, 23). For other social systems, the difference between perception and communication is a problem, one in which perception constantly threatens to impede communication (think, for example, of the tangled relations between emotions, oration, legal rulings, and theater in the modern courtroom). For art, this difference is a resource. Works of art carry out their own communication by staging the relationship between perception and communication in a unique way.

This is most obvious, perhaps, in the art form that uses language as a medium: literature. In literature (and especially in poetry), what is foregrounded is the difference between the text's semantic, denotative dimension and the sensuous, perceptual qualities of language that exceed it (for example, the familiar prosodic elements of rhyme, rhythm, and alliteration). That difference, however, is intended to provoke a *second-order* communication by the artwork itself (what does this difference *mean?*), in which the semantic aspect of the text's words (versus its sonorous or "musical" qualities) is only part of the story. This is why it is often said that poetry cannot be paraphrased. As Luhmann puts it, "Poetry has no use for denotations. Instead, it relies on connotations, employing words as a medium. . . . The poem becomes a unity only at the level of connotation, by exploring the liberties that come with *using words exclusively as a medium*" (2000, 124; emphasis added).

In literature, this use of language as an aural or even graphic, visual medium, nearly emptied of semantic and denotative content, may take a number of forms far beyond the devices of traditional prosody: from the "cut-up" and "fold-in" techniques of Dada in the 1920s, exemplified by figures such as Tristan Tzara; to William S. Burroughs's experiments with randomly cutting and remixing both printed media and audiorecordings of the voice in the 1950s; to the *bruitism* and performance poetry of Kurt Schwitters (one of his poems contains a single letter, *W*, which he "reads" to the audience in a disconcerting array of sonic registers and volumes, from guttural growls to high-pitched screams); and finally to concrete poetry, where the visual shape of the words on the page is paramount, and the playful typewriter experiments of poets such as

A. R. Ammons, whose poem "It's April" anticipates the "emoticons" often used in e-mail communication:

(o (o	a look-see
(o o)	slightly more direct
(—(—	shut-eye
($ (\$	American dream

(1977, 217)

This mobilization of the difference between perception and communication in the services of a *second* communication (that of the artwork itself) is not limited to verbal art, of course. In fact, Luhmann argues, it is the fundamental dynamic of art as such. Art is thus one of those "types of nonverbal communication that realize the same autopoietic structure as verbal communication . . . but are not bound by the specific features of language and thus extend the realm of communications beyond what can be put into words." In this sense, "art functions as communication although—or precisely because—it cannot be adequately rendered through words (let alone concepts)" (2000, 18, 19).

This is clearest, perhaps, in nonliterary art forms that nevertheless make use of language as a medium, and often in very different ways. There is, for example, the groundbreaking work of Joseph Kosuth during the mid- to late 1960s, which investigates the relations between representations and concepts in language, photography, and three-dimensional objects. His work *One and Three Chairs* (1965–67)—comprising a folding chair, a full-scale photograph of that same chair, and a photo-enlargement of the entry for the word *chair* in a dictionary—suggests that language is as important for what it does *not* communicate as for what it does. We find a very different (and perhaps contrary) approach in a series of paintings from the same period by John Baldessari, each of presents a statement painted in black letters on a large white canvas background. In *Everything Is Purged from This Painting but Art; No Ideas Have Entered This Work* (1966–68), the "painting" becomes the mere vehicle for the conceptual matter expressed in language that subsumes it—a language at once dematerialized (as transparent to the conceptual point of the work) and rematerialized (as a painted graphic element).

Later artists such as Barbara Kruger and Jenny Holzer are interested in the nearly overwhelming and, in some sense, unconscious power of words as well, and their work reminds us that one of the unique things about language as a medium for nonliterary art (versus, say, the medium of paint or video) is that it retains its semantic dimension after being "remediated" (to use Bolter and Grusin's term) in the artwork. Kruger and Holzer remind us how the language landscape of everyday life is in itself iconic, littered with prepackaged phrases, shibboleths, and bits of "common sense" that are part of a larger process of social and ideological reproduction. In her series *Truisms*, from the late 1970s, Holzer deployed hundreds of one-liners in a variety of settings and media—from cheap paper posters plastered around Manhattan, to T-shirts, to huge electronic displays in Times Square (where viewers would expect to see advertising or news headlines)—to force viewers into an active role in constructing the work's meaning, rather than simply consuming the languagescape in which they live. Viewers who read such statements as "A positive attitude means all the difference in the world" or "Absolute submission can be a form of freedom" are not only forced to judge whether the sayings are sincere or ironic; they are also confronted with their generic quality as forms of discourse. Language here communicates a semantic content, to be sure, but is also used as a medium to communicate *more* than it communicates.

The use of language as a medium in art need not, however, be limited to its written or graphic form. This is most obvious in music, perhaps, but it is also true of contemporary works such as Gary Hill's video piece *Remarks on Color* (1994). Here, a fifty-minute color video on a large screen is composed of a tight shot of his eight-year-old daughter Anastasia reading aloud from a book of the same title by philosopher Ludwig Wittgenstein. The piece is fascinating for many reasons, not the least of which is the contrast between Wittgenstein's philosophical meditations on language in the most abstract sense (and specifically on how the inability of language to describe color tells us something about language as such), and the unique rhythms of the child's voice, the misreadings and asynchronicity between her intonation and the text's denotation, as she reads a text she understands imperfectly at best. (In one well-known instance, she misreads "angles" as "angels.") Here, the use of the nongeneric, embodied materiality of the voice in the act of *parole* is quite different from what we find in Schwitters's work, and we are left with a host of questions: What is the "text" here? Wittgenstein's book? The girl's audible reading of it? The difference between the two? If language fails here, as Wittgenstein suggests it does in the face of color, does it fail in the same way? For the same reasons?

These questions, and the ethical and ontological issues deriving from them, which we touched on at the outset, are animating concerns for contemporary artist Eduardo Kac, who operates at the intersection of multiple practices and genealogies, including conceptual art, performance art, and bio-art. Kac (pronounced *katz*) often makes use of genetic and organic materials (including living plants and animals) alongside technologies of communications and "telepresence" such as the Internet, remote-viewing apparatuses, video links, and so on. One of the characteristic gestures of his work is to establish a kind of transcoding or, conversely, a jarring disjunction between quite diverse media, dramatizing the disarticulation of meaning and language that we have been discussing, and foregrounding the model of code, *grammé*, and program to explore how far it can be extended across diverse media, how it bears upon the evolutionary and adaptive futures of biological, ecological, and communicational or social systems.

One of his projects, *Genesis* (1998–99), is particularly pertinent to many of the issues we have been discussing. Kac took from the King James Version of the Old Testament a verse (Genesis 1:28) that reads, "Let man have dominion over the fish of the sea, and over the fowl of the air, and over every living thing that moves upon the earth," translated it into Morse code, and then translated the Morse code into *genetic* code using a rule in which the dashes of Morse code became thymine (T), the dots cytosine (C), the spaces between words adenine (A), and the spaces between letters guanine (G). He used this translation to create the genetic sequence for an "artist's gene" which was synthesized in the lab and then incorporated into bacteria displayed in a Petri dish in the gallery space. In the gallery itself, the three different texts/codes, along with a large overhead image of the bacteria, were projected onto the walls, while an original musical composition based upon the "artist's gene" and using "DNA music synthesis" played in the background. The bacteria could also be viewed over the Internet, and online participants could remotely activate an ultraviolet light in the gallery that caused mutations in the bacteria, and thus in the genetic code, and finally in the biblical text itself (Kac 2005, 249–51). For Kac, "the ability to change the sentence is a symbolic gesture: it means that we do not accept its meaning in the form we inherited it and that new meanings emerge as we seek to change it" (252).

Many things could be said about this work, but for our purposes what is most interesting is that it dramatizes the disjunction of meaning (here, genetic and Morse code, but also, interestingly enough, the mathematically formalizable code of music) and the specific medium of language, then uses that difference in the services of the second-order communication of the artwork itself, one that depends upon the irreducibly complex interactions between code, program, and *langue*, on the one hand, and the contingent, contextual events of *parole*, as articulated by remote viewer/participants, on the other. And both of these points are foregrounded as *ethical* issues in at least a double sense: not only as they bear upon the role of informatic systems in the control, production, and evolutionary futures of biological and ecological systems, but also (and less obviously) as they implicate certain traditional notions of authority that derive from the assumptions about the relations of language, concepts, and consciousness that we have been discussing.

As for the latter, *Genesis* both puts to use and finally undermines the assumption that the presence of the voice (or "phonic substance," to use Derrida's phrase) is a guarantor of the authority or validity of concepts embodied in language—an idea that finds its corollary in the idea of the Word as *presence* that grounds the entire "ontotheological tradition" whose contradictions Derrida is at pains to disclose (1981, 10). In the original biblical inscription from Genesis, for example, the pronouncement is taken by believers to be the "voice of God" (offered in the "imperative voice," no less); indeed, the Word is taken to be authoritative insofar as there is an *absence* of mediation between the voice of the divine and what Derrida calls the "exteriority" of language itself. And yet, as Kac's own three-tiered work of translation is calculated to remind us, those "exterior" elements that are responsible for the "voice" before us are almost infinite in their complexity and historicity. For example, as Kac notes in an essay on the project, he selected the King James Bible specifically "as a means of highlighting the multiple mutations of the Old Testament and its interpretations," underscoring the fact that this translation was itself literally "a translation of many translations." Moreover, he notes, if we want to take seriously the "authority" of the text's "source," we need to know that the earliest versions of the text we now call "the Bible," first fixed on written scrolls between 1400 BCE and 100 CE, have "no spaces between words and sentences, no periods and commas, and no chapters." These were added as "subsequent translations and editions attempted to simplify and organize the text—that is, to arrest its continuous transmutation—only to generate more versions" (2005, 261n1). Here, Kac's work reminds us that language is both form *and* medium: form, because were it not so, no translation of any sort would be possible; medium, insofar as the exteriority and materiality of the linguistic and textual form always intervenes, in an irreducibly complex way, between us and the text's meaning. And this, as we have already noted, has profound implications for the supposed authority of the speaking subject.

At the other end of the project, as it were, the work disrupts the idea that meaning is simply the expression of an internal psychological state; it insists, in Luhmann's terms, on the irreducible difference between psychic and social systems. On the one hand, it invites remote participants to "express themselves" in apparently the simplest, most unproblematic way possible: the binary code of "click/no click" on the computer mouse that activates the UV light near the bacteria. Remember, though, that the light causes mutations in the genetic material, directing it away from its "original" state, and thus implicitly altering the biblical text. The viewer is thus drawn into an exercise of the very "dominion" she is resisting and implicated in the ethical complexities involved in activating the link between meaning, code, and authority. If the viewer *does* intervene in the process, "he changes the sentence and its meaning but does not know what new versions might emerge" (252); he becomes an agent not of meaning (conceived as the direct expression and effect of his psyhic interior)—not simply replacing one Word with another—but of *mutation* brought on by the unpredictable, complex interactions of factors external, and yet integral, to the utterance that eventuates from his decision.

What must now strike us is the radical disjunction between what the artwork itself signifies in its second-order communication, which makes *use of* language and code as a medium, and the changes in the codes and texts themselves, which produce the "new" version of Genesis—changes that are both minimal and, strictly speaking, nonsensical: "*Let aan have dominion over the fish of the sea and over the fowl of the air and over every living thing that ioves ua eon the earth.*" Clearly, the meaning of Kac's *Genesis* cannot be reduced to the alteration of a few letters; it is not, strictly speaking, linguistic at all. In fact, in a very real sense, the meaning of the work can be located *nowhere*. This irreducibility of the meaning of the work to its perceptual substrate is ironically underscored by the inscription of the "final product" on a pair of laser-etched granite "Encryption Stones," which themselves allude ironically to the twin stone tablets on which, in biblical lore, the Ten Commandments were etched by the hand of God, in a direct transcription of his voice as heard by Moses on Mount Sinai—a paradigmatic instance of the "ontotheological" tradition we have already touched on above. Yet the stones also allude, Kac suggests, to the Rosetta Stone, whose discovery by Napolean's army in 1799 (man's dominion, indeed!) made possible translation between the three languages—Egyptian hieroglyphics, demotic script, and ancient Greek—that were inscribed there (255–56).

Kac's own *Encryption Stones* and their three "languages" thus remind us that the dream of translation, of complete transparency between one language and another, has always been with us. But the stones also remind us that such a dream carries with it a risk, one that is dramatized in the seductive and facile dream of "the Book of Life" (always close at hand in discussions of the genetic code): a dream that carries with it the ancient danger of the very "dominion" that Kac's biblical text enunciates. So perhaps it is less the idea of code than of *master* code—in which all languages would be one, in which consciousness and communication could be bodied forth in all their simultaneity and transparency—that

Eduardo Kac, *Encryption Stones*, 2001. Laser-etched granite (diptych), 20 x 30 inches each. Collection Richard Langdale.

Kac's work is calculated to disrupt. And perhaps—to return to the issues with which we began—the "dominion" that bases itself upon that notion of language might change if our notion of language itself changes.

References and Suggested Readings

Ammons, A. R. 1977. *The Snow Poems*. New York: Norton.

Bateson, Gregory. 1972. *Steps to an Ecology of Mind*. New York: Ballantine. See esp. "Cybernetic Explanation," "Redundancy and Coding," "Form, Substance, and Difference."

Bolter, Jay David, and Richard Grusin. 2000. *Remediation: Understanding New Media*. Cambridge, MA: MIT Press.

Derrida, Jacques. 1974. *Of Grammatology*, trans. Gayatri Chakravorty Spivak. Baltimore: Johns Hopkins University Press.

——. 1981. "Semiology and Grammatology: Interview with Julia Kristeva." In *Positions*, trans. Alan Bass, 15–36. Chicago: University of Chicago Press.

——. 1982. "Différance." In *Margins of Philosophy*, trans. Alan Bass, 1–28. Chicago: University of Chicago Press.

——. 1988. *Limited Inc.*

——. 1989. *Of Spirit: Heidegger and the Question*, trans. Geoffrey Bennington and Rachel Bowlby. Chicago: University of Chicago Press.

Kac, Eduardo. 2005. *Telepresence and Bio Art: Networking Humans, Rabbits, and Robots*. Ann Arbor: University of Michigan Press.

Luhmann, Niklas. 1994. "How Can the Mind Participate in Communication?" In *Materialities of Communication*, ed. Hans Ulrich Gumbrecht and K. Ludwig Pfeiffer, 371–88. Stanford, CA: Stanford University Press.

———. 1995. *Social Systems*, trans. John Bednarz Jr. with Dirk Baecker. Stanford, CA: Stanford University Press, 1995.

———. 2000. *Art as a Social System*, trans. Eva M. Knodt. Stanford, CA: Stanford University Press.

Maturana, Humberto, and Francisco Varela. [1992] 1987. "Linguistic Domains and Human Consciousness." In *The Tree of Knowledge: The Biological Roots of Human Understanding*. Boston: Shambhala/New York: Random House.

Osborne, Peter, ed. 2002. "Word and Sign." *Conceptual Art*. London: Phaidon.

Rorty, Richard M., ed. [1967] 1992. *The Linguistic Turn*. Chicago: University of Chicago Press.

Saussure, Ferdinand de. [1915] 1959. *Course in General Linguistics*. Ed. Charles Bally, Albert Sechehaye, and Albert Riedlinger. Trans. Wade Baskin. New York: McGraw-Hill.

Wittgenstein, Ludwig. 1958. *Philosophical Investigations*. Oxford: Blackwell.

17 :: LAW

PETER GOODRICH

The relation between law and the media is best depicted in terms of a radical ambivalence. The First Amendment to the U.S. Constitution guarantees freedom of expression, and the Supreme Court is unequivocal in its apparent hostility to all forms of censorship. The right to free speech reigns symbolically over the airwaves and the Internet. On the other hand, the interests of national security, the Patriot Act, and the general and amorphous war on terror permit an expansive yet shadowy realm of surveillance and policing of all communications. Since the Radio Act of 1927 the airwaves have been subject to regimes of licensing and ex post facto control of content through fines and other less direct threats and sanctions. Lobbying, private lawsuits, threats of legislation, corporate self-governance, and consumer boycotts have all also contributed to a rigorous self-policing of the media, gauged both to avoiding conflict with the legislature and to appeasing vaguely defined norms of "the public interest," meaning morality, decency, and propriety, while avoiding vulgarity, prurience, and offence. Wherever possible, in the words of Justice Stevens, law seeks to "channel behavior" rather than directly to prohibit or prescribe.

The key to understanding the tension between law and the media lies in the recognition that law itself functions as a symbolic system or, in an old juridical expression, as a theater of justice and truth. Law enacts in a highly visible and profoundly theatrical form the authoritative drama of social self-presence, the offices and roles of public life, the proper channels and forms of serious or simply visible social discourse. It is as a symbolic discourse, as the most basic or structural form of imagined community, that law both regulates and competes with the other discourses of social self-presence. Put simply, the symbolic function of law is first that of establishing a hierarchy of discourses with the image and other signs of legality reigning at its pinnacle. The licit image of law and of lawful discourse operates as a primary icon of sociality, as the embodiment of the moral order of the imagined community, and is pitched above and, where necessary, against competing claims to social rationality or threats to the sovereign law and indigenous order of established institutions and their extant moral creed. Only where the channeling function, the self-discipline of the media, fails to prevent perceived threats to the symbolic order of law and its customary norms of quiescent morality does the law intrude directly upon the media. When it does so, it is always also acting to preserve its own image and the status of law as a higher and separate order of discourse. This essay will begin by examining the foundational character of law as a medium, as a symbolic and discursive social enterprise, and then move to analyze how law directly and indirectly governs other discourses and media.

Dogma, Doctrine, and Decision

There is one antique and undisputed common law power to summarily imprison, meaning to convict and sentence without trial. It inevitably concerns the public image of law and is termed "contempt of court." Anyone who acts in such a way as to embarrass the court, or behaves in a manner calculated to lessen its authority or dignity can be punished immediately, an exercise of judicial power "coeval with the law itself," intended to protect the public image and symbolic stature of legal personnel and proceedings. A legally unexceptional illustration can help frame the point.

The plaintiff, Orlando Thomas, appeared in Clay County Court to pay a fine for a suspended driver's license and an expired inspection ticket.[1] Nothing much. He was informed by Judge Guest, however, that there was a pending public profanity charge against him as well, and the judge proceeded immediately to trial on the latter charge. Thomas was found guilty and fined. On his way out of the courtroom he called the judge a "son of a bitch" and was thereupon placed under arrest for contempt of court. He was taken in handcuffs before the judge and asked if he understood that he was being held in contempt of court. He remained silent, whereupon the judge became upset and ordered that he be placed in jail. Thomas was led from the courtroom but before leaving directed another obscenity toward the judge. "At this point Judge Guest came down from the bench and physically attacked Thomas." The pair were separated and Thomas was taken to jail. On appeal, his contempt conviction was upheld. That Judge Guest had attacked him may have been a judicial mistake, misconduct even, but the plaintiff's contempt of court was unaffected by that and certainly not expunged by the fact that he had enraged the bench. The argument that the insult had been ad hominem—directed to the man and not to the judge in his official capacity—also failed.

The judge is not a person but an office. What the judge does as judge is invested with a dignity and authority, a *maiestas* or majesty, that not even the judge in his personal capacity can suspend. Add to this that the lead-up to the altercation was the determination that the defendant was guilty of "public profanity," an offence against the order of both church and secular law, and the symbolic role of the legal order comes into clearer view. It is not simply that the social order and the legal order are structurally separate and potentially opposed spheres, but that the function of law includes maintaining and, when necessary, reimposing or reinventing and policing the hierarchy of symbolic orders, the diversity of sites of public discourse or mediated expression. The legal order is not any order, nor is legal writing, to borrow a phrase, the work of any scrivener's boy in his master's shop. The law is a dogmatic order, it expresses and promulgates the articles—the axioms—of social faith and should be approached initially precisely in terms of the symbolic forms of social presence and the gravity of its modes of expression.

The social presence of law is distinctively monumental. It belongs within the written city and first confronts the citizen in the form of architectural tropes. The places from which law speaks are set apart from the street and emblematically protected by elevated entrances, classical columns, Latin inscriptions, statues, murals, guards, and often enough the figure of *Iustitia*, the deity of Justice, portrayed as a blindfolded—mutilated—woman holding out a sword and scales.[2] To this we can add the panoply of other guardians, the portraits, lists, books, and then also the raised bench, the judicial throne, the separating bar, the foreign languages, court dress, and the various enclosures and secret doors that form the essential paraphernalia of agonistic trial and its attendant legal rites.

The social drama of jurisdiction serves to map and enforce the various forms of legal competence, the official places from which law speaks through the sovereign or its delegates. Juridification, the creeping presence of law in all the media of communication, in the intimate public sphere, in the unconscious, is visual, plastic, and frontal. Law operates first through images of its difference, through symbols of its separation from the social: the iconic expressions of law, the multiple representations of legitimate modes of social being, are pitched against the idols or false images of the outlawed, the *homo sacer*, and currently the terrorist, the order of being that barely exists outside of civility and its synonym, law.[3] Clearly this antinomic opposition replicates the classical history of religious discourses, which pitch light against darkness, good against evil, and reason against falsehood and deceit.

The imposing physical presence of law, its architecture, its symbols, the aesthetic of its visual impositions, obviously separates and protects a distinctly emblematic identity and order of knowing. Lawyers inhabit their own world. Their knowledge is internal to their discipline, their methods peculiar to their madness. The lawyer scholar of the early modern era was regularly represented as an "addict" of law, as someone saturated in norms, an individual who, in one fine early description, is "so full of law points, that when they sweat it is nothing but law; when they breath it is nothing but law, when they sneeze it is perfect law, when they dream it is profound law. The book of Littleton's Tenures is their breakfast, their dinner, their boier [tea], their supper and their rare banquet."[4] The jurist addict loved law jealously and exclusively, he loved law alone, or as one early critic put it, "You would love law, but *sine rivali* [without rivals], you would reign, but alone, *hinc illae lachrymae* [hence all these tears]."[5]

Legal control of the image of law—the professional cosseting of the rites of rule within foreign languages, obscure argots, the formalism and the simple verbosity of legalese—has protected and distanced law both from internal critique and from any effectively informed popular challenge. Nor is the protection of law's self-promulgated image simply a matter of disciplinary cunning, of an impenetrable aesthetic and linguistic code. It is also a matter of legal regulation, whereby the image of the law, the authority of judgment and specifically of the figure of the judge, is jealously protected, not only through the summary jurisdiction of contempt of court, but also by rules that govern the presence of cameras and the reporting of cases *sub judice*, or under judicial deliberation. Countless rules and conventions, norms of public order, tacit codes of dress and conduct exist to regulate the proper image, as the maxim goes, of a justice that "must not only be done but must be seen to be done." Of which we can say that the image of law is central to legality and intrinsic to the letter of the law, here understood not simply as the word—the *ipsissima verba*—of the positive norms, but also as the missive, the medium of legality, the writ or sending of decrees.

The primary image of common law, its ambulant visual presence, is embodied in and expressed through the figure of the judge. The judge is the bearer of the oracles, the custodian of an antique and continuing prior knowledge or precedent, not merely the rule but the *nomos* of law. This *nomos*, to borrow from early Greek sources, refers to a method, a melody or rhythm that precedes positive law and makes it possible. If we move to ask how common law captures the imagination of its subjects, how it grasps the affect and generates the consent of its citizens, how it civilizes—literally from *civilis*, those subject to the *corpus iuris civilis*—then the fundamental importance of the representation of law, its aesthetic and rhetorical traditions becomes evident. In Roman law the law of persons was explicitly *ius imaginum*, the law of images, and common law, while it does not use that particular expression, adopts the same foundational principle of legal personality as a fictive mask, a figural and theatrical form. Society and subject are alike instituted legally, structured according to the legal institutional categories of persons, actions, and things. To be a person, to act in the world, requires use of the "forms of action," the symbolic rites of familial role and public office, accession to the *vincula* or bonds of law.

The *nomos*—or foundational and always prior appropriation that justifies law, its absent origin, its arcane and mysterious source in God or nature or moral creed—still gains direct expression in the rites and inscriptions that surround and inaugurate the presence of law. There is a visible system of iconic imitation. The sovereign, to use the words inscribed over the national archive in Washington, DC, carries all the texts of the law in its breast—*omnia scrinia habet in pectore sua*. There the father of social rule still reigns. It bears still the power of life and death, both *regia* and *patria potestas*, the power to state both norm and exception that constitutes the embodiment of governance. Note also the use of services—the Red Mass before the opening of the Supreme Court term, for example, or the State Opening of the British Parliament—the interpellation or cry as the judge enters the courtroom (some variant on "Oyez, oyez, oyez, all rise"), and the residual forms of dress and of address ("your honor") that mark the continuance of ritual and the importance of appearance within the modern law. It is indelibly marked by its imperial roots, its social paternity, the homonymy of spiritual and secular when it comes to matters of legality as represented in and through the image of the father as the medium through which law appears.

The prevalence of the image of paternity resides as much as anything else in the fact that the father—*haec imago*, this image, as the divines used to say—cannot be everywhere present. The order of images stems, in other words, from the need to provide signs of authority that can be ambulant and present throughout a jurisdiction—an area of territorial competence—in which the sovereign lawmaker cannot always or even often be physically or literally present. The sovereign, that is, has usually to appear in images, and specifically in the multiple and itinerant images of his children or followers. Law appeared through its signs. It was self-consciously represented as a hieroglyphic tradition, a matter of an initiate knowledge and an essentially hidden sanctity. On one side, this meant that law was intrinsically bound to sovereign judgment, to the obscure diktats, the "fiats and fuits" of the lawgivers who pronounced the case law and precedents, technically the unwritten law. On the other side, it meant that access to the law itself could only be by way of the symbols or other hieroglyphs, latterly the opaque texts, through which the interior knowledge of the judges was represented and promulgated. This dramatically symbolic role of legal communication is captured in the well-established notion that "the words of the law may be compared to certain images called *Sileni Alcibiadis*, whose outward feature was deformed and ugly, but within they were full of jewels and precious stones."[6] In this respect, it is emblematically interesting that the image of Justice, *Iustitia*, comes to be represented as blindfolded at precisely the time that Renaissance lawyers were describing an unwritten and age-old law. The image emblematizes legality, pure judgment, but also portrays a judge who does not look without for external support but within for an interior and invisible truth.[7]

The argument of the early modern common lawyers was that law was a language of truth, a venerable tradition of books and "communal opinions of the Bar," maxims and cases that should be preserved always in their original and pristine forms, and so best kept away from the adulteration of actual use. The language of law was *vocabula artis*, and in it Lord Chief Justice Coke said we will find "many words that cannot defend themselves *in Bello Grammaticali*, in Grammatical Warre, and yet are more significant, compendious and effectual to express the true sense of the matter than if they were expressed in pure Latine."[8] We must, as the Romans used to say, have faith in our instruments, *de fide instrumentorum*, which means trusting to the books of the law and the interpretations of the judges although we ourselves, the populace, will never be able to assess them. In fact, according to Coke, it would be positively disadvantageous if a nonlawyer were to read the text of the law and then, believing erroneously that he understood it, land himself in penury and ruin. Error in a single letter could and often did wreak havoc and exclude a suit, invalidate a plea, or negate a transaction. The language of law, these carefully preserved terms of art, was written to posterity and not to the present age nor to the audience present and living. The lawyer does not speak but is spoken through.

Law is prior judgment, it is always and already in existence and so merely awaiting enunciation. It is habitually presented in the passive voice and in the mode of indirect speech. The judge as archetypically portrayed not only judged with downcast eyes but spoke as a medium, "in the name of" an absent source of law, not as author but as a custodian and promulgator of texts. To this we can add that the image of law itself, preserved and purveyed by its professionals, its "actors," is that of distant and absolute written instruments, of tables, writs, books, dooms, and codes. Derrida's famous proposition that writing precedes speech is nowhere more evident than in law. The law is in the books or it doesn't exist. The code encodes, and while it makes the law visible and public in one sense, apparently there for all to see, whole and socially present, visibility is not the same thing as intelligibility. Anyone untrained in law who seeks to resolve a legal problem on their own will rapidly experience lexical and textual disorientation. The pattern of lay encounters with the raw instruments of legality, the texts of law, is one of intellectual confusion leading to existential helplessness, and likely culminating not too far off in physical exhaustion or simple admission of incapacity.

The Anti-Aesthetic

The early and continuing form of preservation of the symbolic distinctiveness of law can be read in the history of movements to reform it. The earliest attempt to reform English law came with the Statute of Pleadings of 1356. It legislated that oral pleas should be in English rather than French, and recorded (enrolled) in Latin. The statute itself, however, is written in French and had no appreciable impact upon the bar or upon practice. It sounded politically appealing but was legally nugatory. That was it in terms of formal attempts at reform until the interregnum Parliament of 1650 passed *An Act for Turning the Books of the Law, and all Proces and Proceedings in Courts of Justice, into English*. Again, the statute itself was far from accessible. Every technical term was either Latin or French, and the act was repealed the first year after the restoration of the Crown. The Commonwealth died and with it died the short-lived hopes of the English revolutionaries that law could be a genuine and vernacular expression of popular will. In the immortal words of John Cooke, the lawyer who prosecuted Charles I and sent him to the scaffold for tyrannicide: "We fought for the public good and would have enfranchised the people and secured the welfare of the whole groaning creation, if the nation had not more delighted in servitude than freedom."[9]

The defense of the esoteric and essentially hidden character of legal texts was as much as anything else a successful attempt to wrest the image of legality from the domains of mundane use. Its majesty resided in its distance, its truth lay in the protection of the site from which it was enunciated, and this entailed ritual solemnization of the texts through which the law was made to speak. Here again, we should recall the religious background to legal debate. The common law was and is a Christian tradition. Its maxims of equity were first formulated and pronounced by bishops, and its relation to images was comparably complex. The Roman tradition captured this well in the notion that the image is *veritas falsa*—a "false truth."[10] What did this mean? That law promulgates fictions. That images are necessary: they convey the majesty of law to the populace, they are signs the illiterate can comprehend and fear, they are *liber pauperum*, poor men's books, but they are appearances rather than realities, figures or metaphors rather than plain spoken truths. The image was effective, it got things done. It provided the figure of the truth, but the truth itself was elsewhere, absent, a function of the prototype, of the divinity of which all else was a shadow or pale reflection. For that reason, the lawyers were hostile to imagery even as they depended upon it. That is the paradox of legal communication. It is a rhetoric pitched against rhetoric. It is technically an antirrhetic, a polemical genre of words delivered against images and against the figurative use of words. Its survival depends upon dissimulation, upon fictions and images that have to be presented as icons, as images that are the necessary and direct medium of truth, images that are not images at all.

In common law parlance, the judge speaks from a site of truth, a space beyond images: *res judicata pro veritate accipitur*. Such then is the beginning place of law, that of an irrefragable and iconic excess of images, an origin that is portrayed through an impossible image, an interior and inscrutable belief that places all other knowledge within a hierarchy of imitative forms. Knowledge either belongs within, and evidences obedience to the legal hierarchy of places and modes of knowing, or it is illicit, undignified and idolatrous. Lawyers refused and continue to refuse reform of legal language. It must and should remain esoteric, professional; except in limited instances where plain English has been imposed by the legislature to protect consumers, the boilerplates, the standard forms— antique, foreign, and prolix—continue. So too at the level of images.

The *Digest*, the textual code of early Roman law, contains a fragment that is much to the point. It stipulates that any Roman citizen who "appeared on the stage to act or recite" was subject to the penalty of *infamia*, meaning loss of citizenship or civil death.[11] It is a structural moment because what is at issue is precisely the assertion of control over social self-representation, the image of serious speech or of presence and meaning. Theater was too close to law to be allowed, too competitive with the drama of trials to be comfortable, and in the case of tragedy in particular, too proximate in theme and content to take place without careful control and frequent censorship. What the *Digest* stipulated as a universal ban, which lasted some two centuries, is repeated frequently in episodic proscriptions of theater, anti-aesthetic interventions that litter the history of the legal form and get repeated in more subtle ways in the rules that govern and closely regulate the interpretation and dissemination of legal texts.[12] Transactions involving speech are constitutionally privileged, supposedly immune from state intervention, yet law creeps into the operation of all media to preserve power, to channel identity, to protect children, to reflect and enforce standards, and to maintain public order. On the margins of social communication, the search for a medium that forces nonregulation is ever present, a utopian quest (a "hacker manifesto," as it were), but the historical and juridical truth is that these escapes are momentary. No one escapes the institution, at least not for long.[13]

Regulation

Government and media are yoked, often tragically, in the architecture of sovereignty.[14] Laws may on occasion be passed to protect property rights, freedom of expression, minority interests, cultural diversity, or freedom of information, but all of these rights pass though the vice of judicial interpretation and are subordinate to the interests of law and the security of governance. The modern history of regulation stems from the Printing Act of 1662. It introduced into common law a system of licensing of printers that replaced the earlier system of Royal Privileges granted to publishers. The act stipulated that there could be no publishing without government authorization, and the importation and sale of printed matter was also regulated, specifically so as to prohibit the circulation of any material offensive to the church, the government, or the corporations. Although the language of regulation has changed and is somewhat less direct, the current system of licensing the media in the United States can best be understood in the same broad terms; the Radio Act of 1927 and its progeny, the Communications Act of 1934, have their roots in the earlier Printing Act.

The Communications Act established the Federal Communications Commission (FCC), which historically licensed the broadcast media according to criteria of "citizenship, character, and financial, technical and other qualifications of a broadcast licensee." In the broadest of terms, the licensee is supposedly a fiduciary and the spectrum a public resource. Foreign interests are therefore limited in their capacity to own U.S. broadcast interests, both because of national interest and because the relation of owner to audience is putatively one of trust and community service. Such standards are, however, disappearing forms. The governing criterion of licensing and regulation is the indefinable concept of the public interest. Licenses are allocated, supposedly, pursuant to character qualifications following consideration not only of, say, applicants' criminal records, but also of the amorphous notion of their morality. The concept is so elastic as to be either comedic or tragic, depending upon one's political perspective. Shopping channels are deemed to be operating in the public interest because they satisfy public demand, and so are protected speech. Meanwhile, character qualifications and moral concern are used to threaten broadcasters for even momentary lapses. While there is no prior review of the content of broadcasts, sanctions do await those who air proscribed material, even passing uses of indecent words, or images as trivial as a breast glimpsed during a concert. The audio beep may lack the gravity or extent of the black band of the Soviet press, but it is just as surely the sign of the censor. The likelihood or fear is that as regulation comes increasingly to be applied to the various bandwidths of the Web a similar control over character and offense, most generally to governmental, legal, and corporate interests and loyalties, will be asserted.[15]

It might seem that the image of law and the preservation of the ritual sites of legal enunciation and enactment are marginal to the regime of regulation and the markets for ideological and political loyalty that the increasingly global technologies of communication mediate. That is in one way true. Law is itself simply a medium for effectuating the commercial and political interests of communication concentrations. Government in the United States may not be obviously or immediately involved in implementing standards of public interest in broadcast programming insofar as there is no government-owned channel or medium, but the legal imposition of vaguely stated standards often has the effect of limiting expression and controlling content. The abstract and shifting concept of the public interest is brought to bear by the FCC and the courts both to protect cultural identity and freedom of expression and to sanction transgressions of the loosely defined normative boundaries of free speech. A good example of this process can be found in the development and demise of the "fairness doctrine."

This doctrine was developed by the FCC and, as described in the "fairness primer" of 1964, imposed on the licensee, when presenting issues of public importance, "an affirmative duty generally to encourage and implement the broadcast of all sides of controversial issues" with a view to achieving "fairness" through balance. This assurance, however, was constrained by corporate control of principal media outlets and the vision of the public interest and public issues they believed would best sell to the consumer. Short-lived public interest movements did push the FCC to act as a guardian of the public conscience and of civil rights in the 1970s and early 1980s, but the longer-term trend was toward what one court termed a "limited right" of access. The Supreme Court decision on campaign financing in *Buckley v. Valeo*, which determined that neither federal nor state law can restrict how much money a candidate spends on his or her own campaign, was effectively the death knell for pluralist access, in that wealth could buy overwhelming advantage in access and expression of interest, including of course ownership of the media themselves.[16] It thus consigned the fairness doctrine to the museum of regulation, a relic of a liberal era superseded by the complexities of scale and asset management internal to megalithic corporate concentrations or sidelined by political infomercials and other quasi-legal interactions between lobbying groups and voter-oriented symbolic acts of reprimand or sanction. As the traditional standards evaporate, the FCC now effectuates government interest through a permissive regime of media self-discipline, a free-for-all of access and expression for the wealthily enfranchised, along with a more shadowy regime under the cover of moral and military interventions.

The other face of the equation is that the legal medium of regulation contains a message. The ever-present threat of intervention *in terrorem*, of material being adjudged offensive by the Federal Communications Commission, or of a license being revoked, governs content and limits freedom of expression. The key source of modern case law on this issue is the Supreme Court decision in the case of the broadcast of a satiric monologue titled "Filthy Words," authored and performed by comedian George Carlin.[17] Prompted by a complaint, the FCC ruled that the language used in the monologue was "indecent" and prohibited by section 1464 of Title 18 of the U.S. Code, which forbids the use of any "obscene, indecent, or profane language." While the commission did not impose formal sanctions, it did state that the order would be "associated with" the Pacifica Foundation's licensing file and that any subsequent complaints would reopen the question of sanctions, including fines and revocation of license. The majority of the Supreme Court upheld the determination. Previous case law had determined only that obscene materials were outside of the Constitutional protection of free speech "because their content is so offensive to contemporary moral standards." In the present case, however, the content of the respondent's broadcast was merely "vulgar, offensive, and shocking" because of its use of "words dealing with sex and excretion." Could this content, by analogy with the cases on obscene content, be regulated?

The court notes first, at a purely normative level, that "it is a central tenet of the First Amendment that the government must remain neutral in the marketplace of ideas." If the offensiveness of Carlin's monologue could be traced to its political content or satirical bent, then protection might be required. But such was not the case. Utterances such as Carlin's "are no essential part of any exposition of ideas, and are of such slight social value as a step to truth that any benefit that may be derived from them is clearly outweighed by the social interest in order and morality." Having determined that "Filthy Words" lacked literary merit and was bereft of scientific and political value and of "seriousness," it was a short step for the court to uphold the FCC sanction while claiming that the object of the prohibition was not the content of the monologue but the form.

The case is important for a number of reasons, of which two merit mention here. First, note the disjunction between norm and application. The court resoundingly announces that the First Amendment requires neutrality in the realm of ideas. Freedom of thought and expression are asserted, affirmed, even lauded throughout the judgment. Nothing in the decision will impact negatively upon the content of discourse or the liberty of the airwaves. That said, the decision then holds that Pacifica can be sanctioned and even have its license removed ex post facto for having broadcast a satirical comedy routine on the puerility and prudishness of prevailing norms of linguistic propriety. Second, note the mode of regulation, the channeling of behavior through manipulation of the statutory language. Previous law had interpreted section 1464 as being restricted to the obscene, defined as being of "prurient interest." The additional terms, "indecent" and "profane," were included simply as synonyms or subspecies of obscenity. Now, however, the Court reads the "and" linking the three terms as disjunctive rather than conjunctive, and so is able to apply a different standard to indecent language. Such a little word, such big effects. Through such manipulations of vague juridical standards—public interest, social order, and morality as the criteria by which the sanctioning of word and image is legitimated—the hidden sources of legal regulation of the media, the portentous yet also seemingly commonsense legitimacy of the mode of governance, becomes apparent. The norms of freedom reign in the discourse of law and court, while tacit norms, sanction, and threat reign in the domain of practice.

The dissonance between norm and practice that is witnessed in relation to indecent expression helps explain both the punitive and frequently opaque character of legal governance and the protective and occasionally libertarian role and rulings of the court. The sanctioning of satire is made possible through exactly the same legal means—the judicial capacity for extension and invention—as are used to expand or restrict civil rights, the protection of minorities, the prohibition of hate speech, equal air time, and freedom of information. The courts will do what they view as appropriate and morally right because the general standards of common law and the freedom allowed through interpretation permit a host of novelties. The constants are the method of regulation and the rules of legal reasoning. The general freedom that the court exhibited in the *Pacifica* case can be traced to the overarching power of the sovereign to intervene and seize media and materials in moments of *iustitium*, or self-defined emergency. When the public interest in social order and morality is displaced by the national security interest then the law effectively dispenses with the usual restraints of text and interpretation. The declaration of this exception allows for a wide range of interventions and appropriations of media time. Section 215 of the Patriot Act (as amended March 2006) also provides for a wide power of intervention to seize materials. Such legislation, however, is simply the tip of the iceberg. What matters in practical terms are Department of Justice guidelines, FBI practices, and executive orders for wiretapping and surveillance that are subject to no effective external legal oversight but simply to the vagaries of political opinion, if or when exposed.

Law stands down where the issue is either directly or indirectly that of the preservation of the image of the sovereign, understood here in terms of national security or public interest in its strongest of senses. The logic of such distancing of law from the regulation of government control of communication is a paradoxical one. The legal system as a dogmatic order is a part of the armature of sovereignty, itself a member of the body that legal restraint would here be applied to or exercised upon. For the courts to control the sovereign at the level of images would be for the courts to attack a member of their own body. What is at issue in the practices of law enforcement as applied to the communications industry is a reading of the signs of dissent or hostility to the prevailing order of government and law. Where the issue is not one of direct hostility, and it seldom is, then the dimension of concern is the image of reverence, the respect for rites that the communications offer. The criterion then is not offensiveness but rather attitude as a predictor of belligerence or subversion.

Measured against the inaccessibility of law and its atemporal media of communication, all other social speech is secondary and by law must be accessible to legal scrutiny and disencryption. As the technological capacities of communication expand exponentially, the powers of surveillance and censorship require equal expansion. That is a primary interest of government, and the 1994 Communications Assistance to Law Enforcement Act requires "all telecommunications common carriers to ensure that new technologies and services do not hinder law enforcement access to the communications of a subscriber" (47 U.S.C. §§1001–1021). In other words, and whatever the expense, telecommunication carriers, satellite providers, Internet service providers, and search engines cannot install encryption technologies that would resist governmental tapping. The other side to the obscurity of dogma and the inaccessibility of legal communication, its coded character and initiate quality, is the requirement of the transparency of all other carriers and codes. It is illegal to import encryption/decryption technology for the same reason.

Case and Conclusion

I have endeavored to trace a dual aspect to the relation between media and law. Law is a primary medium of social communication and has a distinct and special status as the site of social self-representation. The law's control of its own image is the model upon which the regulation of other modes of communication are modeled. That is the lesson of legal history and the paradoxical consequence of disseminating law in loud and visible yet opaquely foreign linguistic and plastic forms. The subtle and not so subtle armature of the legal form, the stringent protections afforded its social modes of presence and articulation, allow the construction of a theater of justice and truth, a realm of legal fictions, of false truths, within which the image of law and the dogmas of doctrine are preserved and passed on to posterity according to rules that are peculiarly their own. I will end with a curious but simple example drawn from the law that directly governs the visibility of justice.

The case is from 1936 and was heard in Alberta. The legal issue raised, as formulated by counsel for the appellant, was whether a judge who withdraws himself from the proper public court appointed for hearing trials, and deliberately sits in a place where the public will not find him, is "acting as a judge at all, or . . . does he demit his capacity as a judge and cease to be a judge?"[18] This is already a primarily symbolic question, a matter of proper image. Can a druid be a druid without his gown? Or, ask the question by way of the Reformation maxim: "take off the paint of Rome and you undo her." If a judge sits outside of court, if justice literally cannot be seen to be done because the judge has absconded into the private sphere, is law undone?

In the Alberta case, the judge in an uncontested divorce proceeding, unattended by any trace of publicity, had taken it upon himself to hear the action during the "luncheon interval" in the courthouse judges' law library. Neither the judge nor counsel were robed. The library was private, as indicated by a sign on its outer door. (As the appellant's counsel put it, this was more than a hearing in camera, because in such cases a sign saying "In Camera" would be displayed.) Upon commencement of the proceeding the judge declared, in the best counterfactual legal mode and despite the absence of any member of the public, "I am sitting in open court," thus acknowledging the tradition in which every trial has to be open to every subject. The hearing of trials in public, an earlier court had pronounced, "is so precious a characteristic of law" as to be "the salt of the constitution." For a judge to sit as a judge, he or she must hear the case in open court or hear arguments that legitimate the exclusion of the public and determine accordingly whether to proceed in camera or not.

The decision of the appellate court, the aptly named English Privy Council, proceeded according to the normal logic of legal fictions. The majority opinion begins by observing that the word "private" on the library door meant that "the learned judge on this occasion, albeit unconsciously, was . . . denying his Court to the public in breach of their right to be present." To this it added the legally obvious observation that "the actual presence of the public is never of course necessary," but that does not obviate the conclusion that on this occasion "the public must be treated as having been excluded from the library." The judge then reiterates and insists, in fine and flowing prose, that the trial of cases "shall always take place, and in the fullest sense, in open court." To this he adds, with a touch of genuine legal class, "it is pessimi exempli" (the worst of examples) that "for the trial of an undefended divorce case the gown of ceremony should be discarded." This leads to the conclusion that there has been a serious breach of legal decorum and "the inroad upon the rule of publicity made in this instance—unconscious though it was—[is] one not to be justified, and now that it has been disclosed . . . must be condemned so that it shall not again be permitted."

It sounds full of principle. Justice must be visible; no decision without a hearing in open court; no sentence, injunction, remedy, or decree without the constraint of visibility and the rectitude of appearances. After all of which one might suppose that the decision in question would be overturned, that the case would be remitted for a public hearing. But the fulsome expression of the norm has no immediate bearing upon the facts of the case. What is said need not impact upon what has been done. The legal construction of facts is often stranger than fiction, or more precisely it is legal fiction, the domain of the promulgation of an alternate reality based upon the precedents and other forms of law. The appellant, the former spouse who had not attended the private hearing, wanted the divorce decree overturned. The court refused. The irregularity had no impact upon the procedure or outcome. The court saw no reason to nullify the nullity decree and so let it stand.

There are reasons of law of which reason knows nothing. The symbolic order had been infracted, the image of justice tainted by a trial that took place in a private library. And image, as we have seen, is everything and nothing in law. Image, and here indeed norm or principle, exists in its own special domain, in the dogmatic sphere of legality in its purest form. Put it like this. The image of justice as public and open is of the very essence of legal dogmatics—the salt of the constitution. As such, as an image, it must be preserved inviolate and untouched for posterity. It belongs to the realm of norms and cannot be undone. So much so that it had to be lengthily reiterated and loudly affirmed in the case in question. Nothing matters more for law than the image of the visibility of justice. Sitting in a private library infracted, albeit unconsciously, that dogma, that settled and unimpugnable law. No getting around it. But what also has to be posited is the distance between dogma and reality, between the pristine norms of law and the argot or mire of judicial judgment. The norm was here expounded through the exception. That, in sum, is the paradox of legality, or more concretely, and borrowing from Foucault, the irony of the legal medium: law is said, is said again, and remains to be said. That is because the dogmatic regime acts emblematically rather than in the particular. The real is secondary to the image, the case is of no significance when measured against the onward march of the system of norms. Dogma is dogma. It doesn't die. And the law, as the cliché goes, is the law.

Notes

1. *Orlando Thomas v. State of Mississippi* 734 So. 2d 339 (1999).
2. For a discussion of blindfolded justice, see Martin Jay, "Must Justice Be Blind? The Challenge of Images to the Law," in *Law and the Image: The Authority of Art and the Aesthetics of Law*, ed. C. Douzinas and L. Nead (Chicago: University of Chicago Press, 2000). The major study is Robert Jacob, *Images de la Justice: Essai sur l'iconographie judiciaire du Moyen Âge à l'âge classique* (Paris: Léopard d'Or, 1994). There is also C.-N. Robert, *La Justice dans ses décors* (Geneva: Droz, 2006).
3. This theme of the "antirrhetic" foundation of law is pursued in Goodrich (1995). The notion of the *homo sacer* is elaborated in Giorgio Agaben, *Homo Sacer: Sovereign Power and Bare Life* (Stanford, CA: Stanford University Press, 1998); the common law version is from the early English legal treatise writer Bracton, who defines the outlaw as *caput lupinum*, or wolf's head (*De Legibus*). For an interesting discussion of this and other imagery, see Desmond Manderson, "From Hunger to Love: Myths of the Source, Interpretation, and Constitution of Law in Children's Literature," *Law and Literature* 15 (2003): 87–141.
4. William Fulbeck, *A Parallele or Conference of the Civil Law, the Canon Law, and the Common Law of this Realme of England* (London, 1618), fol. B2a.
5. Abraham Fraunce, *The Lawiers Logike* (London, 1588), vii.
6. William Fulbeck, *A Direction or Preparative to the Study of Law* (London, 1589).
7. See Peter Goodrich, "Justice and the Trauma of Law," *Studies in Law, Politics, and Society* 18 (1998): 271.

8. Sir Edward Coke, *Institutes* (London, 1629), I c 6r.

9. The story is detailed in Geoffrey Robertson, *The Tyrannicide Brief* (London: Chatto & Windus, 2005).

10. Andreas Alciatus, *De Notitia Dignitatum* (Paris, 1651). Discussed in Peter Goodrich, *Languages of Law: From Logics of Memory to Nomadic Masks* (London: Cambridge University Press, 1990).

11. This text is discussed in Peter Goodrich, "Law," in *Encyclopedia of Rhetoric*, ed. Thomas Sloane (New York: 2001).

12. Jean-Jacques Rousseau, *Letter to M. d'Alembert on the Theatre* [1758] (Ithaca: Cornell University Press, 1970), is the most famous rehearsal of political and moral of arguments against the theater.

13. McKenzie Wark, *A Hacker Manifesto* (Cambridge, MA: Harvard University Press, 2004).

14. See Monroe Price, *Television, the Public Sphere, and National Identity* (Oxford: Oxford University Press, 1995).

15. See Monroe Price, "The Market for Loyalties: The Electronic Media and the Global Competition for Allegiances," *Yale Law Journal* 104 (1994–95): 667.

16. *Buckley v. Valeo* 24 US 1 (1976).

17. *Federal Communications Commission v. Pacifica Foundation* 438 U.S. 726 (1978).

18. *McPherson v. McPherson* [1936] AC 177.

References and Suggested Readings

Cormack, B. 2008. *A Power to Do Justice: Jurisdiction, English Literature, and the Rise of Common Law*. Chicago: University of Chicago Press.

Douzinas, C., and L. Nead, eds. 1999. *Law and the Image: The Authority of Art and the Aesthetics of Law*. Chicago: University of Chicago Press.

Goodrich, P. 1995. *Oedipus Lex: Psychoanalysis, History, Law*. Berkeley: University of California Press.

Goodrich, P., et al., eds. 1998. *Law and the Unconscious: A Legendre Reader*. London: Macmillan.

Hutton, C. 2009. *Language, Meaning and the Law*. Edinburgh: Edinburgh University Press.

McVeigh, S., ed. 2008. *The Jurisprudence of Jurisdiction*. London: Routledge.

Moran, L., et al., eds. 2004. *Law's Moving Image*. London: Cavendish.

Price, M. 2002. *Media and Sovereignty: The Global Information Revolution and Its Challenge to State Power*. Cambridge, MA: MIT Press.

Sherwin, R. 2000. *When Law Goes Pop: The Vanishing Line between Law and Popular Culture*. Chicago: University of Chicago Press.

Vismann, C., ed. 2008. "Law and Visual Culture." Special issue. *Parallax* 49.

18 :: MASS MEDIA

JOHN DURHAM PETERS

Media are symbolic connectors consisting of three interrelated dimensions: message, means, and agents. Every medium has a "what," a "how," and a "by/to whom." This triad—sign-content, delivery device, and authors and audiences—can be described in a variety of vocabularies. In the once dominant language of information theory, every medium has a message, a channel, and senders and receivers. In the field of media studies, media are seen as constellations of programs, institutions and technologies, and audiences. In computer language, media consist of data, processors, and user-interfaces. Whatever the terminology, it is definitionally crucial that media involve some version of these three aspects, though there can be great variety in the way they are configured. A religious ritual and a newspaper, for instance, both deliver messages but of such different orders that each might be said, from the perspective of the other, to have no message at all: the ritual lacks current information just as the paper provides no lasting orientation. Again, a medieval manuscript and a satellite both deliver material over time and space, though one delivers old, slow matter to a few at a time and the other new, fast matter to many at once; though both can sustain large audiences, the manuscript's audience will be assembled piecemeal over time while the satellite may reach a large portion of the planet's population simultaneously.

The most radically minimal definition of media would require only the second term of the triad—a connecting or processing apparatus of some sort—leaving messages and people as add-ons. Indeed some influential theorists go in this direction. For Marshall McLuhan the medium is the message, the channel being so dominant that it overwhelms any specific "content" it might carry. For Friedrich Kittler human beings ("so-called people" as he famously puts it) are adjuncts to media systems, not their owners or authors. We might build on the theoretical stringency of such scholars by defining messages and users broadly and unsentimentally and by taking this triad as an analytic device rather than a fact of nature. Even though the apparatus—the how—must take conceptual primacy in the last instance, it is useful to understand media as a threefold system of content, channel, and creature.

Mass media are a subset of media in general. Face-to-face interaction, for instance, involves the medium of the human body; its content might be seen variously as mind, personality, desire, or culture, its delivery system as voice, hands, face, or ears, and its authors and audiences as humans, gods, ancestors, or other beings held to be animate. There is no form of communication, except perhaps among angels as dreamt of by some theologians, without a medium. Though there are conditions (explored below) in which embodied face-to-face speech can function as a mass medium, normally the face-to-face setting is the baseline against which mass media are contrasted. In personal interaction particular content is typically addressed to one or a few usually familiar recipients, and the media of delivery are of local range and short duration. (Notions of content and medium, it might be noted, are in this case retrojections from more expanded systems.) With mass media, communication differentiates into distinct roles: the delivery device multiplies both messages and opportunities for their reception, the audience expands to include strangers, and content must be adapted accordingly. The relationship among participants becomes loosely coupled, distanced, or otherwise problematic. Indeed, the differentiation of author (who sends) from audience (who receives) is an artifact of the increased complexity of mass media; in everyday conversation, people are interchangeably senders and receivers.

Note the application of our three analytic variables: the generalization of content, the spatiotemporal expansion of means, and elective relations among communicants. Defining mass media in these terms accommodates most well-known forms of mass media—the printing press, newspapers and magazines, radio and television, cinema, and the Internet—while also showing that these are by no means the only or most important mass media in human history. The rest of this article is dedicated to explicating each of the three aspects one by one.

Indefinite Forms of Address

Since no sign can have a purely private meaning without thereby ceasing to be a sign, there is at a deep philosophical level no such thing as an utterance addressed to a unique audience.[1] Even the most private and arcane codes are susceptible to being understood by people who are not parties to the interaction. In any act of communication there is potential for spillage. In a face-to-face setting talk may be overheard by unauthorized listeners (eavesdropping), be passed along to third parties (breach of confidence), or fail to hit its desired unique target (misunderstanding). What Charles Sanders Peirce calls the "general" and "vague" quality of all signs means there is a potential for indefinite address in any signifying practice; indeed, the power of a single sign to couple with more than one person is precisely what makes communication possible in the first place. In this sense all communication is mass communication. Features that are particularly pronounced in mass media, such as address gaps and context ruptures, can be visible within face-to-face talk as well.[2] At least since Homer's "winged words," talk's potential for wild dissemination has been appreciated.

Even so, much face-to-face talk is designed for specific actors and contexts and does not travel well outside of those bounds. The talk of intimates can seem like a secret code to the uninitiated. Whatever the philosophical continuities of talk and media, there are some key practical differences. As conversational analysts have shown in compelling detail, everyday talk is delicately designed for the emergent context of interaction. Most talk is an artisanal craft that exquisitely customizes its products for the richly ordered worlds of specific everyday settings. Only a few people are authorized participants in most everyday talk.[3] Historically, mass media have lacked the ability to speak to people as individuals or to tailor speech to the context of its reception. They produce standardized rather than customized communication, designing content by guesswork and probability. The failure rate of their attempts to connect communicatively with recipients would be considered psychotic in everyday interaction. Madness was defined by Erving Goffman as "situational impropriety,"[4] yet we tolerate violations of conversational etiquette from television sets and radios that we never would from people: they jabber away in their obsessed monomania all day and night without any sense for the specific context of their listeners or the norms of conversational turn-taking. That radio and television are so well received in everyday life is a tribute to the ingenuity of their programmers, who face the task of designing symbolic material that has decent odds of traveling well among mixed audiences in an unknowably diverse array of situations. Uncertainty of reception and generality of context are key facts facing the design of mass-media content.

One solution to the puzzle of unknowable audiences is simply to address everyone, without exception. Open address anticipates the untraceable destiny of the message's delivery. We might call this address *ad humanitatem*. Addressing all humanity, however, is not the same as

reaching it. Rulers, scholars, heralds, prophets, and poets have been crying to one and all since time immemorial, but actually reaching the entire
species depends not only on mass delivery but also a common tongue.
King Nebuchadnezzar sent a decree, we read in the book of Daniel, "to all
people, nations, and languages." Whether they all received or understood
it, the text does not say; again (in terms of our triad), mass address is not
the same as mass delivery or mass accessibility. Before we leap to modern
electronic media and the dream shared by early film theorists and film-
makers of pictures as a universally intelligible hieroglyphic language, recall the Christian ambition of preaching the Gospel "to every creature"
and the notion of Pentecostal translation into all languages. Well before
Gutenberg and Edison, Buddhist, Christian, and Muslim evangelists had
stunning success in delivering their message to mass audiences, one by
one. Indeed, people can serve as mass media when they deliver a more or
less unified message to vast numbers—with the advantage that they can
fine-tune content to local circumstance.[5] In a different way, live gather-
ings such as courts, theaters, and political assemblies have long served
as voice-based media of mass communication, publicly and impersonally
disseminating messages to many or "all."

Though some theorists treat mass media as if they are only capable of
open or abstract or monologic modes of address, there are other strategies as well. "The public" has always been a mix out of which various subgroups may be summoned, and mass media need not always address *all*;
they can also address *some*. They often speak "to whom it may concern,"
acknowledging an imperfect fit between the actual and intended audience: this form of address authorizes receivers to ignore stray messages.
One of the oldest forms of address in advertising, the *siquis* (if anyone)
formula, goes back to the Romans.[6] Public postings for lost or found
items, for instance, call to all to find the one. The project of segmenting
mass audiences is much older than modern demographics; modern niche
marketing typically uses delivery mechanisms to sort audiences, an elaboration on the self-sorting invited by "to whom it may concern." People
with a message to share have long resorted to strategies of address to
sort the few from among the many fish that the nets of mass delivery pull
in. Again, religion is a useful antecedent: the early Christian notion of
the *ekklēsia* (imperfectly translated as "church") suggests a select group
united not in space and time but in belief.[7]

Another kind of address we can call the *sit notum omnibus presenti-
bus* strategy: in declaring "be it known to all present," a message equates
the receiving audience with the intended audience, hailing everyone
who falls within its range as presumably "concerned." This mode of ad-

dress admits the impossibility of reaching everyone and takes what it can get. If you can't be with the one you love, as the song says, love the one you're with.

Finally, mass media can address just one or a few. Jorge Luis Borges's stunning story "The Garden of the Forking Paths" concerns, among other things, a spy on the run in World War I England who must somehow get a message to his handler in Germany before he is caught. Consulting a telephone book, he chooses a man whose surname matches the target he must designate, goes to his house, and kills him. The wires and papers light up with news of the enigmatic murder, but only the handler gets the coded message. Many heard, but only one understood. The notion that the mass media are full of secret messages is usually thought paranoid, but peer-to-peer transactions have long been enabled by mass media, through, for example, classified ads in the newspapers, dating sites on the Internet, and other variants on the *siquis* formula. Mass media can enable point-to-point connections amid the large scatter of apparently wayward messages.

Address, then, is one of the three main ways in which mass media attempt to filter the destiny of messages. Of course, mass delivery is not the same as mass address. Radio (and later television) broadcasting made address-to-all obsolete at the same time that it made delivery-to-all possible. As Paddy Scannell arrestingly demonstrates, the rise of broadcasting in Britain and elsewhere meant not the beginning but rather the end of mass communication, at least as a mode of address. Nineteenth-century public communication in print and public address often treated the public as vast, anonymous masses. But when broadcasters used such modes of talk—political pulpit-pounding, for example, or reedy preaching—they failed miserably to connect with listeners. Though radio created a live audience of unprecedented size, the audience did not feel itself to be large and anonymous. On-air speakers had to learn how to speak intimately to people assembled in the privacy of their homes.[8] The resulting adaptation to the new domestic environment heralded a sea change in twentieth-century public communication, away from abstract, martial modes of address toward conversational, chatty, informal, personal, and "feminine" styles of talk—a style mastered by politicians from Franklin Roosevelt through Ronald Reagan and beyond.[9] Instead of "to whom it may concern," the dominant form of broadcast address is "especially for you."

Styles of address, in sum, are a strategy to manage mass media's unpredictability of delivery and the irascible character of audiences. Mass media do not traffic only in mass address: they may target messages to all, some, few, one, or no one in particular. Broadcast talk speaks to all-as-one; speech to a king or queen addresses one-as-all.

Extended Delivery Systems

The two key aspects of mass delivery are range and duration (space and time). Media for spreading messages over long distances have existed for as long as people have had legs. Word-of-mouth is one of history's great mass media; indeed, the ancients personified the oral media of rumor and fame as deities. As noted above, institutionalized forms of oral speech (oratory, theater) have long served as mass media. To maintain the stability of a message over large swaths of time and space, however, writing—a means of fixing the text—was necessary. Writing can serve as a kind of monument—an external memory device. It was, after language itself, the first major rupture in the history of communication. Writing makes the temporal and spatial range of messages potentially unlimited (notwithstanding the obvious barriers of literacy and shared language). It separates reader and writer and thus complicates modes of interaction between them.[10] In Plato's *Phaedrus*, Socrates complains about writing in terms that are strikingly relevant for later mass media: it is unresponsive, saying the same thing over and over; it simulates intelligence and personal care but cannot interact with a reader; it is indiscriminate in its audiences, speaking to anyone who happens upon it; it disrupts memory and the interactive intensity of dialogue.[11]

In terms of space, writing—coupled with word-of-mouth communication—enabled geographically huge religious and cultural empires well before the modern transportation and communication revolutions of the nineteenth century. The printing press, the first application of mass production to communication in history, changed, not the durability of writing, but its ability to reach large numbers.[12] Within two weeks of Luther's posting of his ninety-five theses in 1517, for instance, all of Germany knew about it—something unthinkable before the printing press. His gesture was theatrically designed to set tongues wagging: it was not a personal communication between one monk and the church but a message addressed to all Christendom. Printing's influence was not only on the literate. It opened up new worlds of story and information to many in early modern Europe via a wide variety of performers, priests, teachers, and other mediating figures.[13] If spatial range and audience size are the criteria, there were certainly mass media in the sixteenth century; the coupling of literate and oral systems created a kind of national broadcasting network, albeit one that operated on a much slower pace than radio or television. Though the printing press did not alter the speed of delivery—printed matter, like anything else, depended on transportation by land and water—its innovation was in scale: it brought about the possibility of huge collectives mentally united as national imagined communities.[14]

If we define broadcasting as a form of dissemination that connects dispersed people via a common text at a more or less common time, then writing and printing both allowed for forms of broadcasting avant la lettre. The Passover Haggadah is a text that tells the story of the Jewish people and clearly helped maintain cultural continuity over nearly two millennia of the Jewish diaspora. Every year, according to a shared calendar, the dispersed community gathers virtually for a program—broadcast, by this definition—that not only unites its members across space but historically as well. (There can be broadcasting across time as well as space; every monument does this.) The Haggadah is perhaps the most distinctive of many ancient texts that have held groups together at a distance.[15] The Protestant Reformation, in league with its historic partner the printing press, had another form of regularly scheduled broadcasting. The church was a network with many stations; Sunday morning was the time, the vernacular Bible the program. Of course just because a text is commonly available does not mean that its interpretations will be commonly shared. Same text, many readings: the lesson of Protestantism is relevant for mass media in general. And just because twentieth-century broadcasting has been sponsored largely by the market and the state does not mean that other institutions (such as religion) have not sponsored other modes of it at other times.

The historical tendency of the past two centuries has been to push the speed of delivery to zero and size of audiences to infinity. (That delivery speed could never be reduced quite to zero was the basis of one of the twentieth century's most important conceptual revolutions: Einstein's theory of relativity.[16]) The precision of temporal coordination has increased greatly: If old forms of broadcasting such as the Passover or Sunday school brought their communities together on the same ceremonial day, radio and television can gather millions in the same second. Speed is money: the Rothschilds built their banking empire in the early nineteenth century in part by using carrier pigeons to get a crucial edge on breaking news, and finance still turns on small advantages in time. The temporal intervals of communication have continued to shrink, down to the nanoseconds by which central processing units of computers bill usage. With electrical telegraphy in the 1840s, followed by telephony in the 1870s and wireless in the 1890s, nearly simultaneous contact at a distance became possible for the first time. Despite its early history of party lines open to all listeners, the telephone eventually became a medium for reciprocal and confidential point-to-point exchange; and despite its early history as a form of uniquely addressed wireless telegraphy, radio eventually became a medium for one-way one-to-many broadcasting. The newspaper, which always had mixed modes of communication, led the way with huge growth in terms of audience size in the nineteenth century. The biggest newspapers in the early nineteenth century had print runs only in the thousands, but the one million barrier was broken in the 1890s. By the 1930s radio enabled a simultaneous national audience, and by the late 1960s worldwide television audiences were thinkable. The historical achievement of modern mass media has been the dual conquest of simultaneity and of social scale. The realization and manipulation of communication to national and world populations in real time is a distinct marker of modernity, whose political, economic, and cultural meaning many thinkers since the early twentieth century have been struggling to grasp.[17]

Modern mass media have not only extended and sped up communication; they have increased or reinforced its internal varieties. A mass audience of radio or television is a collective united in time but dispersed in space. The viewers of a televised event, say, the World Cup, may be spread across the world, but they all attend to the same thing at the same time. The Internet tends to configure mass audiences in an inverse way: spread out over time but united at a single point in space—at least if we accept the prevalent spatial metaphors for the Internet. One Web "site" may accumulate millions of hits ("visits"), but each hit occurs at the private pleasure of an individual user at his or her terminal. In this sense, the Internet resembles media such as newspapers, books, and films, which group their audiences into looser time windows than classical broadcasting. Perhaps even more, it recreates the much older logic of pilgrimage, a mass audience that grows over time, assembling one by one at a particular site at its own speed and for its own purposes. The pilgrim—at Mecca, Lenin's tomb, or Google—interacts personally with a site that is designed to accommodate many, knowing perhaps that millions have gone before and millions will come after. Today, mass communication—understood as messages addressed and delivered to everyone at once—seems but one rare species among diverse shapes and sizes of media forms.

The waning of mass delivery to whole populations has been much commented on since the last two decades of the twentieth century. Many interpreters lament a historic trend away from mass or public media toward personal or private ones, supposing a consequent loss of civic or social engagement.[18] This lament is a revisionist reading of the mass society theory that prevailed in the 1950s: what was once seen as bad (huge, anonymous audiences all attending to the same programs) is now seen as good (society provided with a common culture). In the broadcast era, the fear was the loss of individuality in the lonely crowd; in the narrowcast era, the fear is the narcissism of the "daily me." It is misleading, however, to paint mass address to everyone-at-once as the historic norm. Early in the era of radio and television broadcasting, program syndication loosened the grip of the single schedule, and the video recorder was the first in a long line of devices since the 1970s that has freed audiences from the networks' spatiotemporal grid. Classical broadcasting—simultaneous national address—is arguably a great historical exception in the history of communication, and it prevailed only for around fifty years in the mid-twentieth century in industrial countries. "Senders" have rarely wanted to waste money and messages on extraneous eyes and ears. The hunt for the right audience has always had to make do with clumsy delivery mechanisms. Just because media can now attain a higher degree of demographic resolution than they could fifty years ago does not make this the first time communicators have reached over the many for the one or the few. Once advertisers dreamed of "the one-to-one future" in which all promotions would be uniquely personalized.[19] But this is not only a growing reality; it is an ancient practice. The oldest and still most effective media of persuasion are human beings—salesmen, missionaries, campaigners, and peers—and they have always tailored mass content to individuals. Delivery systems that slice up fine demographic groupings try to mimic the erstwhile flexibility of human-based mass communication.[20] Here again, what seems novel in communication often apes forgotten historical styles. Indeed, it is characteristic of so-called new media to return to the oldest (bodily) media, such as voice, face, and hands, so important for video art and mobile telephony alike.

Mass delivery has great diversity in time and space, scale and speed. Means of delivery can unite audiences in time but scatter them in space (classical broadcasting, text-based diasporas); scatter them in time but unite them in space (the Internet, pilgrimage); unite them in both space and time (assembly); or scatter them in both space and time (writing and printing). In each case, space and time are matters of degree. All of these mixtures are bona fide species of mass media, and we should not let one particular model monopolize our thinking. Broadcast radio and TV, classical Hollywood cinema, and the general interest press are indeed remarkable forms, but there is no reason to universalize their features as the essence of all mass media. Planetwide simultaneous delivery is the limit point of a whole ecology of mass mediation. Communicators have probably tried to deliver their messages to everyone at once only when they had something to tell or sell to everyone; much of the history and practice of mass media involves remarkably diverse efforts to identify and deliver messages to select subgroups of different scales. The history of mass communication is less the story of one speaking to all than of few speaking to some.

Loose Coupling of Sending and Receiving

Though not all face-to-face talk is reciprocal (think of scoldings) or personal (think of dealings with police), a key feature is its interactive constitution by participants in real time. Anything the person being scolded or arrested does or says can influence how events will unfold; even utter passivity may be taken as a comment that will draw praise or further reprisals. The famous dictum that "you cannot not communicate" separates face-to-face interaction from mass media with great precision. With mass media, people can "not communicate" with great ease. Television viewers at home can mock the TV, ignore it, throw projectiles at it, or turn it off—all without consequence as far as the television is concerned. Scannell notes a quandary for the early BBC: what if men listening to a royal wedding over the radio left their hats on? In Westminster Abbey the etiquette would be clear, but what kind of social contract does a home audience have with a distant live event? What kind of communication situation is it in which interaction is suspended and audience members have such liberty to come and go as they please? Though there is no necessary correspondence between sender and receiver in mass media, there are many ways that the gap gets filled. Audience liberty is managed in many ways. In the case of broadcasting, ratings mechanisms have sought a statistical picture of audience behavior and size, with varying success. With Internet "cookies," it is much easier to track what kind of engagements people have with remote environments, though the mystery of what happens at the other end of a sending still remains: just because a television set was turned on or Web site was visited does not mean that anyone really saw it, understood it, will remember or act upon it. At some level, receivers usually have the final say in what they attend to. The sender and the receiver are insulated from each other by factors such as scale, technology, or decorum. Attention, interest, desire, and action are the final frontiers for mass communication and no one, thank goodness, has found a way to engineer them all the time.

The very notion of an audience—a group that hears without speaking—owes to the distended configuration of communication peculiar to mass media. A change in size implies a change of shape: this law of form is highly relevant for communication. The assembly in ancient Athens, for instance, gave all participants the theoretical right to speak, but few took the risk to put themselves on the line before thousands of their peers. A rough natural differentiation of communication into specialized roles—say, speakers and hearers—occurs with increases of scale. Yet how such differentiations are deployed is also a political and historical choice. The telephone, in the multiple address of the party line, was at first a kind of broadcast medium; the radio was at first a point-to-point medium with amateur wireless operators. Radio in some countries can still serve as a public forum in which many voices speak. Raw technology is probably less important than the ways it gets implemented and configured. The fact that mass communication has typically been studied in terms of few speaking to many (as with radio and TV) rather than many speaking to few (as in strikes, votes, petitions, boycotts, protests) shows an ideological bias toward standing power: indeed, there are many forms of mass communication in which senders, and not just receivers, are large collectives. The configurations of communication favored by such influential institutions as the BBC, CBS, and NBC do not exhaust ways for thinking about mediated relations at a distance.[21]

Simple dissemination without interest in reception is quite rare. Most senders want to know what happens to their messages. There are various methods of disciplining reception. One is to guarantee delivery, on the model of certified mail. Another is to establish collective forums and rituals for reception. Mao did not trust people to read his little red book on their own; rather, he organized regular reading breaks for the workers. In theory, radio could have taken cinema's path of congregated reception in specially dedicated places; policy makers in 1920s Germany, for instance, favored what they called "Saal-Funk" (assembly-hall radio) over private home listening. Messages can also contain implied instructions for reception: laugh tracks and the sound and spectacle of roaring crowds are among the techniques used in broadcasting to loop the home audience into the scene. Much film theory in the 1970s and 1980s concerned itself with how the camera guides the psychodynamics of looking along highly ideological lines. The audience can also be disciplined by gate requirements, such as passwords or linguistic competence, that certify them as authorized receivers. Critical race theory and feminist media analysis have heightened sensitivity about how some kinds of messages systematically exclude certain kinds of people as legitimate recipients.

As Luhmann argues, media that operate in conditions of spatiotemporal extension often seek to guarantee connection through rewards and inducements; he calls these *Erfolgsmedien*, or success-media. Early radio personalities, for instance, organized fan clubs, contests, and promotions to elicit correspondence from listeners; a few lucky winners might even get to appear on the show and briefly assume the role of performer instead of spectator. Most media systems today not only send naked messages, they accompany their messages with threats, promises, fantasies, and sometimes cash. There are a variety of ways that senders manage the conditions of reception.[22]

There is no ideal version of the mass audience, no paradigm case; there is only a family variety of possibilities. To return to our starting triad, the three key dimensions for mass media are address, availability, and access. Messages are filtered by how they are encoded, distributed, and received. A message distributed to all may be addressed to or readable by only a few; a message addressed to all may be distributed to or readable by only a few; and a message received by all may have been addressed or distributed to a few. The most transparent alignment of address, availability, and access is probably found in physical assemblies. The broadcast audience, despite its hegemonic hold as the very type of mass communication, is a deviant case, especially in its curious mismatch between availability (to many) and address (to few). The notion of public and completely open dissemination to all is a normative ideal: in the real practice of scattering words, images, and sounds across distances (of space, time, culture, and trust) to diverse groups, filters are highly prized expedients.

A Final Observation

Typically mass media are the playthings of institutions. They are expensive to run, usually require distinct castes with specialized knowledge (scribes, programmers, "talent") to operate them, and are of great strategic importance politically, economically, culturally, and otherwise. Rarely in history have mass media operated apart from the central power sources of a social order, and they are typically under the management of the palace, the market, or the temple.[23] Where mass media are, there is usually power. Kings have always jealously controlled the rights to reproduction and multiplication—whether of words, coins, likenesses, or babies. Harold Innis would remind us that different kinds of power prefer different kinds of media. Media that span space are usually under the control of soldiers and merchants and lend themselves to political and economic empires; media that span time are usually under the control of sages and priests and build religious empires of memory or hope. Space-binding media usually tend to the profane and time-binding ones to the sacred. Though such generalizations are suggestive for creating analytic grids, we should never lose a supple sense for the intricacies of particular cases. This article is a plea for an approach to mass media that is at once philosophically general and pragmatically particular, one that can range across cases and history without mistaking particularly dominant forms as the essence of all mass media. The three criteria given above for mass media—address gaps, spatiotemporal range, and problematized interaction—count equally well for twentieth-century broadcasting and the decrees of ancient kings. No one talked back when Ozymandias proclaimed the vastness of his dominion. Power is perhaps the ultimate mass medium: it speaks to whom it will, multiplies symbols across space and time, and immobilizes audiences.

Notes

1. On the intricacies of mass address, see Paddy Scannell, "For Anyone-as-Someone Structures," *Media, Culture and Society* 22 (2000): 5–24, and Warner (2002, 65–124).

2. John Durham Peters, *Speaking into the Air* (Chicago: University of Chicago Press, 1999).

3. For one statement, see Emanuel A. Schegloff, "Whose Text? Whose Context?" *Discourse and Society* 8, no. 2 (1997): 165–87.

4. Erving Goffman, *Interaction Ritual* (Chicago: Aldine, 1967), 141.

5. Herbert Menzel, "Quasi-Mass Communication: A Neglected Area," *Public Opinion Quarterly* 35 (1971): 406–9.

6. Geoffrey N. Leech, *English in Advertising: A Linguistic Study of Advertising in Great Britain* (London: Longmans, 1966), 168.

7. Peter Simonson, "Assembly, Rhetoric, and Widespread Community: Mass Communication in Paul of Tarsus," *Journal of Media and Religion* 2 (2003): 165–82.

8. Paddy Scannell, "Introduction: The Relevance of Talk," *Broadcast Talk*, ed. Paddy Scannell (Newbury Park: Sage, 1991), 1–9; Paddy Scannell and David Cardiff, *A Social History of British Broadcasting* (Oxford: Blackwell, 1991).

9. Kathleen Hall Jamieson, *Eloquence in an Electronic Age* (New York: Oxford University Press, 1988).

10. Niklas Luhmann, *Die Gesellschaft der Gesellschaft* (Frankfurt: Suhrkamp, 1997), chap. 2. For a helpful account in English of Luhmann's views on the evolution of media, see Geoffrey Winthrop-Young, "On a Species of Origin: Luhmann's Darwin," *Configurations* 11 (2003): 305–49.

11. Peters, *Speaking into the Air*, chap. 1.

12. The three great inventions hailed in the Renaissance—printing, gunpowder, and the mariner's compass—all originated in East Asia. The Koreans and Chinese are still vying for priority regarding the printing press.

13. Natalie Zemon Davis, "Printing and the People," in *Rethinking Popular Culture*, ed. Chandra Mukerji and Michael Schudson (Berkeley: University of California Press, 1991), 65–96.

14. Benedict Anderson, *Imagined Communities: Reflections on the Origins and Growth of Nationalism*, 2nd ed. (New York: Verso, 1991). Anderson's thesis is strikingly foreshadowed by Marshall McLuhan, "Technology and Political Change," *International Journal* 3 (1952): 189–95.

15. See Menahem Blondheim, "Why Is This Book Different from All Other Books? The Orality, the Literacy, and the Printing of the Passover *Haggadah*," paper presented at the Institute for Advanced Studies, Hebrew University, Jerusalem, November 2004; Paul Frosh, "Telling Presences: Witnessing, Mass Media, and the Imagined Lives of Strangers," *Critical Studies in Media Communication*, 23, no. 4 (October 2006): 265–84.

16. John Durham Peters, "Space, Time, and Communication Theory," *Canadian Journal of Communication* 28 (2003): 397–411.

17. John Durham Peters and Peter Simonson, *Mass Communication and American Social Thought: Key Texts, 1919–1968* (Boulder: Rowman and Littlefield, 2004).

18. A representative statement of this view, now partly retracted by the author, is Cass Sunstein, *Republic.com* (Princeton: Princeton University Press, 2001).

19. Joseph Turow, *Breaking Up America* (Chicago: University of Chicago Press, 1997).

20. See James R. Beniger, "Personalization of Mass Media and the Growth of Pseudo-Community," *Communication Research* 14 (1987): 352–71; Stig Hjarvard, "Simulated Conversations: The Simulation of Interpersonal Communication in Electronic Media," *Northern Lights*, vol. 1, ed. Anne Jerslev (Copenhagen: University of Copenhagen Press, 2002), 227–52.

21. Raymond Williams, *Television: Technology and Cultural Form* (New York: Schocken, 1974), chap. 1.

22. Elihu Katz and Mihaela Popescu, "Supplementation: On Communicator Control of the Conditions of Reception," in *European Culture and the Media*, ed. Ib Bondebjerg and Peter Golding (Bristol, UK: Intellect Press, 2004), 19–40.

23. Carl Couch, "Markets, Temples, and Palaces," *Studies in Symbolic Interaction* 7 (1986): 137–59.

References and Suggested Readings

Fairclough, Norman. 1995. *Media Discourse*. London: Edward Arnold.

Innis, Harold A. 1951. *The Bias of Communication*. Toronto: University of Toronto Press.

Merton, Robert K., with Marjorie Fiske and Alberta Curtis. [1946] 2006. *Mass Persuasion: The Social Psychology of a War Bond Drive*. New York: Howard Fertig.

Neuman, W. Russell. 1991. *The Future of the Mass Audience*. Cambridge: Cambridge University Press.

Peters, John Durham. 2001. "Mass Audiences." In *Encyclopedia of Rhetoric*, ed. Thomas O. Sloane, 68–72. Oxford: Oxford University Press.

Scannell, Paddy, ed. 1991. *Broadcast Talk*. Newbury Park, CA: Sage.

Stappers, James G. 1983. "Mass Communication as Public Communication." *Journal of Communication* 33, no. 3:141–45.

Warner, Michael. 2002. *Publics and Counterpublics*. New York: Zone.

Webster, James G., and Patricia F. Phelan. 1997. *The Mass Audience: Rediscovering the Dominant Model*. Mahwah, NJ: LEA.

Williams, Raymond. 1958. "Conclusion." In *Culture and Society*. New York: Columbia University Press.

19 :: NETWORKS

ALEXANDER R. GALLOWAY

In the tragedy *Agamemnon* Aeschylus describes two types of networks. The first, an actual communications network, is described in detail but remains off stage. The second, a meshwork of traps, while visible and present is but a symbol of larger machinations. The communications network is a chain of fire beacons, spanning a few hundred miles, that carries the message of the fall of Troy back to Argos, thus warning of the victor Agamemnon's imminent homecoming. "Ida first launched his blazing beam; thence to this place / Beacon lit beacon in relays of flame" (281–83), Clytemnestra explains, describing each of the dozen nodes in the overland chain.[1] "They blazed in turn, kindling their pile of withered heath, / And passed the signal on" (294–95). But later, upon the return of Agamemnon to his hearth, a second net is deployed, this one a "vast voluminous net" (1382) used by Clytemnestra to ensnare her husband and bring about his ruin. This voluminous net, later decried by the chorus as a "foul spider's web" (1492) finds form in a symbol: the sea of purple textile created by Clytemnestra and her weavers to adorn the threshold of the house, upon which Agamemnon is eventually convinced to tread, against his better judgment.[2] With that silken step Agamemnon is, as Aegisthus gloats in the final lines of the play, "tangled in a net the avenging Furies wove" (1580), his fate at Clytemnestra's bloody hands all but sealed. Sensing that her wait is nearly over, the coy betrayer entices Agamemnon with mock concern:

> Why, if my lord received as many wounds as Rumour,
> Plying from Troy to Argos, gave him, he is a net,
> All holes! (866–68)

Indeed, the image of the hero as netting, materializes in the play's final scenes as Agamemnon's body is perforated three times. Before it is recounted by Clytemnestra, the murder, and the weaponized net necessary for its consummation, is foreseen by Cassandra:

There, there! O terror! What is this new sight?
A hunting-net, Death's weapon of attack!
And she who hunts is she who shared his bed. (1114–16)

Networks thus oscillate between two related but incompatible formal structures. On one side, the chain of triumph; on the other, the web of ruin.

In *Agamemnon* the chain of triumph is linear, efficient, and functional. It is contagious and additive as it moves. The lighting of one hilltop beacon does not dim or dilute the previous node but effectively compounds it. The chain of triumph is communicative and telepresent. It is directional. It follows a chain of command. It is constitutive of reality rather than destructive of it. And perhaps most evocative: the chain of triumph is made of pure energy. It is Iris and Hermes combined.

The web of ruin is none of these things. It is a nonlinear mesh, not a linear chain, designed to ensnare and delimit even the most intractable opponent. It is commonly characterized as a swarm, or a pack of animals, unknowable in quality and innumerable in form. The divine referent is not Iris or Hermes but the Furies. Less concerned with connectivity, the web brings with it a flood of insatiable persecution. This net is not a tonic, tethering together distant elements, but a solvent set on dissolving those ties. It follows the network of fire beacons, and the web undoes the chain. Only Clytemnestra's net can trap Ilium's conqueror, eviscerating the house of Atreus.

In *Agamemnon*, the first play of Aeschylus's Orestes trilogy, the Furies are mentioned only in passing. In the third play, *The Eumenides*, the Furies saturate the narrative so fully that they are personified in the chorus, an actual character but one that can only be represented by a multiplicity of bodies. What were three in Virgil are twelve in Aeschylus (in Euripides they are fifteen). In tragedy the chorus is generally a signifier for the social community. It is not a synonym for "the masses" or "the people" but simply "the group." This makes *The Eumenides* unusual, for what were stern, scolding elders in *Agamemnon* and clamoring female maidservants in the second play, *The Libation Bearers*, have in the third devolved into a personification of vengeance itself, but in a divine, which is to say nonhuman, form. This is no longer the "group" but the swarm. The web of ruin, symbolized in the first two plays by Clytemnestra's textiles— her weaponized nets and sea of purple fabric, but also the tentacles of fabric forming the straightjacket-like robe used to subdue Agamemnon (what Orestes in *The Libation Bearers* calls "a trap, not of iron, but of thread"; 493)—this web of ruin is no longer a symbol but an incarnation of networked presence itself. The Furies are the web of ruin personified.

Hermes (as the chain of triumph) appears in *The Eumenides* too, if only for an instant, shepherding Orestes in his travel from Delphi to Athens. So while Athena and the concept of justice dominate the final play, the Furies indicate the lingering threat of networked forms of being (if not networked vengeance).

+ + +

I begin this discussion of networks with classical texts for several reasons. The first is to introduce, from the foundations of Western literature, the two tropes of the chain of triumph and the web of ruin, which are helpful for understanding the power of networks both then and now. The second is to put in question, at the outset, the assumption that networks are exclusively endemic to the late twentieth and early twenty-first centuries and, more pointedly, that networks are somehow synonymous with the technologies of modernity or postmodernity, such as the telegraph or the Internet.

The third reason is to broach the question of the internal inconsistency or inequity of the network form (what contemporary network theorists call the "power law," or nonrandom, distribution of network assets such as links). There are many kinds of networks; they are not internally simple, nor globally uniform. Some networks are rigid and hierarchical, while others are flexible and resist hierarchy. Some networks, like the chain of triumph, tend to create order; others, like the web of ruin, to dissolve it. In the hands of the American military, networks are classified not only as communications tools but as weapons systems, while in the hands of antiglobalization activists, networks are mobilized as tools for disruption and evasion. Thus, I mean to point out the differences between different kinds of networks, both in their architectonic shape and in their values and motivations, but also to point out that different network forms might be in conflict with one another and, indeed, might be specifically derived to exploit or disrupt other network forms (just as terrorist networks exploit global networks of travel, mobile communications, and mass media). "It is worth recalling at this point," wrote Michel Foucault, "the old Greek adage, that arithmetic should be taught in democracies, for it teaches relations of equality, but that geometry alone should be reserved for oligarchies, as it demonstrates the proportions within inequality." Hence we should remember that the networks described by graph theory, the topological cousin of geometry, are not at all immune to questions of internal inconsistency or inequity.[3]

A final reason is to define networks not as abstract concepts describing shape or structure, but as specific technologies of power, organization, and control. Admittedly my opening citations are literary in nature, but the networks described in Aeschylus (the chain of hilltop beacons, the hunter's net) are concrete, material technologies. And in each case the networks in question, be they chains of triumph or webs of ruin, are the material bearers of power as it appears in the world. Nets are tools for hunting and fishing, but they are also weapons used in warfare alongside the shield and the bow. This is crucial to one's present understanding—that networks are often symbols for, or actual embodiments of, real world power and control. So as tropes the chain of triumph and the web of ruin do not constitute a holistic theory of networks but rather two windows into the various forms of networked organization, both structural and political.

+   +   +

The English term *network* is a compound formed from the Old Saxon words *net*, an open-weave fabric used for catching or confining animals or objects, and *werk*, both an act of doing and the structure or thing resulting from the act. (In Aeschylus the term is *diktyon* [διχτυον], a network, system, or grid.) In media studies the term appears most often in analyses of communications technologies. In this context, networks refer to broadcast technologies for creation and distribution such as radio and television networks, telecommunication technologies such as telegraph and telephone networks, and information processing and transfer systems such as the Internet. Networks are significant, too, in material and industrial systems (logistical networks for commodity flows, transportation networks of various kinds), the biological and life sciences (ecology, neuroscience, genetics), and several branches of mathematics (graph theory, topology). In the social sciences and humanities, sociology and anthropology study networks in social and cultural contexts, and economics in the analysis of markets, while fields such as semiotics view language and culture as complex networks of meaning-making and exchange.

Certain connotative assumptions tie together these many different uses of the term. First, networks are understood as systems of interconnectivity. More than simply an aggregation of parts, they must hold those parts in constant relation. Thus a forest is not a network, but a forest's *ecosystem* is. A population is not in itself a network, but a population engaged in a market economy may well be. Second, networks assume a certain level of complexity. Simple systems are almost never understood as networks, but it is almost programmatic that complex systems—protein signaling inside cells, flows of global capital—be characterized as such. Thus it is no wonder that networks often serve as allegorical indices for many different types of complex systems in the contemporary landscape.

In addition to the classical tradition mentioned at the outset there exists a constellation of influences from modern science and philosophy that inform today's cybernetic, networked environment. "If I were to choose a patron saint for cybernetics out of the history of science, I should have to choose Leibniz," wrote Norbert Wiener, the MIT mathematician and defense researcher (1965, 12). Indeed from the early modern period both Leibniz and Spinoza articulate prototypical approximations of machinic and networklike arrangements. Leibniz, with his *Monadology*, describes a smooth, universal network of "monads," each of which is singular but contains within itself a mirror of the totality. In the *Ethics* Spinoza identifies a universal substance, from whose infinite attributes thought and extension emerge to form the human body. The affections of the human body superimpose onto substance a distributed network of relations and counterrelations, a theory further developed by the French philosopher Gilles Deleuze. In the twentieth century Ludwig von Bertalanffy, with the science of general systems theory, and Wiener, with the science of cybernetics, helped describe open and closed systems, how subsystems are nested within systems, and how communication and control pass from one part of a system to another. In roughly the same period Claude Shannon and Warren Weaver put forth their information theory which defined communication in terms not solely of semantics but of the relative integrity of symbolic patterns and the amount of unpredictability contained in the languages used to construct those patterns (see chapter 11, "Information"). In mathematics, graph theory is also a key influence. It provides a vocabulary for understanding networks, known simply as graphs, as groups of nodes and links.

Cybernetic systems are essentially communication networks in which information may pass between system components, effecting their ongoing states. Wiener's influential book *Cybernetics, or Control and Communication in the Animal and the Machine*, looked across disciplines—from electrical engineering to neurophysiology—and suggested that human, animal, and mechanical systems were united in their ability to handle input and output data in the ongoing management of the system (see chapter 10, "Cybernetics"). A central aspect to such cybernetic systems was feedback, which implied a degree of self-reflexivity in any web of relationships.[4] Information, for Wiener, is a statistical choice from among the "noise" of the surrounding world, and as such it implies an apparatus with the ability to instantiate the very act of choice or selection.[5] Wiener refers to this ability as "control by informative feedback." Like Aeschylus's chain of triumph, networks in Wiener are always efficient and directed. They are machinic in nature and act to better integrate complex assemblies of bodies and technologies into functional, systemic wholes.

Wiener formed the term *cybernetic* from the Greek word *kubernetes*, or "steersman," alluding also to the nineteenth-century writings of Clerk Maxwell on "governors" which he suggests is a Latin corruption of the same Greek term.

While Wiener was doing cybernetic research on antiaircraft ballistics, his colleague Claude Shannon was doing telecommunications research for Bell Labs. Much of Shannon's work with Warren Weaver is acknowledged as the foundation for modern telecommunications networks, and can be said to have paved the way for the idea of the ARPAnet in the late 1960s. Shannon's work, while much less interdisciplinary than Wiener's, resonated with cybernetics in its effort to define "information" as the key component of communications technologies (indeed, Wiener cites Shannon's work directly). Shannon and Weaver's information theory emphasized the quantitative view of information, even at the expense of considerations of quality or content. As they state, "information must not be confused with meaning. In fact, two messages, one of which is heavily loaded with meaning and the other which is pure nonsense, can be exactly equivalent, from the present viewpoint, as regards information" (1963, 8). Such a hard-nosed technical view can still be seen today in the Internet's implementation of packet-switching, in which chunks of data are fragmented and routed to destination addresses. While these data packets can be interpreted to reveal content, the technical functioning has as its implicit priority the delivery of quantity X from point A to point B.

If both cybernetics (Wiener) and information theory (Shannon) imply a quantitative, statistical view of information networks, a third contemporaneous approach offers a slight alternative. Trained as a biologist, Ludwig von Bertalanffy developed a "general systems theory" that differs significantly from the views of Wiener or Shannon (see chapter 9, "Communication"). Wiener viewed human, animal, and mechanical systems together from an electrical engineering perspective, while Shannon viewed human users as separate from the communications technologies they used. By contrast, von Bertalanffy stressed the view of human or technological systems from a biological standpoint. In doing so, he elaborated theoretical distinctions between open and closed systems and showed how subsystems are always nested within larger systems (a model that would be adopted wholesale in the layered construction of Internet protocols). As he states:

> The organism is not a static system closed to the outside and always containing the identical components; it is an open system in a quasi-steady state, maintained constant in its mass relations in a continuous change

of component material and energies, in which material continually enters from, and leaves into, the outside environment. (1976, 121)

This view has several consequences. One is that while von Bertalanffy does have a definition of "information," it plays much less of a role in the overall regulation of the system than other factors. Information is central to any living network, but it is nothing without an overall logic for utilizing it as a resource. In other words, the logics for the handling of information are just as important as the idea of information itself.

Another consequence is that von Bertalanffy's systems theory, in its organicist outlook, provides a means of understanding information in biological terms, rather than those of engineering or communications. This is not to suggest that systems theory is in any way more accurate or successful than the theories of Wiener or Shannon. But what the genealogies of cybernetics, information theory, and systems theory do show is that an informatic worldview entails an ambivalent relation to the material world. On the one hand, information is seen as abstract, quantitative, reducible to a calculus of management and regulation—this is the disembodied, immaterial conception referred to above. On the other hand, cybernetics, information theory, and systems theory all show how information is immanently material, configured into military technology, communications media, and even biological systems.

The preponderance of scientific literature on cybernetic interconnectivity and associative systems outlined here, coupled with the emergence of the World Wide Web (a specific set of networking technologies including the HyperText Transfer Protocol [HTTP] and HyperText Markup Language [HTML] developed by Tim Berners-Lee in 1990–1991), resulted in an explosion of both popular and academic writing on the subject in the mid-1990s. This bookshelf includes what Geert Lovink calls "the libertarian values of pre-dotcom Internet pioneers"—Richard Barbrook's critique of the "Californian Ideology," Mark Dery's hallucinatory reportage, John Perry Barlow's "Declaration of the Independence of Cyberspace," and Eben Moglen's "dotCommunist Manifesto"— but also everything from popular books on chaos and complexity in the information economy (Kevin Kelly, Esther Dyson, Ray Kurzweil, Nicholas Negroponte), to theories of emergence and self-organization (Steven Johnson, Manuel DeLanda), to theories of the virtual (Pierre Lévy, Mark Poster, Brian Massumi), and cyber law (Lawrence Lessig, Yochai Benkler).[6] Influenced by cultural studies, critical theory, and science and technology studies, scholars such as Espen Aarseth, Jay Bolter, Wendy Hui Kyong Chun, Richard Grusin, Marina Grzinic, Donna Haraway, Katherine Hayles, Lev Manovich, Lisa Nakamura, Sadie Plant, Allucquère Rosanne Stone, and

Sherry Turkle have written about networks from the perspective of on-line identity formation, nonlinearity and interactivity, network aesthetics, hermeneutics, and the social uses of software.[7] Another influential discourse achieving prominence in this period comes at the intersection of social network theory, graph theory, and topology. With its roots in Leonhard Euler's 1736 proof of the insolvability of the "seven bridges of Königsberg" puzzle and the "small world" experiments of twentieth-century psychologist Stanley Milgram, contemporary debates in social network theory address issues such as network growth and topological change, the random or nonrandom distribution of links across networks, and the clustering and interconnectedness of network subgroups.[8]

+ + +

While networks and discourse on networks are not new, what distinguishes the present moment may be that normative claims about different network architectures and their internecine struggles have reversed themselves. If the old scenario was one in which the web of ruin, in the form of the distributed network, was perceived as a solvent or threat vis-à-vis more centralized control (i.e., the notion that the Orestes trilogy is fundamentally about Athenian justice), then the new scenario is one in which the web is perceived as entirely vital, even necessary. One is witnessing, as Peter Galison succinctly puts it, a "war against the center."[9] The web of ruin has finally outclassed the chain of triumph. Today the Furies are the operative divinity, not Iris or Hermes. This is the case across the board, for hegemonic forces but also for more progressive political movements. One might speak of the new social movements of the 1960s and their decentralized structures, what Jo Freeman so interestingly assessed in her 1970 essay "The Tyranny of Structurelessness."[10] But in the same breath one must admit that the Hardt-Negrian notion of empire—"a dynamic and flexible systemic structure that is articulated horizontally"—is formally identical to the very movements intent on abolishing it.[11] "We're tired of trees," wrote Deleuze and Guattari. But it did not take long for those same words to be spoken in the highest echelons of the transnationals, or behind the closed doors of the Pentagon, or deep within other former bastions of pyramidal hierarchy.

The "war against the center" is, indeed, evident in a variety of milieus worth sketching out here in greater resolution. In doing so, however, it is imperative that any critical appraisal of the Web or of networks remain dissatisfied with making speculative, "broadband" claims, what Lovink calls the unfortunate quest for a General Network Theory (a quest I myself have no doubt pursued). Thus it is necessary to delve into some of the more technical and historical details implicit in the trope of the web of ruin. By this I mean the assumption that, following Clytemnestra's model, networks have the potential to dehierarchize, disrupt, and dissolve rigid structures of all varieties. This thread runs from Hans Magnus Enzensberger's chart of emancipated versus repressive media, to Deleuze and Guattari's "rhizome," to Galison and his "war against the center" (or, essentially, against centralized networks), and even to RAND researchers John Arquilla and David Ronfeldt and their theory of "netwar."[12] All these thinkers adopt the Clytemnestra model; they assume that networks exist in an antagonistic relationship to authority, that networks are the sole form of organization that can possibly threaten entrenched, fortified power centers.

This trend was articulated distinctly in the 1960s by Paul Baran (1964), who conceived of the distributed network, an extremely complex network topology that contains within it a curious synthesis of both the web of ruin and the chain of triumph. The distributed or "mesh" network is spread out horizontally with a large number of links connecting all nodes. No single node acts as master of the network. Each node making local decisions about network topology and message sending, thus spreading organization and control is integrated broadly across the entire mesh. Baran contrasted the distributed network from the centralized or "star" network, which is characterized by a singular hub with a number of branches extending to peripheral nodes. A third form, the decentralized network, is a mixture of the first two: it combines a number of hierarchical star subnetworks, the hubs of which are interconnected via backbone links into a larger amalgam. The distributed network, distinct from its centralized and decentralized cousins, is a specific architecture characterized by equity between nodes, bidirectional links, a high degree of redundancy, and a general lack of internal hierarchy.

For sending messages, Baran's distributed network relies on a technology called packet-switching, which allows messages to break themselves into small fragments. Each fragment, or packet, then finds its own way to its destination. Once there, the packets reassemble themselves to create the original message. The ARPAnet, started in 1969 by the Advanced Research Projects Agency (ARPA) at the U.S. Department of Defense, was the first network to use Baran's packet-switching technology. (Note that the term *packet-switching* was invented, not by Baran, but by British scientist Donald Davies, who, without knowing of Baran's work, also invented a system for sending small packets of information over a distributed network. It was Baran's affiliation with RAND and his proximity to the newly emerging ARPA network in America that solidified his historical legacy.) At the same time, Leonard Kleinrock published his research on network flow and queuing theory. Kleinrock's focus was to analyze

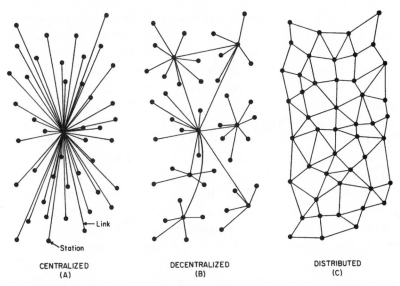

CENTRALIZED
(A)

DECENTRALIZED
(B)

DISTRIBUTED
(C)

Centralized, decentralized, and distributed networks. Baran (1964). Copyright 1964 by Rand Corporation. Reproduced with permission.

stochastic flow through networks, which is to say, flow that is not steady or predictable but in which "both the time between successive arrivals to the system and the demand placed on the channel by each of these arrivals are random quantities."[13] Kleinrock's research on queuing would become important for the design of network nodes such as routers.

During the 1970s and 1980s the ARPAnet, later dubbed the Internet, benefited from the drafting of a number of technological standards called protocols. A computer protocol is a set of recommendations and rules for implementing a technical standard. The protocols that govern much of the Internet are contained in what are called RFC (Request for Comments) documents. The expression derives from a memorandum titled "Host Software," sent by Steve Crocker on April 7, 1969, which is known today as RFC 1. The RFCs, published by the Internet Engineering Task Force (IETF), are freely available (archived online in a number of locations, they may be retrieved via a normal Web search) and are used predominantly by engineers who wish to build hardware or software that meets common specifications. Since 1969, a few thousand RFC documents have been released, and they, along with a larger constellation of global technological standards, constitute the system of organization and control known as protocol. Protocols are systems of material organization; they structure relationships of bits and atoms and how they flow through the distributed networks in which they are embedded.

While he did not invent automated communications networks, I consider Baran to be the "father" of protocological systems, not simply because of his position in the historical emergence of distributed networks, but because he explicitly understood that distributed networks create new, robust structures for organization and control; they do not *remove* organization and control. Compared to pyramidal hierarchies, networks are indeed flimsy, ineffective, and disorganized. But this relationship of asymmetry is precisely what, in the long run, makes networks so robust. The web of ruin can be highly effective. Baran understood that the Cold War model relied upon a decentralized system of targets—cities, and military bases, mostly—and so, if a new targetless model of organization could be rolled out (the smooth, distributed network), a new strategic advantage could be gained. Distributed networks have become hegemonic only recently, and because of this it is relatively easy to lapse back into the thinking of a time when networks were disruptive of power centers, when the guerilla threatened the army, when the nomadic horde threatened the citadel. But this is no longer the case. The distributed network is the new citadel, the new army, the new power.

+   +   +

In closing, I would like to identify a few details of networked media that have important ramifications for a critical theory of the network form.

The first is that, following Shannon and Weaver, informatic networks are relatively indifferent to semantic content and interpretation. Data is parsed, not "read" in any conventional sense. Media objects are defined at the intersection between two protocols (two technologies) but not as a result of some human being's semantic projection onto that data. This is readily illustrated via McLuhan's notion that any new medium contains within it older media: film contains still photographs as frames, a Web page contains images and text, and so on. With digital media McLuhan's principle has become law. Since all is information, any recognizable "content" is merely the artificial parsing of that substrate data into predictable, template-driven chunks. This can be seen in the concept of a checksum, a simple numeric signature that appears in all network messages. A checksum is computed from scanning the "content" of a message, not realized via any bona fide act of "reading." Any machinic understanding of content is derived as an epiphenomenon of human behavior, as seen in the page rank algorithms used by search engines. Following the argument above that the Furies have replaced Hermes (and perhaps Iris too) as the operative divinity, this might be referred to as the antihermeneutic tendency of networks. In short, a new model of reading will have to be explored, one that is not hermeneutic in nature but instead based on cybernetic parsing, scanning, rearranging, filtering, and interpolating. This new model of reading will need to be based on an immanent or machinic notion of software. The question now is not simply *logos* (discourse) but *ergon* (work). Networks are not simply textual entities, they are entities in a constant labor with themselves.

The second ramification is what might be called the political tragedy of interactivity. Interactivity and network bidirectionality was famously held up as a sort of utopia by Bertolt Brecht in his short fragments on radio, and later reprised by Enzensberger as the heart and soul of an "emancipated" media. Today, however, interactivity is one of the core instruments of control and organization. Like the web of ruin, networks ensnare in the very act of connection. Yet like the chain of triumph, networks are exceedingly efficient at articulating and conveying messages bidirectionally (this is what graph theory terms an "undirected" graph). Today, organisms must communicate whether they want to or not. This is essentially why "communication" and "control" are inextricably linked in Wiener's concept of cybernetics. Organisms are "captured," to use Phil Agre's terminology, using any number of informatic codes and rubrics. Clicks are accumulated. Behaviors are mined for meaningful data or tracked for illegal data. Even the genome is prospected for rare or otherwise useful sequences. Enzensberger's desire to change the media from the unidirectional model of fascism to the bidirectional model of radical democracy was laudable, and germane to the political movements of the time. Yet today bidirectionality is not the saving grace it once was thought to be, due to the incorporation of bi- and multidirectionality into the networked technologies of control and organization. Today, interactivity means total participation, universal capture. The chain of triumph is not a monologue but a multilogue.

The third ramification is the tendency for software to privilege surface over source, while at the same time championing sources as absolutely essential even when hidden. What does this mean? Software is often understood as existing on various levels. At the level of authorship, it exists as "source code," a human-readable text that contains commands written in a high-level computer language such as C++. When this source code is compiled, these commands are translated into machine-readable code called an executable application, consisting of basic commands that can be understood by the hardware of the machine. This application creates a third modality, the "runtime" experience of the user who launches and runs the software. These three modalities—source, executable application, and interface—are crucial aspects of any computer technology. The interface is often considered to be primary, as it determines the actual experience of the software as it relates to a user. Yet the executable mode comprises the actual machinic commands necessary for the software to function. But at the same time, the executable is merely the result of a machinic compilation of the source code, which is thus the essential recipe or score for the realized work. So for software "source" to work it must appear in a form it is not (the executable), only then to be experienced in a third form different entirely from the other two. This is what might be called the occult logic of software: software hides itself at exactly the moment when it expresses itself most fully. As Wendy Hui Kyong Chun notes in her work, code is never merely a source; it is always a "resource."

The tendency for software to privilege surface over source has led to social movements promoting open source software (a type of software in which both source code and executable are made available to users). Yet this surfacing effect is insidious, and reappears even within so-called open source software. There is a design approach in computer science known as encapsulation, whereby code is segregated into modular units, sometimes called objects or libraries, with which one interacts via interfaces. In this sense, software itself acts like a network, a network of message-sending simulated entirely within an abstract informatic space. The software objects are the nodes in the network and messages are sent via an "edge" consisting of any two object's interfaces. The interface acts as the sole conduit for communication into and out of the object or library. The source of the object or library itself is hidden. Computer scientists use encapsulation for a variety of reasons, all of them practical. It makes the code easier to maintain and simpler to implement. The practice pervades a whole variety of computer languages and programming environments, including open code software. The open source movement, then, is not enough; something like an "open runtime" movement might also be required, in which the dialectic of obscurantism and transparency, a longtime stalwart in aesthetics and philosophy, is interrogated as a central problem, if not *the* central problem, of software. The paradox of networked relations is thus the following: the networked other is always obscured, but experiencing the essence of the other, even in its obscurity, is assumed to be the ultimate goal of any networked relation. For example, in the discourse of complexity theory it is the very obscurity of the networked totality that is first posited, only to be overcome, via the phenomenon of "emergence" into the new spiritual essence of the "collective intelligence."

A fourth and final ramification of this new, topsy-turvy relationship between the chain of triumph and the web of ruin is that it suggests new scenes of political interest. There are a number of options possible in this regard. Using the network as a fulcrum, I will suggest two avenues: (1) political questions that issue from a formal congruency "within" the network, and (2) political questions that issue from the space of the "without."

One of the basic qualities of a net—the gaps or holes that allow, in the case of fishing, water and smaller objects to pass through—is neglected by topology and graph theory. Graph properties are topological in nature; the edges are infinitely elastic, meaning that a graph's nodes can be moved at random, producing networks that look completely different but are still isomorphic. Connectivity between nodes outweighs any spatial concern. For example, it is possible for a parallelogram and a rectangle to be isomorphic in graph theory, whereas in geometry this is not the case (except in the special instance of the parallelogram with all right angles). In general, the geometry of the space in which a graph is embedded does not indicate anything meaningful about the graph. From this we may assert that graph theory has no theory of the gap. Graphs are nets without holes. Or at least they are nets in which the specific shape and quality of the holes (which do exist) have no consequence whatsoever. Graphs assert the hole, but only as an exclusion from the whole, as something that is present but unable to act. Graphs are nets for which the "offline" has been prohibited from discourse. They "suspend" the hole, both in an ontological sense and literally, as a suspension hanging from webs of knots and thread. Of course this is a feature of graph theory, not a shortcoming.

But it may also be a liability. Thus one may identify today a number of new scenes of political interest that come from without. These are movements that speak from the position of the holes in the graph. Perhaps in a former time this was called Ludditism. Today, with the general augmentation of network technologies throughout social space, it encompasses all exclusionary and extra-network concerns: Agamben's notion of "bare life"; the politics of imprisonment, extradition, and habeas corpus (today's "dark" prisons take a cue from Devil's Island and the former penal colonies); the initiative by the West to "wire" Africa; Mehdi Belhaj Kacem's notion of being "imprisoned on the outside"; precarious labor and post-Fordism; biometrics and the expansion of what counts as empirically measurable and semiologically expressive data (following the tragedy of interactivity described above); the question of topographical resolution in the field of geography; and so on. The primary issue here is the notion of intelligibility. Who or what is excluded from networked presence? What are the necessary conditions in any specific situation for an entity to be excluded from the network? What price must be paid in exclusion? What *larger* price must be paid for inclusion? "Before the law sits a gatekeeper," wrote Kafka.

On the other hand, one may cite all the network-centric diagrams for political resistance viable under modernity and the passage into postmodernity: grassroots organizations, guerrilla warfare, anarcho-syndicalism, and other rhizomatic movements. These are all "formally within" the network mode because they are themselves formally constituted as distributed or decentralized networks of some kind or another.[14] (One may also argue that it is the very formal asymmetry of the rhizomatic movements vis-à-vis centralized antagonists that provides the basis of the rhizome's potency, but that is the topic of another essay.) Yet after the powers-that-be have migrated into the distributed network as well, thereby co-opting the very tools of the former left, new models for political action are required. A new exploit is necessary, one that is as asymmetrical in relationship to distributed networks as the distributed network was to the power centers of modernity, or as Clytemnestra's "vast voluminous net" was to Agamemnon's militaristic efficiency. But this new exploit is never outside the network, it is always formally within it. Thus certain intra-anti-network movements have also emerged. An example is Hakim Bey's model of the temporary autonomous zone, or, following the example of the Furies, the Electronic Disturbance Theatre's system of online electronic swarming. In the realm of the nonhuman, computer viruses and worms have innovated, perhaps totally haphazardly, a new model of intra–anti-network infection and disruption that takes advantage of the homogeneity of distributed networks and their ability to propagate information. At the same time hackers seek out logical exploits in networked machines that allow for inversions and modulations in the normal functionality of those machines.

These techniques are not yet fully formed and in many cases are politically naïve if not retrograde, as with the case of the virus. Yet they do begin to sketch out a new model of networked organization and, via silhouette, an image of a counternetwork practice that is entirely native to the network form. Coupled with the scenes located outside of or at the borders of the network, as well as the "problem" of interactivity, the matter of surfaces and sources, and the antihermeneutic impulse, one begins to see the spectrum of issues at play in a critical theory of the network form.

Notes

1. Parenthetical citations refer to line numbers from the Greek text. The translation is from Aeschylus, *The Oresteian Trilogy*, trans. Philip Vellacott (New York: Penguin, 1956).
2. The concordance between textiles and spiderwebs is noted again later in Ovid with the story of Arachne, the haughty weaver maiden whom Athena transforms into a spider: "her hair and then her eyes and ears fell off, and all her body sank. And at her sides, her slen-

der fingers clung to her as legs. The rest is belly; but from this, Arachne spins out a thread; again she practices her weaver's art, as once she fashioned webs" (book 6, lines 141–45). Ovid, *Metamorphoses*, trans. Allen Bandelbaum (New York: Harcourt, 1993), 183. Arachne reappears in Dante (*Inferno*, canto 17; *Purgatorio*, canto 12) as an allegorical figure for the poet himself, undone at the hands of his own artistic creation. The thread used to weave the pictorial textile becomes a noose with which Arachne tries to hang herself in defiance of the goddess. But the noose becomes a web again, referring back to the "spinning" of the artist, be it of tales or tapestries.

3. Michel Foucault, *The Archaeology of Knowledge* (New York: Pantheon, 1972), 219. As branches of mathematics, geometry and graph theory are as different as they are similar. They share the Euclidean concepts of point and line (translated to *vertex* and *edge* in graph theory), yet being essentially topological, graph theory lacks any concept of angle (between lines) or polygonal surface area (the holes or gaps between strands of the net) both of which are central to Euclidean geometry. One counterexample in which the geometry of the graph's embedded space matters is the planar graph, which is a graph drawn so that no edges intersect except at nodes. Yet even the planar graph is topologically elastic in ways prohibited in classical geometry.

4. Wiener describes feedback as follows: "It has long been clear to me that the modern ultra-rapid computing machine was in principle an ideal central nervous system to an apparatus for automatic control. . . . With the aid of strain gauges or similar agencies to read the performance of these motor organs and to report, to 'feed back,' to the central control system as an artificial kinesthetic sense, we are already in a position to construct artificial machines of almost any degree of elaborateness of performance" (1965, 27).

5. "Just as the amount of information in a system is a measure of its degree of organization, so the entropy of a system is a measure of its degree of disorganization; and the one is simply the negative of the other" (Wiener 1965, 11).

6. See Benkler (2006), as well as Geert Lovink, *My First Recession* (Rotterdam: V2, 2003), 12; Richard Barbrook and Andy Cameron, "Californian Ideology," and John Perry Barlow, "A Declaration of the Independence of Cyberspace," in *Crypto Anarchy, Cyberstates, and Pirate Utopias*, ed. Peter Ludow (Cambridge, MA: MIT Press, 2001); Mark Dery, *Escape Velocity* (New York: Grove Press, 1996); Eben Moglen, "The dotCommunist Manifesto," http://emoglen.law.columbia.edu/publications/dcm.html (accessed November 5, 2005); Kevin Kelly, *Out of Control* (New York: Perseus, 1995); Esther Dyson, *Release 2.0* (New York: Broadway, 1997); Ray Kurzweil, *The Age of Spiritual Machines* (New York: Penguin, 1999); Nicholas Negroponte, *Being Digital* (New York: Knopf, 1995); Steven Johnson, *Emergence* (New York: Scribner, 2002); Manuel DeLanda, *A Thousand Years of Nonlinear History* (New York: Zone, 2000); Pierre Lévy, *Becoming Virtual* (New York: Plenum, 1998); Mark Poster, *What's the Matter with the Internet?* (Minneapolis: University of Minnesota Press, 2001); Brian Massumi, *Parables for the Virtual* (Durham: Duke University Press, 2002); and Lawrence Lessig, *Code and Other Laws of Cyberspace* (New York: Basic, 2000).

7. See Chun (2005) and Hayles (1999). Also Espen Aarseth, *Cybertext* (Baltimore: Johns Hopkins University Press, 1997); Jay Bolter and Richard Grusin, *Remediation* (Cambridge, MA: MIT Press, 2000); Marina Grzinic, "Exposure Time, the Aura, and Telerobotics" in *The Robot in the Garden*, ed. Ken Goldberg (Cambridge, MA: MIT Press, 2000); Donna Haraway, *Simians, Cyborgs, and Women* (New York: Routledge, 1991); Lev Manovich, *The Language of New Media* (Cambridge, MA: MIT Press, 2001); Lisa Nakamura, *Cybertypes* (New York: Routledge,

2002); Sadie Plant, *Zeros + Ones* (New York: Fourth Estate, 1997); Allucquère Rosanne Stone, *The War of Desire and Technology at the Close of the Mechanical Age* (Cambridge, MA: MIT Press, 1996); Sherry Turkle, *Life on the Screen* (New York: Simon & Schuster, 1997).

8. For a good overview of social network theory and graph theory, see Barabási (2002).

9. Peter Galison, "War against the Center," *Grey Room* 4 (Summer 2001): 7–33.

10. Jo Freeman, "The Tyranny of Structurelessness," http://www.jofreeman.com/joreen/tyranny.htm (accessed January 4, 2006).

11. Michael Hardt and Antonio Negri, *Empire* (Cambridge, MA: Harvard University Press, 2000), 13,

12. See Deleuze and Guattari (1987) and Arquilla and Ronfeldt (2001). Also Hans Magnus Enzensberger, "Constituents of a Theory of the Media" in Noah Wardrip-Fruin and Nick Montfort, Eds., *The New Media Reader* (Cambridge, MA: MIT Press, 2003); Galison, "War Against the Center."

13. Leonard Kleinrock, *Communication Nets* (New York: Dover, 1964).

14. This is analogous to how "noise" is defined in information theory. One might romantically think that noise is some postmodern godsend to combat the rigidity of digital code. However, in information science, noise is not the opposite of information, defined by Shannon and Weaver as the amount of entropy in message construction. Simply put, more noise (generally) means more information. Hence noise is an intra-informatic problem, not an extra-informatic problem.

References and Suggested Readings

Arquilla, John, and David Ronfeldt. 2001. *Networks and Netwars: The Future of Terror, Crime, and Militancy*. Santa Monica, CA: RAND.

Barabási, Albert-László. 2002. *Linked*. New York: Perseus.

Baran, Paul.1964. *On Distributed Communications*. Santa Monica, CA: RAND.

Benkler, Yochai. 2006. *The Wealth of Markets*, New Haven, CT: Yale University Press.

Chun, Wendy Hui Kyong. 2005. *Control and Freedom*. Cambridge, MA: MIT Press.

Deleuze, Gilles, and Félix Guattari. 1987. *A Thousand Plateaus*. Minneapolis: University of Minnesota Press.

Hayles, Katherine. 1999. *How We Became Posthuman*. Chicago: University of Chicago Press.

Shannon, Claude, and Warren Weaver. 1963. *The Mathematical Theory of Communication*. Chicago: University of Illinois Press.

Von Bertalanffy, Ludwig. 1976. *General Systems Theory: Foundations, Development, Application*. New York: George Braziller.

Wiener, Norbert. 1965. *Cybernetics, or Control and Communication in the Animal and the Machine*. Cambridge, MA: MIT Press.

20 :: SYSTEMS DAVID WELLBERY

The sociological systems theory of Niklas Luhmann is of compelling interest for media studies because it offers a capacious yet precise notion of media equipped with multiple conceptual linkages. Indeed, one feature that distinguishes Luhmann's theory from those of such classical social theorists as Durkheim, Simmel, Weber, Mead, and Parsons is the centrality it accords to media-theoretical considerations. This is not surprising, since Luhmann holds events of communication (and not, for example, individuals, groups, or actions) to constitute the elements of which social systems consist. His inflection of the concept of media is, however, sufficiently original and complex to warrant explication.

The obvious place to start is with the concept of "system" itself. Yet already here we must pause for a moment to note that Luhmann's theory does not operate with insular concepts that purport to refer to real-world entities. Rather, all his leading terms are formulated within and as distinctions. Of course, every concept rests on distinctions (otherwise it would lack definition, hence content), but in Luhmann's work this semantic fact is not submerged; it is brought to the foreground and made methodical. "Draw a distinction!" This initial imperative of George Spencer Brown's *Laws of Form*, a crucial reference text for Luhmann, is executed again and again across his work. Nowhere is this more evident than in the case of the theory's titular concept, which we encounter not as a freely standing notion, but as one side of a distinction: system/environment. Whereas most uses of the concept of system are merely reminders to think holistically and (beyond this rhetorical function) to remain theoretically anodyne, Luhmann's differential employment of the term bears far-reaching conceptual ramifications. The locus of its generative capacity is the border that separates and relates system and environment from/to one another. No system can exist in (conceptual or real) independence from its environment. Systems, in fact, arise when they draw a boundary between themselves and their environment: when their operations establish a limit that distinguishes what is proper to the system itself from the milieu within which the system operates. Systems emerge as autonomous operative concatenations that extend themselves by continuously redrawing the distinction between internal operations and external events. Moreover, just as systems are relative to a particular environment, so environments are relative to systems. There is no single, all-inclusive environment, and no single, all-embracing viewpoint from which such a total environment might be described. The environment is a different one according to the system-reference with respect to which it is observed.

It is useful to parse this in terms of an example. Take a university class on media studies. If we say that this class, as it unfolds in time, constitutes a social system, that is typically interpreted to mean that the individual human beings in the room are somehow "unified" to make a larger whole, as in the famous frontispiece to Hobbes's *Leviathan*. The social system is conceived in terms of the distinction part/whole, an observational ploy that quickly leads to familiar discussions on tired themes such as "the individual and society." From the point of view of Luhmannian systems theory, however, the social system we are dealing with here is not made up of people at all; it is, rather, the ongoing, recursively self-validating, self-correcting, and in every case, self-referring series of communicative events. Such social systems, anchored in face-to-face situations and therefore relatively ephemeral, are called "interactions," and they are well known to that branch of media studies devoted to research on oral communication. But the point we are interested in here is the thrust of the system/environment distinction generally. What is the environment of the social system constituted in the class meeting? Well, it's just everything else, including the physical-natural environment and the conscious life of the active and passive participants in the class. The people in the room are not components (parts) of the social system, but factors within its environment. Here it becomes abundantly clear that the boundary separating system from environment involves a drop-off in complexity. The social system of the "class" cannot account for (much less contain) everything in its environment: not the minor fluctuations of room temperature, not the fluctuating personal feelings of each student. Only if it can reduce the complexity of the environment can the system establish itself as a linked set of operations. Thus, not everything that enters into Jack's mind (say, the soreness of his ankle) or Jill's (say, her overdue cell phone bill) will find its way into the communicative interaction, and if it did, if everyone attempted to say everything on his or her mind at every moment (an absurd, but telling surmise), then the social system of the class would disintegrate, collapsing into the blather of consciousnesses that constitutes (a factor of) its environment.

In comparison to its environment, every system is a simplification; there can be no point-for-point correspondence between system and environment. Precisely this reduction of complexity, achieved by contingent selection, enables the system to build up internal complexity (in the example at hand, a reticulated, semantically rich discussion). But let us return for a moment to the minds of Jack and Jill. They are not, as we noted, "parts" of the social system (which consists solely of the linked communications constituting the class discussion) but features of its environment. Each of these minds, however, is a system in itself (in Luhmann's terminology, a "psychic system," the elements of which are "thought-events") and for each of these psychic systems (linkages of affect, mood, perception, recollection, etc.) the environment will be a different one. And of each environment it is true that, although it includes systems of various sorts (psychic, social, biological, mechanical), it is not itself systematic. The consciousnesses of Jack and Jill do not together form one system, although it is certainly possible, as the nursery rhyme intimates, that Jack and Jill participate in their own system of communicative intercourse. By the lights of the system/environment distinction, then, even so simple a context as a college classroom ramifies into a complex and shifting array of perspectives. One is reminded of Leibniz's universe of monads, each of which is "windowless," each of which represents, from its unique vantage, the entire world. In Luhmann's pluriverse, however, there is no master monad—no god—to coordinate all the individual world-versions.

As our example shows, Luhmann's systems theory makes room for various kinds of system. But two sorts—psychic systems and social systems—are at the core of his theoretical interest; he was, after all, a sociologist by trade (see chapter 9, "Communication"). What the two systems have in common is, first of all, that their respective elements—"thoughts" and "communications"—are "events" and, as such, evanescent, passing out of existence with their occasions. There is something here of the pragmatic emphasis on the "present as the locus of reality," in George Herbert Mead's phrase, and this emphasis sometimes betrays a sense of crisis. Both psychic and social systems confront, without respite, the problem of getting to the next moment, to the next event that will ratify their existence, even as it, in turn, evaporates, raising anew the problem of systemic reproduction or continuation. To grasp the audacity of Luhmann's vision, one must have a feel for the airy insubstantiality of systems that consist only of events. In order to perdure, they must bind one moment to another, bridge the abyss of temporal transition with threads of continuity. And this brings us to the second feature held in common by psychic and social systems, while distinguishing them, for example, from machines and organisms. They are able to achieve the work of temporal binding across a discontinuous series of events because their operations occur within the medium of meaning (*Sinn*). Delicate filaments of meaning tie the events of which psychic and social systems consist together, providing linkages forward and backward in time. Like organic systems (cells, immune systems, brains), psychic and social systems are *autopoietic*, themselves generating the elements of which they consist. But here the notion of autopoiesis, first formulated by Varela and Maturana in the context of biology, is generalized to include nonorganic systems, systems whose elements have no protoplasmic basis but are, as noted above, events within the medium of meaning.

We have arrived at the first, and perhaps most important, occurrence of the concept of "medium" within the framework of systems theory: the claim that the feature distinguishing psychic and social systems from all other autopoietic systems is the fact that they constitute themselves within the medium of meaning. Psychic and social systems represent evolutionary achievements, emergent realities, and the branching within the network of evolutionary pathways that marks the inauguration of their joint itinerary comes about at that point where meaning (as opposed, for instance, to electrical or chemical processes) becomes the "stuff" of which the constitutive elements are made. To unpack this claim, it is necessary to clarify what Luhmann means by "meaning." His starting point is Husserl's phenomenology of perception, in particular the doctrine that whatever is given to consciousness as a perceptual datum refers to a horizon of other, nonactualized perceptions. In Luhmann's redaction, the datum/horizon structure is definitive of meaning in general. Meaning is the referential excess that carries (from the Latin *ferre*, to bear or carry) each presentation beyond itself to other presentations. In Luhmannian patois this is captured by the dictum, meaning is the unity of the difference of actuality and potentiality. We may gloss this as defining meaning not as a self-standing ideal entity, but as a dynamic relation: a relation, because any occurent phenomenon within the space of meaning is what it is only by virtue of its relations to other possible phenomena; dynamic, because this very relationality has the effect of propelling the system's operations from one meaning actualization to another, and so forth. Thus, every event of meaning bears (once again: *ferre*!) references to prior actualizations as well as to potential future actualizations. For readers of Derrida, this interlacing of trace and deferral is familiar as the very nature of semiosis. For Luhmann, however, the structure is not limited to sign-use, but permeates all of conscious and social life. Moreover, Luhmann is interested not in pointing out how meaning thus conceptualized provides the critical leverage necessary to "deconstruct" various traditionally held "metaphysical" views, but rather in showing how, within the airy and volatile medium of meaning, our psychic and social lives take shape. That involves a rather complicated story. For the moment, however, we can hold on to this point: because meaning refers beyond its present actualization to prior and posterior meanings, it provides a solution to the problem of temporal binding alluded to above. Systems that consist of events can, if those events take form within the medium of meaning, maintain basal self-reference—and hence maintain themselves—across the chasm of temporal discontinuity. Finally, the datum/horizon structure of meaning makes possible the reduction of complexity that is required if the psychic or social system is to distinguish itself from its environment. Dealing in meaning events, the system can, as it were, hold the world's complexity in abeyance without, however, eliminating it altogether and thus rendering it inaccessible. Meaning events are postponements, they put off attention to other possible meanings while a particular meaning is in focus but, at the same time, hold open the possibility of treating other aspects of the virtualized world complexity later. For psychic and social systems, procrastination is the precondition of action.

If, as systems theory claims, meaning is a medium, then we shall need a general theory of media in order to give that claim some conceptual grip. Luhmann finds access to such a theory in an essay on the physical preconditions of perception by the psychologist Fritz Heider. Once again, we begin by drawing a distinction, this time between "form" and "medium"; and once again we shall endeavor to keep the interdependence of the two terms (no form without a medium and vice versa) in view. This distinction, as Luhmann employs it, yields what might be termed the Friday theory of media. For what distinguishes media from forms is that the former consist of loosely coupled elements, whereas the latter bring those elements into a rigid coupling. Consider a stretch of sand on an apparently uninhabited island. As such, it just is what it is: sand. However, if I, like Crusoe, happen to encounter a footprint in it, it becomes a medium bearing a form. The grains of sand—"loosely coupled" in the sense of having no fixed arrangement and being susceptible to rearrangement—are brought into a particular array that exhibits the form "human footprint." Friday has left his trace and this trace is a datum that is itself distinguished from, but related to other data ("animal spoor," "wind swirl"). The footprint is a "rigid coupling" of the loosely coupled elements (the grains of sand) in the sense that not just any indentation in the beach will do. The sand thus becomes a medium when it is imprinted with, receives, or comes to bear the form; and the footprint becomes a form when the loosely coupled elements of the medium are brought into an alignment that makes a difference ("That's Friday's footprint, not the footprint of a turtle!").

The form/medium distinction ramifies along several paths within the conceptual network of systems theory. At this juncture, however, it is useful to highlight a particular point that contrasts sharply with, indeed contradicts, a fundamental assumption of many varieties of media studies. Call this assumption the "materiality thesis." To see how systems theory militates against the notion that to investigate media is, in some sense, to investigate bottom-line materialities, let us apply our Friday theory to the case of spoken language. We start with the range of possible sounds producible by the physiological apparatus of tongue, teeth, vocal cords, oral cavity, lungs, and so on. In his *Course on General Linguistics* Saussure pictured this tonal amalgam as a wavy sound-sea, a salient image of loose coupling. If from this reservoir of tonal possibilities we select certain rigid couplings of features such that just these combinations are taken as distinctive, then we can generate the phonemic system specific, say, to English. One combination yields the phoneme /p/, another the phoneme /t/. Since the tonal features must be combined in a certain way to yield a sound recognizable as /p/ and in another way in order successfully to proffer a token of /t/, phonemes are indeed "forms" in the sense of our Friday theory. Taken in isolation, phonemes obey no constraints as to their possible combinations, but we can, of course, "rigidify" certain concatenations (for example: /pat/ or /tap/), while leaving others to fall into insignificance (/pttttpap/). This means, of course, that the phonemes, when viewed in the context of the physiologically available tonal possibilities, are "forms," but, when viewed with respect to a superior level of "forms" (the morphemes), are a "medium" (reservoir of loosely coupled elements). This situation, of course, continues to obtain as we move upward through the levels of lexeme, phrase, sentence, text, and discourse. From the perspective of systems theory, then, the terms *form* and *medium* are relative; what counts as a medium will depend entirely on the plane of analysis selected. On this model, media studies is free to investigate meanings while nonetheless remaining true to itself, and the theoretical alternatives of Platonism and materialism can both be consigned to the junk heap of outmoded thought.

We now have enough pieces of the puzzle in place to consider the relationship between "consciousness" (equivalent, in Luhmann's terminology, to "psychic system") and "communication" (the operation characteristic of "social systems"). There is an inherited, both commonsensical and philosophically dignified view that communication is grounded in consciousness in the sense that to communicate is to externalize in speech or in writing something that is mental, say, a meaning, a thought, and to do this in such a way that another consciousness can wean the meaning from its external vehicle and reactualize it as thought. Luhmann's view, however, is that consciousness and communication are each autopoietic systems that reproduce themselves by reproducing the elements of which they consist, thought-events and communication-events respectively. If this is the case, it is wrong to imagine that conscious thoughts can enter into communication or, for that matter, that communications can enter consciousness. As autopoietic systems, both consciousness and communication are operationally closed to their environments; they operate solely with those elements they themselves produce. One cannot, therefore, consciously communicate. Only communication—the social system—can communicate; communication just is the operation social systems perform. (I note in passing that there is something akin here to the so-called private language argument made philosophically crucial by Wittgenstein. And I note further that, from a Luhmannian point of view, the consequence that some commentators have drawn from that argument—namely, that meaning must be defined socially rather than in terms of the purported mental fact of "having a meaning"—is vacuous, for the "social" itself is operation with meanings as articulated in communications.) If systems theory describes things this way, however, then it would still seem to owe us an account of the relation between mind and meaning or, in its own terms, consciousness and communication. For certainly communication is not possible apart from the participation of conscious systems (unless the term is expanded to include machine-to-machine "communication"), if only for the reason that communicational media, such as speech and writing, require perception to be effective. But if consciousness and communication are autonomous (autopoietic) systems, operationally closed to one another, then how do they interact?

This is where the notion of "structural coupling" enters, and it is a notion that must prove central in any attempt to develop a full-blown systems-theoretical version of media studies. Structural coupling occurs at the border between autonomous systems and enables them to affect one another without, as it were, entering into each other's (after all, autonomous) operations. This indirect affection occurs via an interface to which the operations of both systems are attached. Language is just such an interface, not the only one, but certainly the most important (see chapter 16, "Language"). As we noted above, language is to be conceived as a complex hierarchy of form/medium relations, and it may very well be true that, in every case, structural couplings occur via such multileveled formations. If so, then an important upshot of systems theory would be a complication of the concept of "medium" itself. Be that as it may, it should be clear that, from the point of view of systems theory, language is not a system. There are no self-constituting operations that language as such performs. This way of describing things marks an important distinction between systems theory and all varieties of structuralism. In fact, given the emphasis in systems theory on such notions as "event," "contingency," and "improbability," the concept of "structural determination," so dear to the sociological tradition, falls into desuetude. But this is a subsidiary point. The thought that deserves emphasis in the present context is that language enables (is the medium of) a structural coupling between consciousness and communication in such a way that what is inaccessible to both, namely occurent thought for communication and communicative exchange for consciousness, can take effect without violating either system's autopoietic closure. In this sense, language (but prior to it gesture, facial expression, etc.) enables communication to emerge as a reality sui generis despite the radical heterogeneity of conscious systems; it enables consciousness, we might say, to support communication. But it also, and equally importantly, allows communication to discipline consciousness, to lend thematic continuity to its desultory meanderings. Here the theoretical salience of the concept of "media" (more specifically, form/medium hierarchies) as enabling structural coupling comes clearly into view: structural coupling is the condition of the coevolution of consciousness and communication. Nonetheless each remains operationally closed to the other: consciousness doesn't communicate, nor is communication absorbed by thought.

We have thus far referred to the operation of communication as the mode of operation of social systems but have neglected to characterize it with respect to its internal constituents. The distinction in question here is a threefold one: the "utterance" or "conveying"; the information; and the understanding that distinguishes these two. Thus, a communication comes about when Ego understands that Alter has conveyed some information. Consider the man who at dinner pushes a boiled potato to the edge of his plate. His wife understands this as a communicative utterance ("he's telling me something") that is correlated with the information that the potato is cold. Of course, it's possible that the wife has identified an utterance act that didn't really occur; the husband, after all, is constantly shoving food about with his fork. And it's likewise possible that the wife's understanding construes a bit of false information (the potato is actually too hot), or attributes to the husband a motive in making the utterance ("he's suggesting I'm a lousy cook") that the husband didn't actually have (he wanted to intimate a general sense of dissatisfaction with his life). These possibilities highlight the improbability of communication, embedded as it is in what Luhmann, following Talcott Parsons, calls the "double contingency" of the social situation. Whoever has experienced the morass of misunderstanding into which scenarios kindred to our dinner-table example tend to sink will appreciate the force of this concept. Double contingency marks the improbability that something like sociality should come about at all. Since the triple selections (of utterances, of information, of understandings) are contingent on *both* sides and all of the components could therefore be otherwise, the least likely of outcomes would seem to be ongoing communication. Such improbability is the primary datum of systems theory.

Systems-theoretical accounts of social phenomena, then, cannot aspire to be deterministic. Instead, systems theory employs a mode of inquiry that Gregory Bateson termed cybernetic explanation. Given the contingency of the start-up situation (the fact that a large number of outcomes are possible), we ask, How is it that this one outcome, improbable as it is, comes about? The answer typically points to redundancies or constraints, both of which limit the improbability of a certain outcome. How is it that the wife knows her husband is telling her the potato is cold and that she's a lousy cook? How is it, given everything else his gesture could mean, including nothing at all, that she makes the right selection and allows the couple's nightly marital quarrel to commence on schedule? Perhaps because he's said the same thing a thousand other ways already, starting with the gasp he expelled as he sat down at the table. Perhaps because in this household marital conversation, whether its theme is food, sex, or income, operates with the code values: adequate/inadequate. Redundancy and constraint achieved through binary codes are modes of ensuring the continuity of systemic operations despite the contingency of selections. They do not eliminate contingency and in fact are unintelligible apart from it. There will always be variations, unforeseeable outcomes, and surprises. Indeed, the very life of psychic and social systems depends on this, and increasingly so as internal complexity (hence redundancy and constraint) is enhanced. The intellectual comedy of cultural analyses that find a bit of social determinism here and a bit of individual agency there or link the two in some sort of circular causality can finally be abandoned. Systems theory provides a radically nondeterministic model of explanation consonant with such adjacent disciplines as decision theory or evolutionary theory. For this reason, media studies, which not infrequently succumbs to the false allure of technological determinism, might find an introductory course in the forms of cybernetic explanation salutary.

As we have seen, the most fundamental linkage between the concepts "system" and "medium" resides in the fact that psychic and social systems autopoietically produce the elements of which each consists in the medium of meaning. Generally speaking, then, meaning is the medium in which individual thoughts (in the case of psychic systems) and communications (in the case of social systems) occur as forms. With the introduction of specific media, this universal form/medium relationship can exfoliate in different ways, achieving rather reticulate hierarchies. This was illustrated in terms of the "medium" of language. Systems-theoretical analysis, however, is also functional analysis, examining not merely the inner structure of media but also their contribution to the solution of problems that systems face. Recalling our dinner-table scenario, we note that, because the communication takes form in the medium of gesture (shoving the potato to the edge of the plate), it is so encumbered with ambiguities that it is not even clear whether communication is occurring at all. How different would the situation be if the husband had said, "This goddamn potato is cold as hell." Then there would be no question as to the fact that a communication was intended, and its purport, too, would be difficult to misinterpret. The function of language for the ongoing autopoiesis of social systems, then, is that it provides a specialized medium that differentiates communication from all other activities (such as pushing food around one's plate). Moreover, it is the internal structure of the linguistic medium that makes it so apt as a solution to the problem of securing understanding. As we have seen, language is hierarchically articulated. On the level of the form/medium relations that produce the phonemic system (one could, of course, add, intonation, meter, etc.), it provides a low-cost (producible without much energy expenditure) repertoire of differences that are easily discriminated perceptually and couples these in higher-order forms (morphemes, lexemes, sentences) capable of boundless semantic complexity. In this sense, language embodies the difference between "utterance" and "information" that must be "understood" if communication is to take place at all. Further, it is natural to assume that this medium will evolve and gain in complexity along with the coevolution of consciousness and communication it (qua structural coupling) makes possible. This is a large topic, but the methodological point I wish to illustrate should be clear enough. In systems theory, functional analysis and analysis in terms of form/medium relations are intricately intertwined, and this conceptual linkage provides the bridge to investigations of social and cultural evolution. Functions are not causal determinations, but correlations of problems and solutions. Needless to say, each solution brings with it new and unforeseen problems. From the perspective of systems theory, there is no respite, and certainly no utopia, no ideal state.

Thus far, we have oriented our discussion principally in terms of oral communication. What happens when writing is introduced? Here we do not mean "writing" in the sense of the "arche-writing" made current by Derrida, a sense that bears, as noted above, similarities to Luhmann's notion of meaning (*Sinn*). We are concerned, rather, with writing in its straightforward empirical sense, as a notational system, and our theoretical points of reference are the pioneers of research on the orality/literacy divide: Goody and Watt, Havelock, and Ong (see chapter 21, "Writing"). Obviously, the systems-theoretically relevant point in this connection is the fact that writing extricates communication from its ensconcement in interaction. No longer tethered to the face-to-face situation, communication can operate at spatial and temporal distances; it can build up a capacious archive (memory); it can develop specialized vocabularies and genres; it can complexify its hierarchy of form/medium relations; it can expand the range of culturally available semantic alternatives. All this is perfectly evident. It is well known that the emergence of the ancient civilizations is tied to the invention of writing, much as the emergence of the modern era is unthinkable apart from the technologization of writing in print. The interesting question from the point of view of this essay is whether the conceptual tools of systems theory provide a means of perspicuously organizing and interpreting the ongoing empirical research in this area. And the same question can be raised with respect to the technological media and telecommunications. We might formulate the issue in terms of synthetic power. To what degree does systems theory provide a framework that allows for an integrative approach to media studies in both its theoretical and its historical dimensions? The contention advanced in the foregoing paragraphs is that, at least on the level of conceptual articulation, systems theory indeed has a great deal to offer. And on the historical side, several recent contributions have demonstrated the fecundity of the systems-theoretical paradigm. In Anglo-American and French discussions, however, systems theory is viewed, for the most part, as marginal and recondite. Only the gods of academic fashion know whether this situation will change.

This brings me to my final point, appropriately hypothetical. If systems theory is taken seriously as a viable paradigm for research in media studies, then something like a conceptual metamorphosis will occur. Media studies will emerge from its cocoon of specialization, free itself from its fixation on specific "materialities," sensory channels, and coding procedures (analog/digital), and take flight as a general inquiry into the structure and evolution of communication. An adumbration of what such an expansion of its domain of study might mean can be glimpsed in connection with a further notion developed within systems theory, that of "symbolically generalized media of communication." This notion addresses problems akin to those mentioned above in connection with the double contingency of the social situation. If we consider the burgeoning complexity of communication achieved with the spread of writing, we can immediately see that the problem of the improbability of communication (double contingency) is immeasurably aggravated. With its detachment from the contextual supports inherent in the face-to-face situation (e.g., perceptually transparent deixis, gesture, shared and unshakable semantic presuppositions), communication sets sail on a sea of improbability that calls forth, if communication is to have any chance of succeeding, the establishment of innovative types of constraint. These constraints tie the selection of the communication with the motivation to take it up and continue the communicative process. This they accomplish by establishing situation-transcendent (hence "generalized") frameworks that consign the communicative transaction to its own domain of application condensed in an overarching "symbol." Examples of such symbolically generalized media include power (and law), love, art, money, and truth. These are media in the sense elaborated above. That is, they are tracts of "meaning" susceptible to analysis in terms of form/medium relations. Money, for example, is a reservoir of loosely coupled elements capable of accepting forms (prices). The crucial feature of symbolically generalized media is that they reduce the improbability of communication by allowing for its adjudication in terms of a binary code. To participate in economic exchange within the medium of money is to accept the alternative payment/nonpayment as the criterion for evaluating any particular communicational outcome. It is a commonplace of social theory that modern society—as opposed to tribal society, with its segmental differentiation, and feudal-aristocratic society, with its stratified differentiation—is functionally differentiated into specialized, task-defined spheres: science, law, economy, family, education, art, and so on. The systems-theoretical notion of symbolically generalized communication media brings out the additional point that such functional subsystems crystallize around specific media (e.g., money in the case of the economic system). But to say that money, love, and power are media is to expand that notion well beyond its present horizon of pertinence.

Systems theory offers compelling arguments in favor of accepting this extension of the media concept, as well as a repertoire of distinctions (consciousness/communication, form/medium, system/environment, operation/observation) that secure the precision of its employment. If, however, such a reconceptualization is undertaken, then media studies itself will be transformed. Under the new theoretical regime, it will amount to much more than a description of the materialities and technologies involved in the reproduction, storage, and transmission of voice, writing, and image. Indeed, a systems-theoretically informed media studies will not establish itself as a "discipline" or "field" at all. One might think of its status as that of a transdisciplinary operator: a methodology for recasting and correlating a range of local inquiries. For the lesson of systems theory is that media are—in multiple and complexly imbricated ways—constitutive features of the operation of psychic and social systems generally. This lesson does not circumscribe a region of epistemological objects so much as it opens an analytical perspective on the entirety of our social and cultural lives and an account of their ongoing evolution.

References and Suggested Readings

Bateson, Gregory. 1972. *Steps to an Ecology of Mind*. New York: Ballantine.

Luhmann, Niklas. 1976. "Generalized Media and the Problem of Contingency." In *Explorations in General Theory in Social Science: Essays in Honor of Talcott Parsons*, ed. Jan J. Loubser, Rainer C. Baum, Andrew Effrat and Victor M. Lidz, 2:507–52. New York: Basic Books.

———. 1982. *The Differentiation of Society*, trans. Stephen Holmes and Charles Larmore. New York: Columbia University Press.

———. 1989. *Ecological Communication*, trans. John Bednarz. Chicago: University of Chicago Press.

———. 1990. *Essays on Self-Reference*. New York: Columbia University Press.

———. 1994. "How Can the Mind Participate in Communication?" In *Materialities of Communication*, ed. Hans Ulrich Gumbrecht and K. Ludwig Pfeiffer, trans. William Whobrey, 370–87. Stanford, CA: Stanford University Press.

———. 1995. *Social Systems*, trans. John Bednarz with Dirk Baecker. Stanford, CA: Stanford University Press.

———. 1997. *Die Gesellschaft der Gesellschaft*. 2 vols. Frankfurt am Main: Suhrkamp.

———. 1998. *Observations on Modernity*, trans. William Whobrey. Stanford, CA: Stanford University Press.

———. 2002. *Theories of Distinction: Redescribing the Descriptions of Modernity*, ed. William Rasch. Stanford, CA: Stanford University Press.

Maturana, Humberto R. 1981. "Autopoiesis." In *Autopoiesis: A Theory of Living Organization*, ed. Milan Zeleny, 21–33. New York: North Holland.

Mead, George Herbert. 2002. "The Present as the Locus of Reality." In *The Philosophy of the Present*, 35–60. Amherst, NY: Prometheus Books.

Spencer Brown, George. 1979. *Laws of Form*. New York: Dutton.

21 :: WRITING

LYDIA H. LIU

A bone, a pebble, and a ramskin . . . Thus an inventory of primordial objects that James Joyce evokes in his novel *Finnegans Wake* to distinguish writing from other media. The setting forth of writing in this manner draws our attention to the stark muteness of three-dimensional tokens or two-dimensional surfaces on which all inscriptions begin and end. This insight is worth pondering insofar as it permits us to reckon with the biomechanics of writing as a technology. But is writing not a system of representation like other visual and verbal codes? Yes, there is no doubt about it, and we will address the symbolic function of writing in due course. As we launch into the subject, it is important to keep it in mind that writing came into existence first and foremost as a technology—an early invention that made first civilizations, empires, long-distance trade and communication, and urbanization possible. From clay tablets to microchips, writing involves at least a twofold process of preparing material surfaces on which signs or codes are to be inscribed and of coordinating the human motor skills (or prosthetic robot arms) required to make the inscription.[1] In the age of informatics and computer technology, writing increasingly penetrates the biomechanics of human speech to the extent that sound, including speech, is now being turned into an artifact, a notable example being text-to-speech (TTS) synthesis.[2] The colossal amount of written and printed record and electronic information stored in data banks, libraries, museums, archival centers, and global communication networks further indicates how much the technologies of writing and print have evolved to shape modern life and the future of humanity, with major implications for our planetary and interplanetary ecology.

Civilization is unthinkable without writing.[3] This common observation entails a critical reevaluation of the concept of civilization itself (and of barbarity) which lies beyond the scope of this essay.[4] Insomuch as the presence or absence of writing is always evoked, explicitly or implicitly, as a positive index in the ranking of human societies and their intellectual attributes, we need to come to a basic understanding of what writing is and what it does and ask why the stakes are generally very high in discourses on this subject.[5] In this essay, we identify and discuss six key registers concerning writing and consider their implications for understanding politics, technology, history, and socioeconomic organization: (1) How much do we know about the origins of writing? Is the question of origin inevitable and important? (2) In what sense is literacy central to political governance and imperial projects, past and present? What kinds of social, territorial, and political control are exercised on a population by the ruling class, the state, or empire through writing? (3) By what script and visual medium is writing to be known or knowable? How do alphabetical and nonalphabetical writing, on the one hand, and mathematical and cryptographic symbols, on the other, compare in the context of a broader semiotic conception of the visual/verbal/spatial production of meaning? (4) How did writing evolve from antiquity to the invention of print and mass media? This bears upon the technological dimensions of writing that open the dialectic of orality and literacy to further inquiry in light of mechanical (re)productions of the audiovisual sensorial continuum. (5) Is writing a visual representation of speech? This familiar issue brings a number of different positions into play, including structural linguistics, metaphysics, and grammatology; our discussion will highlight the relevance of these positions to some of the other registers treated in this essay. (6) Finally, in what ways does digital media transform the idea of alphabetical writing to take us where we are, or into what media theorist Marshall McLuhan termed "a global village"?

The past century has witnessed spectacular archaeological discoveries that make it easier than ever for scholars to map out the writing systems of the world and hypothesize their origins. Whereas the iconographic origin of writing is widely observed across civilizations, scholars disagree as to how one might interpret ancient iconic signs, such as petroglyphs or Amerindian pictographs, as instances of writing. The beginnings of Mesopotamian writing, or proto-cuneiform, are commonly dated to the end of the fourth millennium BCE, the first consonantal alphabet in Phoenicia to 1200 BCE, and the adoption of alphabets in Greece to 750 BCE.[6] Direct archaeological evidence suggests that a well-developed form of Chinese writing already existed in the last quarter of the second millennium BCE.[7] The evidence brought to light thus far has given scholars good reason to believe that the earliest scripts were invented separately in different parts of the world by at least four sedentary civilizations characterized by urbanization, division of labor, and a surplus economy: Mesopotamia, Egypt, China, and Mesoamerica.

I. J. Gelb, who defines writing as "a system of human intercommunication by means of conventional visible marks," sees iconic signs as the precursor to full writing systems and terms such signs "semasiographs."[8] Florian Coulmas believes that a major conceptual shift took place when the visual representation of an object began to be differentiated from a system of writing that transcribed the *name* of the object.[9] (Coulmas's emphasis on "objects" and their nominal properties, however, appears to rule out the consideration of graphic movement or a "syntactic" understanding of graphism.) The widespread use of the rebus principle in early logographic developments would have corresponded to this conceptual shift.[10] In general, scholars who are keen on developing a general concept of writing on the basis of linguistic theory have tended to downplay the importance of iconicity and to treat non–language-related instances of graphism as nonwriting.[11] The majority of them insist that, regardless of scripts, all full writing systems (broadly classified as alphabetic, syllabic, logographic, or phonographic), must meet the criterion of adequate phonetic representation of language.[12] Is this view of writing defensible from the standpoint of media and semiotic considerations? Since our immediate focus here is media and writing rather than phonetic symbolism narrowly conceived, it behooves us to open the issue to broad social vistas beyond the horizons of linguistic representation. The issue of phonocentrism is something we will deal with later, but suffice it to mention that the anxieties surrounding the role of iconicity in writing in the West are not new and have been subjected to critique by many philosophers, historians, and literary theorists, the foremost among whom was the late French philosopher Jacques Derrida.

Our knowledge of the earliest beginnings of writing is necessarily restricted by the precarious state of archaeological evidence and by the condition of a posteriori record keeping that hinges on the existence of writing. Whereas the exact circumstances of how and why writing was invented may never be known, all ancient civilizations appear to have been acutely aware of the earthshaking significance of such inventions. This is amply attested by the universal accounts of the mythical origins of writing. Egyptian documents name Theuth of Hermopolis as the inventor of writing, for which their king Thamus, according to Plato in *Phaedrus*, both applauded and criticized him.[13] In Mesopotamia, the god Nabu was revered by Sumerian scribes as the inventor of writing. Nabu's emblem consists of a table and a stylus in the shape of a single wedge or two wedges, the lower pierced by the upper one. In ancient Chinese legends, Cang Jie's invention of writing is said to have caused Heaven to rain millet and ghosts to wail in the night.[14] In India, where primacy has been attached to transmitting the sacred Vedic texts orally from one generation to another, writing was highly esteemed in its antiquity. Ganesh, the elephant-faced god of wisdom, was credited with the invention of writing and is said to have broken off one of his tusks to use as a pencil.[15]

These legends bear witness to the magical power of writing and the upheavals caused by its introduction into societies previously dominated by oral communication, but they tell us little about how and why writing emerged. Since no direct means exist that will give us firsthand knowledge about prehistoric language and the origin of writing, scholars have speculated on the basis of available evidence or by analogy with so-called primitive or preliterate societies in the present day. Of the multifarious theories they have advanced, André Leroi-Gourhan's paleontology of writing offers some of the most interesting theoretical speculations to date. In his book *Gesture and Speech*, Leroi-Gourhan examines the evidence of excavated fossil anthropoids preceding *Homo sapiens* to gather clues about their tool-making and symbol-making activities. Dating what he calls "the birth of graphism" among the late Palaeoanthropians to roughly 35,000 BCE, he notes neurological linkages between the hand/tools and the face/language, as well as their simultaneous participation in the construction of communication symbols:

> Humans, though they started out with the same formula as primates, can make tools as well as symbols, both of which derive from the same process or, rather, draw upon the same basic equipment in the brain. . . . As soon as there are prehistoric tools, there is a possibility of a prehistoric language, for tools and language are neurologically linked and cannot be dissociated within the social structure of mankind. (1993, 113)

Leroi-Gourhan believes that graphism and language have never been mutually exclusive, just as gesture has always paralleled speech in the development of mind and language. This insight appears to anticipate the notion of arche-writing (*arche-l'ecriture*) that Derrida would develop later, which contests the predominant view that writing is a secondary symbolic system vis-à-vis speech.[16] More importantly, Leroi-Gourhan's emphasis on the mutual embeddedness of human labor and symbol making renders the narrow issue of "the origin of writing" a moot point. The more meaningful question we must pose is, What were the prehistoric conditions of labor, symbol making, and social organization that contributed to the evolution of humans and their civilizations (see chapter 5, "Memory")? To this question no one has a definitive answer, but the angles provided by the question itself may guide us toward a better understanding of observable traces of comparative conditions in ancient civilizations.

The magical power attributed to writing by the mythological accounts we have observed provides some useful hints as to how theocratic and imperial authorities in ancient Egyptian, Sumerian, Chinese, Mesoamerican, and other ancient civilizations might have exerted control or monopoly over the written sign and written document. Just as literacy is about access to power and upward social mobility in modern society, writing in ancient civilizations marked the social division between those who had access to knowledge and power and those who did not. The complexity of social organizations in Egyptian, Babylonian, and Chinese civilizations—often associated with record keeping, accumulated wealth, religious power, commerce, law and treaty making, and so on—conferred special prestige upon writing and, by extension, scribes. Priests, who were often scribes, sometimes held a monopoly of knowledge through which they dominated the organizations of political power. When Hammurabi completed the transition from Sumerian script to Akkadian and made the Semitic language official, he claimed that he had received the laws from the god of justice in order to subordinate the ecclesiastical establishment to civil courts.[17]

Insomuch as writing as social practice cannot be separated from religion, law, politics, and commerce, it is inextricably associated with the emergence of new spatial/temporal configurations and new forms of geopolitical consciousness (see chapter 7, "Time and Space"). If "the city as a form of social organization is unknown among oral cultures," writing is so much more linked with empire making, because spatial expansion and bureaucratic centralization presuppose efficient communication across long distances.[18] Harold A. Innis suggests that the monarchies of Egypt and Persia, the Roman Empire, and the city-states should be understood as products of writing (Innis 1972, 10). In China, writing was the first thing that drew the attention of the first emperor, Qin Shi Huang of the Qin Dynasty (221–206 BCE), upon his successful imperial conquest. The emperor outlawed a multiplicity of scripts that had existed before his rule and imposed a standard script (the square-block characters still in use today), standard orthography (the minor *zhuan*, or seal calligraphy) and standard legal codes and bureaucratic procedures, along with uniform weights and measure, uniform coinage, uniform imperial road widths, and so on, all in the service of centralized rule. Thus began a more than two millennia of imperial historiography in China, an unbroken record unique among world civilizations. This deep historiography would have been unthinkable outside of a textual tradition supported by successive imperial rule and a standard written script.[19]

Weights, measures, and currency presuppose accurate numerical notation and record keeping, which appear to have played a seminal role

The Mayan vigesimal numerical system consists of three symbols: a dot (one), a dash (five), and a shell (zero).

in the development of ancient writing. The striking predominance of numerical notations—using pebbles, tallies, tokens, and clay containers (*bullae*)—in some of the earliest recorded commercial transactions, which date back ten thousand years, has caused some theorists to view mathematics as the earliest precursor to writing.[20] Rather than evolving, as many suppose, from pictograph to syllabic writing and then to phoneticization, writing systems could have emerged from a much more complex set of semiotic situations than the single need to record human speech. This conjecture is tangentially supported by the etymology of the Phoenician word *spr*, to which the English word *scribe* (and its Latin root and Greek equivalent) can be traced. The Phoenician word descended originally from the verb *to count* and did not acquire the meaning *to write* until later.[21] This shared ancestry for "inscription" and "counting" sheds interesting light on the alphabet as an alphanumerical system in addition to being a phonetic tool. In ancient Greek, as in other ancient writing systems, the function of the alphabet was already constrained by the requirement of mathematics, because the twenty-four letters of the alphabet plus three additional alphanumeric signs (digamma, koppa, sampi) notated unspoken mathematical concepts based on the enneads of the Egyptian numerical system. In short, the twenty-seven Greek characters were part of a total semiotic universe of writing and reasoning that encompassed phonetic representation but went well beyond it.[22]

In ordinary parlance, "alphabet" is used interchangeably with "script" on the one hand and "writing system" on the other. It is helpful to maintain careful distinctions among these terms to avoid confusion when we discuss writing. For instance, when the Greeks adapted the conventional Phoenician Semitic consonantal alphabet and Cypriote syllabary to their spoken language, what they imported into Greek was not a writing system but foreign scripts out of which they created a new writing system. By Coulmas's definition, writing systems are language-specific whereas scripts typically are not—there have been far fewer scripts than writing systems in the world. A script may coincide with a single writing system, such as the Korean phonetic script *Han'gul*, which is used for no other language, but the opposite is often true. The *Devanagari* script in India, to take an example, is used for a variety of languages, such as Hindi, Nepali, and Marathi. Alternatively, Hindi and Urdu are virtually the same spoken language, but Hindi is written in *Devanagari* whereas Urdu is written in Perso-Arabic script.[23] The (Chinese) square-block character script has been adopted to create a great variety of writing systems in Asia: Japanese, classical Korean, Vietnamese, among others, including some obsolete ones. The Roman alphabet, in the course of Christian evangelization and modern colonialism, has been adapted to numerous languages in Africa, Asia, and the Americas. For instance, the Wade-Giles system and, more recently, the *Pinyin* alphabet (with twenty-one consonants and fifteen vowels/diphthongs)—used to transcribe the phonemes of written Chinese characters for the purpose of standardized translation, school pedagogy, and, increasingly in our time, access to global "electracy" (literacy in electronic media), which is primarily coded in English—are not themselves writing systems but notational scripts based on the Roman alphabet.

From the viewpoint of biomechanic media, the dissemination of writing has been accompanied by an impressive variety of instruments of inscription, ranging from bones, shells, clay, bronzes, stone, papyrus, parchment, bamboo, silk, wood, brushes, quills, and ink, all the way to the invention of paper, print or typography, and chips for electronic processing. Different mediums have no doubt made their imprints on writing, reading, and bookmaking. Tsuen-Hsuin Tsien suggests that the predominantly downward strokes of written Chinese characters and the vertical, right to left, arrangement of lines have to do with the material and tools of writing before the invention of paper in China in 105 CE. The hand holding the writing brush (by a right-handed scribe) was constrained by the grain of bamboo and wood surfaces and by the narrow strips, which allowed only a single line of characters.[24] Likewise, Egyptian hieroglyphs, when chiseled on stone monuments, were carefully formed and decorative in shape when compared with writing on papyrus, which permitted cursive or hieratic forms to develop and accommodated rapid writing (Innis 1972, 16). Papyrus, parchment, and paper each gave rise to specific forms of manuscript culture that have greatly affected the forms of political organization in history.[25] Commenting on the Roman Empire, Innis suggests that "the written tradition dependent on papyrus and the roll supported an emphasis on centralized bureaucratic administration," whereas parchment as a medium in medieval Europe helped give the church a monopoly of knowledge through monasticism.[26] The ecclesiastical monopoly was greatly weakened by the introduction of paper and printing from China, which led to the rise of vernacular literatures and nationalism in Europe.[27]

The spread of Buddhism in China prompted the invention of woodblock printing early in the eighth century. Large-scale productions of printed books and their dissemination across Asia facilitated widespread socioeconomic transformations that would eventually sweep across the whole world. Movable type was invented in China in 1041–1048 CE.[28] Interestingly, besides the printing of Buddhist scripture, this technology was adopted in the printing of the earliest paper currency, within decades of the invention of paper money in China around this time, which suggests that the standardization and serialization of metal type also served the needs for the organization and control of early modern economy in Asia.[29] Following the introduction of paper manufacture to Europe, block prints also began to appear in European cities in the latter part of the fourteenth century as a result of the westward expansion of the Mongol Empire. The adaptability of the alphabet to movable type and large-scale machine industry translated gradually into the rise of universal literacy, newspapers, vernacular fiction, advertising, and new forms of trade and politics. Observing the tremendous effects of printing on the transformation of psychic and social life in Europe and elsewhere, Marshall McLuhan pointed out in *The Gutenberg Galaxy* that "the invention of typography confirmed and extended the new visual stress of applied knowledge, providing the first uniformly repeatable commodity, the first assembly-line, and the first mass-production."[30] The mechanization of scribal art introduced a new level of "repeatable precision that inspired totally new forms of extending social energies."[31] In English literature, as W. J. T. Mitchell demonstrates in *Picture Theory*, this typographic imagination gave rise to William Blake's innovative poetic idiom and "a visible language of graphic and typographic signifiers" (1994, 129).

Writing and its relation to visuality lie at the heart of a long-standing philosophical discourse on writing, scripts, language, representation, and truth in the West.[32] In *Phaedrus*, Plato's ambivalence about writing shows up in his distrust of visual arts in general and his fear that writing might supplant or destroy memory (which, not surprisingly, anticipated the kinds of anxieties that followed upon the introduction of print in fifteenth-century Europe and the personal computer in our time; the fantasy about downloading the human mind or memory into the computer resonates with that fear).[33] The accidental discovery of Egyptian hieroglyphs in the eighteenth century gave further impetus and a comparative spin to the discourse on visuality and writing as Europeans, in the course of colonial travel and exploration, became increasingly aware of the existence of archaic scripts and nonalphabetical writing.[34] From then on, the history of writing began to assume an evolutionary guise or what Mitchell characterizes as "a story of progress from primitive picture-writing and gestural sign language to hieroglyphics to alphabetic writing 'proper'" (1994, 113). Thus, Jean-Jacques Rousseau hypothesized in *The Origin of Language* that "the depicting of objects is appropriate to a savage people; signs of words and of propositions, to a barbaric people, and the alphabet to civilized people."[35] Dr. Johnson called the Chinese "barbarians" on a sliding scale of evolutionary progress for the reason that "they have not an alphabet."[36] The superiority of the alphabet to pictographic, syllabic, and ideographic scripts is generally attributed to its unique ability to represent speech.[37]

This colonial, evolutionary theory of writing has posed numerous obstacles to a clear understanding of the relationship among visuality, writing, and language. Not only does it misrepresent nonalphabetical writing as a failure in the teleological march toward phoneticization, but it simultaneously obscures the process whereby alphabetic writing has evolved as an alphanumerical technology from antiquity to the rise of informatics. As we know, alphabetic letters are no less visual symbols than nonalphabetic writing but, compared with the latter, are much easier to learn and to reproduce. The linearity, simplicity, and analytical powers of alphabetical writing have facilitated its dissemination around the world, although the same phonetic function is also capable of suppressing the spatial, architectonic, and gestural dimensions of human communication. The modernist poet Ezra Pound saw the limitations and tried to mitigate them by incorporating nonalphabetic characters in his English verse. Depending on how one frames the issue and what social functions one expects writing to fulfill, there are advantages and limitations to both alphabetical and nonalphabetical forms of writing that need not be elaborated here. From the hindsight of informatics, the singular advantage enjoyed by alphabetical writing over nonalphabetic writing is the algorithmic potentials of alphabetic letters with respect to cryptography, machine, and mathematics, which overshadow its much touted power of phoneticization with respect to human communication. If the simplicity of phonetic representation were the telos of human communication, then literature, art, and rhetoric would have been superfluous to the making of civilizations, but the same simplicity greatly aided the invention of Morse code, informatics, and machine language, which we will discuss below.

Due to the ambiguous status of alphabetical letters with regard to phonetics and visuality, informatics and modern linguistics often proceed from very different theoretical assumptions about alphabet writing. Whereas algorithmic thinking revolves around the numerical or ideographic potentials of alphabetical writing, modern linguistic theory has inherited much of the phonocentrism of earlier European evolutionary theories. In the *Course in General Linguistics* (first published by his students in 1916), Ferdinand de Saussure inaugurated structural linguistics, formalizing a systematic approach to the study of language with an emphasis on synchronic structure. The linguistic sign, in his definition, consists of a signifier and a signified. The signifier is a discrete linguistic element, such as the sound unit known as the "phoneme," or a graphic image, but it primarily assumes the material aspect of the sign in the form of a sound image. The signified consists of a conceptual image or idea which is arbitrarily fixed onto the sound image, arbitrarily in the sense that no natural correspondence exists between sound and concept. The relation between signifier and signified and their relation to other signs within the system determine the differential value of each sign. According to Saussure, synchronic analysis can shed important light on the diachronic understanding of language change as well:

> Let there be no mistake about the meaning that we attach to the word 'change'. One might think that it deals especially with phonetic changes undergone by the signifier, or perhaps, changes in meaning which affect the signified concept. That view would be inadequate. Regardless of what the forces of change are, whether in isolation or in combination, they always result in a *shift in the relationship between the signified and the signifier*.[38]

This insight enabled Saussure to analyze linguistic meaning as a differential function of the signifier and the signified rather than as a result of natural correspondence between symbol and idea. This powerful explanatory model enabled the French anthropologist Claude Lévi-Strauss to launch structural anthropology, which would transform the discipline of anthropology in the West for several decades. In structural anthropology as in linguistics, speech is primary, suggesting immediacy, presence, identity, and authenticity, whereas writing, a secondary system of representation, figures deferment, absence, difference, and inauthenticity (even though Saussure was not unaware of instances of writing such as the rebus, the anagram, and the written letter). Derrida dubs the structuralist's preoccupation with phonetic inscription "logocentric" and discerns in its operation a supplementary logic that simultaneously excludes writing from the linguistic system and relies on alphabetical writing to enable phonemic analyses.[39]

But writing persists in spite of the linguistic sign. Jacques Lacan troubles the Saussurian sign by performing a psychoanalytical reading of the signifier in his famous seminar on Edgar Allen Poe's detective story "The Purloined Letter." He demonstrates that the stolen letter in the story signifies and circulates among the various agents without the help of any particular signified. As a pure signifier, the letter's movement, displacement, and retrieval alone can support the full weight of a fictional drama about royal intrigues and detective interventions.[40] Poe, of course, had been fascinated by cryptographic code and other pure signifiers in his time. The central enigma of another of his celebrated stories, "The Gold-Bug," for example, presents itself as a textual problem: How to crack an unknown code to find the hidden treasure? Curiously, the code—handwritten on a piece of parchment—consists of not only familiar numerals, letters, and punctuation marks but typographical symbols (*, ¶, ‡, †, etc.) that would have been rare or nonexistent in manuscript (parchment) culture but are abundant in typography—which was the medium of Poe's story. Friedrich Kittler's contention that Lacan's theoretical apparatus was indebted to the evolution of modern media technologies might easily be extended to explain Poe, whose passion for typography and cryptoanalysis anticipated the arrival of information theory in our own time. For Lacan, the symbolic enjoys the status of typography, whereas the real and the imaginary correspond, respectively, to phonography and film (Kittler 1999, 18). In the other words, the typewriter, gramophone, and film provide the conceptual and technological framework within which Lacanian psychoanalysis begins to make sense. Kittler reminds us further that Nietzsche "changed from arguments to aphorisms, from thoughts to puns, from rhetoric to telegram style" when he became the first philosopher to use a typewriter (1999, 203).

Through print and electronic media, alphabetic writing has come to dominate the world of communication. McLuhan was quick to grasp the implications of this development and termed the phonetic alphabet a "cool and uniform visual medium" for good reason.[41] Intuitive reflections on the function of the phonetic alphabet seem to support the impression that letters stand for the sounds of speech. But what sounds? C. K. Ogden, the architect of BASIC English along with the literary critic I. A. Richards, once complained about the irregularities of phonetic representation in English, stating that "the vowels represent not 7 sounds but 54, the 26 letters of the alphabet giving a total of 107 values, or with the vowel digraphs ('each', 'ou', etc.) and multigraphs ('eau', etc.) 280." Compounding the burden of 280 sound values and their various combinatorial units are the statistical hurdles at the level of English vocabulary. "To distinguish all these in a vocabulary of 20,000 words, or even 2,000," says Ogden, "necessitates an amount of drudgery which has given phoneticians and advocates of synthetic languages their opportunity."[42]

Leaving aside the contested theory of which discrete units of speech or phonemes can phonetically be represented by which letters (as in the case of /ks/, written as one letter, x, in English), there is also the cognitive question of how the written code relates *meaningfully* to the linguistic image in the mind. In a cybernetic leap of faith, Norbert Wiener and his colleagues experimented with the idea of bypassing both hearing and vision so that deaf-mutes could arrive at instant comprehension of verbal signs through touch rather than gesture. Their experiment brings to mind Rousseau's description in *The Origin of Language* of how traders in India conducted business by taking each other by the hand, varying their grip in such a way as to perform secret transactions in public, unobserved by others and without uttering a single word.[43] That is to say, sight, hearing, and speech need not to be present for communication to take place. Wiener's experiment rested on a similar premise about communication, except that it also involved a translation of acoustic signals in the form of physical vibrations in the air, which, fed through a tactile device, would correspond to an experience of meaning in the receiver's mind.[44] Even so, Wiener's sensory prosthesis begs the question of how the tactile code relates to the conceptual processes in the mind.

Cryptography and information theory tried to get around the cognitive issue by working exclusively with alphanumerical symbols in a mathematical remapping of communication. Alan Turing and Claude Shannon uniformly took the printed letters of the English alphabet as their point of departure. Shannon, the inventor of information theory, approached English as a statistical system, which he termed "Printed English," and subjected alphabetic writing to algorithmic thinking and engineering on behalf of informatics. This peculiar English is composed of the twenty-six-letter alphabet (A to Z) plus a twenty-seventh letter that mathematically codes "space." In other words, Printed English is an ideographical alphabet with a definable statistical structure. As a postphonetic system, it functions as a conceptual interface between natural language and machine language. This postphonetic construct is predicated on the symbolic correspondences between the twenty-seven letters and their numeral counterparts in lieu of mapping the letters onto the phonemic units in the spoken language. The alphanumerical correspondence not only facilitates the encoding of messages in information systems but also enables a rethinking of the idea of communication. The centrality of printed symbol for technology has something to do with the fact that, to use Friedrich A. Kittler's words, "in contrast to the flow of handwriting, we now have discrete elements separated by spaces" (1999, 16). The "space" symbol in Printed English is a conceptual figure, not a visible word divider as is commonly observed in some writing systems. The sign may show up as a negative value or as the visible absence of letters, but the twenty-seventh letter is just as likely to be mathematically represented by "o" as by one or two types of electric pulse on a transmission system. This letter owes its existence to the statistical, rather than visual or phonemic, parameters of symbols. It has no linguistic meaning insofar as conventional semantics is concerned but it is fully functional as a meaningful ideographical notion.

Nietzsche made a prescient remark in 1878: "The press, the machine, the railway, the telegraph are premises whose thousand-year conclusion no one has yet dared to draw."[45] As one of the most significant inventions since World War II, Printed English is a direct offspring of telegraphy because it is based on a close analysis of Morse code conducted by Shannon himself. In his pathbreaking essay "A Mathematical Theory of Communication" published in the *Bell System Technical Journal* 1948, Shannon laid the statistical foundation of information theory. Two years later, he published another article called "Prediction and Entropy of Printed English," which further elaborated the experimental work in connection with his earlier work. These studies suggest numerous connections with Shannon's code work in World War II, when he had investigated the statistical aspects of alphabetic writing in cryptoanalysis and helped design secrecy systems at Bell Laboratories for the U.S. military. As a discrete, ideographic symbol, Shannon's twenty-seventh letter is meaningful precisely in this cryptographic sense. As if mirroring cryptography, Printed English has a corresponding, translated text in numerical symbols. The original text "with an alphabet of 27 symbols, A, B, . . . Z, space, has been translated into a new language with the alphabet 1, 2, . . . 27."[46] This conception lays the theoretical foundation for what would become digital technology in computer science. Through a built-in mechanism of alphanumerical translation, Printed English achieves its ultimate ideographic embodiment in the mathematical figuring of o/1 binary oppositions.[47]

In our time, the alphabet seems more thoroughly and universally digital than it has been. Be it word processing, digital imaging, genetic engineering, interactive games, or simulated and actual warfare, we are living in the midst of a digital revolution that is dissolving older conceptual boundaries and introducing new ones. Digital media transform contemporary civilization by turning one of the oldest technologies—alphabetic writing—into a universal coding system to unlock the mind and the secret of life itself (see chapter 8, "Biomedia"). It seems that the spatial/temporal coordinates of our future cognitive world will evolve into ever intensified interdependence of human and machine or similar kinds of prosthetic conditions enabled by digital media. But as Mitchell's discussion of image and media in chapter 3 suggests, "digital imaging may be uncovering yet another layer of the perceptible cognitive world that we will recognize as having always been there." Indeed, the numerical function of the alphabet has been there since antiquity, and yet we are so used to thinking of alphabetic writing as a phonetic system of transcription that Shannon's treatment of the English alphabet as a total ideographic (algorithmic) system may still come as a shock. At the same time, digital technology is converting nonalphabetic writing systems such as Chinese into a kind of subcode of global English. Once again, a tower of Babel is being erected on the promised land of universal communicability, machine translation (MT), or machine-aided translation (MAT), a dream that is forever haunted by the memories of a not so distant oracle.

Notes

1. The six-dot matrix within which characters are differentiated in Braille is a formal mechanism that relies on spatial rather than visual arrangement. For a discussion of writing as the organization of graphic space, see Harris, *Signs of Writing* (1995, 45).

2. TTS, a branch of artificial intelligence, is one of the areas where the relationship between writing and speech can be fruitfully investigated for both engineering and theoretical purposes. See Richard Sproat, *A Computational Theory of Writing Systems* (Cambridge: Cambridge University Press, 2000).

3. The shared Chinese and Japanese *kanji* word *wenming* ("civilization"; literally, "illumination through text"), with its positive emphasis on *wen* or "text/textuality," brings out the etymology of writing more forcefully than the Latin equivalent. *civilis*.

4. For helpful reference on the subject, see Jack Goody, *The Domestication of the Savage Mind* (Cambridge: Cambridge University Press, 1977).

5. For example, Jacques Derrida discerns an inherent ethnocentrism in anthropological discourse on writing in his reading of "A Writing Lesson" by Lévi-Strauss in which the latter describes his fieldwork among the "innocent" Nambikwara tribe. See "The Violence of the Letter: From Lévi-Strauss to Rousseau" in Derrida, *Of Grammatology*, trans. Gayatri Chakravorty Spivak (Baltimore: The Johns Hopkins University Press, 1971), pp.101–40.

6. The Phoenicians are often credited as the inventors of the alphabet. M. O'Connor argues, however, that "the Phoenicians did not 'invent' the alphabet. A variety of scripts (and peoples) were involved in the diffusion of the alphabet around the region, even if the Phoenicians played a major role in the process." See Peter T. Daniels and William Bright, eds., *The World's Writing Systems* (Oxford: Oxford University Press, 1996), 96.

7. A vocabulary of more than four thousand written characters and/or words has been brought to light by archaeologists. These were inscribed on the oracle bones used by the royal houses for divination and are regarded as the royal archives of the period. Only about half of the characters have been successfully decoded thus far. From the evidence of these oracle bone inscriptions, it is clear that the earliest beginnings of Chinese writing go much further back, but there is considerable controversy over the dates due to the lack of direct archaeological evidence. Much of this controversy also hinges on how one views writing. Recently, the journal *Antiquity* published a field report by archaeologist Li Xueqin and his Chinese and American collaborators, who speculate tentatively that the antiquity of Chinese writing might be dated to the seventh millennium BCE. Li Xueqin et al. "The Earliest Writing? Sign Use in the Seventh Millennium BC at Jiahu, Henan Province, China," *Antiquity*

77, no, 295 (2003): 31–44. For representative works on this subject, see David N. Keightley, "The Origin of Writing in China: Scripts and Cultural Contexts," in *The Origins of Writing*, ed. Wayne M. Senner (Lincoln: University of Nebraska Press, 1989), 170–202.

8. I. J. Gelb, *A Study of Writing* (Chicago: University of Chicago Press, 1963). Gelb provides some of the most influential taxonomies for twentieth-century theories of writing and coined the term *grammatology*, which Derrida later adopted in his philosophical work. See also Coulmas, *The Writing Systems of the World* (Oxford: Basil Blackwell, 1989), 1.

9. See Coulmas, *Writing Systems: An Introduction to Their Linguistic Analysis* (Cambridge: Cambridge University Press, 2003), 192–96.

10. The term *logograph*, which was Gelb's coinage, means word writing. It is widely adopted to distinguish a written sign that transcribes a word unit rather than a sound unit in speech. The rebus principle involves a process of phonetic abstraction whereby the graph of one word is borrowed to transcribe another word on the basis of homophony although the two words are semantically unrelated. A modern example in English is "U2" used as shorthand for "you, too" or "you two."

11. For a systematic critique of the mutual exclusion of picture and word in the West, see Mitchell, (1994), esp. chaps. 1–3.

12. John DeFrancis has been one of the most vocal defenders of this view. See his book *Visible Speech: The Diverse Oneness of Writing Systems* (Honolulu: University of Hawaii Press, 1989), especially the chapter "A Critique of Writing about Writing," 211–47.

13. It bears pointing out that in Plato's account, Socrates also attributed the invention "of number, arithmetic, geometry, and astronomy, of games involving draughts and dice" to the deity Theuth. See Plato, *Phaedrus*, trans. Robin Waterfield (Oxford: Oxford University Press, 2002), 68–69.

14. For analysis of early Chinese legends about the origin of writing, see William G. Boltz, *The Origin and Early Development of the Chinese Writing System* (New Haven: American Oriental Society, 1994), 129–38.

15. Coulmas, *Writing Systems of the World*, 5.

16. In a footnote to the preface to *Of Grammatology*, Derrida states that the first part of his book, "Writing before the Letter," was originally written in 1965 as an essay in response to the publication of three important works, one of which was Leroi-Gourhan's *Le geste et la parole* (1965).

17. See Innis (1972, 31–32). For the impact of writing on the concept of "law" and "justice," see Jon Stratton, "Writing and the Concept of Law in Ancient Greece," *Visible Language* 14, no. 2 (1980): 99–121.

18. Coulmas, *Writing Systems of the World*, 7.

19. For a detailed study of the role of writing in early imperial China, see Mark Edward Lewis, *Writing and Authority in China* (Albany: State University of New York Press, 1999).

20. J. D. Bernal, *Science in History*, 4 vols. (London: C. A. Watts, 1971), 119. See also D. Schmandt-Besserat, "The Earliest Precursors of Writing," *Scientific American*, 238 (1978): 50–59.

21. See C. Bonnet, "Les scribes phoenico-puniques," in *Phoinikeia Grammata*, ed. Cl. Baurain, C. Bonnet, and V. Krings (Namur: Société des Etudes Classiques, 1991), 150.

22. See Dimitris K. Psychoyos, "The Forgotten Art of Isopsephy and the Magic Number KZ," *Semiotica* 154, no. 1 (April 2005): 209.

23. Daniels and Bright, *World's Writing Systems*, 384–90.

24. Chinese recorded history indicates that Cai Lun (Ts'ai Lun), an official of the imperial court, first reported the invention of paper to the emperor in the year 105 CE, but recent archaeological findings place the actual invention of papermaking a couple of hundred years earlier. Tsuen-Hsuin Tsien, *Written on Bamboo and Silk: The Beginnings of Chinese Books and Inscriptions* (Chicago: University of Chicago Press, 2004), 204.

25. Parchment is made from the treated hides of calves or sheep; papyrus is a natural product, sliced from the stem of the papyrus plant; and paper is manufactured by chemical process from rags or plant fibers. For a detailed account of the invention of paper in China, see Tsien, "Paper and Paper Manuscripts," in *Written on Bamboo and Silk*, 145–74.

26. See Innis (1972, 107, 135).

27. Innis mentions that "Greeks began to use paper in manuscripts in the twelfth century and Italians in the thirteenth century, but it was sparingly used, in spite of the very high cost of parchment notably in the thirteenth century, until the fifteenth century" (1972, 138–39).

28. Bi Sheng (or Pi Sheng, ca. 990–1051) employed clay types when he first invented movable type. Historical documents suggest that wooden and metal types began to appear in China as early as the thirteenth century, although surviving prints from prior to the fourteenth century are rare. By the fifteenth century bronze movable type had been widely adopted in China and Korea, but for aesthetic, technical, and socioeconomic reasons, movable type could not compete with the popularity of block prints in China until the end of the nineteenth century. For an account of the rise of early woodblock printing to the spread of printing from movable type as well as Gutenberg's exposure to this technology before 1456, see Joseph Needham's series Science and Civilization in China, specifically vol. 5, pt. 1, *Paper and Printing* by Tsien Tsuen-Hsuin (Cambridge: Cambridge University Press, 1985), 201–22, 313–19.

29. For up-to-date and detailed research, consult Pan Jixing's book in Chinese, *Zhongguo jinshu huozi yinshua jishu shi* [A history of metal movable type and printing technology in China] (Shenyang: Liaoning kexue jishu chubanshe, 2001).

30. Marshall McLuhan, *The Gutenberg Galaxy: The Making of Typographic Man* (Toronto: University of Toronto Press, 1965), 124.

31. Marshall McLuhan, *Understanding Media: The Extensions of Man* (Cambridge, MA: MIT Press, 1994), 172.

32. Derrida's method of deconstruction in *Of Grammatology* has centered on this problem.

33. For Derrida's insightful reading of this foundational text, see "Plato's Pharmacy," in *Dissemination*, trans. Barbara Johnson (Chicago: University of Chicago Press, 1981), 61–155.

34. Walter Ong, *Orality and Literacy: The Technologizing of the Word* (New York: Routledge, 1982), 80.

35. Jean-Jacques Rousseau, *On the Origin of Language*, trans. John H. Moran and Alexander Gode (Chicago: University of Chicago Press, 1966), 17. Ironically, the decoding of the Rosetta Stone (1799) twenty years after Rousseau's death relied on the phonetic principle (the rebus) for its success, after pictographic interpretation had come to a dead end.

36. James Boswell, *Life of Johnson*, 6 vols., ed. G. B. Hill and L. F. Powell (Oxford: Oxford University Press, 1934), 3:339, as quoted in David Porter, *Ideographia* (Stanford, CA: Stanford University Press, 2001), 76.

37. This view is also shared by McLuhan in *Understanding Media*, 83–84.

38. See Ferdinand de Saussure, *Course in General Linguistics*, trans. Wade Baskin (New York: McGraw-Hill Book Company, 1966), 74–75.

39. For Derrida's critique, see "Linguistics and Grammatology" in Derrida (1971, 27–73). By no accident did Roman Jakobson and Claude Lévi-Strauss follow the same logic in their subsequent development of structural poetics and structural anthropology. They privileged speech and linguistic systems and treated their object of analysis, whether poetry or society, as a closed system of relations governed by rules. For Derrida's reading of Lévi-Strauss and Rousseau, see "Nature, Culture, Writing" (ibid., 95–140).

40. Jacques Lacan, "The Purloined Letter," in *The Seminar of Jacques Lacan*, book 2, *The Ego in Freud's Theory and in the Technique of Psychoanalysis, 1954–1955*, ed. Jacques-Alain Miller, trans. Sylvana Tomaselli (New York: W. W. Norton, 1991), 191–205.

41. McLuhan, *Understanding Media*, 84.

42. C. K. Ogden, *Basic English: A General Introduction with Rules and Grammar* (London: Kegan Paul, Trench, Trubner & Co., 1935), 21. BASIC (the acronym stands for British, American, Scientific, International, and Commercial) consists of a vocabulary of 850 common English words.

43. Rousseau, *On the Origin of Language*, 9–10.

44. Norbert Wiener, *The Human Use of Human Beings* (New York: Da Capo Press, 1950), 168–70.

45. Friedrich Nietzsche, *Human, All Too Human: A Book for Free Spirits*, trans. R. J. Holingdale (Cambridge: Cambridge University Press, 1986), 378.

46. Claude Shannon, "Prediction and Entropy of Printed English," *Bell System Technical Journal*, January 1951, 56.

47. For a detailed account of Shannon's work, see my article "iSpace: The Theory Machine after Joyce, Shannon, and Derrida," *Critical Inquiry* 32 (spring 2006): 516–50.

References and Suggested Readings

Bernal, Martin. 1990. *Cadmean Letters: The Transmission of the Alphabet to the Aegean and Further West before 1400 B.C.* Winona Lake: Eisenbrauns.

Coulmas, Florian. 2003. *Writing Systems: An Introduction to Their Linguistic Analysis*. Cambridge: Cambridge University Press.

Derrida, Jacques. 1971. *Of Grammatology*, trans. Gayatri Chakravorty Spivak. Baltimore: Johns Hopkins University Press.

Donald, Merlin. 1993. *Origins of the Modern Mind: Three Stages in the Evolution of Culture and Cognition*. Cambridge, MA: Harvard University Press.

Harris, Roy. 1995. *Signs of Writing*. London: Routledge.

Innis, Harold A. 2007. *Empire and Communications*. Boulder: Rowman & Littlefield.

Kittler, Friedrich. 1999. *Gramophone, Film, Typewriter*, trans. Geoffrey Winthrop-Young and Michael Wutz. Stanford, CA: Stanford University Press.

Leroi-Gourhan, André. 1993. *Gesture and Speech*, trans. Anna Bostock Berger. Cambridge, MA: MIT Press.

Mitchell, W. J. T. 1994. *Picture Theory*. Chicago: University of Chicago Press.

Schmandt-Besserat, Denise. 1997. *How Writing Came About*. Austin: University of Texas Press.

Contributors

BILL BROWN, the Edward Carson Waller Professor at the University of Chicago and a fellow of the Chicago Center for Contemporary Theory, teaches in the departments of English and Visual Arts and serves as a coeditor of *Critical Inquiry*. Along with essays on material culture and the role of inanimate objects in everyday life, he has published *The Material Unconscious* (1996) and *A Sense of Things: The Object Matter of American Literature* (2003). He edited "Things," a special issue of *Critical Inquiry* (Fall 2001), since expanded and published as a book. He is currently at work on *Objects, Others, and Us*.

BRUCE CLARKE is professor of literature and science at Texas Tech University. His *Posthuman Metamorphosis: Narrative and Systems* (2008) reads the contingencies of systems in modern and contemporary literary and cinematic narratives of corporeal transformation. Other publications include *Allegories of Writing: The Subject of Metamorphosis* (1995); *Dora Marsden and Early Modernism: Gender, Individualism, Science* (1996); *Energy Forms: Allegory and Science in the Era of Classical Thermodynamics* (2001); *From Energy to Information: Representation in Science and Technology, Art, and Literature*, coedited with Linda Dalrymple Henderson (2002); and *Emergence and Embodiment: New Essays in Second-Order Systems Theory*, coedited with Mark Hansen (2009). With Manuela Rossini, he is preparing the *Routledge Companion to Literature and Science*.

JOHANNA DRUCKER is the inaugural Bernard and Martin Breslauer Professor of Bibliography in the Department of Information Studies at UCLA. She has published extensively on the history of written forms, typography, design, and visual poetics within the twentieth-century avant-garde. In addition to her scholarly work, Drucker is internationally known as a book artist and experimental visual poet. Recent titles include *Sweet Dreams: Contemporary Art and Complicity* (2005); *Graphic Design History: A Critical Guide*, with Emily McVarish (2008); *Testament of Women* (2006); *Combo Meals* (2008); and *SpecLab: Digital Aesthetics and Speculative Computing* (2009).

ALEXANDER R. GALLOWAY is an author and programmer. He is a founding member of the software collective RSG and creator of the Carnivore and Kriegspiel projects. *The New York Times* recently described his work as "conceptually sharp, visually compelling and completely attuned to the political moment." Galloway is the author of *Protocol: How Control Exists after Decentralization* (2004), *Gaming: Essays on Algorithmic Culture* (2006), and, with Eugene Thacker, *The Exploit: A Theory of Networks* (2007). He teaches at New York University.

PETER GOODRICH is professor of law and director of the Program in Law and Humanities at Cardozo School of Law, Yeshiva University, New York. He is author most recently of *The Laws of Love: A Brief Practical and Historical Manual* (2008), and editor of *Law, Text, Terror: Essays for Pierre Legendre* (2008) and *Derrida and Legal Philosophy* (2008). His current work addresses the visual culture of law and the changing media of its transmission and interpretation.

DAVID GRAEBER, an anthropologist, is the author of *Lost People: Magic and the Legacy of Slavery in Madagascar* (2007), *Toward an Anthropological Theory of Value* (2001), *Fragments of an Anarchist Anthropology* (2004), *Possibilities: Essays on Hierarchy, Rebellion, and Desire* (2007), and *Direct Action: An Ethnography* (2008). He is current a reader in social anthropology at Goldsmiths, University of London, where he is working on a history of debt.

MARK B. N. HANSEN is professor in the Program in Literature, the Visual Studies Initiative, and Information Science and Information Studies (ISIS) at Duke University. His books include *Emergence and Embodiment: New Essays in Second Order Cybernetics*, coedited with Bruce Clarke (2009); *Bodies in Code: Interfaces with New Media* (2006); *The Cambridge Companion to Merleau-Ponty*, coedited with Taylor Carman (2005); *New Philosophy for New Media* (2004); and *Embodying Technesis: Technology Beyond Writing* (2000). His recent work has focused on the experiential significance of the computational revolution and how computation has transformed the architecture of knowledge in academe and in culture more broadly. His current book project explores the correlation of media and temporalization in digital networks.

N. KATHERINE HAYLES, professor in the Program in Literature, the Visual Studies Initiative, and Information Science and Information Studies (ISIS) at Duke University, teaches and writes on the relations of science, technology, and literature in the twentieth and twenty-first centuries. Her books include *How We Became Posthuman: Virtual Bodies in Cybernetics, Literature, and Informatics* (1999), which won the Rene Wellek Prize for Best Book in Literary Theory; *Writing Machines* (2002), which won the Suzanne Langer Award for Outstanding Scholarship; *My Mother Was a Computer: Digital Subjects and Literary Texts* (2005); and *Electronic Literature: New Horizons for the Literary* (2008). She is currently at work on a book entitled *How We Think: The Transforming Power of Digital Technologies*.

JOHN JOHNSTON is professor of English and comparative literature at Emory University. His publications include *The Allure of Machinic Life* (2008), *Information Multiplicity: American Fiction in the Age of Media Saturation* (1998), and *Carnival of Repetition: William Gaddis' "The Recognitions" and Postmodern Theory* (1990). He was the editor and translator of *Literature, Media, Information System: Essays by Friedrich A. Kittler* for the series Critical Voices in Theory and Culture (1997).

CAROLINE JONES studies modern and contemporary art, with a focus on its technological modes of production, distribution, and reception. Professor of art history and director of the History, Theory, Criticism Program in the Department of Architecture at MIT, she has also worked as an essayist, filmmaker, and curatorial consultant, most recently with MIT's List Visual Art Center, which published her *Sounding the Subject/Video*

Trajectories (2007). Other publications include *Sensorium* (editor, 2006); *Eyesight Alone* (2005); *Machine in the Studio* (1996); and *Picturing Science, Producing Art*, coedited with Peter Galison (1998). A frequent contributor to *Artforum*, Jones's current research on globalization informs her next book *Desires for the World Picture: The Global Work of Art*.

LYDIA H. LIU is the W. T. Tam Professor in the Humanities and professor of Chinese and comparative literature at Columbia University. Her work explores translation theory, the movement of words, images, and artifacts across civilizations, and the evolution of writing, textuality, and media technology, with a current research focus on writing, psychoanalysis, and digital media. She has published numerous books and articles in English and Chinese, including *Translingual Practice* (1995), *The Clash of Empires* (2004), and an edited volume titled *Tokens of Exchange: The Problem of Translation in Global Circulations* (1999).

W. J. T. MITCHELL is the Gaylord Donnelly Distinguished Service Professor in the Department of English Language and Literature and in the Department Art History at the University of Chicago. He is editor of the interdisciplinary journal *Critical Inquiry*, a quarterly devoted to critical theory in the arts and human sciences. A scholar and theorist of media, visual art, and literature, he is associated with the emergent fields of visual culture and iconology. His publications include: *What Do Pictures Want? The Lives and Loves of Images* (2005), *The Last Dinosaur Book: The Life and Times of a Cultural Icon* (1998), *Picture Theory* (1994), *Art and the Public Sphere* (1993), *Landscape and Power* (1992), *Iconology* (1987), *The Language of Images* (1980), *On Narrative* (1981), and *The Politics of Interpretation* (1984).

JOHN DURHAM PETERS is the F. Wendell Miller Distinguished Professor of Communication Studies and International Studies at the University of Iowa. He is the author of *Speaking into the Air: A History of the Idea of Communication* (1999) and *Courting the Abyss: Free Speech and the Liberal Tradition* (2005), as well as diverse essays on the philosophy of communication and cultural history of media.

BERNARD STIEGLER, director for cultural development at the Institute of Research and Innovation at the Pompidou Center in Paris, is a philosopher, associate professor at the Compiègne University, and professor at Goldsmiths College in London. He has served as codirector of the Institut National de l'Audiovisuel (INA) and director general at the Institut de Recherche et Coordination Acoustique/Musique and is president of the political group Ars Industrialis, which he cofounded in 2005. Of his more than twenty books, *Technics and Time*, volumes 1 and 2, and *Acting Out* are available in English, with *For a New Critique of Political Economy* (forthcoming). His work, inspired by phenomenology, Derrida, Simondon, Deleuze, and Foucault, considers the disruption of philosophical and political questions by contemporary technology and attempts to set forth an organology and pharmacology of the contemporary world.

EUGENE THACKER is the author of *Biomedia* (2004); *The Global Genome: Biotechnology, Politics, and Culture* (2005); *The Exploit: A Theory of Networks*, with Alexander Galloway (2007); and the forthcoming *After Life*. He has also previously collaborated with RSG (Radical Software Group), Biotech Hobbyist, and Fakeshop. Thacker is associate professor in the School of Literature, Communication & Culture at the Georgia Institute of Technology.

BERNADETTE WEGENSTEIN, an Austrian linguist and filmmaker, is associate research professor in the Department of German and Romance Languages and Literatures at the Johns Hopkins University, where she teaches media and film theory. She is the author of *Getting under the Skin: Body and Media Theory* (2006), *The Cosmetic Gaze: Body Modification and the Construction of Beauty* (forthcoming), and numerous articles on body criticism, performance art, and film theory, and editor of "Reality Made Over: The Culture of Reality Television Makeover Shows," a special double issue of *Configurations* (2008). In 2006 she formed her own production company, Waystone Productions LLC. Her first documentary is *Made Over in America* (2007).

DAVID WELLBERY is the LeRoy T. and Margaret Deffenbaugh Carlson University Professor at the University of Chicago, where he teaches in the departments of Germanic Studies and Comparative Literature, the Committee on Social Thought, and the College. He is also director of the Center for Interdisciplinary Research on German Literature and Culture. His book publications include *Lessing's Laocöon. Aesthetics and Semiotics in the Age of Reason* (1984) and *The Specular Moment: Goethe's Early Lyric and the Beginnings of Romanticism* (1996). He is editor in chief of *A New History of German Literature* (2004).

GEOFFREY WINTHROP-YOUNG is associate professor of German at the University of British Columbia. His research interests include media theory, posthumanism, and science fiction. His books and edited projects include *Friedrich Kittler zur Einführung* (Hamburg: Junius, 2005), and he is currently working on an examination of posthumanist thought titled *Media, Systems, Spheres: Probing German Posthumanism*.

CARY WOLFE, the Bruce and Elizabeth Dunlevie Professor of English at Rice University, is the founding editor of the University of Minnesota Press series Posthumanities. His books and edited collections include *Critical Environments: Postmodern Theory and the Pragmatics of the "Outside"* (1998); *Observing Complexity: Systems Theory and Postmodernity*, with William Rasch (2000); *Animal Rites: American Culture, the Discourse of Species, and Posthumanist Theory* (2003); *Zoontologies: The Question of the Animal* (2003); and *What Is Posthumanism?* (2009).

Index

architecture, media, 30–31

Aristotle: on *aesthesis*, 91; Alberti draws on, 4; on biology, 121; defining space and time objectively, 106, 111; on dramatic performance, 40; as media theorist, ix; on mimesis, xix; temporal privileged in art by, 104; treatise on time, 111

Arnold, Matthew, 8

ARPAnet, 285, 288, 289

Arquilla, John, 288

art, 3–18; abstract, 10, 12, 105; artist seen as gifted individual, 4–5; avant-garde, 10, 96; Benjamin on reproducibility of, 11, 37, 54, 70, 187; body, 20; as changing field of vision, 54–55; conceptual gamesmanship in, 11–12; as conventional, 12; defamiliarization seen as effect, 10; as democratic medium, 9; experimentation with new media in, 46; as exploitation of the medium, 3; as giving formal expression to imaginative thought, 4; "high" versus "low," 13; as holistic, integrated alternative to industrialism, 8; versus ideology, 12; images raised to status of, 38; Industrial Revolution as foundational moment for modern, 3; installation, 15, 97; as instrument of cultural change, 8; language in, 241–48; materiality as increasing emphasis in, 9–10; Minimalist, 14, 40; modern, 11–15; the noise is the art, 164, 170; performance, 13, 15, 96; printing challenges identity of, 5, 7; and reformation of the senses, 97–98; Romantic contrast between mechanistic labor and artistic innovation, 6–7; for sale, 4; as secular religion, 7; senses and genres of, 93–94; sound, 98; spatial, 101, 102–5; symbolically generalized media in, 308; technology abused and manipulated in, xviii–xix; temporal, 101, 102–5; "underground," 96; as way of paying attention, 18. *See also* fine art

Art (Bell), 10

art-for-art's-sake, 9

artificial intelligence, 27, 44, 199, 202–3

artificial life, 27, 203

Arts and Crafts movement, 8

Ashby, Ross, 146

Athens, assembly of, 276

audience: growth in size of, 273; loose coupling of sending and receiving, 275–77; styles of addressing, 267–71; waning of mass, 273–74

audio beep, 258

Auroux, Sylvain, 66

Austin, J. L., 140

automata, 200–201, 203, 212n5

automatism, 183

autoperception, 25–26

autopoiesis: in art, 242; in consciousness and communication, 303; information and meaning reconnected with, 147–48; operational circularity of, 141; in social and psychic systems, 238, 300, 306; virtuality and, 149

avant-garde, 10, 96

"Avant Garde and Kitsch" (Greenberg), 12

Babbit, Irving, 93

Balderston, John, 60n2

Baldessari, John, 242

Balzac, Honoré de, 8

Baran, Paul, 288, 289–90

Barbrook, Richard, 286

Barlow, John Perry, 286

barter, 219–23; as emerging in cases of currency breakdown, 225; seen as economically fundamental, 218

Barthes, Roland, xix

Bateson, Gregory, 157, 165, 235–36, 237, 240, 305

Baudrillard, Jean, 28, 50, 110

Baumgarten, Alexander Gottlieb, 91

BBC, 275, 276

Beadle, George and Muriel, 121

Beatles, 164

Beck, Jeff, 169

Beck, Julian, 96

Beecroft, Vanessa, 15

"Behavior, Purpose and Teleology" (Rosenblueth, Wiener, and Bigelow), 145

Bell, Clive, 10

benday dots, 45

Benjamin, Walter: on fragmentation of experience, 28; materialist phenomenology of, 59; as media theorist, ix, xvii; on optical unconscious, 46; on reproducibility of work of art, 11, 37, 54, 70, 187, 188; Simmel heard by, 52; on space and time transformed photography and phonography, 104; "The Work of Art in the Age of Mechanical Reproducibility," 11, 187

Benkler, Yochai, 286

Bergson, Henri: on body in organization of images, 25–26; embodied phenomenology of, 59; on internal time consciousness, 106–7, 108, 109, 110; *Matter and Memory*, 25; *Time and Free Will*, 107

Berkeley, George, 91

Berliner Phonogramm-Archiv, 184

Bernard, Claude, 73

Berners-Lee, Tim, 286

Bertalanffy, Ludwig von, 284, 285–86

Bey, Hakim, 294

bibliographies, 76

bidirectionality, 291

Bigelow, Julian, 145

bills of exchange, 228

biocomputing, 58

biocybernetics, 37

biofeedback, 29

bioinformatics, 58, 118

biology: boundary between technology and, 58; evolution applied to technical systems, 209–12; genetic code, 119–21, 123–28, 244; as information, 118–23, 125, 126–27; molecular, 119–21. *See also* biomedia; biotechnology

biomedia, 117–30; biology and technology come together in, 58; consequences of, 124–26; critical assessment of, 126–29; defined, 123; image-production technology in, 37; notion of information complicated by, 126; principles of, 122–24

biotechnology: activities falling under rubric of, 117–18; biology and information integrated in, 117; principles in development of, 122; subindustries of, 125

bioterrorism, 125–26

Birmingham school of cultural studies, xxi

Blake, William, 6, 10, 104, 317

Blanc, Louis, 220

blindfolded justice, 251, 254

blindness, 89–90

Blindness and Insight (De Man), 89

bloodwealth, 224

Blur building, 30–31

body, 19–34; as aesthetic object, 20; being versus having, 21; in cognitive science, 25, 27; constituting power of, 19, 29; corporeal imagination, 60; Descartes on mind and, 23–24; as dynamic process, 20; as earliest media of human expression, x; embodiment distinguished from, 20–21; female, 20; gendered, 28–29; as ground for assessing materiality of media, 57–58; healing, 22–23; images as housed in, 41, 46; imbrications of space, time, and embodiment, 111–12; information operating in conjunction with, xii, 148, 150; McLuhan on media and, xiii; medieval attitude toward, 22; as medium, 19–34, 153–55; mind-body dualism, 23–24, 27, 55, 189; modification, 20; as object versus agent of experience, 21–23; passivity attributed to, 19; in phenomenology, 25–26; in psychoanalysis, 25; taken as a given, 19; as wetware, 191. *See also* brain; embodiment; senses

body ego, 25

Bolter, Jay, xiv, 242, 286

Boltzmann, Ludwig, 160, 161, 162, 201

Borges, Jorge Luis, 80, 270

Boxer, Philip, 149

Braille, 323n1

brain: computers as electronic brains, 199; as grayware, 191; imaging of, 50; as model for computers, 208; and the senses, 91; uploading into a computer, 146

Brecht, Bertolt, 291

Breughel, Pieter, 5

bridewealth, 224–25

broadcasting: all-as-one address in, 270–71; as analogic orthothetical mnemotechnique, 76; concentration of means of production in, 78; as delivery system, 272–73; fresh information required in, 78–79; networks, 283; regulation of, 257–62; simultaneous national address as historical exception, 274; waning of mass audience, 273–74. *See also* radio; television

Brooks, Rodney, 154

Brown, George Spencer, 297

Bubbles (Millais), 7–8

Buckley v. Valeo (1976), 259

Burke, Edmund, 99n12
Burroughs, William S., 241
Butler, Judith, 28–29
Bynum, Caroline Walker, 22
Byron, Lord, 6

Cage, John, 96
camera obscura, 39, 41
Cang Jie, 312
Canguilhem, Georges, 84n9, 121–22
capital, financialization of, 229, 230
capitalism: cognitive/cultural, 67, 71; consumable novelty required in, 77; and mid-century modernism, 95; printing in advent of, 76; temporal standardization in, 109
Carlin, George, 259–61
carrier pigeons, 272
Cassirer, Ernst, 51, 52
Castoriadis, Cornelius, 60
cathedrals, 36
Cavell, Stanley, 183
Cayley, John, 152
celebrity culture, 14
Celera Corporation, 118
centralized (star) networks, 288, 289
central processing unit (CPU), 206, 207–8
Cézanne, Paul, 10
Chance and Necessity (Monod), 121
Chang, Briankle G., 139, 140–41
Chargaff, Erwin, 120
checksum, 290
Cheret, Jules, 9
Chicago School of Media Theory, 57
Chinese medicine, traditional, 23
Chinese script, 311, 316, 318, 323, 323n7
Chomsky, Noam, xvi, xvii
chromosomes, 124
Chun, Wendy Hui Kyong, 286, 292
cinema. *See* film (cinema)
Clapton, Eric, 169
Clark, Lygia, 98
classified ads, 270
Clinton, Hillary, x
Clokr (Klingemann), 182
cloning, 37, 125
clothing, 30, 31
CoBrA, 12
codes: digital, 45; genetic, 119–21, 123–28,

244; Shannon's work in World War II, 322; tactile, 321
coding problem, 120
cognitive science, 25, 27
coinage, 226, 227, 228
Coke, Sir Edward, 254
Cold War, 290
collage, 11, 13
Color Field painting, 95
commodification, 52–53, 180
common law, 252–53, 254, 255–56
communication, 131–44; alphabetic writing dominates world of, 320; analogue versus digital systems of, 235; computer as model for, 196–97; conceptual amplification of, 132; consciousness in, 302–3, 304; constitutive model of, 133, 138; context required for, 167; defined, 131; DNA as system of, 121; effective, 137; etymology of, 131–32; face-to-face, 267, 268, 275, 298, 308; goal of, 139; industries of, 78; information and, 136–39; internal constituents of, 304; Jakobson on, 134–35; Luhmann on, 141–43, 238, 240, 241, 242, 297, 303; materiality of, 50, 55–58, 138; media associated with, 132–33; modern informatic sense of, 132; paradox of legal, 256, 262; postmetaphysical approach to, 140; real-time, 135–36; Shannon on, 120, 133–34, 136, 138, 142, 188, 201–2; and social systems, 139–43; surveillance and policing of, 249; symbolically generalized media of, 307–8; transmission model of, 132–33, 140; transport associated with, 133; two formal models of, 132–33. *See also* cybernetics; language; media; networks; writing; telecommunications
Communications Act of 1934, 257
Communications Assistance to Law Enforcement Act of 1994, 261–62
communication satellites, 86n34, 266
Communism: economic exchange in, 220–21, 223, 230n2; idols in, 37
complex adaptive systems, 149
complexity theory, 292
computability, 203–4
computational reembodiment, 27

Dada, 11, 13, 241
Darwinian evolution, 210
Dasein, 26, 108
datum/horizon structure, 300, 301
Davies, Donald, 288
Davis, Gray, x
Debord, Guy, 50
debt, 225, 226, 227, 228, 229
decadent sensibility, 9
decentralized networks, 288, 289, 294
deconstruction, 136, 233, 238, 301, 325n32
decorative art, 3, 4
defamiliarization, 10, 11, 186
Delacroix, Eugene, 6
DeLanda, Manuel, 286
Deleuze, Gilles, 66, 68, 110, 284, 287
delivery systems, 271–75
De Man, Paul, 89
dematerialization, 50, 51–55, 58, 60n2
Denis, Maurice, 9–10
Derrida, Jacques: on arche-writing, 176, 307, 313; on communication, 135, 239; concept of writing of, ix; deconstruction of, 233, 238; on *différance,* 69, 109, 135, 176, 236, 237, 240; on *grammé,* 236, 244; on insightful blindness, 89; on language, 233, 236–37; on Lévi-Strauss's "A Writing Lesson," 323n5; on logocentrism, 319; *Memoirs of the Blind,* 89; on metaphor in philosophy, 141; on metaphysics of presence, 237; on the natural and the cultural, 29; on no interiority preceding exteriorization, 70; *Of Grammatology,* 29, 69, 233, 324n16, 325n32; on phonic substance, 237, 245; on phonocentrism, 312; on Plato on anamnesis and hypomnesis, 69, 71; "Plato's Pharmacy," 69; on Saussure, 236, 237; on semiosis, 300; on space and time, 109; on technical exteriorization of memory, 65–66; on transcendental signified, 237; on writing preceding speech, 255, 313
Dery, Mark, 286
Descartes, René, 23–24, 55, 88, 98n2, 106, 121, 166
design, 8–9
détournement, 13
Devanagari script, 316
dialectical materialism, xx–xxi

Dialectics of Enlightenment (Adorno and Horkheimer), 187
Diderot, Denis, 92–93
différance, 69, 109, 135, 176, 236, 237, 240
differential analyzers, 205
digital art, 16
digitization: alphabet as thoroughly and universal digital, 322; cinematic metaphor for digital data, 179; and dematerialization, 53–54; ecology of hypomnesis, 81–84; embodiment in digital revolution, 27–33; experiential reunification in, 176; of images, 35, 43–47; in memory aids, 64–66; memory from writing to, 75–78; new media containing older media, 290; preservation of electromagnetic texts, 158; relevance of technological developments in law, 239; transmission and storage as simultaneous in, 136. *See also* computers
Diller + Scofidio, 30–31
discretization, 70
disembodiment, in cybernetics, 27, 55
distributed networks, 288, 289, 290, 294
divided line, 89
DNA, 119–21, 122, 123–28, 137, 202
double contingency, 305, 308
doubt, Cartesian, 88, 98n2
Doyle, Richard, 119
dualism, mind-body, 23–24, 27, 55, 189
Duby, Georges, 23
Duchamp, Marcel, 11–12, 13, 241
duration, 107
d'Urbano, Alba, 31–33, 32
Durkheim, Emile, 52, 297
Dyson, Esther, 286

Eckert, J. Presper, 205, 206, 212n9
economic exchange. *See* exchange
education, politics of forgetfulness in, 77–78
EDVAC, 205, 206
Egginton, William, 22
Ego and the Id, The (Freud), 25
egoism, 227
Egyptian hieroglyphics, 316, 317
Einstein, Albert, 111, 272
Eisenstein, Elizabeth, 76, 175–76
electronic art, 16
Electronic Disturbance Theatre, 294

industrialization: art as alternative to industrialism, 8; defined, 76; emergence
of, 76; as generalization of mnemotechnological reproducibility, 68; hyperindustrialization, 68–69, 71; industrial
economy of information, 78; industrial
hypomnesis, 82, 83, 84; Industrial Revolution as foundational moment for
modern art, 3; modernity associated
with, 52; of the symbolic, 82
infectious diseases, emerging, 125–26
information, 157–71; Bertalanffy on, 286;
biology as, 118–23, 125, 126–27; and
biomedia, 123, 126; the body as informational medium, xii, 148, 150; as commodity, 78; and communication, 136–
39; computer processing of, 199, 200;
contemporary techniques for processing, 76; as created or destroyed at will,
157; in cybernetics, 145, 148, 200–201;
as difference which makes a difference,
165; entropy, 138, 161–63; exchange of,
219; hierarchization of, 80; industrial
economy of, 78; informatics of domination, 137; materiality and, 55–56, 165–
67; mathematical definition of, 161;
memory and, 78–81; quantification of,
157, 160; quantitative aspect of, 120;
speed-of-light transmission of, 79; utterance versus, 303, 305; as virtual, 157–
58. *See also* information theory
information theory: alphanumeric symbols in, 321; in biology, 120, 121; in cybernetics, 146, 147; on feedback, 168;
general systems theory compared with,
286; information seen as skeleton key,
137; Saussure's linguistics compared
with, 158–60; Shannon in, 120, 137, 146,
147, 158, 201–2, 205, 284, 285, 321, 322;
Wiener in, 146, 147, 163, 200–201, 284
Ingham, Geoffrey, 226
Innis, Harold A., 187, 188, 277, 314, 325n27
innovation: dialectics of media, 173, 174;
factors driving media, 46–47; formal, in
the arts, 10; in image production, 37–
38; in measuring space and time, 101–2;
media entangled in cycles of, xviii; media studies as obsessed with, xvi; Romantic contrast between mechanistic
labor and artistic, 6–7

installation art, 15, 97
instrumentality, 127–28
interactions, 298
interactivity, political tragedy of, 291, 294
interest rates, 226
interfaces, 79
International Human Genome Sequencing
Consortium, 118
Internet: age as one of hypomnesis, 64,
83; ARPAnet, 285, 288, 289; audience
dispersed in time, 273; Communications Assistance to Law Enforcement
Act of 1994 and, 262; computer development spurred by, 209; cookies,
275; cultural and gender difference
masked on, 28; dating sites, 28, 270;
factors driving invention of, 46–47;
freedom of expression on, 249; hypertext as having no place, 158; literature
on, 286; loose coupling of sending and
receiving in, 275–77; many-to-many
connectivity on, 180–82; as network,
283; packet-switching in, 285; and
pictorial turn in modern culture, 37;
Shredder 1.0, 56–57; social networking sites, 180, 181, 182, 183; space and
time transformed by, 104; Web 2.0, 175,
180–82
Internet Engineering Task Force (IETF),
289
interpretation, 150–51
intersubjectivity, 139–41
In the Name of God (Hirst), 15
invention: media studies as obsessed with,
xvi. *See also* innovation
iPods, 64, 83, 184, 239
Iroquois, 224
ishotmyself.com, 28
Islands of Consciousness (Klingemann),
182
"It's April" (Ammons), 242
Iusticia, 251, 254

Jacob, François, 120, 121
Jakobson, Roman, 134–35, 140, 326n39
Jameson, Fredric, 105–6
Japanese prints, 10
Jargon of Authenticity, The (Adorno), 109
Jaspers, Karl, 231n5
Jetée, La (film), 47

jewelry, 20

Johannessen, Jon-Arild, 149

Johnson, Samuel, 318

Johnson, Steven, 286

Jonas, Hans, 20–21

Jonson, Ben, 104

Jorn, Asger, 12

Joyce, James, 310

Judd, Donald, 14

judges, 251, 252, 253, 254, 256, 262–63

justice, blindfolded, 251, 254

Kac, Eduardo, 243–48

Kacem, Mehdi Belhaj, 293

Kaluli, 222–23

Kant, Immanuel: on autonomy of art, 6; on Baumgarten on aesthetics, 91; on passiveness of the body, 24; on perception, 26; and sensation and thought, 88; Simmel's view of art and, 55; on space and time, 103, 104, 106, 109; on things themselves, 51

Kapp, Ernst, 196

Kaprow, Allan, 96

Kay, Lily, 119, 120, 121

Keller, Evelyn Fox, 119

Kelly, Kevin, 286

Kenny, Vincent, 149

Khlebnikov, Velimer, 10

King James Version (Bible), 244, 245

Kirschenbaum, Matt, 56

Kittler, Friedrich A.: on autonomy of technics, 177–78; on city as medium, 60n3; on communication and media, 136; on digitization, 54; on discrete symbols separated by spaces, 321; on economics of media, 181; on end of age of media, 106; on "eyewash," 44; *Gramophone, Film, Typewriter,* vii, xxi, 88, 165, 176, 177, 320; on information and matter, 165–66; on Lacan on Poe, 320; McLuhan as influence on, xii; on media and the body, xiii, 88, 98n1; on media as determining our situation, vii, xv, xxi–xxii, 59, 155; as no longer "media theorist," 195; on people as adjuncts to media, 266; on software, 193, 195; on standardization by media, 176; on stereo development, 46; technological determinism of, xiv; "There Is No Software," 193; on

translating any medium into another, 195

Klein, Yves, 13

Kleinrock, Leonard, 288–89

Klingemann, Mario, 182–83

KnoWear, 30

knowledge industries, 67, 68

Koons, Jeff, 15

Korean language, 316

Korperwelten (Hagen), 153

Kosuth, Joseph, 242

Kracauer, Sigfried, 52, 54

Krauss, Rosalind, xvi–xvii

Kroker, Arthur and Mariluise, 28

Kruchenyk, Aleksei, 10

Kruger, Barbara, 242–43

Kurzweil, Ray, 27, 154, 286

Kwakiutl, 223

Lacan, Jacques, xix, 25, 33, 149, 166, 319–20

Laclau, Ernesto, xxi

Lamarckianism, 73, 210

Landing Home: Geneva (Fujihata), 112

Langton, Christopher G., 158

language, 233–48; in art, 241–48; for biomedia, 128; as dialogical, 82; as differential and negative system, 235–36; as form and medium, 245; Friday theory of media applied to spoken, 302; genetic code and, 119; *langue,* 158, 159, 234, 244; linguistic construction of observer in language communities, 149; Luhmann on, 238–41; as medium, 306; object-centered view of, 234; *parole,* 158, 159, 234, 244; profane language, 259–61; Saussure's linguistics, 158–60, 165, 233–35, 236; as specifically human, 233; structural coupling in, 303–4; structural linguistics, 134–35, 311, 319; systems theoretic approach to, 237–41; two fundamental dimensions of, 158, 234. *See also* speech; writing

Language of Life, The (Beadle and Beadle), 121

Language of New Media (Manovich), 179

langue, 158, 159, 234, 244

Laocoön: An Essay on the Limits of Painting and Poetry (Lessing), 6, 102, 105

Latour, Bruno, 133, 153, 195

law, 249–65; anti-aesthetic interventions in, 256–57; common, 252–53, 254, 255–56; contempt of court, 250–51; fictions promulgated by, 256, 262, 263; as hieroglyphic tradition, 253–54; image of, 252–54, 258, 262, 263–64; images and, 256; monumental social presence of, 251–52; paradox of legal communication, 256, 262; paternal image in, 253; as prior judgment, 254–55; reform of esoteric language attempted, 255–56; regulation, 257–62; relevance of technological developments in, 239; religious background of legal debate, 255–56; rituals of, 253, 258; Roman, 253, 256; symbolically generalized media in, 308; symbolic function of, 249–50, 251
Laws of Form (Brown), 297
lawyers, 252, 256
Leibniz, Gottfried Wilhelm, 101, 106, 197n3, 284, 299
Lem, Stanislaw, 137–38, 157
Lenoir, Timothy, 59
Leonardo da Vinci, 5, 102
Leroi-Gourhan, André, xiii, 65, 70, 72–73, 196, 209, 313
Lessig, Lawrence, 286
Lessing, Gotthold, 6, 93–94, 99n14, 102–3, 104, 105
"Letter as Such, The" (Khlebnikov and Kruchenyk), 10
Le Va, Barry, 14
Levine, Sherri, 15
Lévi-Strauss, Claude, 218–19, 319, 323n5, 326n39
Lévy, Pierre, 158, 286
LeWitt, Sol, 13
Lewontin, Richard, 119
Libation Bearers, The (Aeschylus), 281
libidinal energy, 73
library catalogs, 76
licenses, broadcast, 257–58
life: artificial, 27, 203; concept of life itself, 121–22, 123, 127, 128. *See also* biology
Life Itself: Its Origin and Nature (Crick), 121
linguistics, structural, 134–35, 311, 319
linguistic turn in philosophy, 233
Linnaeus, Carolus, 121
Linux, 207
Lippard, Lucy, 13

literature, language as medium in, 241–42
lived experience (*Erlebnis*), 107
Lives of the Artists (Vasari), 5
"live" transmission, 79
Living Theater, 96
Locke, John, 91, 131
"Logical Calculus of the Ideas Immanent in Nervous Activity, A" (McCulloch and Pitts), 145–46, 212n10
logic circuits, 205
Logic of Life, The (Jacob), 121
Logic Theorist, 199
logocentrism, 319
logographics, 72, 312, 324n10
Louis, Morris, 12
Lovink, Geert, 286, 287
Ludditism, 293
Luhmann, Niklas: on communication, 141–43, 238, 240, 241, 242, 297, 303; on double contingency, 305; and form/medium distinction, 301–2; on language, 237, 238–41; on meaning, 238, 239, 240, 300–301, 303, 307; psychic and social systems contrasted by, 238, 240, 245, 299–300, 302; on re-entry, 238; on success-media, 276; systems theory of, 141, 238, 297, 299
Lukács, Georg, xx, 52, 60n6
Luther, Martin, 76, 271

machine translation, 323
MacKay, Donald, 146–47, 150–51, 212n2
Mac OS, 207
Macy Conferences on Cybernetics, 146
magnetic resonance imaging (MRI), 50, 153
Malevich, Kasimir, 10
Malraux, André, 54
Manet, Edouard, 9
manipulation: of images, 44; of information, 164
Manovich, Lev, 45, 136, 164, 179, 286
Manzoni, Piero, 13
Mao Zedong, 276
Marker, Chris, 47
market economy: in early agrarian empires, 225–26; exchange in, 217–18; governments make possible, 226; as imaginary projection, 222; rational choice theory generalizes, 219

Marx, Karl: in Communist pantheon, 37; on determination, xxi; dialectical materialism of, xx; and hypomnesic nature of technics, 71; materialism of, 58; on modernity and abstraction, 50; modes of production as critical concept for, ix; on money, 52, 53, 230; on proletarianization, 70–71; on technological influence on senses, 95

Marxism: in Situationist International, 13; uniting media studies with, xxi. *See also* Marx, Karl

masking, 20

mass culture: demassification, 84; fine art versus, 12, 14; massification, 52

mass media, 266–79; addressing audience in, 267–71; apparatus-dependent reproducibility in emergence of, 70; best-known forms of, 267; Chomsky's "propaganda thesis" regarding, xvii; delivery systems, 271–75; demassification of, 84; and fine art, 3, 5, 7, 11, 13, 14, 17; geographical differences in, 38; images in, 35–48; loose coupling of sending and receiving, 275–77; *media as collective singular tied to emergence of*, xi–xii; new media encompass new inflections of, 184; powerful institutions control, 277–78; purified signals in, 95; Schwarzenegger as depicted in, x; space and time transformed by, 104; as subset of media in general, 267; three dimensions of, 266–67, 277; waning of mass audience, 273–74. *See also* broadcasting; newspapers

mass production: Benjamin on art and, 11; in Duchamp's artworks, 12, 13; printing as first application to communication, 271, 317; versus unique, hand-executed originals, 7

Massumi, Brian, 45, 286

Master/Slave dialectic, 90, 99n7

materialism, xx–xxi, 50, 58–60

materiality, 49–63; in analysis of media, 151; of communication, 50, 55–58, 138; dematerialization, 50, 51–55, 58, 60n2; of embodiment, 56; as increasing emphasis in art, 9–10; and information, 55–56, 165–67; materialism, xx–xxi, 50, 58–60; specific meaning of, 49

materiality-effect, 51–52

materiality thesis, 302

"Material Texts" book series, 61n16

Mathematical Theory of Communication, The (Shannon and Weaver), 133–34, 136, 138, 201, 322

mathematics: graph theory, 282, 284, 287, 293, 295n3; in invention of writing, 315; topology, 287, 293. *See also* information theory

Matter and Memory (Bergson), 25

Matthai, Heinrich, 119

Maturana, Humberto, 147, 149, 202, 237, 300

Mauchly, John, 205, 206, 212n9

Mauss, Marcel, 220, 221, 227

Maxwell, James Clerk, 138, 160, 285

Maxwell's demon, 137–38

Mayan vigesimal numerical system, 315

McChesney, Robert, xvi

McCulloch, Warren, 145–46, 148, 152, 206, 212n10

McLuhan, Marshall: on artists as in forefront of experimentation with new media, 46; Bolter and Grusin's remediation of, xiv; on clothing as extension of skin, 31; on coupling media form and media use, 175; on dual function of media, 21; on global village, 311; *The Gutenberg Galaxy*, 175, 317; on media and transport, 133; on media as extensions of man, xii–xiii, xvii, 21, 29, 88, 97, 98n1, 151, 174–75, 186, 266; on medium as the massage, 16–17, 135, 167; on medium as the message, x–xi, 175, 188; Merleau-Ponty compared with, 26; on narcissism and media-induced narcosis, 186; on new media containing older media, 290; on news as always bad, 35; on phonetic alphabetic, 320; on printing's socioeconomic significance, 317; on print in transformation to visual culture, 42–43; Starr fails to refer to, xvi; on synthesis of fractured media, 188; as technical determinist, xvii, 59, 175; *Understanding Media*, x–xi, 31, 98n1, 174–75, 186

McPherson v. McPherson (1936), 262–64

McTaggart, J. M. E., 111

Mead, George Herbert, 297, 299

meaning: in cybernetics, 150–51; Luhmann on, 238, 239, 240, 300–301, 303, 307; as medium, 301, 306; in Saussure's linguistics, 158–59, 234; in Shannon's definition of information, 146, 202, 285, 290. *See also* signifier and signified

Meat Joy (Schneeman), 96

media: computers as, 152, 153, 186; computers dissociate technics from, 178–83; as configurations of space, time, and embodiment, 111–12; as coproducing that which takes place, 80–81; defining, 151; as determining our situation, vii, xv, xxi, 59, 155; as dynamic, historically evolving environment, xiv; end of age of, 106; etymology of, xi; as extensions of man to McLuhan, xii–xiii, xvii, 21, 29, 88, 97, 98n1, 151, 174–75, 186; form/medium distinction, 301–2, 306, 307; four levels of analysis of, 151–52; law and, 249–65; materiality of, 49–63; as mediated, xv; as the message to McLuhan, x–xi, 175, 188, 266; minimal definition of, 266; multidimensional, triangulated approach to, x, xix–xx; ontological dimension of, xiii–xiv; as perspective for understanding, xxi–xxii; preservation of, 158; regulation of, 257–62; self-policing of, 249, 250; as singular noun, x, xi–xii, xx; as technical form or formal technics, ix; three dimensions of, 266–67, 277; two trajectories of, 135–36. *See also* biomedia; communication; mass media; media studies; mediation; medium; new media

media architecture, 30–31

media ecology, xxiin1

media studies: as amorphous, vii–viii, xv; attention to materiality in, 59; computers as problem for, 187, 197; cybernetics as central orientation of, 145, 152; emergence of, vii, x; failure to communicate across borders of, xvi–xvii; institutionalization of, vii, 196; invention and innovation as obsessions of, xvi; materiality thesis in, 302; McLuhan's redirection as foundational for, xi; as mediator, xix–xx; memory as keyword in, xvii–xviii; origins of, 186–87; and rematerializing of media, 56; systems-theoretic

approach's effect on, 307–9; taxonomies of, viii; uniting Marxism with, xxi

mediation: in dialectical materialism, xx–xxi; in face-to-face communication, 16; gendered body as instance of, 28–29; in Hegelian idealism, xx; of images, 25–26; of information, xi; in Kantian theory of knowledge, 51; media as mediated, xv; mediality is always already intermediality, 188; media studies as mediator, xix–xx; new media mediate the conditions of, 181; pedigree of, xx; political, ix; theoretical questions regarding, viii

medical imaging, 22–23

medium: art as exploitation of the, 3; body as, 19–34, 153–55; definitions of, xi; as designating minimal relationality, xii; of exchange, 217–18; and media as singular noun, xi, xii, xx; middle term of syllogism as, xix; senses as first, 88; theoretical questions regarding, viii. *See also* media

Medium, The (Zweig), 16, 17

Memoirs of the Blind (Derrida), 89

memory, 64–87; artificial aids to, 64–66; computer, 204, 206, 207; computers as exteriorization of, xvii; conservation of, 80; displacement of initial instrumentality of, 81; as epiphylogenesis, 72–75; as finite, 65; grammatization, 66, 70–71, 72, 74; industrial exteriorization of, 66–68; and information, 78–81; as keyword in media studies, xvii–xviii; mental images in, 41; Mnemosyne, 102; recollection, 108; selectivity in, 80; technics as vector of, 73; third layer of, 73–74; writing and, xvii, 67, 75–78, 173, 271, 317. *See also* anamnesis; hypomnesis

Meno (Plato), 65, 74, 75, 99n11

mental images, 41

Merleau-Ponty, Maurice, 26, 58

metalingual function, 134, 140

Michelangelo Buonarroti, 5

Microsoft, 194

Milgram, Stanley, 287

Millais, John Everett, 7–8

MIMD (multiple instruction, multiple data) configuration, 208

mind: as autopoietic system, 141; images as mental things, 41; intersubjectivity,

139–41; thoughts as immaterial, 49. *See also* consciousness; memory

mind-body dualism, 23–24, 27, 55, 189

Minimalist art, 14, 40

Minsky, Richard, 16

Mitchell, W. J. T., 317, 318, 322

mixed media, 42

mixed reality, 148

Mnemosyne, 102

mnemotechnics, xvii, 70, 72, 74–75

mnemotechniques, 65, 67, 75, 76

mnemotechnologies, 65, 67–68, 74

Möbius strip, 33

modernism: midcentury, 95, 98; modern art, 11–15; time associated with, 105

modernity: abstraction associated with, 50, 52; conception of embodiment in transition to, 23–24; pictorial turn in modern culture, 37–38; printing in emergence of, 307; senses in mid-twentieth-century, 95–96, 98. *See also* modernism

Moglen, Eben, 286

molecular biology, 119–21

monads, 197n3, 284, 299

Mondrian, Piet, 10

Monet, Claude, 9

money: in axial age, 226–27; coinage, 226, 227, 228; as credit accorded the future, 81; delinked from coercive institutions, 228; delinked from religious institutions, 229; earliest forms of, 225; in early agrarian empires, 225; Marx on, 52, 53, 230; as master trope for abstraction and rationalization, 52; mediatory power of, 53; in Middle Ages, 227–28; origins of, 223–25; paper, 228, 229, 317; precious metals as, 218, 223, 225, 226, 228–29, 230; primitive currencies, 230; symbolically generalized media and, 308; as ultimate medium of exchange, 218; virtual, 229

Monod, Jacques, 120, 121

moon landing, 96–97

Moore, Gordon E., 213n16

Moravec, Hans, 27, 146, 154

Moreau, Gustave, 10

Morowitz, Harold, 152–53

Morris, Robert, 14

Morris, William, 8

motion pictures. *See* film (cinema)

Mouffe, Chantal, xxi

movable type, 38, 175, 317, 325n27

movie camera, factors driving invention of, 46, 47

MP3 players, 150

MRI (magnetic resonance imaging), 50, 153

Mulder, Arjen, 194–95

multicore processors, 207–8

muses, 102

MySpace, 180

mythograms, 75

Nabu, 312

Nakamura, Lisa, 286

nanomedicine, 58

Napier, Mark, 56–57

narrowcasting, 274

Ndalianis, Angela, 29

Nebuchadnezzar, 269

negative feedback, 168

negentropy, 202

Negri, Antonio, xxi, 287

Negroponte, Nicholas, 286

Nelkin, Dorothy, 119

neoclassical economics, 219

Neoconcretismo, 98

netwar, 288

networks, 280–96; architectures, 287–90; centralized (star), 288, 289; connotative assumptions of, 283; decentralized, 288, 289, 294; distributed, 288, 289, 290, 294; etymology of term, 283; in industry, 283; networked computers, 180–83; paradox of networked relations, 292; plurality of types of, 282; "power law" distribution of assets in, 282; protocols, 289–90; pyramidal hierarchies contrasted with, 290; ramifications of, 290–94; Shannon in development of, 285; social networking sites, 180, 181, 182, 183; as technologies of power, organization, and control, 282–83; two types of, 280–81; Wiener on, 284–85. *See also* Internet

neural nets, 212n10

neurofeedback, 29

neuron, McCulloch-Pitts, 146, 148, 152, 212n10

Newell, Alan, 199

new media, 172–85; in artistic tradition, 15; cultural and computer layers of, 179; deconstruction of communication and representation by, 136; as destabilizing, 173; embodiment in, 27–33, 57–58; index changing vocation of media itself, 183; long series of "new media" revolutions, 177; materiality of, 56; as mediating the conditions of mediation, 181; as new in new way, 181; old new media, 184; as presenting refashioned and improved versions of other media, 56; as range of technical, aesthetic, and social developments, 183–84; signifier-signified relationship reconfigured by, 55; as singular and plural, 172–73; stakes of issue of newness of, 172

newspapers: audience growth, 273; benday dots in images, 45; classified ads in, 270; as delivery device, 266; Internet compared with, 273; *media* as collective singular tied to emergence of, xi; new social spheres and communities created by, 7; press agencies, 78, 80; space and time transformed by, 104; verbal and visual images in, 43

Newton, Isaac, 101

Nietzsche, Friedrich, 320, 322

Nightingale, Andrea Wilson, 90

9/11, 81

Nirenberg, Marshall, 119

Nixon, Richard, 229

noise, 163–64; as the art, 164, 170; defined, 138; information versus, 120, 138–39; as infra-informatic problem, 296n14; in Shannon's information theory, 120, 201, 202; signal-to-noise ratio, 202; as signature of the real, 166; as source of new patterns, 168; in Wiener's information theory, 200, 284

nomos, 252–53

noncommercial exchange, 219–23

Nora, Pierre, 77, 79

nucleotide bases, 120

numerical notations, 315

Nutrasweet, 42

Obama, Barack, x

Observing Systems (von Foerster), 147

Ockham, William of, 93

Of Grammatology (Derrida), 29, 69, 233, 324n16, 325n32

Ogden, C. K., 3, 320

Oiticica, Hélio, 98

"On Computable Numbers with an Application to the Entscheidungsproblem" (Turing), 197n1, 203

"On Defence of Poetry" (Shelley), 6

One and Three Chairs (Kosuth), 242

On Painting (Della Pintura) (Alberti), 4, 46

open source software, 292

operating systems, 190–91, 193, 194, 207

oral media, 271

Orgel, Leslie, 120

originality, 4, 14

Origin of Language, The (Rousseau), 318, 321

Ovid, 294n2

Pacifica Foundation, 259–61

packet-switching, 285, 288

Page, Jimmy, 169

Panofsky, Erwin, 39, 104–5

Pantone color-matching system, 99n18

paper, 316–17, 325n25

paper money, 228, 229, 317

papyrus, 316, 325n25

"Paragraphs on Conceptual Art" (Le-Witt), 13

parallel processing computers, 206, 207–8, 213n14

parchment, 316, 325n25

parole, 158, 159, 234, 244

Parreno, Philippe, 15

Parsons, Talcott, 297, 305

party lines, 272–73, 276

Pask, Gordon, 145, 149

Patriot Act, 249, 261

Paulson, William R., 139, 162, 163

PDAs (personal digital assistants), 64, 67, 112

Peirce, Charles Sanders, 39, 42, 43, 44, 268

penny press, 7

perception: autoperception, 25–26. *See also* senses

performance art, 13, 15, 96

Perkin-Elmer, 118

personal digital assistants (PDAs), 64, 67, 112

personal media, 84

perspective, artificial, 38

Peters, John Durham, 132

Phaedo (Plato), 76

Phaedrus (Plato), 65, 67, 69, 71, 173, 271, 312, 317

Pharmaceutical Research Manufacturer's Association, 125

pharmacogenomics, 125

phatic function, 134

phenomenology, 25–26, 59

Phenomenology of Internal Time Consciousness (Husserl), 107

Phenomenology of Perception (Merleau-Ponty), 26

philosophy: antipathy to technics in Western, 65, 176; coinage seen as instrumental in Greek, 227; cultural context of Greek, 90; empiricism, 91–93; German Idealism, xx, 6; linguistic turn in, 233; metaphor in, 141; phenomenology, 25–26, 59; question of memory in origins of, 71, 72; sense versus thought distinguished in, 88, 94

"Philosophy of Composition, The" (Poe), 6

Philosophy of Fine Art (Hegel), 6

Phoenician alphabet, 311, 315, 323n6

phoneticization, 318

phonocentrism, 312, 319

phonography: as analogic orthothetical mnemotechnique, 76; autonomy of technics in, 178; Berliner Phonogramm-Archiv, 184; evolution of, 79; print's "writing monopoly" ended by, 166; as representational (inscription and storage focused), 135–36, 164; space and time transformed by, 104; stereophonic sound, 46, 47

photography: as analogic orthothetical mnemotechnique, 76; commodification and, 52–53; contact with material world attributed to, 53; digital images compared with, 44; evolution of, 79; print's "writing monopoly" ended by, 166; as representational (inscription and storage focused), 135–36, 164; space and time transformed by, 104; unseen and overlooked realities revealed by, 46

photomontage, 13

Photoshop, 44

Picasso, Pablo, 11, 39

Picturedisco (Klingemann), 182

Picture Theory, The (Mitchell), 317

piercing, 20

pigments, synthetic, 94, 99n16

pilgrimage, 273, 274

Pinyin system, 316

Pitts, Warren, 146, 148, 152, 212n10

Plant, Sadie, 286

Plato: on anamnesis, 64, 65, 72; cave allegory of, 40, 45, 88–90; *Gorgias*, 72; on hypomnesis, 67, 68, 72; *Meno*, 65, 74, 75, 99n11; *Phaedo*, 76; *Phaedrus*, 65, 67, 69, 71, 173, 271, 312, 317; philosophy begins with, 71, 72; on Prometheus and Epimetheus, 173–74; *Protagoras*, 173; on space and time, 102, 104; on writing, 173, 271, 317

"Plato's Pharmacy" (Derrida), 69

podcasting, 84

Poe, Edgar Allan, 6, 319–20

poetry, 241

Polhemus helmet, 148

Pop art, 13–14

positive feedback, 168

Poster, Mark, 55, 286

posthumanism, xiii, 27, 44, 136

Postimpressionism, 10

Postman, Neil, xxiin1

postmodernism: on art, 15; in reformation of senses, 97; space associated with, 106

potlatches, 223

Pound, Ezra, 318

power law, 282

Praxiteles, 4

precious metals, 218, 223, 225, 226, 228–29, 230

"Prediction and Entropy of Printed English" (Shannon), 322

preestablished harmony, 197n3

press agencies, 78, 80

Prince, Richard, 15

Printed English, 321–22

printing: art's identity challenged by, 5, 7; as delivery system, 271–72; ecclesiastical monopoly on knowledge broken by, 317; Eisenstein on consequences of, 175–76; end of "writing monopoly" of, 166; Hazlitt on French Revolution and, xv–xvi; mass-circulation printed

printing (*continued*)
matter, 7; McLuhan on consequences of, 175; modernity's emergence tied to, 307; movable type, 38, 175, 317, 325n27; preservation of printed texts, 158; print as visual, 42; social and psychic life affected by, 317; standardization of linguistic marks in, 176; in synthesis of linguistic memory, 75–76; woodblock, 5, 317, 325n27

Printing Act of 1662, 257

Printing Press as an Agent of Change, The (Eisenstein), 175–76

prints, 5, 10

profane language, 259–61

proletarianization, 71

Prometheus, 173–74, 176

proprioceptive senses, 89–90

prosthetic extension, 26

prostitution, 224–25

Protagoras (Plato), 173

protocols, 289–90

psychedelia, 99n18

psychoanalysis, 25, 80

public art, 9

public interest, 257, 258, 260, 261

"Purloined Letter, The" (Poe), 319–20

Pynchon, Thomas, 110, 131, 139

Qin Shi Huang, 314

Quastler, Henry, 120

radio: all-as-one address in, 270–71; as analogic orthothetical mnemotechnique, 76; audience dispersed in space, 273; audience growth, 273; "communication" refitted by, 132; in evolution of telegraphy and phonography, 79; loose coupling of sending and receiving in, 276–77; mixed audience addressed by, 268; near-simultaneous delivery possible with, 272; as originally point-to-point, 273, 276; and pictorial turn in modern culture, 37; program syndication, 274; as real-time, 136; space and time transformed by, 104

Radio Act of 1927, 249, 257

radio-frequency identification (RFID), 111, 148

RAM (random access memory), 206, 213n12

RAND Corporation, 288

random access memory (RAM), 206, 213n12

random-access search systems, 76

rational choice theory, 219

Reagan, Ronald, 270

realism, 8, 55

Real Presence, 22

rebus principle, 312

"Recent Contributions to the Mathematical Theory of Communication" (Weaver), 158

reciprocity, 218, 219, 221, 222, 230n2, 275

recollection, 108

reductionism, 119, 127–28, 193

re-entry, 238, 239

referential function, 134

Reformation, 76, 176, 271, 272

regulation, 257–62

religion: art as secular, 7; King James Bible, 244, 245; and legal debate, 255–56; and money, 227–28, 229; printing breaks ecclesiastical monopoly on knowledge, 317; Real Presence doctrine, 22; Reformation, 76, 176, 271, 272

Remarks on Color (Hill), 243

Rembrandt van Rijn, 5

Renaissance, artist seen as gifted individual in, 4–5

Renan, Ernest, 77

Renfrew, Colin, 51

Request for Comments (RFC) documents, 289

Research Centre for Material Digital Culture (University of Sussex), 56

RFID (radio-frequency identification), 111, 148

Rheinberger, Hans-Jörg, 119

rhizomatic movements, 294

Rich, Alexander, 120

Richards, I. A., 3, 320

Ricoeur, Paul, 110–11

Riemann, Bernhard, 107

Roman alphabet, 316

Roman law, 253, 256

Romanticism: on artist as at odds with society, 5, 6; on artistic imagination and

tion in, 305; as functional analysis, 306; on language, 237–38; of Luhmann, 141, 238, 297, 299; media studies affected by adopting approach of, 307–9; "medium" concept in, 300; as nondeterministic, 305; rise of computer parallels rise of, 196; social systems, 298–300; structural coupling in, 303; on symbolically generalized media of communication, 307–8; on writing, 307

Tagnautica (Klingemann), 182
tally-sticks, 227–28
tattooing, 20, 75
taxation, 226
technics: autonomy of, 177–78; computers dissociate media from, 178–83; co-originality with the human, xiii; Freud ignores constitutive role of, 73; the human and, xiii, xxii, 65, 176, 177, 196, 197n2; hypomnesic nature of, 71; media as technical form or formal, ix; mnemotechnics, xvii, 70, 72, 74–75; as originary milieu of epiphylogenetic memory, 75; technicity of computational networks, 181; transcendental technicity, 180; as vector of memory, 73; Western philosophical antipathy to, 65, 176. *See also* technology
Technics and Time: The Fault of Epimetheus (Stiegler), 65, 176
technology, 115–214; in analysis of media, 151; artists abuse and manipulate, xviii–xix; biological evolution applied to, 209–12; boundary between biology and, 58; bypassed technologies, 172; causation attributed to, xv–xvi; computer development, 199–214; as essentially human, 65; exteriorization of the living, 73; inextricability of the social and, 133; innovations in image production, 37–38; *logos* versus *technē*, 72, 74; memory and, xvii; mnemotechnologies, 65, 67–68, 74; technological determinism, xvii, 59; technological estrangement, 97; technological unconscious, 110, 179, 181; writing as, 310. *See also* biotechnology; computers; printing; telecommunications

telecommunications: Communications Assistance to Law Enforcement Act of 1994, 261–62; as dematerializing and multiplying the media, 132; networks, 283, 285. *See also* radio; telegraphy; telephony; television
telegraphy: body and thought separated by, 57; "communication" refitted by, 132; freedom of choice in, 159; near-simultaneous delivery possible with, 272; networks, 283; and phonography in development of telephony, 79; press agencies made possible by, 78; Printed English as offspring of, 322; as real-time, 136; time and space shrunk by, 104; as transmission focused, 164
telephony: becomes point-to-point medium, 273; near-simultaneous delivery possible with, 272; networks, 283; party lines, 272–73, 276; as real-time, 136; Shannon's diagram of communication system draws from, 134; telegraphy and phonography in development of, 79; as transmission focused, 164
television: all-as-one address in, 270–71; audience dispersed in space, 273; audience growth, 273; concentration of means of production in, 78; in evolution of photography, 79; loose coupling of sending and receiving in, 275–77; *media* as collective singular tied to emergence of, xi; mixed audience addressed by, 268; as mnemotechnology, 68, 76; near-simultaneous delivery possible with, 272; and pictorial turn in modern culture, 37; program syndication, 274; as real-time, 136; space and time transformed by, 104
Telstar, 86n34
terminals, 79
text-to-speech (TTS) synthesis, 310, 323n2
Thacker, Eugene, 58
theater: Electronic Disturbance Theatre, 294; Living Theater, 96; Roman citizens barred from, 256–57
theme parks, 29
theôria, 90
"There Is No Software" (Kittler), 193
thermodynamics, second law of, 138, 160–61

Web, the. *See* Internet
Web 2.0, 175, 180–82
Weber, Max, 50, 52, 76, 192, 297
Wegenstein, Bernadette, 154
Weissmann, August, 74
Weston, Edward, 15
wetware, 191–92; in biomedia, 123; as obstacle in cognitive science, 27, 191; as relational term, 191; in trinity with software and hardware, 191–92
What Is Life? (Schrödinger), 119, 121
Whitman, Walt, 170
Who Wrote the Book of Life? (Kay), 119, 120, 121
Wiener, Norbert: "Behavior, Purpose and Teleology," 145; *Cybernetics*, 120, 146, 200, 284; "cybernetics" coined by, 145, 285; cybernetics defined by, 163; on cybernetic systems, 120; electrical engineering perspective of, 285; on feedback, 200, 284, 295n4; on freedom of choice in information systems, 159; *The Human Use of Human Beings: Cybernetics and Society*, 202; on information and probabilities, 161; in information theory, 146, 147, 163, 200–201, 284; on Leibniz, 284; on negative entropy, 202; on networks, 284–85; Shannon's theory compared with that of, 202, 212n3; tactile code of, 321
Wikipedia, viii
wikis, 180
Wilde, Oscar, 9
Wilkins, Maurice, 119
William of Ockham, 93
Williams, Raymond, xxi, 58–59
Windows (operating system), 193–94, 207
Wittgenstein, Ludwig, 39, 140, 233, 243
Wolfram, Stephen, 150, 155
women: bridewealth, 224–25; female body, 20; feminine styles of talk, 270. *See also* feminism
Wood, J. E. H., 3
woodblock printing, 5, 317, 325n27
"Word as Such, The" (Khlebnikov and Kruchenyk), 10

word-of-mouth communication, 271
"Work of Art in the Age of Mechanical Reproducibility, The" (Benjamin), 11, 187
World Wide Web. *See* Internet
writing, 310–26; ancient civilizations' emergence tied to, 307; archaeological discoveries regarding, 311–12; civilization as unthinkable without, 310–11, 323n3; in conquest of space and time, 102; defined, 312; as delivery system, 271; Derrida on arche-writing, 176, 307, 313; digital memory aids compared with, 64; evolutionary theory of, 318; full systems, 312; as grammatization, 70; iconic signs, 42, 43, 311–12; ideogrammatic, 67; invention of, 311; key questions regarding, 311; magical power attributed to, 312–13; and memory, xvii, 67, 75–78, 173, 271, 317; mythical accounts of origins of, 312–13; nonalphabetic, 317–18; Plato on, 173, 271, 317; relationship of verbal and visual media, 43; Saussure elevates speech above, 237; scripts distinguished from writing systems, 315–16; social divisions marked by literacy, 314; and speech, 237, 255, 311, 313, 315; systems theory and, 307; as technology, 310; theocratic and imperial power associated with, 314; tools and materials of, 316–17; twofold processes of, 310; weights, measures, and currency in invention of, 314–15. *See also* alphabet
"Writing Lesson, A" (Lévi-Strauss), 323n5

Yates, Frances, 76
Youngblood, Gene, 96–97
YouTube, 180, 181

Ziman, John, 210–11
Zinjanthropus boisei, 72–73
Zizek, Slavoj, 28
Zola, Emile, 8
Zweig, Janet, 16, 17